传播·地缘·政治
丛书主编：赵月枝　张志华

数字化衰退：
信息技术与经济危机

Digital Depression:
Information Technology and
Economic Crisis

〔美〕丹·席勒（Dan Schiller）/ 著
吴畅畅 / 译

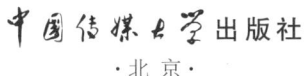
·北京·

总　序

世界正经历500年未有之大变局。

2008年资本主义体系性危机的爆发，不但宣告了美国主导的新自由主义全球化霸权的破产，而且使区域、国家、民族、阶级、种族、性别等各个层面的权力关系在更广的地域范围和更复杂的交错中剧烈地分化与重构。2013年，联合国开发计划署在人类发展报告《南方的崛起》中指出，按购买力平价，巴西、中国和印度三国2012年的经济总产出已与加拿大、法国、德国、意大利、英国和美国这六个传统北方工业强国的GDP总和相当，这是150年来首次出现的情况。然而，在2016年G20杭州峰会上，中国国家主席习近平提及，世界基尼系数已经达到0.7左右，超过了公认的0.6"危险线"；在2017年达沃斯论坛上，乐施会（Oxfam）的报告更是显示，截至2016年，全球8大富豪所占有的财富总值与占全球总人口一半的36亿最贫穷人口的总财产相当。毫无疑问，以欧美为中心并以种族主义、殖民主义和帝国主义为特征的世界资本主义体系及其文明等级论，在遭遇20世纪民族革命、社会革命和文化革命的碰撞后，正面临新的、更为深刻的内爆与挑战。

与此同时,自20世纪80年代以来全球资本主义的信息化和数字化转型,使信息和传播成了正在展开的世界地缘政治和社会文化政治斗争的核心场域。从半岛电视台和今日俄罗斯电视台(RT)的先后崛起到中国媒体的"走出去"努力和"互联互通"在"一带一路"战略中的关键位置,从维基解密的揭露、斯诺登的曝光到互联网全球治理领域的博弈,从2010年谷歌退出中国大陆市场到2016年欧洲议会通过《欧盟反击第三方宣传的战略传播》决议案和美国出台《波特曼—墨菲反宣传法案》,从阿拉伯世界的"推特革命"到社交媒体在2016年美国大选中的重要作用,信息与传播领域的权力关系重构正在国家、市场和社会各个层面全面展开,信息与传播在国家和区域内外的地缘政治和社会文化政治变迁中的关键地位得到进一步强化。

尽管20世纪的"冷战"早已被宣告结束,互联网也早就将世界各个角落更加密切地联系在一起,但是,世界并不是平的,历史更未终结。进入21世纪以来,不同资本主义国家之间、不同政治和社会文化体系之间、不同世界愿景之间的摩擦和冲突日趋激烈,全球和区域间的地缘政治斗争和社会文化政治斗争更加复杂,新形式的冷战与热战的硝烟不断在世界历史空间弥漫开来。"地球村"内,恐惧与希望并存,惶惑与理想齐飞。一方面,作为资本主义世界体系中的霸权国家,美国凭借其强大的军事力量和在信息传播领域的优势,以更为直接的强权手段努力维系其遍及全球的既得利益。另一方面,与民族主义框架内和国家间的冲突相互交织,不同社会文化背景下的反资本主义力量也在世界各地集聚:从政治、经济、社会、文化和生态各个层面展开历史性的斗争。

在全球资本主义进入结构性危机,全球人心求变并急切吁求新的未来可能性的历史当口,在人类再一次面临"社会主义还是野蛮状态"抉择的关键时刻,传播领域如何结构性地内在于这一过程,以及传播过程如何被世界各地不同的权力主体所掌握,借以维系、强化或者挑战不公正的全球秩序和不平等的社会权力关系,已然是当下传播研究者必须面对的重大而又急迫的问题,而网络时代传播政治的全球性和跨国性特征以及传播研究的西方中心主义倾向,则迫切需要我们广纳基于不同地缘视角的最新学术成果。

鉴于此,我们在独家翻译出版美国伊利诺伊大学出版社"信息地缘政治"书系相关书目的基础上,吸收国内学者从地缘、社会文化与政治角度分析中外传播现象的著作,推出融中外优秀研究成果于一炉的"传播·地缘·政治"丛书。我们希望藉敏锐的问题意识、开阔的研究视野和前沿的研究方法,为国内传播学术界以动态的、历史的、整体的多维视角分析全球传播现象竭尽绵力,以促进中国传播学术的创新和范式转型,推动全球传播秩序和社会传播关系的公平与公正发展,开启"新地球村"的想象。

谨序。

赵月枝 张志华

目 录
contents

导论：矛盾时刻 /1

第一部分 数字资本主义上升为危机

第 1 章　网络的连接性与劳动体系 ／3

第 2 章　网络化的生产与重建的商品链 ／18

第 3 章　网络化的金融化 ／35

第 4 章　网络化的军事化 ／51

第二部分 传播的重组

第 5 章　历史的序幕 ／67

第 6 章　网络通信商品链 ／76

第 7 章　服务与应用程序 ／117

第 8 章　赞助商制度的"复苏" ／129

第 9 章　衰退中的增长？ ／148

第 10 章　奋力寻求增长 ／154

第 11 章　新的外交政策的必要措施 ／163

第 12 章　关注商业：美国商务部与互联网 ／172

第 13 章　超越以美国为中心的互联网体系？ ／187

第 14 章　积累与遏制 ／218

第 15 章　从地缘政治到社会政治冲突 ／238

导论:矛盾时刻

在发达的信息通信技术的中心地带美国,悖论式地爆发金融与经济危机,影响至今。作为硅谷与好莱坞的大本营,加州可能是美国(危机)重灾区①。2013年年末,硅谷中心加州圣何塞市削减社会服务,任由路面凹坑无人管理,并计划取消工人的健康福利②。

事情原本不应该这样。数十年来,我们被灌输这样的想法:信息通信技术成为总体经济的增长点。从发端于1960年代的后工业社会理论到1990年代流行的"新经济"学说及其发展,无一不是关于信息通信技术的再生性特质(regenerative benefit)的公共话语。随着我们进入网络化的信息社会,美好的未来向我们徐徐展开;前途永远是光明的。然而,恰恰是美国这位数字体系与服务的历史驱动者,使世界陷入自1930年代以来旷日持久的经济衰退之中。

2007年12月爆发的经济衰退演变成一场全面的恐慌。2008年9月至10月,在金融危机的最低谷,13家美国最大的金融机构中有12家面临着两周内即将垮台的危险。然而,这场危机的规模是全球性的,无论是英格兰银行还是巴西央行,欧洲央行还是韩国的中央银行,它们在绝望中求助于"美元流动性"③。美联储主席伯南克向金融危机调查委员会表示,"哪怕把经济大萧条算进去",这段时期"也是全球历史上最糟糕的一次金融危机"④。美国政府干预的力度前所未有,相继出台35项救市计划,耗资23.7万亿,试图阻止金融体系的崩溃⑤。紧急情况稍有所缓解,可仍无法阻挡国内与国际经济出现混乱局

---

① Richard Walker, "The Golden State Adrift," *New Left Review* 66 (November/December 2010):5–30.
② Rick Lyman and Mary Williams Walsh, "Struggling San Jose Plans to Cut Worker Benefits," *New York Times*, September 24,2013.
③ Neil Irwin, "Fed's Aid in '08 Crisis Stretched Worldwide," *New York Times*, February 24,2014.
④ Financial Crisis Inquiry Commission, *The Financial Crisis Inquiry Report* (New York:Public Affairs,2011),354. The most persuasive account is Leo Panitch and Sam Gindin, *The Making of Global Capitalism* (London:Verso,2012),301–30. Carrying forward through late 2012, though with less analytical bite, is Robert Kuttner, *Debtors' Prison:The Politics of Austerity versus Possibility* (New York:Knopf,2013).
⑤ Neil Barofsky, *Bailout:An Inside Account of How Washington Abandoned Main Street While Rescuing Wall Street* (New York:Free Press,2012),162.

面。产值、贸易、投资一律大幅度缩水。2009年经济危机依然继续,然而,冷静的分析家只用一种更为克制的语调形容彼时的局面:一场"经济大衰退"(recession)、"第二次经济大紧缩"(contraction),甚至是一次"不那么严重的经济萧条"①。

2009年6月,美国国家经济研究所对外宣称经济开始复苏②。关于经济萧条的讨论开始减少,可金融风暴与经济停滞的症状始终没有消退。2010年,官方宣布,15.1%的美国人(4 620万人口)生活在贫穷线以下,这是半个多世纪有记录以来人数最多的一次③。全世界仍然处于这场金融与经济危机的余威中。2011年《金融时报》刊文指出,"既然经济活动并没有大规模持续减少,那么严格来说,现在已经不存在经济萧条了";然而,这一跨国媒体的论调紧随凯恩斯,它凸显了"另一种类型的经济萧条:长期持续的次优(经济)活动,尽管政府出台强制性的财政与货币政策……低于峰值的经济生产、负的实际政策利率、高失业率与政府赤字破坏性地混杂在一起"④。这一症状没有消停,依然存在,并把全球经济推向了两位批判分析家所说的"无尽的危机"⑤的泥沼中。

倘若这场金融危机的基础条件明确,那么我们需要指出,随着它进入第7个年头,"经济衰退"这个词只是偶尔地出现在公共话语中。极少数像克鲁格曼这样大无畏的经济学家坚持使用这一词语⑥。经济学家布拉德福德·德龙(J. Bradford DeLong)比较了"当前的危机"与"经济大萧条",在此基础上他得出结论,"没有什么比它更'不重要'的了"⑦。然而,这些却成了例外之见。2013年冬至2014年初,经济报道大肆宣扬"经济不景气"、高"失业率"、"止步不前的"的家庭收入、交易"疲软"、"缓慢的经济增长"⑧,"通

---

① Carmen M. Reinhardt and Kenneth S. Rogoff, *This Time is Different: Eight Centuries of Financial Folly* (Princeton, N. J.: Princeton University Press, 2009).
② National Bureau of Economic Research, available at http://www.nber.org/cycles/sept2010.html (accessed January 10, 2014).
③ Matt Kennard and Shannon Bond, "Number of Americans in Poverty at Highest in 50 Years," *Financial Times*, September 14, 2011.
④ "Bipolar Bearish," The Lex Column, *Financial Times*, May 13, 2011.
⑤ John Bellamy Foster and Robert W. McChesney, *The Endless Crisis: How Monopoly-Finance Capital Produces Stagnation and Upheaval from the USA to China* (New York: Monthly Review, 2012).
⑥ Paul Krugman, "The Big Shrug," *New York Times*, June 10, 2013. 也请参见 Kuttner, *Debtors' Prison*, 36; Paul Krugman, *End This Depression Now* (New York: Norton, 2012).
⑦ J. Bradford DeLong, "The Second Great Depression," *Foreign Affairs* 92, no. 4 (July/August 2013): 159.
⑧ Brian Blackstone, "Euro Zone Braces for Stagnation," *Wall Street Journal*, June 21, 2013; Annie Lowrey, "I. M. F. Trims Global Growth Forecast as Emerging Markets Lag," *New York Times*, July 10, 2013; Julia Werdigier, "Jobless Rate Will Continue to Increase in Europe, O. E. C. D. Forecasts," *New York Times*, July 17, 2013; Neil Shah, Ben Casselman, and Jon Hilsenrath, "Tepid Growth Restrains Fed," *Wall Street Journal*, August 1, 2013.

货紧缩"①,美国资本投资"放缓"②,有可能出现的"互联网泡沫"③,新出现的"市场抛售"现象④,以及"新的"金融危机⑤——尽管持续的经济不景气并未导致社会共识的形成,即我们实际上正在经历一场经济大萧条。同样,这场经济大萧条的余威及其深远影响也没有引起人们关注。

这场危机主要表现为财政压力与经济不景气。由于既存的结构性关系日趋紧绷,并开始分崩离析,经济政策的出台刻不容缓。但是倘若当前的政治经济结构不只是遭到破坏,失去活力,倘若它还在经历着一场影响深远的结构转型,倘若在寻求恢复常态的各种短期举措之后我们正处于一种过渡的阶段,事实上它正改变我们关于常态的概念,那么,一切将去往何方?1930年代的经济大萧条能够预见性地回答上述问题。

在美国,1930年代的政治动员推动政府史无前例地采取应对措施。这些措施直接导致美国资本主义的重建,并激活民主化实践。相反,在面对经济大萧条时,日本与德国却孕育出法西斯主义的国家动员和军事扩张主义。经济大萧条在国内,尤其在国际上引发激烈冲突:相互敌对的国家以及社会阶级之间竞相重建全球政治经济体系。

关于经济大萧条的另一历史特征虽不被人所熟知,但值得强调:经济大萧条为再生性生产活动(客观上)提供庇护场所。迈克·伯恩斯坦(Michael A. Bernstein)的研究表明:1930年代,在美国的化工、建材、石油、烟草、食品以及非电力机械等工业领域,经济活力一直没有消退⑥。尽管营利性投资逐渐流入上述以及其他新兴产业当中⑦,这一新兴的增长极也只是在数年剧烈的社会变动之后才开始从整体上推动经济发展。在1929年金融崩溃与第二次世界大战结束之间,美国采取紧急措施重新调整国内阶级关系;重新调

---

① Claire Jones, "Deflation Fears Spark Shock ECB Rate Cut," *Financial Times*, November 8, 2013; Robin Harding, "IMF Warns of Growing Threat from Deflation," *Financial Times*, January 16, 2014; Claudia Jones and Chris Giles, "ECB Poised for Battle to Ward Off Deflation," *Financial Times*, January 27, 2014.
② Ed Crooks, "US Capital Spending Set to Slow to Four-Year Low in Sign of Caution," *Financial Times*, January 24, 2014.
③ Farhad Manjoo, "Beware of Tech Bubble, Maybe," *Wall Street Journal*, December 30, 2013; Nick Bilton, "If It Looks Like a Bubble and Floats Like One...," *New York Times*, November 25, 2013; David Streitfeld, "In Silicon Valley, Partying Like It's 1999 Once More," *New York Times*, November 27, 2013.
④ Delphine Strauss, John Paul Rathbone, and Jonathan Wheatley, "Argentine Peso Plunges amid Emerging Markets Sell-Off," *Financial Times*, January 24, 2014.
⑤ Annie Lowrie, "Household Incomes Remain Flat Despite Improving Economy," *New York Times*, September 17, 2013; Shawn Donnan, "Trade to Remain Sluggish, Says Unctad," *Financial Times*, September 13, 2013; David Jolly, "World Economy Growing Unevenly, O.E.C.D. Says," *New York Times*, September 3, 2013; Satyajit Das, "Post-Crisis Policies Offer Only Chronic Stagnation," *Financial Times*, September 12, 2013; United Nations Conference on Trade and Development, *World Investment Report* 2013 (New York: United Nations, 2013); John Authers, "Risk of New Crisis Drives Fed Doubts over Taper," *Financial Times*, September 7–8, 2013; Gillian Tett, "Insane Financial System Lives on Post-Lehman," *Financial Times*, September 13, 2013.
⑥ Michael A. Bernstein, *The Great Depression: Delayed Recovery and Economic Change in America, 1929–1939* (Princeton, N.J.: Princeton University Press, 1987), 49, 51.
⑦ Bernstein, Great Depression, 88–89. 也请参见 Alexander J. Field, *A Great Leap Forward: 1930s Depression and U.S. Economic Growth* (New Haven, Conn.: Yale University Press, 2011).

整全球政治经济的结构性关系;并同日渐崛起的后殖民与社会主义国家展开竞争。一面是欧洲与日本帝国的衰落,一面则是势不可当的去殖民主义与民族解放浪潮。

当前的危机可否比得上1930年代的经济大萧条?新的增长极(或营利性积累)正在形成吗?相互敌对的国家是否以各自的方式争夺全球资本主义政治经济体系的主导权?正在启动哪一种重建:重组政治经济体系的工程所描绘出的主要框架是什么?重建(工程)是否有望实现?

数字技术给上述难题的解决带来一线光明。为了梳理这一脉络,我们需要关于当下危机的理论。侥幸生存下来的书店里,充斥着大量分析此次金融灾难的书籍。在表明我的观点之前,我先扼要地叙述一下市面上流行的(关于金融危机的)各类观点。

一份官方报告指出,一段时间的积累后危机才能爆发,这无非证明了一种周期性的趋势。美国金融与经济危机调查委员会(National Commission on the Causes of the Financial and Economist Crisis)宣称,"数年间,引发潜在危机的各种漏洞一直存在。在危机爆发前十年,已有不少迹象显示,金融系统的风险不断增长,没有受到任何限制"。随即,委员会将美国房地产泡沫同"17世纪荷兰的郁金香市场泡沫、18世纪南海泡沫事件以及1990年代的互联网泡沫"[①]进行对比。有影响力的学者与政策制定者直到后来才承认,金融繁荣与萧条并非例外情形,而是(体系固有的)周期性与结构性特征;一篇重要的文献提供了关于几个世纪以来金融系统遭到破坏的复杂的类型学分析[②]。

另一组研究显示出迥然不同的目标,它使我们不再考虑金融系统的发展趋势,而提醒我们应当注意那些已经披露出来的个体犯罪与自私行为,以及机构腐败等现象。这些叙述的背后,是对贪婪、违法勾当与缺乏责任感(等行为)的出离愤怒[③]。

还有一组截然不同的研究超越了既定的金融繁荣——萧条循环,强调结构性趋势:加速的经济发展不平等,金融的去规制化,以及与日俱增的消费者债务。1970年代以来这些趋势日渐明显,并导致政治经济结构愈发有可能爆发经济危机[④]。激进的分析者将这些趋势与"垄断资本"这一具有深远影响的概念联系起来,同时指认经济不景气只是地方性现象[⑤]。我们已经展示了关于这一主题(经济不景气)的不同观点,有学者适时指出,

---

① National Commission on the Causes of the Financial and Economic Crisis in the United States, *The Financial Crisis Inquiry Report* (New York: Public Affairs, 2011), xvi, 3, 4.
② Carmen M. Reinhart and Kenneth S. Rogoff, *This Time Is Different: A Panoramic View of Eight Centuries of Crises* (Princeton: Princeton University Press, 2009).
③ Barofsky, Bail-Out; Simon Johnson and James Kwak, *Thirteen Bankers: The Wall Street Takeover and the Next Financial Meltdown* (New York: Pantheon, 2010); Charles H. Ferguson, *Predator Nation: Corporate Criminals, Political Corruption, and the Hijacking of America* (New York: Crown, 2012).
④ Robert B. Reich, *After-Shock: The Next Economy and America's Future* (New York: Vintage, 2011); Joseph E. Stiglitz, *Free Fall: America, Free Markets, and the Sinking of the World Economy* (New York: Norton, 2010).
⑤ Foster and McChesney, *Endless Crisis*.

哪怕经济的长期不景气也不一定会抑制企业的盈利。对此,亨伍德(Doug Henwood)举出如下材料为证,"1982年以降,包括1997年在内,企业盈利不断上升"①。在2009年6月宣布的"恢复期"的前九个季度中,无论按绝对值计算,还是按国民收入增长的比例衡量,企业利润再次大幅上扬②。

尽管存在上述多种论点,但它们都没有详细阐述技术革命同经济不景气(它已经成为当前资本主义的一部分)所组成的矛盾矩阵模型(contradictory matrix)。自由主义与激进的政治经济学家将经济衰落置于资本主义的当代历史发展之中加以审视,但他们要么忽略或轻视信息通信技术的经济角色,要么不予考虑、弃之如敝屣。例如,亨伍德明确反对信息与传播的经济紧要性,并认为这些领域仅仅代表了一种复杂化的趋势,即无节制的金融投机活动。哪怕有人想要翻查克鲁格曼、斯蒂格里兹(Joseph Stiglitz)或者库特纳(Robert Kuttner)这些自由主义经济学家在新近的论著中关于信息通信技术与因特网的讨论,也是徒然。他们一致地将信息与传播摒除在分析范围之外;相反,(当今资本主义的)两大特征——信息通信技术与经济衰落——之间的关系却始终没有厘清。

当然,还有不少论著大肆渲染信息技术的贡献。然而,这些关于信息社会的神谕般的文献,都避而不谈信息通信技术与资本主义历史发展之间的关联。在过去几十年里,回避这一关联的行为,其实是对特定的意识形态阵营的背叛。后工业与信息理论应追溯到流行于1960—1970年代的理念,即服务业与信息业的增长,以及社会对"智能技术"的接受,将共同推动资本主义产权关系的历史性飞越③。那些对资本主义社会关系的持续性讳莫如深的论调,即便剔除了后工业理论其他一些有问题的特征(problematic features),依旧声势大涨。最典型的例子当属社会学家曼纽尔·卡斯特(Manuel Castells)所提出的"网络社会"理论。卡斯特避免将资本主义简化为一个整体性的概念,以便更好地处理当今世界复杂异质的社会形态。相较之下,雷蒙·威廉斯坚持认为,"不存在某一种生产方式、某一种主导性的社会秩序以及某一种主导性的文化,能够包纳或穷尽人类所有的实践、能量与意图"④。对照卡斯特与威廉斯的研究进路,启示颇深。然而,生产方式与主导性的社会秩序持存至今。卡斯特时常假定,"网络社会"依然是资本主义的一种发展形态⑤;可他的论述矢口不提"资本主义已演变成一种中心式的在场、一种普遍式的形塑力量"这一事实。实际上,卡斯特从他的首本著作开始,便从根本上与资本主义保持距

---

① Doug Henwood, *After the New Economy* (New York: New Press, 2003), 203.
② Kuttner, *Debtors' Prison*, 43.
③ Dan Schiller, *Theorizing Communication: A History* (New York: Oxford University Press, 1996), 161–72.
④ Raymond Williams, "Literature and Sociology: In Memory of Lucien Goldman," *New Left Review* 67 (May–June 1971): 11.
⑤ Manuel Castells, "An Introduction to the Information Age," *City* 7 (1997): 6–16.

离;在《网络社会的崛起》一书中,他首次引入"网络社会"概念,认为它代表了"经济、国家与社会三角关系的一种新的形式"①。

与"网络社会"概念相比,数字资本主义理论显得独树一帜,因为它凸显传播与信息的重要性:它逐渐成为能够承载不断演变的资本主义政治经济结构的新的支撑点②。1990年代末我最早提出这一观点,旨在对"新经济"学说进行拨乱反正,后者滋养并助长了互联网泡沫的连续膨胀。我已表明,美国的资本与资本主义国家在这一蜕变过程(metamorphosis)中,自始至终决定着政治经济的变革方向:一种更倾向于信息通信技术密集型产业的资本主义体系。

那么,我们如何应用数字资本主义这一概念(来分析今天的金融危机)?如何有可能对它稍作调整,以适应并追溯21世纪早期十余年这段经过彻底重构却尚未终结的历史?毫无疑问,这样一种(理论)修正刻不容缓。我们所处的时代不以扩张为标志,而以(经济)紧缩为特质;不以停滞为标志,而以令人昏眩的结构性变革为特质。我们需要修订并拓展数字资本主义概念,以强调社会对网络容量(network capacities)的持续挪用。今天,技术革命被包裹在经济崩溃的外衣之中:数字化衰退何时到来?《金融时报》2013年11月曾以"通缩恐惧"为题,刊载一则头版故事;故事讲述推特的几位创建人在公司首次公开募股后,一夜之间变成亿万富翁的过程,并对他们的好运表示祝贺③。我们如何解释这一虽然显著,却身处经济滑坡的趋势中的相对增长极的出现?什么样的历史动力导致了数字化衰退,它们将去往何方?

对信息与传播在政治经济的主要发展过程中的角色的分析,构成了本书的主题。在第一部分,我归纳出三种功能:透过永不停歇的劳动力重构与不断增加的外商直接投资的循环,资本重组了生产体系;资本同时进入金融领域;大幅上升的军事采购支出。在第二部分,我将考察第四种趋势,即信息与通信行业乱象丛生的重组情况④。数字化体系、设备、服务与应用深植于上述复杂且混乱的趋势之中。对信息通信技术的投资已内生为资本主义发展的一部分,而非与资本主义毫无关系。

然而,资本主义的发展过程却前后相抵,扞格不入。詹明信(Fredric Jameson)指出,"资本是一架穷凶极恶的机器,经常发生故障,并只能费力地借助扩张抽搐(the laborious convulsions of expansion)等方式进行自我修复"⑤。一旦资本主义再次重生,下一次危机

---

① Manuel Castells, *The Rise of the Network Society* (Cambridge:Blackwell,1996),1.
② Dan Schiller, *Digital Capitalism:Networking the Global Market System* (Cambridge,Mass.:MIT Press,1999).
③ Jones,"Deflation Fears"; Hannah Kuchler,Tim Bradshaw,and Arash Massoudi,"Life Is Tweet for Twitter Founders after Company Valued at $30bn," *Financial Times*, November 8,2013.
④ Dan Schiller, *How To Think about Information* (Urbana:University of Illinois Press,2007),36-57.
⑤ Fredric Jameson, *Representing Capital:A Reading of Volume One* (London:Verso,2011),87.

的种子早已深埋于政治经济结构中。那么,一方面,不断崛起的数字资本主义强有力地推动资本的重新积累;另一方面,它也有可能引发天翻地覆的矛盾与张力。正如哈维(David Harvey)所言,"危机趋势从未缓解,它只是四处游窜(move around)而已"①。前一次遭遇质疑的(经济)重构,导致了今天经济的不景气局面;而围绕各种前瞻性的解决途径及其实质的争论不断升温,构成了当前经济不景气的最大景观。此次争论的来源与特点是什么?这是本书第三部分要讨论的内容。

自始至终贯穿全书的主线包括:2007—2008年间数字资本主义破产之因;它的增长极——通信与信息业——参差不齐、非均衡的发展特点;当今旨在赢得经济增长(而不管是哪种类型)而展开的激烈的政治经济冲突与争斗。

商品链

在开始我的分析之旅前,我必须要借用世界体系理论中的一个专有名词:"商品链"。1970年代霍普金斯(Terence Hopkins)与沃勒斯坦(Immanuel Wallerstein)率先提出这一概念,用以"揭示在资本主义世界经济体系——只关注商品在市场上的消费情况——中,一条跨越国界的长链主导了绝大部分生产活动;并且,这一现象贯穿了资本主义世界经济从漫长的16世纪至今的全部历史"②。

有必要对照"商品链"学说与我们更为熟悉的"价值链"概念。后者由哈佛商学院教授迈克·波特(Michael Porter)于1980年代提出,并流传至今。尽管上述两概念不约而同地强调不同产业之间的联系,不过,它们在价值取向上却是南辕北辙;詹妮弗·拜尔(Jennifer Bair)已经指出这一根本性差异。"价值链"既不以劳动力也不以利润率为中心,而是仰仗产业组织与所谓的"附加价值"(value-added),这些价值在产业运作连续的各个阶段产生。与之相反,"商品链"聚焦于劳动的全球性分工在始终处于重构状态的资本积累这一历史背景下如何演化并演变③。行政高管们主动内化了"价值链"理论,而"商品链"准许我们与之保持必要的"分析距离"(analytical distance)。

"商品链"学说旨在联合不同的劳动体系,进而实现能够在全球层面进行分配的生产过程。分析家使用此概念用以研究不同形态的商品:例如谷物等农产品或萃取产品,或

---

① David Harvey, *The Enigma of Capital* (New York: Oxford, 2010), 117.
② Immanuel Wallerstein, "Protection Networks and Commodity Chains in the Capitalist World-Economy," in Frontiers of Commodity Chain Research, ed. *Jennifer Bair* (Stanford, Calif.: Stanford University Press, 2009), 83. 沃勒斯坦一直强调这一点,例如"16世纪资本主义世界商品链的跨国性与20世纪一样,都具有欺骗性", Immanuel Wallerstein, *Historical Capitalism* (London: Verso, 1983), 31.
③ Jennifer Bair, "Global Commodity Chains: Genealogy and Review," in Bair, *Frontiers*, 10-13, 7-9.

者轮船、汽车、电子产品、服务甚至可卡因等制造业的资本货物。即便资本由上至下的规划、国家机构的保护性措施早已相伴相随、成为"日常",但它们既不能预先决定,也无法机械地植入(mechanically implanted)某一特定的商品链的流向与基本特征(constitutive features)①。

"商品链"概念的分析力源自于其外向的包容性,以及对社会关系——生产贯穿于其中——所具有的散布各方、复杂多变等特点的强调。"商品链"的开端是劳动力,劳动者用以维持生计,并且通过"次生链条"(sub-chains),他们自身的劳动构成零部件生产的基础;由此,"商品链"延伸至生产过程,这些半成品仍以产品的其他形式投入使用;链条的终端是装配完毕的成品及其分销与消费。对于詹妮弗·拜尔这些世界体系理论研究者而言,"商品链"概念串联起似乎彼此互不连属、迥然各异的劳动力动员,并视之为资本主义生产的基底(essential substrate)②。因此,我们分析的动机在于,"只有追溯这些商品链的网络构成,我们才能追踪到劳动过程的分工与一体化,并及时把握世界经济生产体系的发展与转型情况"③。

世界体系理论的追随者一直声称,连接不同地区和产业的结构性关系,与盈利各有差别的生产过程的空间分布,暴露出一个根本模式:盈利越多的生产越有可能扎根于富饶的"中心"地带,越有可能受到资本的垄断控制;而盈利越少的生产则不成比例(大规模)地集中在"边缘"地区,此处的"边缘"地区包括殖民地、欠发达地区或新兴市场。从这个角度来说,"地区与地区之间的商品链沿着从边缘地区的产品朝中心地带的产品的方向流动"④。那么,尽管"这些商品链没有片刻静止"⑤,但他们(世界体系理论的追随者)的详细阐述及其逻辑向我们揭示了根深蒂固的结构性不平等现象。霍普金斯与沃勒斯坦认为,"通过这样一种投射的方式,资本主义世界经济自我呈现为一张快速流动的关系网络,它持续不断地再生产基本秩序……或者迄今为止它至少已经再生产了这一整套基本秩序"⑥。

在第三部分,我对这一理论宣称提出质疑。今天,世界体系理论所假设的深层结构——"中心—边缘"模式,在中国以及其他曾处于边缘地区的国家所发生的深刻的资本

---

① Steven Topik, Carlos Marichal and Zephyr Frank, "Commodity Chains in Theory and Latin American History," in *From Silver to Cocaine: Latin American Commodity Chains and the Building of the World Economy, 1500 – 2000*, ed. (Durham, N. C. : Duke University Press, 2006), 14.
② Terence K. Hopkins and Immanuel Wallerstein, "Conclusions about Commodity Chains," in Commodity Chains and Global Capitalism, ed. *Gary Gereffi and Miguel Korzeniewicz* (Westport, Conn. : Praeger, 1994), 49.
③ Terence K. Hopkins and Immanuel Wallerstein, "Commodity Chains: Construct and Research," in Gereffi and Korzeniewicz, *Commodity Chains and Global Capitalism*, 17.
④ Hopkins and Wallerstein, "Commodity Chains," 17.
⑤ Hopkins and Wallerstein, "Conclusions," 50.
⑥ Hopkins and Wallerstein, "Conclusions," 50.

主义转型等事实面前,越发具有某种偶然性色彩。即便如此,世界体系理论的目标却不容置疑:通过探查增长与衰落的另一种循环模式,如何与四处蔓延的商品链中劳动体系的重组之间相互关联,从而对资本主义世界经济的发展节奏有所洞察。援引霍普金斯与沃勒斯坦的洞见,"围绕支柱型产业而展开的研究,可以依据'商品链网络'推翻重来"[①],当前的核心问题在于,如何更充分地将网络与信息通信技术纳入我们对商品链的研究之中。

该问题不仅仅停留在学术层面。实际上,对垄断资本而言,如何使网络体系融入商品链已普遍成为垄断资本的当务之急,事关全局。我认为,考虑到资本对网络容量的持续挪用,商品链同时吸纳从地方到跨国的生产过程,永无停歇地处在分解与重组的循环模式中[②]。那么,数字资本主义不仅为我们正在经历的历史转折时期命名,也向我们提供了一个宏大的概念框架,以帮助我们更好地理解这一进程。数字资本主义的概念指向五百年历史长河中一次新的变革,后者体现为如下趋势:资本延长使用雇佣劳动,资本寻找商品化的新场所并时常遭遇挑战,变化无常的资本危机,以及甚嚣尘上的金融投机行为催生了经济萧条与衰退。因此,数字资本主义完全可以与"工业资本主义"相提并论;工业资本主义的说法最早出现于19世纪,用来描述英格兰与其他地区出现的机器生产及其导致的影响深远的政治经济革命。再次强调,数字资本主义的特殊性必须置于持久的结构性趋势与历史危机趋势中加以审视,而不能假定与后者相脱离,或推断数字资本主义脱胎于后者。

本书建诸我一以贯之的研究,并借用其他学者的研究文献,通过将数字资本主义概念整合进关于政治经济重返危机的描述中,试图深化这一理论。随着经济普遍陷入停滞状态,以及由此导致的症状在2012—2013年间越发明显,成为持续性的危机,2008年金融恐慌已然中断了数字资本主义这一新的发展阶段。当然,还存在大量的不确定性,但有两点可以确认:1)信息与通信产业对当代数字资本主义的经济贡献,使得数字(化)领域成为根本性的增长极,类似于1930年代初生的消费产业;2)金融投机行为,连同资本全方位地将数字(化)体系整合进当前的政治经济结构之中,两者共同导致了当前的金融危机。

---

① Hopkins and Wallerstein,"Conclusions,"49.
② 正如沃勒斯坦所形容的碎片化的个体生产的"魔盒";碎片化的个体生产构成了更加延长的商品链:"它们不是已知之事实,而是一种社会定义,实际上它们也是持续不断的社会再定义过程",具体请参见 Wallerstein,"Introduction,"Review,*A Journal of the Fernand Braudel Center* 23,no.1(2000):5.

第一部分
数字资本主义上升为危机

第 1 章
网络的连接性与劳动体系

我们这个时代的历史前身并非(1930年代的)经济大萧条时期,而是1970年代早期至中期。哈维①、普拉沙德(Vijay Prashad)②以及其他学者的论著表明,针对1970年代的经济衰退(recession)而展开的修补工作可谓影响深远;而这些修补工作最终导致了2008年的金融危机。我的论述独异于他们的观点,我侧重于讨论过去几十年间信息与传播技术如何成为资本主义发展的"跳动的脉搏"(beating pulse);并且,我把这一转变置于涵盖生产、金融与美国军事行动三大趋势所编织的网络中。1972年至1974年年末,美国股市损失了近一半的市值,使市场体系陷入被称为二战以来最糟糕的经济衰退的困境中③。穆迪(Kim Moody)回忆道,"世界资本主义经济开始探底停滞(ground to a halt),24个最富裕国家的经济增长率从1973年的5%下降到1975年的0"④。不仅美国,整个西欧地区,失业率急速上升,经济不平等(虽然在过去的25年间已经受到遏制)的状况也开始加深。1975年,世界贸易额首次在二战结束后出现大幅下滑⑤。原油价格不再受到英美以及其他帝国主义国家的大石油公司和国家机构的恣意控制,而随着石油输出国组织展示了它们新的政治实力,急速飙升;直至1974年4月的两年内,美国油价足足上升了三成有余⑥。美国逐步升级了在东南亚地区的债务融资之战(debt-financed war),却导致国内通胀压力与日俱增。

二战后西欧与日本重建资本主义,导致出现过剩生产力,而资本主义国家之间也已

---

① David Harvey, *Enigma of Capital* (New York: Oxford University Press, 2010).
② Vijay Prashad, *The Poorer Nations: A Possible History of the Global South* (London: Verso, 2012).
③ Judith Stein, *Pivotal Decade: How the United States Traded Factories for Services in the Seventies* (New Haven, Conn.: Yale University Press, 2010), 102.
④ Kim Moody, *U. S. Labor in Trouble and Transition* (New York: Verso, 2007), 12.
⑤ Stein, *Pivotal Decade*, 127.
⑥ Stein, *Pivotal Decade*, 106-7.

经不再围绕一连串的制造业(如钢铁制造、汽车、化工、纺织与家用电子产品)而展开竞争①。昔日强劲的美国制造业引擎开始熄火,从美国中西部工业基地的满目疮痍便可见一斑。随着竞争与生产力过剩所引发的利润率的不断紧缩②,政治冲突进一步加剧了美国资本的压力。

国际上,"第三世界"的政治规划受到内部矛盾重重的社会主义第二世界的大力支持,并遏制了资本的再生性潜能。许多国家威胁要摆脱美国国务院为它们设定的发展路线。与此同时,美国民安物阜的"黄金时代"渐进结束,雇佣劳动者的日常反抗降低了(资方的)利润率。对于国内数百万人民(不仅包括贫穷的白人还有大量的非裔美国人、墨西哥裔美国人)而言,他们的生活哪怕想勉强符合既定标准,也无异于镜花水月。他们无法公平地享受到良好的教育、医疗卫生、住房以及其他基本的社会福利。可以这么认为,在二战结束后到1970年代早期之间,加入工会的美国工人阶级的薪资与福利待遇得到极大提高,而他们的力量也在慢慢积蓄、逐渐壮大。(相继出现的)民权运动、女权主义运动与反战运动纷纭交错,它们推动了工人阶级(运动)的激进化,促使他们更加激烈地反对那些要求土地使用权的公司管理层以及对工人不闻不问的工会领导者③。在公司高管的眼里,工人们正日益变得令人捉摸不透;后者限制并阻止了(公司的资本)积累战略,威胁将打碎"工联主义"的制度性框架。要知道,这一框架确立了处理劳动关系的基本模式,已经覆盖了1/3由工会代表的美国工人。

1970年代经济危机所展现出的社会轮廓(social contours)与后果,迅速凌驾于任何狭隘地追逐利润的冲动之上。冲突与争斗在各个层面如火如荼地展开:国内,业主及其同盟试图招降桀骜不驯的工人阶级;国际上,他们极力反对由第三世界国家发起的不结盟运动,及其致力于建设的"国际经济新秩序"与"国际信息新秩序"运动④。面对这些来自市场与阶级的压力、或真或假的(工人)叛乱,美国公司开始重建生产运作流程。

资本与资本主义国家一直在寻找大卫·哈维所说的"时空修复"(spatio-temporal fix),又或者如穆迪所说,寻求"恢复原有的利润率与提高竞争力的另一种方式"⑤。这些

---

① 关于该议题的最新的论述,请参见 Robert Brenner, *The Boom and the Bubble: The U. S. in the World Economy* (London: Verso, 2002); and Stein, *Pivotal Decade*. Bennett Harrison and Barry Bluestone, *The Deindustrialization of America: Plant Closings, Community Abandonment, and the Dismantling of Basic Industry* (New York: Basic, 1982) 也颇有价值; and Bennett Harrison and Barry Bluestone, *The Great U-Turn: Corporate Restructuring and the Polarizing of America* (New York: Basic, 1990).

② Stein, *Pivotal Decade*, 115.

③ Jefferson Cowie, *Stayin' Alive: The 1970s and the Last Days of the Working Class* (New York: New Press, 2010); Aaron Brenner, Robert Brenner, and Cal Winslow, eds., *Rebel Rank and File: Labor Militancy and Revolt from Below during the Long 1970s* (New York: Verso, 2010); Thomas Borstelmann, *The 1970s: A New Global History from Civil Rights to Economic Inequality* (Princeton, N. J.: Princeton University Press, 2012).

④ Prashad, *Poorer Nations*; Dan Schiller, *How to Think about Information* (Urbana: University of Illinois Press, 2007), 37–39.

⑤ David Harvey, *The New Imperialism* (Oxford: Oxford University Press, 2003), 87–88; Moody, *U. S. Labor in Trouble*, 13.

"修复"或"另一种方式"导致一场多面且偶然性的转变,而不仅仅是呆板机械的例行活动。普拉沙德指出,"美国政府授权了对其自身经济的重创行为(authorized a major assault on its own economy),以此重塑经济,并遵循德国社会学家桑巴特(Werner Sombart)提出的原则,'置之死地而后生——毁灭中才能诞生新的创造性精神'"①。信息与传播驱动了猛烈(wrenching)的生产变革,它正位于这一"毁灭式创新"的中心。

从头到脚的重建工作事无巨细,例如公司与全部产业内特定工种的内容与劳动的技术性分工,以及原本互不相连(discrete)如今日益可被分割(isolable)的生产过程的选址定位(location)。穆迪指出,这场"巨变"②(卡尔·波兰尼也提出过这一概念)既囊括了资本支出的定位与特点,也包含了投资驱动下劳动力的类型与数量。"全面质量管理"(total quality management)和"企业再造"(re-engineering)所导致的"精益生产"(Lean production)③已成为一句标语,它给那些疯狂攻击现有的常规工作流程的行为,笼罩了一层深思熟虑却非合理的光晕(an unjustified aura of thoughtfulness);这同样也适用于"实时库存"(just-in-time inventory)"团队工作""外包"以及"减员"④等一系列模式的提出。在这些行话背后,降低成本与体制转型,这些我们早已熟悉的变革,就这么单刀直入地闯进美国与西欧国家雇佣劳动者的生活中。同时,在全球南方,生产流程的重组将数以万计的农民与农业小生产者驱赶进雇佣劳动者的行列中。

我将从两个方面讨论这场"巨变":一是劳动过程⑤;二是更宏观的商品链,在其中,劳动力已经被调动集合起来。

当然,生产过程已经不是第一回遭遇重构。英国农业自开端起,资本已迫不及待地甩掉低效率,提高利润率,以及重新掌控那些执拗难训的工人。这并非一条线性与理性的进步之路。主次流程的颠倒(misplaced priorities)、从管理层面(对工人)加以控制的幻想、对生产常规过程的忽视,连同工人的抵制,合力阻碍了资本从整体上实现变革工作(流程)以及驱使工人服从(资本)目的的计划。修正—推迟—调整这一循环模式依然继续。然而,在这些限定条件之下,生产所依赖的劳动过程周期性地进行彻底改革。

---

① Prashad, *Poorer Nations*, 52.
② Moody, *U.S. Labor in Trouble*, 11-36.
③ James P. Womack, Daniel T. Jones, and Daniel Roos, *The Machine That Changed the World: The Story of Lean Production* (New York: HarperPerennial, 1991). Often this was actually only a variation on an older tune. David Harvey, *A Companion to Marx's Capital* (London: Verso, 2010).
④ Moody, *U.S. Labor in Trouble*, 28-34.
⑤ 在赫曼与莫斯可看来,劳动过程应为传播与媒体研究的重要领域,具体请参见 Andrew Herman and Vincent Mosco in "Radical Social Theory and the Communications Revolution," in *Communication and Social Structure*, ed. E. G. McAnany, N. Janus, and J. Schnitman (New York: Praeger, 1981), 58-84.

通过阅读英国工厂检验员报告与议会文件①,马克思试图理解他所处的年代(即英国工厂制度)下高科技劳动过程,进而奠定关于劳动过程发展史的三阶段论。马克思发现,资本主义在劳动过程的范围内设定了一条长期的前进路线:从手工业、制造业到大工业。每一类手工业生产,无论是印刷还是铸造业,都必须仰仗手工业者的技艺水平;在手工劳动中,一名手工业者往往生产出一整件商品,生产力与资本对劳动过程的控制都受到严格限制。劳动过程发展的第二阶段,马克思称之为制造业,主要是指 16 至 18 世纪的欧洲;制造业证明了资本成功地创造了更有效率的劳动分工这一事实。随着时间的流逝,曾是属于单个工人的工作,被分割成若干部分,这样彼此分离的工人只需要重复完成每一项分配给他的任务。马克思阐述,制造业劳动分工的特点在于,此前独立的工人开始服膺于资本的规训,那么,"等级分层"(hierarchic gradation)超越了临时的合作关系,代表了这一转型的劳动过程②。马克思相当尊重这一阶段的发展:制造业最终"(被)当作一种经济的作品,耸峙在都市手工业和农村家庭工业的基础上"③。许多独立的商业贸易,都拥有各自的技艺与运作方式,却不得不满足于"联合劳动"(associated labour)的需求,以实现那些在小作坊工作的工匠们难以企及的生产效率。制造业时代符合亚当·斯密所记载的"劳动的世界"(the world of labor);在亚当·斯密看来,哪怕一根最简单不过的针的制造,也需要多方配合共同完成。

然而,第三种形式即"大工业"的历史面貌,"从根本上"④扭转了劳动过程。不断面对提高劳动生产力的压力,资本"依照它在历史上发现的技术条件"⑤,并非均衡也并非完全地超越了劳动对其的隶属关系。在应用于生产的科学,或被引入生产过程中由能量所驱动的专业化机械设备面前,个体手工业者的技艺黯然失色,并且,手工业的活动,"才不复为社会生产的支配原则":马克思声称,"操纵工具的熟练,和工具一道由劳动者转移到机械上。工具的能率,从人类劳动力之人格的限制中解放出来了。于是,作为制造业分工的基础的技术条件,被扫除了"⑥。

生产工具从工匠的手工台向复杂又相互关联的机器的转变,不仅强迫数十个、数百个乃至数千个相互协作的工人转化成劳动力,更意味着我们必须将生产工具视为劳动过程的根本向量。大工业逐步将"劳动手段转化为仅能共同利用的劳动手段",而这(绝非

---

① Oz Frankel, *States of Inquiry: Social Investigations and Print Culture in Nineteenth - Century Britain and the United States* (Baltimore: Johns Hopkins, 2006), 10, 39 – 71.
② Karl Marx, *Capital*, Volume I: *A Critical Analysis of Capitalist Production* (New York: International, 1967), 360. 本译本使用郭大力、王亚南翻译的《资本论》版本(下同),上海:上海三联书店 2009 年,251 页。
③④ Marx, Capital, I, 368. 选自《资本论》2009 年,257 页。
⑤ Marx, Capital, I, 310. 选自《资本论》2009 年,213 页。
⑥ Marx, Capital, I, 420. 选自《资本论》2009 年,257、295 页。

偶然地）导致"一切生产方式，当作结合的社会的劳动之生产方式使用"，将变得"更加经济"①。

19世纪的英国工厂就是"仅能共同利用的劳动手段"的原型。18世纪末劳动分工与合作已是普遍现象；但从蒸汽机到以化石燃料提供能源的机器等一系列技术创新，史无前例地提高了产量与生产力。历史学家霍布斯鲍姆毫不夸张地指出，"工业革命标志着有文字记载的世界历史上人类生活的最根本转型"②。劳动过程正位于这一转型过程的中心。对此，大卫·哈维总结到，机械技术"使得速度与持续性成为机器系统的内在要素，工人不得不遵守流水生产线的操作流程"③。在马克思看来，19世纪上半叶机器在英国的广泛使用不仅延长了工作日，以保证那些昂贵的设备可以不受打搅，维持嗡嗡运转的状态，也增加了劳动强度④。

工业革命不是一次历史事件，而是持久复杂的历史过程。英国资本家率先投入使用蒸汽机与纺织厂，在此基础上产生并拓展了机器大生产的各种新兴形式：不同产业、劳动过程与地区间的变迁，推动了工业革命的进程⑤。环环相扣的技术创新导致一系列新的消费品与资本货物的产生：缝纫机、木制产品、收割机、自行车与小轿车。受英国工业革命的启发，格伦·波特（Glenn Porter）如是描述19世纪末20世纪初美国工业革命的经验，"工厂组织、专业化机器、精密化生产、可互换零件、共同协调的工作流程与物流（materials flows），并且，冲压与焊接金属的新技术"已成为生产分析、实验与重组的对象⑥。生产技术不断突破之前商品生产的规模。

制造业产量的增长有赖于三大新兴的网络工业（network industry），即交通、能源与电

---

① Marx Capital, I, 763. 选自《资本论》2009年，567页；在《资本论》另一处，马克思对这一过程做了启发性的论述："因为随着劳动对资本的实际上的从属或特殊资本主义生产方式的发展，变成总劳动过程的实际执行者的并不是单个工人，而是日益以社会的规模结合起来的劳动能力；互相竞争的和构成为一台总生产机器的各种劳动能力，以极其不同的方式参加直接的商品形成过程，或者在这里不如说直接参加产品形成过程：有的人多用手工作，有的人多用脑工作，有的人当经理、工程师、工艺师等等，有的人当监工，有的人当直接的体力劳动者或者做十分简单的粗工，于是劳动能力的越来越多的职能被列在生产劳动的直接概念下，这种劳动能力的承担者也被列在生产工人的概念下，即直接被资本剥削的和从属于资本价值增殖过程与生产过程本身的工人的概念下"，From A Critical Analysis of Capitalist Production in Marx, *Capital*, *Volume 1*: *A Critique of Political Economy*, trans. Ben Fowkes, (Harmondsworth: Penguin, 1992), 1039 – 40 (original emphasis). 该段引文没有收录在郭大力、王亚南翻译的《资本论》第一卷里，请参见中共中央马克思、恩格斯、列宁、斯大林著作编译局，《马克思恩格斯全集》（第49卷），北京：人民出版社1985年，100 – 101页：译者注。
② Eric Hobsbawm, *Industry and Empire*: *The Birth of the Industrial Revolution* (New Press, 1999), xi.
③ Harvey, *Companion to Marx's Capital*, 212.
④ E. P. Thompson, "Time, Work – Discipline, and Industrial Capitalism," *Past and Present* 38 (December 1967): 56 – 97.
⑤ David S. Landes, *The Unbound Prometheus*: *Technological Change and Industrial Development in Western Europe from 1750 to the Present* (Cambridge: Cambridge University Press, 1969); Sidney Pollard, *Peaceful Conquest*: *The Industrialization of Europe 1760 – 1970* (Oxford University Press, 1982).
⑥ Glenn Porter, "Foreword," in D. A. Hounshell, *From the American System to Mass Production*, 1800 – 1932 (Baltimore: Johns Hopkins, 1984), xv.

信;它们帮助制造商开拓全国性的产品市场。同样这些基础设施推动了制造业劳动过程的彻底重组①。1885 年至 1890 年,美国工业引入电力,1900 年后引入电力公司的集中发电模式,从而使电力走到了工业重组的前沿。然而,电力取代煤与蒸汽,远不止能源更替这么简单。理查德·杜波夫(Richard DuBoff)指出,与电力传输相比,早期的生产技术、实践与组织方式显得十分突兀,"看起来累赘多余"。于是,电气化成为"制造业升级换代"的支点。"相较于蒸汽机时代,电气时代的生产成本下降,而产量却能更大程度地增长"。对此,杜波夫解释到,"能源装置的细分与流动性导致了劳动、生产资料与资本设备更大范围的结合"②。人们发现,电力不仅能够拆分能源供给,通过发电厂使发电设备分布四处,更能去中心化,强化个体操作的能力。

与之相伴相生的,是信息加工者的持续增长。当我们论及工业革命,映入脑海的可能是肮脏的烟囱、轰鸣的机器以及"不熟练的"工厂工人。不过,哪怕在工业化革命伊始,它也紧紧围绕信息生产、加工与管理等方面而展开。公司信息处理能力的增强,不仅能够处理销售订单,拟订会计与财务方案,并从 19 世纪末开始制订系统性的市场营销与技术调研计划,这些计划取决于国家资本。1919 年,非生产人员已占美国制造业总体队伍的 19%,在接下来的经济危机时期,份额一直在这一数字上下浮动;二战结束后,非生产人员的数量激增,1979 年份额高达 28%③。尤其在电力或电器设备、仪器、化工和石化、机械等科学主导的行业中,这一份额更高;通用电气这些行业领导者所招募的非生产人员的数量,远高于其他小公司④。美国工程师的数量从 1910 年的 77 000 名增长到 1970 年的 120 万人⑤,正是这一时代的典型特征。但是职业变革的范围更为广泛。企业经理,与会计、广告或电信等服务行业从业人员,这些专业的、科技的、文职性质的或管理性职位,都大大扩展了。

1920 年代早期⑥,信息工作者的数量剧增,无疑给美国资本家带来了成本压力。西摩·梅尔曼(Seymour Melman)在一篇发表于 60 年前的文章中颇有洞察力地预见了他称之为美国制造业"行政开支"(administrative overhead)的增加。他发现,1899 至 1947 年

---

① Gary Fields, *Territories of Profit:Communications,Capitalist Development,and the Innovative Enterprises of G. F. Swift and Dell Computer* (Stanford,Calif.:Stanford University Press,2004).
② Richard B. Du Boff,"The Introduction of Electric Power in American Manufacturing," *Economic History Review* 20,no. 3 (December 1967):509 – 10,513,514,518.
③ U. S. Department of Labor,Bureau of Labor Statistics, *Handbook of Labor Statistics*, *Bulletin* 2175,December 1983 (Washington,D. C.:U. S. GPO),table 71,pp. 165 – 68.
④ Mark McColloch, *White Collar Workers in Transition:The Boom Years*,1940 – 1970 (Westport,Conn:Greenwood,1983),15.
⑤ Dale C. Johnson,ed., *Class and Social Development:A New Theory of the Middle Class* (Beverly Hills,Calif.:Sage,1982),197.
⑥ Jorge Reina Schement,"Porat,Bell,and the Information Society Reconsidered:The Growth of Information Work in the Early Twentieth Century," *Information Processing and Management* 26,no. 4 (1990):449 – 65.

间,美国制造业行政人员增长幅度高达485%,共有267.2万人;而生产人员增长幅度只有160%,共有1 201万人。梅尔曼认为行政人员所占比例的增长并非生产效率走低的结果,而是源自于"行政人员所承担的新职能"。他的解释是,这一转变的实质在于,"不同种类的商业行为开始出现,它们统一受控于管理目标之下",正如管理层"在每一个细节上试图控制生产成本、工作强度、产品的市场需求以及企业运作的其他方面"①。其他的研究确证并更新了职场结构的这一发展趋势②。二战结束后数十年间美国外商直接投资的发展,进一步扩大了跨国企业的管理人员与职员队伍,提高了生产技术。那么高级管理者与企业所有者如何能够保持对不断扩展、花销剧增的成本的管控呢?

无论是19世纪末的德国还是20世纪中期的美国,不少激进的学者都对该问题的潜在意义有过思索。哈利·布雷弗曼(Harry Braverman)指出,"行政"或"白领工作""脑力劳动"(德国在19世纪末围绕职业结构的转型所展开的辩论中曾使用这个术语)这一工种已经引发资本家的持续关注。布雷弗曼表明,随着行政的、专业的、管理性或技术工作的重要性日渐凸显,企业高管竭力寻找、确认并采用各种手段,旨在提高工作效率。合理地削减成本与重组职业结构,成为普遍现象。它使更多的女性进入雇佣劳动行列,持续引发劳动分工与工作内容的变革,并越来越把重心放在新的办公科技上。

在杰弗里·奥地利(Geoffrey D. Austrian)看来,重建劳动过程很大程度上有赖于"精确且及时的成本核算",那么,用于机电数据处理的打孔卡机的应用"必须以工作的合理化为前提"③。所以,企业高管通常能够实现利润目标,后者并非仅仅停留在提高劳动生产率这一水平上。纽约中央铁路用打孔卡机取代了1895年起每年几乎四百万张的货运单;据此,纽约中央铁路能够每周而不是每月绘制货运路线与记录收入明细,并依照它复杂的铁路交通网络更有效地安排货物运输④。一战后,随着高官们"确信系统化(管理)"之于办公事务的"必要性",至少有100台新式的办公设备投放到美国市场;1940年代末,这个数字上升到3 000台⑤。机械与机电类办公设备的更新换代——从打字机、直立式档案柜到加法机、计算器以及打孔卡数据处理器,不断改变着劳动过程。然而,劳动过程的

---

① Seymour Melman,"The Rise of Administrative Overhead in the Manufacturing Industries of the United States,1899 – 1947,"*Oxford Economic Papers*,New Series,3,no.1(February 1951),67,90,91,92.
② C. Wright Mills,*White Collar*(New York:Oxford University Press,1953);McColloch,*White Collar Workers*,15,83;Daniel Bell,*The Coming of the Post – Industrial Society*(New York:Basic,1974);Marc Uri Porat,*The Information Economy:Definition and Measurement*,PhD diss.,Stanford University,published by U. S. Department of Commerce,May 1977;Schement,"Porat."
③ Geoffrey D. Austrian,*Herman Hollerith:Forgotten Giant of Information Processing*(New York:Columbia University Press,1982),203.
④ Austrian,*Herman Hollerith*,125.
⑤ Mills,*White Collar*,193.

改变也无法阻挡劳动生产率的节节高升①。

机器的投入使用,让劳动者能够在保证质量的基础上提高大部分商品的产量;可到了1950年代末,依然没有出现可以从根本上转变各种信息处理工作(流程)的技术革命。一面是不断提高的资本密集度预示着工厂装配线上机器使用的日常化与普遍化,另一面却是手工操作(在劳动分工、合作与机电设备的协助下)依然主导着信息处理这一工作领域。设计师仍旧坚持手工设计与绘制草图。秘书们手动打信、整理备忘录与报告(标准速度是1分钟60个单词),并使用直立式档案柜汇总或储存这些资料。小职员与底层管理者"记录"下公司的运作情况,起草与查阅备忘录或其他文件资料,并通过电话或没完没了的面对面会议等方式与高层管理者之间保持互通。在广告行业,所谓的"广告创意人员"围绕不同的推广活动进行头脑风暴,展现了一种混杂着巧舌若簧、矫揉造作与主题鲜明等元素在内的德柏雷(Don Draperish)式的风格,却不失迎合消费者与媒体诉求之心。出纳主任和簿记员手工或使用简单的机器进行复杂的统计运算;一直到1930年代末,政府和企业科层所需要的某些复杂的统计工作才交由女性数学家(female "computers")的核心骨干来完成②。不断膨胀的行政、管理、办公、科技与工程机构所要求的相对较高的人工成本(所有这些流入大公司的"白领"劳动)能够被合理化吗?

当年英国工厂推进集体劳动过程形成的动力(impulse,正如"仅能共同利用的劳动手段"),作为一种决定性的力量(a shaping force),出于大致相同的原因进入到由计算机所主导的劳动过程当中。在20世纪最后数十年至21世纪初,公司重组打破了工厂与产地、办公室与实验室之间正常的合作生产流程。若没有全能的、无远弗届的计算机通讯的"辅佐",这一重组工作恐难以推进下去。

包括互联网在内的网络(当它成为任何企业组织架构的普遍基础时)组成了工具箱。网络支持(network enabled)的工具(tool)的特征在于,它能够帮助那些日益繁复的信息处理工作突破以往手工技艺所受到的限制。无论是人工复印、誊写还是打印,建筑制图还是产品设计,这些手工完成的信息工作在网络支持的共享工具与数据等技术创新的条件下已实现转型。相比于工厂工人而言,办公室职员身上的资本投资急剧增长③。因此,网络使生产工具被转化成"仅能共同利用的劳动手段"这一内在的历史趋势,延续到新的生产实践或以往不被波及的劳动分工领域(previously exemptsegments)当中——例如谷歌的

---

① Margaret Davies, *Woman's Place Is at the Typewriter* (Philadelphia: Temple University Press, 1982); James W. Cortada, *Before the Computer: IBM, NCR, Burroughs, and Remington Rand and the Industry They Created* 1865 – 1956 (Princeton, N. J. : Princeton University Press, 1993); JoAnne Yates, *Control through Communication: The Rise of System in American Management* (Baltimore: Johns Hopkins University Press, 1989); Vincent E. Giuliano, "The Mechanization of Office Work," *Scientific American* 247, no. 3 (September 1982), 149 – 64.

② David Alan Grier, *When Computers Were Human* (Princeton, N. J. : Princeton University Press, 2005).

③ "Office Automation: How Much Is Too Much?" (advertisement), *Wall Street Journal*, August 6, 1985, 11.

搜索与邮件功能、用于文字处理或税务申报的标准化的软件包,或者那些旨在管理企业数据、经过定制的大型软件。随着资本重新规定了各种行业与职位的技术要求,面对不断扩展的系统和应用程序(Across anever - widening front of systems and applications),有时被称为"信息资源共享"的技术推动了劳动过程的质变①。我并非表明上述这些网络工具(network tool)超越了人类技艺;当然,只有发展与培育新技术,才能操作与使用工具。企业信息技术工人与外部供应商跟随技术更新的脚步,提高自身技术水平,并辨别出(identify)那些额外的技能要求。

即便应对1970年代经济低迷局面的措施开始相继出台,布雷弗曼仍在一本具有独创性的著作中,清晰地描述了"彼时大规模涌现的工种如何在办公与服务过程中没有如工厂那般被极端合理化与机械化的情况,尽管这已是大势所趋"②。在此基础上,乌苏拉·胡斯(Ursula Huws)借用布雷弗曼的观点详细讲解(合理化与机械化的)每一步骤。商业组织被解析成几个组成部分。作者检视了每一部分或功能所应具备的"特定的技艺与职责",以及"对包括默会知识在内的工人知识的渐进式的整理"。职责被化约成不同的组成要素,用以"向工人设定行为标准,并通常引入复杂精密的劳动分工体系,由此将更加日常的任务落实到每一个低技术工人身上"。相应地,控制与管理的外部命令形式,与产出测算一样,需要制定并贯彻下去③。

下列三重关系中,网络发挥着重要作用:通过资源共享与任务自动化等形式,提高生产力;增强对那些在此之前不受管控的劳动过程的监管与干预;加强此前互不连属的各个生产过程之间的关联。尼克·戴尔-维泽福特(Nick Dyer-Witheford)认为,办公室、教室、工作室与实验室里被动员起来的劳动者,不仅第一次与生产一线员工,更与代表最终消费者的劳动者产生直接关系④。计算机网络从根本上拓展了劳动过程的范围——依据工厂生产制,马克思相当重视劳动过程。专门服务于协作使用目的的网络化工具(networked tool),体现了标准化的操作流程,并把分布在各地、拥有不同技艺的工人团结起来,推动他们将共享知识发挥到最大的效能。开发协作劳动潜能的前景成为计算机网络发展的最大推动力。1968年,约瑟夫·利克莱德(Joseph Licklider)与罗伯特·泰勒(Robert Taylor)在制定互联网前身阿帕网的试验计划时,曾强调"一台经过精细编程的计

---

① Harry Braverman, *Labor and Monopoly Capital* (New York: Monthly Review, 1974), 9.
② Braverman, *Labor and Monopoly Capital*, 37.
③ Ursula Huws, "Crisis as Capitalist Opportunity: New Accumulation through Public Service Commodification," in *The Crisis and the Left: The Socialist Register* 2012, ed. L. Panitch, G. Albo, and V. Chibber (Pontypool, U. K.: Merlin, 2011), 74, 76 (quote).
④ 彼时,在日本关于信息社会的话语里,实现这些联系是明确目标。具体请参见 Nick Dyer-Witheford, *Cyber-Marx: Cycles and Circuits of Struggle in High-Technology Capitalism* (Urbana: University of Illinois Press, 1999), 20; Tessa Morris-Suzuki, *Beyond Computopia: Information, Automation and Democracy in Japan* (London: Kegan Paul, 1988), 8–13.

算机可以保证使用者既能直接接触信息源,又能充分了解利用这些资源的过程"。他们宣称,由无线电通信连接的多路存取计算机的"革命性"影响,来自于这些系统支持"散布的智识资源"的"共享"进而形成"合作模型"的能力。所谓"合作模型",是指"在建构、维系与使用某一模型过程中所应遵循的合作关系"①。美国国防部高等研究计划署(Defense Advanced Research Projects Agency,DARPA)曾于1969年启动发展阿帕网计划,实际上在这一计划中已然孕育了"资源共享计算机网络"的理念②。

诚如珍妮特·阿巴特(Janet Abbate)所表述的那般,计算机属于体积庞大、成本巨大的设备这一事实,反而推动网络朝共享(信息)处理能力与软件程序的方向发展③——哪怕在1968年,利克莱德与泰勒似乎指向一种更加包罗万象(more overarching)的计算机能力。阿帕网的首要承包商是一家名为BBN的公司,1981年,也正是万维网改变并扩大互联网版图的十年前,该公司在评估阿帕网时,确定无疑地强调资源共享的理念。阿帕网的信息量呈级数增长,从1971年的大约6 000条增长至1977年的1 000万条④。BBN公司发现,伴随着这一增长,阿帕网实现了两项主要目标。首先,它敦促人们开发新技术或发展出新知识,以连接不同计算机,"这样,更为宽泛的互动关系成为可能"。其次,它保障用户"通过资源共享的方式提高并增强计算机的研发能力"⑤。此前,代表不同技术标准的计算机互不兼容;如今,计算机网络使得这些计算机之间能够有效地相互连接,并且,它允许相互连接的任一计算机的用户或程序"可以任意使用其他任何一台计算机上的程序或子系统,而无需修改远程程序"⑥。这一"互动"的意义早已超越了当年美国国防部高等研究计划署的研究计划,而扩展至"全社会"⑦。到了1981年,BBN公司明白无

---

① J. C. R. Licklider and Robert W. Taylor,"The Computer as a Communication Device,"*Science and Technology* 76 (April 1968):22 (original emphasis),27,28,30.
② Licklider and Taylor,"Computer as a Communication Device,"30;要了解立克里德及其分时系统(time – sharing systems),请参见 Arthur L. Norberg and Judy E. O'Neill, *Transforming Computer Technology*:*Information Processing for the Pentagon*,1962 – 1986 (Baltimore, Md.:Johns Hopkins,1996),68 – 118;Janet Abbate, *Inventing the Internet* (Cambridge, Mass.:MIT Press,1999).
③ Abbate, *Inventing the Internet*,96,100,104 – 6.
④ BBN Communications Corporation, Report No. 4799,"A History of the ARPA – NET:The First Decade", prepared for Defense Advanced Research Agency, April 1981,III – 100 – 102.
⑤ BBN,"History of the ARPANET,"II – 2. Norbert and O'Neill, in *Transforming Computer Technology*, state:"ARPANET was a large – scale experiment that was started to solve the problem of resource sharing between computers and among researchers. The goal was to connect computing systems, and through the systems the researchers, so that research could be accumulated and duplication of effort avoided through the sharing of resources and improved communication"(192).
⑥ BBN,"History of the Arpanet,"II – 2. "[V]arious computer systems of different ages and degrees of incompatibility always exist concurrently, which means that some digitized data residing in a computer can't easily be shared with other parts of the enterprise. To be sure, much progress has been made since the late 1960s to address this problem;however, one can reasonably assume it will never be fully resolved." James W. Cortada, *Information and the Modern Corporation* (Cambridge, Mass.:MIT Press,2011),93.
⑦ BBN,"History of the Arpanet,"II – 3. What can best be termed utopian gestures to the wider societal applications of networked tools are also evident in Licklider and Taylor,"Computer as a Communication Device",39 – 40.

误地预测出"(计算机网络)最终对公共或私人部门的计算机使用所造成的深远影响"①。

早在 1960 年代,首次可公开使用的部分电子数据库可以让使用者远程使用那些共享的机读书目数据库与数据文件。正如利克莱德与泰勒所预示的,到了 1970 年代,原本意味着人类思想与情感表达而非软件或信息处理能力的共享的电子邮件,逐渐使那些在大学和军工产业工作的计算机科学家打破地域的藩篱,实现劳动协作。在 1980 年代,局域网的发展深化了共享各类软件工具与办公资源(例如打印机)的趋势;与此同时,在制造业生产领域,所谓的电子数据交换保证了在工厂第一线投入使用的新式机器同工厂与供应商之间的信息流动。迄今为止,广域网使得更大范围的数据库资源与应用程序向更加专有或专属的联机系统(online system)转移。朝向微型或台式电脑终端发展的趋势,深入推进了"使用网络以实现资源共享"这一理念;这一理念早已在各种计算机网络项目中持续得到体现。

如今,管理者、计算机研发人员与工程师等技术人员转向更高层次的问题:如何建立一个完整的计算机网络,而不是彼此隔离的主机电脑。为了实现这一目标,人们已尝试各种截然不同的方法以实现网络创新。实际上,直到 1990 年代早期,主导性的数据通信技术才被正式确定下来。然而,提高(网络)共享能力的过程并非一条直线,而是时断时续的,这在一定程度上决定了哪一类网络系统能够在竞争中脱颖而出。1980 年代早期用于增建被称为"互联网"的协议将互操作性(interoperability)放在首位。互联网系统的"互操作性"能够保障分散各地的用户能够使用共享数据库与应用程序;随着构建万维网的软件相继面世,这一优势得到进一步增强。我们已经到达了一个转折点。互联网不但扩展了可连通功能的范围,也拓宽了准入网络化工具的条件;互联网突破了任何专属的数据通信系统的限制,这使它显得有点难以驾驭。

资本对网络(network connectivity)连接性的占用与专有,实际上彻底改造了大工业的劳动过程:以往因为劳动分工而彼此互不连属的生产部门,被网络整合成集体协作的生产过程,并与更高级的劳动过程直接对接。詹姆斯·科尔塔达(James Cortada)着重指出,不同产业部门和私人公司的采用模式(Patterns of adoption)差别很大②。他强调,"早在互联网被广泛应用之前,商业已开始使用电信网络",并着手对此前投资数十亿的系统进行改革,因此,"大部分的结构性变革已经发生,这些变革甚至至今在互联网领域还没有出现"③。网络所打开的管理选择的范围,几乎覆盖无限时域,因为可重新编程、可无限扩展

---

① BBN, "History of the Arpanet," II-7,8.
② James W. Cortada, *The Digital Hand*, Volume 1: *How Computers Changed the Work of American Manufacturing, Transportation, and Retail Industries* (New York: Oxford University Press, 2004), 24.
③ James W. Cortada, "New Wine in Old and New Bottles: Patterns and Effects of the Internet on Companies," in *The Internet and American Business*, ed. William Aspray and Paul E. Ceruzzi (Cambridge, Mass.: MIT Press, 2008), 415, 417.

的网络是有史以来创造出的用途最广泛的工具之一。

到了1980年代,人们普遍认为,网络使大公司有机会"向其他公司出售有关自己公司运作的副产品——信息",并越来越普遍地"利用公司信息来赢利"①。《商业周刊》吹嘘:大多数美国公司"正逐渐意识到自己占有宝贵的信息资源,这些资源完全可以被用作有效的战略武器"。该杂志进一步指明,"随着这些公司利用信息的手段不断翻新且多种多样,它们可以更好地运作自己的基础性业务,提供各项服务以拓展其业务市场,并能够创造出新的产品或开发新的业务,从而在竞争中脱颖而出"②。在接下来的数十年间,这一发展重心成为主流。

不仅职员、专业、管理和技术工作领域中逐渐引入行政控制体系,大公司对网络的战略性应用还抱有其他目的。首先,它们利用网络,把那些标准化的应用程序外包给特定的供应商,如思爱普(SAP)、甲骨文(Oracle)或美国国际商业机器公司(IBM)。其次,大公司运用网络系统,旨在确立市场优势的结构化形式。许多管理学大师都在讲授如何调用计算机系统以树立市场准入藩篱(例如让顾客对公司软件与服务产生依赖,进而提高转换成本)、改变与供应商的力量均衡关系(通过网络了解供应商的库存情况,帮助通用汽车或通用电气公司降低存货成本),以及开发新的产品与业务以扭转产业间竞争的基本规则③。例如,彭博公司(Bloomberg)创立了一款专属系统,牢牢锁定公司用户,从而比那些金融数据的供应商抢先一步④。再次,公司应用网络系统,旨在降低人力成本。迈克·帕姆(Michael Palm)指出,20世纪初期以来,电话系统以自动(电动机械)开关为基础,奉行自助式销售理念;计算机网络延续了这一理念,保障了大公司将高昂的未付人工成本转嫁到消费者身上⑤。

大部分应用程序耗资不菲,或者它们并未产生预期的效果。然而,商业愈发被计算机网络的连接性所吸引。1980年,美国国际商业机器公司首席科学家估计,美国的劳动人口中,每48位雇佣工人配备一台电脑终端;在美国国际商业机器公司的顾客群体中,每25位雇佣工人配备一台电脑终端;而在该公司内部,每5位雇佣工人配备一台电脑终端(彼时,美国国际商业机器公司已经成为一家所向披靡的高科技公司巨头、美国公司的

---

① Michael E. Porter and Victor E. Millar, "How Information Gives You Competitive Advantage," *Harvard Business Review* 63, no. 4 (July – August 1985):149 – 60; "capitalizing" quote from Irving P. Canton, "Learning to Love the Service Economy," *Harvard Business Review* 62, no.3 (May – June 1984):89 – 97.

② "Business Is Turning Data into a Potent Strategic Weapon," *Business Week*, August 22,1983,92 – 98.

③ F. Warren McFarlan, "Information Technology Changes the Way you Compete", *Harvard Business Review* 62, sno.3 (May – June 1984):98 – 103; "Cost – Cutting that Goes to the Bone," *Business Week*, July 12,1982,65 – 66; Gregory L. Parsons, "Information Technology: A New Competitive Weapon", *Sloan Management Review* 25, no. 1 (Fall 1983):3 – 13.

④ "TRW Leads a Revolution in Managing Technology," *Business Week*, November 15,1982,130.

⑤ Michael Palm, "Phoning It In:Self – Service, Telecommunications, and New Consumer Labor," PhD diss., New York University,2010.

标杆)。他甚至预测,这些"电脑终端"的数量将在未来不断增长①。当然,他的预测被证实。2012 年的一项研究显示,"在最发达的经济体(国家或地区)里,百分百的劳动者被卷入到供应链中,并在日常工作时使用信息技术;这已是稀疏平常的现象"②。

但是,这一奥林匹亚式的观点模糊了网络给工作本身带来的变革。在汽车工业重组专家哈利·夏肯(Harley Shaiken)看来,"计算机技术并没有彻底改变大部分劳动过程"。1984 年,他指出管理系统应用计算机辅助设计(CAD)后可能产生的四大好处:扩大了设计选择的范围,增加了系统修复的机会,使设计能更好地融合在制造过程中,摆脱了时间与空间的部分限制③。计算机辅助设计能够保证设计者可以测试不同的物质、不同的组成部分在应对压力、高温或其他可变条件时的反应,而无需耗费人力、财力建黏土模型来测试。设计者还能够模拟物质的结构与外形,从而在排除重量影响以及腐蚀的可能性的基础上,建立一个引人注目的(虚拟)模型④。随着设计过程的速度的增加,产品开发周期大大缩减⑤。几何建模的技术不断发展,尤其是在立体(3D)建模、部分被预编程序以评估结构特质的工程分析、对每个组成部分如何凭借"机械动力学"相互作用的检验,以及自动绘图技术等方面⑥。

1984 年,通用汽车五分之二的绘图工作都在计算机上进行,数年前,这一份额还不到五分之一;该公司的数学家利用计算机模型来预测某一特定的金属或合金能否被塑造成特定的图案。通用公司的土星汽车,作为世界上第一辆完全采用计算机操作系统的汽车,推动着其他汽车相继采用计算机辅助设计⑦。在随后的三十余年间,计算机辅助设计与计算机辅助工程(CAE)不断改进,应用范围不断扩大,并被整合进汽车开发战略中。哪怕现有的交通堵塞问题有可能被其他问题所取代,也一定要谨慎评价这一技术进展,

---

① Lewis M. Branscomb,"Computer Communications in the Eighties—Time to Put It All Together," International Conference on Computer Communications, Atlanta, Georgia, October 27, 1980, 5.

② Cortada, *Information*, 47.

③ Harley Shaiken, *Work Transformed: Automation and Labor in the Computer Age* (New York: Holt, Rinehart, and Winston, 1984), 218 – 19.

④ "The Car of the Future Will Have New Skin and Bones," *Business Week*, July 29, 1985, 50; Turner Whitted, "Some Recent Advances in Computer Graphics," *Science* 215, no. 4534 (February 12, 1982): 767 – 74; C. A. Hudson, "Computers in Manufacturing," *Science* 215, no. 4534 (February 12, 1982): 818 – 25; and especially, Harley Shaiken, *Work Transformed*, 136 – 246.

⑤ 也请参见 Bob Davis, "Computers Speed the Design of More Workaday Products," *Wall Street Journal*, January 18, 1985; 以及 "Computers in Design and Manufacturing," in *New Pathways in Science and Technology*, U. S. National Academy of Science, 214 – 34 (New York: Vintage, 1985).

⑥ Hudson, "Computers in Manufacturing," 819.

⑦ Electronic Data Systems, Inc., *Annual Report* 1984, 10; "Industry's Hot New Find: The Mathematician," *Business Week*, July 4, 1983, 88; Urban C. Lehner and John Marcom, "Auto Automation: To Battle the Japanese, GM Is Pushing Boldly into Computerization—If the Program Succeeds, It May Dramatically Affect Much of Manufacturing; Leaning on Computer Firms." *Wall Street Journal*, July 9, 1984.

因为它已经引发了一连串的问题。例如,丰田汽车在2010年召回1 100万辆汽车,很大程度上源于它"过度依赖于对其产品与样品的虚拟测试机制"①。企业控制生产进程的同时,也释放了它们自身的非理性行为。

不过,机械化与自动化蔓延到此前彼此互不连属的各个生产过程之中,其渗透程度同马克思主义理论家厄内思特·曼德尔(Ernest Mandel)在1970年代早期所宣称的情况相差无几,即"经济结构的每个部分第一次被彻底工业化"②。在曼德尔提出社会断裂(societal discontinuity)概念之前,管理顾问兼未来学家艾尔文·托夫勒(Alvin Toffler)使用类似的术语,称呼这所谓的"第三次浪潮"或正在兴起的系统革命为"超工业资本主义"(super-industrial capitalism)③。这并非表明网络化的合作模式(以大工业的劳动过程为典型)可以恣意运用于所有的商品链上,而成为一种普世性的现象;它充其量说明人们正在逐步摆脱网络化的合作模式的应用局限性。不同的劳动体系依然存在,新的工种开始出现或增长。然而,支撑劳动协作的计算机网络始终处于不断增强与扩展的状态中。

通过计算机网络形成的协作关系,被视为一种内在的、总体性的特征而与资本主义生产方式无关。简言之,它似乎成为了"天外救星"(a deus ex machina)。互联网保证了不同形式的协作关系(本克拉[Benkler]称之为"大众生产"[peer-production]④),然而,这些协作关系并非植根于寻常百姓。谁在征用共享资源与共同劳动,这是个问题;不同地区的社会行动者会给出截然不同的答案,毕竟,有些地区的行动者比其他地区的行动者拥有更大的权力。倘若让分散各地的人彼此之间形成合作关系的能力是计算机网络的核心价值所在,那么(网络化的合作模式)这一特征则按照剥削关系与劳动分工的结构,分层进入社会。核心问题在于,哪些行动者主导着网络化的合作关系,又为了什么目的。⑤

事实上,企业赢利的主动性一直不会消停,而其他不同(于主流)的网络化项目(networking projects)大部分处于边缘地带。大概从1970年代开始,发达资本主义经济体(国家或地区)的企业高管或管理者们迅速地拓展了他们熟悉的信条,即"大部分工作应当被

---

① John Reed, "Integration of Design Tools Speeds Up Car Production," *Financial Times*, September 29, 2010.
② Ernest Mandel, *Late Capitalism* (London: NLB, 1975), 191.
③ Alvin Toffler, *The Adaptive Corporation* (New York: Gower, 1985); David Noble, *Forces of Production* (New York: Oxford University Press, 1984).
④ Yochai Benkler, *The Wealth of Networks: How Social Production Transforms Markets and Freedom* (New Haven, Conn.: Yale University Press, 2006).
⑤ Graham Murdock, "Political Economies as Moral Economies: Commodities, Gifts, and Public Goods," in *The Handbook of Political Economy of Communications*, ed. Janet Wasko, Graham Murdock, and Helena Sousa, 13-40 (Chichester, U.K.: Wiley-Blackwell, 2011).

视为不同过程的集合体"以及"搜集关于工作流的数据",必须成为"每个人的日常工作环节"①。这一洞见已经在正在转移的(metastasizing)生产系统内部引发了一连串的突发性变革。如何利用网络工具重组企业及其劳动力队伍,在当前资本主义全球化时代已经成为一个基本的参照点。于是,网络在"巨变"过程中发挥着根本性的作用;在这一过程中,资本不但寻求对劳动过程内容的重组,更寻求(正如我们当前所见的)在已经重建了的商品链中,对工业管理程序、空间布置以及生产管理的重组。

---

① Cortada, *Information*, 11,12 – 13.

第 2 章
网络化的生产与重建的商品链

我们必须把数字网络置于资本主义全球化漫长且复杂的过程中加以考察。跨国企业可以追溯到 17 世纪,但直到 20 世纪,它才成为资本的首要表征。制造业的生产能力已经突破先前的局限,这是跨国企业的推动力之一。其他的因素包括:能够更便利地获取廉价劳动力与自然资源;在具有吸引力的国外市场中操纵产品销售与营销的能力渐长。专利法、配额、关税以及国家对出口的其他限制,同样刺激了资本主义企业在美国大本营之外建厂、开矿、设立营业部或开辟种植园[1]。当然,运输成本的降低与二战以来美元的强势地位这些因素也不容忽视[2]。经济史学家朱迪思·斯坦(Judith Stein)指出,早在 1958 年至 1965 年间,"美国公司海外投资增长率已高于国内 50%"。1965 年,新的外商直接投资占美国橡胶生产总投资的 34%,占运输设备制造投资的 25%,占化工制造投资的 25%,占电力机械制造投资的 21%[3]。

二战结束后数十年里,美国领导人周旋于欧洲帝国主义者与反殖民主义民族解放运动者之间,渔翁得利;同时,美国资本也成为跨国投资的重要来源。可以肯定的是,美国的外商直接投资的分布并不均衡,主要集中在少数地区。过去一个世纪里作为美国势力范围的拉丁美洲,获得美国的外商直接投资的份额虽不算多,却不可忽略;中东的石油资源也吸引到不少美国的外商直接投资。由于非洲仍是欧洲传统的势力范围,因此它并未吸引多少美国外商投资。日本的产业政策谨慎有序,在限制外商直接投资方面毫不手

---

[1] 1960 年代美国企业利润约占全球利润总额的 5%,截至 2007 年,这一数字飙升至 25%,请参见 Ed Yardeni, citing U. S. Commerce Department figures in Timothy Appel,"Overseas Profits Provide Shelter for U. S. Firms," *Wall Street Journal*, August 9, 2007. 也请参见 David Harvey, *Enigma of Capital* (New York: Oxford University Press, 2010).

[2] Mira Wilkins, *The Maturing of Multinational Enterprise* (Cambridge: Harvard University Press, 1974), 411–39.

[3] Judith Stein, *Pivotal Decade: How the United States Traded Factories for Services in the Seventies* (New Haven, Conn.: Yale University Press, 2010), 12. 另外两本见解深刻的著作包括 Martin Hart-Landsberg, *Capitalist Globalization: Consequences, Resistance, and Alternatives* (New York: Monthly Review, 2013);以及 Leo Panitch and Sam Gindin, *The Making of Global Capitalism: The Political Economy of American Empire* (London: Verso, 2012).

软。正如印度在1990年代之前的几十年里,尼赫鲁政府及其继任者一直主张进口替代原则。除去个别情况,苏联与中华人民共和国基本上没有吸纳资本主义国家的投资。如今美国的跨国资本将亚非拉的自然资源整合进它的商品链中;但那时,美国外商直接投资只是流向美国之外的少数几个地区,首要的正是欧洲。北大西洋的两端,构成了战后资本主义全球化的主轴;工厂制品、固定设备与资金流在这些地区来回流动。然而,1970年代以来,外商直接投资模式及其关联的商品链开始遭遇戏剧性的变动。

随着日本与德国战后重建的相继启动,以及汇率波动、安抚产业工人阶级与保护本国资本的国家政策的出台,资本主义国家或地区间的相互竞争再次出现,推动资本主义全球化迈向新的阶段。这一阶段也受到以下趋势的影响:产能过剩情况的不断恶化,以及由此引发的供求失衡(供给增长与需求减少之间的不匹配)。对资本而言,重组(经济)工作犹如箭在弦上,势在必行。在卡特政府时期(1977至1980年四年间),美国的外商直接投资不断飙升[1]。1980年美国总统大选,罗纳德·里根当选总统,这更助推了外商直接投资的增长。美国政府及其主导的多边机构强制通过各项政策,旨在保障资本投资的自由度。

商品链在空间上的重构这一历史过程,令人忧心忡忡;它充斥着各种矛盾与复杂的历史后果。随着美国对制造业的外商直接投资越来越倾向于低劳动力成本的东亚国家或地区,(制造)零部件的本地供应商开始崭露头角。香港、韩国、中国台湾与新加坡一跃成为全球制造业的重镇;它们(想当然地)认为自己能够在资本主义全球化过程中分到一杯羹,并逐渐与其他贫穷国家或地区区别开。可关键的是,它们的市场份额越来越多地返回至美国本土。一份出版于1985年的报告显示,"国外工厂大规模生产的商品再次出口至(美国)国内市场或其他出口市场,这一最早出现于1960年代末的现象正成为国外制造业的本质特征"。报告强调,它已被视为更宏大的重新制定企业生产与供给战略的一部分:"1977年,美国在亚洲的子公司的总销售额中超过25%返回到美国本土,而1966年这个数字还不到10%"[2]。整体而言,到1978年为止,发展中国家制造业出口至富裕国家的总额中,美国占据一半以上的份额。正如斯坦所说,"庞大的美国市场已成为美国盟友出口产业的安全阀,后者迅速成为美国在经济上有力的竞争者"。美国经济的"历史角色"在于,它"自始至终扮演着世界其他国家或地区市场的救命稻草的角色"[3]。美国市场处于"世界经济需求的来源"这一举足轻重的地位,不仅反映了窄化的经济关系,更要归因于(美国)在政治与战略上的精打细算、步步为营。冷战背景下,美国将无可匹敌的

---

[1] Jeffrey A. Frieden, *Global Capitalism: Its Fall and Rise in the Twentieth Century* (New York: Norton, 2007), 371.
[2] Joseph Grunwald and Kenneth Flamm, *The Global Factory: Foreign Assembly in International Trade* (Washington, D. C.: Brookings Institution, 1985), 3.
[3] Stein, *Pivotal Decade*, 174 (LDC exports to U.S.), 8 ("safety valve"), 156 ("first and last resort").

国内市场与经济政策作为"胡萝卜",引诱其他国家进入其势力范围,并让它们与社会主义阵营相脱离。

苏联社会主义的崩溃,以及中国重新进入如今被称为"全球资本主义"的体系之中等这些历史事件,不仅使资本主义全球化获益匪浅,更深刻地改变了它的进程。1997 年,跨国企业的生产总值高达 8 万亿,约占全球生产总值的 25%;联合国贸易和发展委员会(the United Nations Commissionon Trade and Development)2000 年指出,"跨国生产已横跨不同国家、部门、产业与经济领域"①。1980 至 2008 年间,发达资本主义国家的公司加大对外直接投资的存量,从 0.5 万亿上升到 13.623 万亿,增长率远远超过通货膨胀率②。兰兹伯格(Hart – Landsberg)特别指明,一系列投资与自由贸易协定的签署,是这一进展背后(movement)不可缺少的政治推动者③。

然而,倘若当前外商直接投资可以四处流动,那么外商直接投资的源头(sources)也开始多样化或重新进行调整(recompose)。二战结束初期,跨国资本不断壮大;除美国外,英国、德国、日本、荷兰、法国、意大利以及其他发达国家相继涌现跨国资本。然而,从1990 年代到 21 世纪初,少数却不容忽视的外商直接投资来自于韩国、中国台湾、香港、印度、新加坡、巴西、墨西哥以及中国(中国的对外直接投资从 2007 年每年 200 亿美元增长至 2012 年每年 840 亿美元,仅次于美国与日本④)。迄今为止,美国的海外直接投资总额仍居世界第一,但美国也仅仅只是排名第一(only first among equals)。2010 年,联合国贸易和发展委员会声称,"全球危机并未阻碍生产的国际化趋势"⑤(尽管兼并与收购以及贸易出现停滞⑥,外商直接投资总量降低⑦),但生产模式不断发生改变。2012 年,发展中国家吸收的外商直接投资首次超过发达国家,正如联合国贸易和发展委员会所说的"新兴的投资者国家"的外商直接投资占全球总量的比例越来越高,接近于 1/3⑧。2000 年,金砖五国⑨的外商直接投资总量只有 70 亿美元,2012 年这一数字已经飙升至 1 450 亿美元,占全球总量的 10%⑩。

资本主义全球化在商品链中锻造了数不胜数的新的链接,并与生产和贸易的激进变

---

① United Nations Conference on Trade and Development [UNCTAD], *World Investment Report* 2000 (New York: United Nations, 2000), 3.
② Peter Nolan and Jin Zhang, "Global Competition after the Financial Crisis", *New Left Review* 64 (July/August 2010): 101.
③ Hart – Landsberg, *Capitalist Globalization*, 90 – 130.
④ UNCTAD, *World Investment Report* 2013, *Country Fact Sheet: China*, available at at http://unctad.org/sections/dite_dir/docs/wir2013/wir13_fs_cn_en.pdf (accessed January 10, 2014).
⑤ UNCTAD, *World Investment Report* 2010 (New York: United Nations, 2010), xviii.
⑥ Helen Thomas, "Tax Fears Prompt M&A Rush," *Financial Times*, May 16, 2011.
⑦ UNCTAD, *World Investment Report* 2013.
⑧ UNCTAD, *World Investment Report* 2013, vii.
⑨ Brazil, Russia, India, China, and South Africa.
⑩ UNCTAD, *World Investment Report* 2013, 2.

化亦步亦趋。世界贸易组织总干事于2011年写道，"今天，原产国这个概念可以废弃不用……没有国家可以单独制造汽车或商用飞机"①。对于大公司而言，中间组件（intermediate components）可以本土制造，或外包生产，离岸出境。顶级承包商可能与跨国公司自己的装配工厂协同生产，而那些二三线承包商则不得不想方设法进入延长的商品链中。生产的碎片化改变了"贸易"的真正含义。贸易不再是指集中于不同国家的独立生产者之间的交易行为，而是指原材料、组件、半成品与商品在子公司及其承包商、销售商之间的流动情况。2012年，跨国公司通过它们的子公司、承包商与独立供应商，协同完成了全球近五分之四的贸易额②。作为这一体系的顶端，千余家举足轻重的跨国公司彻底改变了它们所主导的商品链。

40年前，两位具有敏锐眼光的学者撰文指出，"跨国生产的革命性意义在于，卫星通讯与集装箱运输等技术创新，使得四处散布的生产机构可以（从观念上）被整合进全球工厂之中"③。他们笔下的"集中化科学的进步"使跨国企业在总部进行生产协调与控制成为可能，这是因为（诚如他们所观察到）"集中化科学主要建立在对传播的复杂控制的基础之上"④。1982年，布鲁斯通与哈里森（Bluestone and Harrison）进一步补充道，"自由宽松的技术环境保证了大型企业能够同时运营数百家小型、分散在各地的工厂，而不是少数政治上弱不禁风、大型的地方企业"。这完全颠倒了人们长期视为理所当然的事物的自然秩序，即"对生产的集中化控制与大型工厂的生产行为的集中化之间的关系"⑤。对此，兰兹伯格如是评价，"无论在横向还是纵向上，企业着手将生产过程分解成更为精细的部分，并将这些分离的环节置放在两个或更多的国家中完成，以搭建跨境的生产网络（体系）"⑥。

就本质而言，资本协调与控制分散各地的生产流程，并非一种新的现象。哈德逊湾公司（the Hudson's Bay Company）伦敦总部的一位负责人早在1680年就开始尝试远程管理其加拿大北部分公司的经理人与职员⑦。信息网络并不是保障产业重新调整其运营模

---

① Pascal Lamy, "'Made in China' Tells Us Little about Global Trade," *Financial Times*, January 25, 2011.
② UNCTAD, World Investment Report 2013 Overview, x, available at http://unctad.org/en/PublicationsLibrary/wir2013overview_en.pdf (accessed January 10, 2014).
③ Richard J. Barnet and Ronald E. Muller, *Global Reach: The Power of the Multinational Corporations* (New York: Simon and Schuster, 1974), 27-28.
④ Barnet and Muller, *Global Reach*, 40, 42.
⑤ Bennett Harrison and Barry Bluestone, *The Deindustrialization of America: Plant Closings, Community Abandonment, and the Dismantling of Basic Industry* (New York: Basic, 1982), 178. 麻省理工学院某位管理分析师对计算机通信如何"减少时空对组织设计的限制"有更为具体的论述，请参见Peter G. W. Keen, "Telecommunications and Business Policy: The Coming Impacts of Communication on Management," CISR no. 81, Sloan WP no. 1266-81 (Cambridge, Mass.: MIT Center for Information Systems Research, 1981), 27.
⑥ Hart-Landsberg, *Capitalist Globalization*, 91.
⑦ Michael O'Leary, Wanda Orlikowski, and JoAnne Yates, "Distributed Work over the Centuries: Trust and Control in the Hudson's Bay Company, 1670-1826," in *Distributed Work*, ed. Pamela Hinds and Sara Kiesler (Cambridge, Mass.: MIT Press, 2001), 27-54.

式的唯一技术条件。19世纪晚期的铁路与输电网络,以及当今的燃气涡轮、柴油引擎与集装箱运输,都发挥着类似于信息网络的作用①。然而,现代协同生产机制的分散与重组,根本上有赖于数字连接性的大体量、通用等特性。有时(并不是通常情况下)在被切割得支离破碎、分散四处的劳动过程之中或之间,组建出高度集中(Dramatically heightened)的企业。这一重组过程可能横跨从工程研究到最终装配、从后台业务到售后服务等各个环节。它经常将"低值"功能外化并交由承包商承担,后者"仅仅"需要保障不同零部件在不同时间节点的及时运送(delivery)。通常来说,在公司战略的整体规划下,更多类型的工作被派往更多地方加以完成。反过来,除了工作场所的自动化,数字网络被赋予了一种新型的区位流动性(locational flexibility)。哈利·夏肯在1984年就已捕捉到这一转型过程的实质,"计算机技术能够帮助我们整合生产体系内部各个相互分离的环节……从设计师到流水生产线,各个层面的管理者,以及从底特律到圣保罗的地理空间"②。随着网络使工业管理程序、选址以及生产过程中不同环节的相互关系变得更加具有弹性,跨境的商品链似乎进入到一个永恒创新与变动的阶段之中。

经理与管理人员高度关注这一"进化"过程,并从商业媒体上追踪其发展动向③。"供应链管理"的专业知识开始大量出现,物流等新兴领域里的企业领导者名录相继出版;2010年,苹果公司拥有的复杂精细的供应商网络"被普遍视为最高级有效的网络之一"④。真正的突破性进展屈指可数;然而,它们并不能保证利润率,甚至是安全性。一定程度上,基于网络技术而实现的突破性进展,(反而)使大公司更容易受到自然灾害、政治风险以及其他偶然性因素的干扰。1990年代,一位记者曾指出,"所有产业都在实行及时供应链制度(just-in-time supply chains),指望生产技术能够提高生产效率"。因此,2003年,当美国国土安全部出台规定,要求托运方有义务在货物进入美国领土(视乎采取陆路、铁路还是水路的方式)前4至24小时之内上报边境官员时,及时供应的主干线(major artery)正遭到破坏(destabilized);对此,这位记者问道:"实现及时供应制度是否越来越困难?"⑤同样,2011年,日本地震、海啸以及随后泰国遭遇的半个世纪以来最严重的一次水灾,摧毁了美国上千家制造商平稳却脆弱的物流系统。福特、丰田等汽车制造商与戴尔等台式机制造商身在其列,难逃此劫⑥。其他形式的混乱情况也能对公司造成重

---

① 布鲁斯通(Bluestone)与哈里森(Harrison)称之为美国去工业化过程中的"被动技术"(Permissive technologies)。
② Harley Shaiken, *Work Transformed: Automation and Labor in the Computer Age* (New York: Holt, Rinehart, and Winston, 1984), 217.
③ Tim Scannell, "'Fortune' Survey Finds No Loss of Corporate Control in Move to DDP," *Computerworld*, March 23, 1981, 10–11.
④ Paul Taylor, "Supply Chain Is a Strategic Discipline," *Financial Times Connected Business*, January 26, 2011.
⑤ Daniel Altman, "Uncertain Economy Hinders Highly Precise Supply System," *New York Times*, March 15, 2003.
⑥ Ben Bland and Robin Kwong, "Sunken Ambitions," *Financial Times*, November 4, 2011.

大影响。有媒体披露,美泰公司的中方合同制造商使用铅基油漆,该公司(受舆论压力)不得不在 2007 年召回市面上近百万件玩具①。尽管苹果公司在业界长期享有"最优方法"的美誉,可仍然被"其承包商残酷剥削年轻工人"的新闻杀得措手不及。于是,物流领域迅速形成了一项专业化共识:"供应链拿管理在冒险"。

信息通信技术产业引领生产体系的捆绑化(parcelized)、贸易的内部化以及出口再次向富裕国家的集中化等风气之先。摩根·斯坦利的亚洲区执行主席史蒂芬·罗奇(Stephen Roach)早在 1988 年就已指明,"大量集中于信息技术领域的资本支出,偏向于(信息技术的)进口。当前,国外生产的高新技术资本货物占美国市场份额的 25%"②。2001 年,这一效应加剧。《华尔街日报》记者叶伟平在报道中指出,"零部件从流水生产线到组装成电脑、路由器或手机之前,有可能来回跨越国境数次。美国国内新购买的电脑有 60% 来自进口"③。在叶伟平看来,该现象具有重大的经济意义,因为美国对国外生产的半导体与电脑配件的消费量远高于原油。

过去数十年间,资本主义全球化再度兴起。在此过程中,网络也具有了更加重要的战略意义。代表美国大型企业利益的商业游说组织"商业圆桌会议"曾强调,(全球化与网络之间的)紧密关系在 1985 年就已初露端倪:"以前是每家工厂独立生产整系列产品,如今的情况是,一家工厂生产某一类产品,甚至某一基本零部件,而其他工厂负责将零部件组装成特定产品。这一生产方式有赖于总公司旗下不同分公司之间畅通的信息流动。同样,在其他国家进行生产也有赖于对(该公司)共同数据库的使用……毕竟,一件产品无法在两套完全不同的设计规格下生产出来"④。

在不同国家的工厂大量采购半成品、调度与跟踪复杂且四处分散的生产流程,以及对成品的销售与营销,所有这些环节必须步调一致。不断扩展的网络功能,以及宽松的网络使用环境,本质上是相互关联的,因为"每一步骤都需要大量信息与之配合"⑤。网络重建了商品链,网络自身呈现了各种复杂性,然而,这些复杂性并不只是技术层面上的。

1987 年,两位分析家阐释道,"政府就网络管理出台的各项政策,将极大地影响国家实现还是错过那些可持续性的、竞争性的经济增长的各种可能。在相关政策的指导下,

---

① Paul Taylor, "Supply Chain."
② Stephen S. Roach, "Dark Side of a Capital – Spending Boom," *Wall Street Journal*, June 2, 1988.
③ Greg Ip, "Tech Bust: What Goes Around, Comes Around," *Wall Street Journal*, July 16, 2001.
④ The Business Roundtable, "International Information Flow: A Plan for Action" (New York: Business Roundtable, January 1985), 10 – 11, quoted in Herbert I. Schiller, "National Sovereignty and the World Business System," paper presented to *the International Political Science Association*, XIII World Congress, Paris, July 19, 1985, 10 – 11.
⑤ James W. Cortada, *Information and the Modern Corporation* (Cambridge, Mass.: MIT Press, 2011), 36.

电信网络得以兴建。这些网络在配置、使用目的以及产业发展的潜能上,各不相同"①。从1970年代至1980年代起,大企业就已要求政府放松对使用网络系统与专用设备的管制,抵制政府对它们的专属网络的服务与数据流的各种限制。并且,它们在跨国运营过程中继续贯彻这一(放松管制的)原则②。到1990年代,(放松管制的)现象已经无处不在。甚至在万维网流行之前,互联网正在成为跨国资本的"攻城之锤",或者"特洛伊木马",旨在实现它们的域外网络自由化项目③。

自由化的推进,打开了资本投资的闸门。信息通讯产业的投资(spending),最终提振了全球消费(expenditure)的"士气":高达10万亿的资金投入(reckoned in),占世界国内生产总值的6%至7%④。企业或公司在网络建设上的投入(spending),占与网络有关的所有支出的最大份额⑤(信息通讯技术的消费支出[consumer spending]的市场份额不到三分之一[29%],商业与政府则占71%⑥)。特别是制造业,已成为最需要信息通讯技术的主要部门。美国耐用与非耐用产品制造商在2009年金融危机时期,仍花费多达300亿美金购置信息通讯设备与软件,这使它成为美国网络系统与应用软件的商用需求的第三大主体(source of business demand)。

汽车工业形象地向我们展示了制造业如何不断地引进数字技术,并推动我们把资本主义全球化与受薪(wage-earning)工人阶级的全球性重构连接起来。

数字化汽车

鲜为人知的是,1980年代早期,美国有十大城市凭借美元投资,完成了全市整体计算机配备项目。底特律是其中之一。全球最大的汽车制造商——通用汽车对外宣称,1984年公司收入已达840亿美元,旗下员工约75万人——三分之二的员工在美国境内。此外,美国通用拥有超过三千家供应商,美国制造业的中流砥柱非其莫属。通用子公司通用汽车金融服务公司自1918年起,开办汽车贷款业务。如今,该公司已有314家分支机构,其中253家在美国境内。1970年代,美国通用内忧外患:内有员工抗争,外有日本竞争对手所带来的市场压力。于是,它启动了一项庞大持久的项目——在汽车生产的每一

---

① Stephen S. Cohen and John Zysman, *Manufacturing Matters: The Myth of the Postindustrial Economy* (New York: Basic, 1987), 193.
② Dan Schiller, *Telematics and Government* (Norwood: Ablex, 1982).
③ Dan Schiller, *Digital Capitalism: Networking the Global Market System* (Cambridge: MIT Press, 1999), 37–50.
④ Cortada, Information, 80.
⑤ 例如,美国电话电报公司在电话业务上的收入有一半来自其公司或企业客户。具体请参见 Andrew Parker and Paul Taylor, "Tough Calls Are Queuing Up for AT&T's Chief Executive," *Financial Times*, July 19, 2010.
⑥ Cortada, *Information*, 80.

环节里推广信息通讯技术。此番决策必须放在更大的背景下进行审视:以美国通用为首的制造商,保罗·沃克尔(Paul Volcker)掌管联邦储备银行后决意采取紧缩政策以解决通胀问题的金融系统,与直接碾压(工人)集体协商权利与社会项目的里根政府,合力降低了工人的生活水准,压缩他们的权力诉求。

正如报章评论所言,"管理通用信息流,犹如管理某一个小国家的信息流"①。通用汽车安装了25万台电话机对运营情况进行管控,每月不同部门的员工要进行800万次长途通话。一份1984年出版的年度报告显示,汽车制造商在内部企业数据处理、沟通与办公自动化等方面投入的总资金高达20亿美元(另一位作者指出为60亿)②。彼时,通用汽车正着手推动美国有史以来最大的一次技术、人力与资本资源(capital resources)的转型③。

美国通用这一汽车巨头在1984年耗费25亿美元收购美国顶级计算机服务提供商"电子数据系统"(EDS)。作为"不同系统的整合器",电子数据系统接掌大任,将通用汽车内部碎片化、功能上彼此分离的数据处理与沟通系统整合起来并进行合理化。在通用汽车的要求下,电子数据系统横跨企业庞大复杂的结构,打造出在线连接系统,以完成订单、航运、金融、库存与材料管理。这样,已经建成的"自动化的各个岛屿"相互桥接起来。通用汽车的工程师开发出一套所谓的"制造自动化协议"(Manufacturing Automation Protocol),以保证此前工厂里互不连属的机器之间,以及与通用汽车中央计算机设备(据说包括上百台大型主机)之间能够交换与共享信息④。通用汽车专属的电子数据交换系统将众多供应商与其自身的设计、制造与销售系统相连接⑤。它成为首家配备专属的超级计算机(在此之后全球大约有百余台超级计算机)的制造商。超级计算机主要用于三维建模、空气动力测试与模拟模型等。通用汽车在五十铃、铃木、发那科、丰田、衍射(Diffracto)、科技知识(Teknowledge)、克劳士比与大宇等集团或企业里都持有股权,帮助

---

① Ann Knight of Paine, Webber, in Daniel F. Cuff, "General Motors Goes Courting," *New York Times*, May 19, 1984.
② Electronic Data Systems Corporation, 1984 Annual Report, 10; "GM Moves into a New Era," *Business Week*, July 16, 1984, 49.
③ Martin Anderson, writing in Technology Review in 1982, quoted in Cortada, *Digital Hand*, vol. 1, 134.
④ Richard Brandt, "Finding the Missing Link in Automation," *Business Week*, June 17, 1985, 39; Sydney Shaw, "Pact Signed for Standards on Computers," *Washington Post*, April 25, 1984; "Communication Barriers in the Factory Are Falling," *Business Week*, May 14, 1984, 148 – 52; "A Push to Make Computers Talk to Each Other," *Business Week*, May 7, 1984, 37 – 38; Urban C. Lehner and John Marcom Jr., "To Battle the Japanese, GM Is Pushing Boldly into Computerization," *Wall Street Journal*, July 9, 1984; Marjorie Sorge and Michelle Krebs, "New Automation Setup Due for GM Plants," *Automotive News*, March 18, 1985, 26, 43, 45.
⑤ James W. Cortada, "New Wine in Old and New Bottles: Patterns and Effects of the Internet on Companies," in *The Internet and American Business*, ed. William Aspray and Paul E. Ceruzzi (Cambridge, Mass.: MIT Press, 2008), 393;有关美国汽车工业的总体发展,请参见 Cortada, *Digital Hand*, vol. 1, 131 – 39.

它们研发机器人、人工智能与机器视觉系统，以及管理咨询服务与各类软件①。最终在1985年，通用汽车耗资52亿美元，并购美国最大卫星制造商"休斯飞行"。通用汽车借助休斯飞行的（既得）优势，连接并整合其复杂丛生的跨国运营业务，例如分布在36个国家的超过200家主要生产基地，包括多达5 000家经销商、供应商与财务办公室在内的额外站点②。以上这些表明，通用汽车的确在计算机化与工厂机器人配置上毫不吝惜，甚至挥金如土：1979年至1984年间就已耗资数十亿，到了2008年共计花费900亿美元，令人咋舌③。

通用汽车在网络建设方面的巨额投资，改变并延展了汽车工业的劳动过程，壮大了通用汽车旗下分布广泛的部门同其合作伙伴之间的数据流；不过，这一投资引发的实际后果却并不合意。通用汽车试图完成整合其庞大的信息系统这一雄心勃勃、看似连贯一致的战略计划最终被无情地搅碎：它在1996年卖掉电子数据系统；到了2009年，通用汽车所吹嘘的系统整合工程也只能保证它"需要花费数周（时间）而非数日"来汇总其公司资产负债表。"管理人员不得不在全球范围内发电子邮件，然后把分布在不同国家的分公司传来的报告东拼西凑，整合成最终报表。"④然而，尽管存在这样或那样的问题，通用汽车的网络化工程（与其他大型制造商一样）确实决定性地拓宽了资本主义全球化进程。20世纪末，在网络的助推或加持下，产业化发展能够摆脱此前的地域限制，并能在全球范围内充分利用工资劳动力所形成的新的蓄水池。

工资关系一直是资本主义发展的基石。在同样的历史情境中，域外网络迫不及待地实现了现代化发展并不断扩展。苏联社会主义的垮台、中国对资本主义的拥抱以及第三世界政治蓝图的失败⑤驱使成千上万的工人或直接或间接地与资本相互关联。秉持新自由主义立场的顶级杂志《经济学人》承认中国"史无前例地动员国内劳动力，这成为过去半个世纪间最大的经济事件"⑥。据国际劳工局（International Labour Office）估计，1980至

---

① Business Week,"GM Moves,"48 – 54,esp. 49;General Motors,"How to Use Computers Intelligently"(advertisement), *Wall Street Journal*,May 4,1987. For a different example, one rooted in the television manufacturing industry, see Jefferson Cowie, *Capital Moves: RCA's Seventy – Year Quest for Cheap Labor* (Ithaca,N. Y.:Cornell University Press,1999).
② Amal Nag and Roy J. Harris Jr.,"GM's Winning Offer for Hughes May Set Heavy – Industry Trend," *Wall Street Journal*, June 6,1985;General Motors,"How to Use Computers Intelligently."
③ 1979至1984期间，330亿美元用于"重建"，具体请参见Business Week,"GM Moves";General Motors,"How to Use Computers Intelligently";以及Steven Rattner, *Overhaul:An Insider's Account of the Obama Administration's Emergency Rescue of the Auto Industry* (Boston:Houghton Mifflin,2011),15.
④ Rattner, *Overhaul*,185.
⑤ Vijay Prashad, *The Darker Nations* (New York:New Press,2007).
⑥ "What a Waste," *Economist*,May 13,2013,14.

2007年间,全球劳动力从19亿增长至31亿,增长率高达63%[①]。日渐扩大并急速变化的工薪阶层,已成为当代世界的基本特征。跨国资本对劳动力的调动,为全球制造业在当今时代的重组与制造业产出的大幅度增长,奠定了坚实的基础。

通用汽车这样的制造商实施网络化战略,旨在整合高科技生产体系。制造商试图改良生产体系,并将之扩展到设置在贫穷国家的出口加工区。夏肯所描述的1990年设立在墨西哥边境的美墨联营工厂[②]可为例证。跨国制造商主导研发、设计、营销以及总装等环节,与此同时,(在全球范围内)分布广泛的承包商或外包商运营的工厂承担起生产零部件的职能,并最终完成总装环节。这一快速变化的生产体系,仰仗于深植其中的网络(结构),不仅对资本更对劳动力产生了深远且痛苦的影响。

托尼·史密斯(Tony Smith)指出,"信息技术已经使企业能够更加密切地(intimately)协调生产与销售环节",导致"核心/周边这一不对称的经济权力网络的形成,后者可以保证公司核心圈掌控生产环节与信息流动,并能够把经济负担转嫁给附属企业(ring firms),由此实现对(附属)企业工人的充分剥削"[③]。一方面,这一"权力不对称"尽管不能保证相应的利润回报,却将自动化与自助服务(self-service)推向史无前例的水平。实际上,生产能力过剩正潜在地威胁企业利润率。因此,在20世纪的最后几十年间,通用汽车的利润高低起伏,变化不定,而它在北美的汽车销售份额已然下降[④]。另一方面,如大卫·哈维所言,网络化的生产与"血汗工厂、家庭劳动制、散工制、分包/转包制以及类似的劳动体制"有关。并且,哈维断定这一多样性(multiformity)导致"不同劳动体制之间的竞争,它们之间的竞争已经成为资方"争夺过剩产能(surplus generation)与销售主动权时"对抗劳方的有力武器"[⑤]。同样,金·穆迪(Kim Moody)也抱有类似的观点。他指出,企业把信息技术与"外包、雇佣临时工制、老式的提高生产速度以及延长工时等老派的工作组织形式"[⑥]相结合。经济差异并非均衡地分布于全球;相反,世界范围内不平等现象四处蔓延。

队伍不断壮大的工薪阶层,对富裕国家的劳动力(主要是制造业工人)形成的压力与日俱增。1978年至1983年间,美国工人的实际工资下降了10%;从1979年开始,美国劳

[①] International Labour Office, *Economically Active Population Estimates and Projections*, 5th ed., rev. 2009, in John Bellamy Foster, Robert W. McChesney, and Jamil Jonna, "The Global Reserve Army of Labor and the New Imperialism," *Monthly Review* 63, no. 6 (November 2011):21.

[②] Harley Shaiken, *Mexico in the Global Economy: High Technology and Work Organization in Export Industries* (La Jolla: Center for U.S.-Mexico Studies [University of California, San Diego], 1990); "Free Exchange: Chains of Gold," *The Economist*, August 4, 2012, 68.

[③] Tony Smith, *Technology and Capital in the Age of Lean Production* (Albany: State University of New York Press, 2000), 117.

[④] Martin Anderson, writing in *Technology Review* in 1982, quoted in Cortada, *Digital Hand*, vol. 1, 134.

[⑤] David Harvey, *A Companion to Marx's Capital* (London: Verso, 2010), 225–26.

[⑥] Kim Moody, *Workers in a Lean World: Unions in the International Economy* (London: Verso, 1997), 86.

动力价值不断下跌,直至20世纪末①。美国工人阶级不但要为愈演愈烈的收入与财富不平等现象而战,还不得不围绕这一现象所代表的经济剥削问题展开斗争②。于是,低收入、派遣制或兼职就业情况纷纷出现,意大利经济学家甚至在前沿产业或发达市场经济体中发现"朝不保夕族"③的存在。大卫·哈维仔细梳理了这一后果所产生的双重不稳定效应:资本对"工资钳制"(wage repression)的追逐超乎想象;低收入意味着当前资本也不得不应对世界最富裕市场中所出现的消费者需求日渐减弱的问题④。随着汽车工业发展的起落不定,这一矛盾性的压力(contradictory stress)正逐年累月地积聚起来。

在美国本土,汽车生产体系的重组产生了灾难性的后果。2008年,通用汽车在全球34个国家中生产汽车,但如今它只掌控装配环节,直接雇佣的工人数量只有24.3万名,这个数字只是它半个世纪前雇佣工人数量的三分之一,并且,美国本土的雇佣工人数量不到9.1万名⑤。美国汽车工人总量仍然过百万,可大部分人受雇于独立的零部件供应商,还有部分工人替丰田、日产、本田、现代等在美国设立分支机构的国外汽车公司打工⑥。

1980年至2009年间,国外汽车公司在美国成立的零部件供应商与装配工厂主要分布在印第安纳和田纳西州这样的"劳动权利"(right-to-work)地带⑦,这绝非偶然现象。但它不仅仅与这些"闯入者"有关。一位激进的汽车工人兼作家格雷格·肖特维尔(Gregg Shotwell)在上世纪末曾指出,通用汽车1999年将生产汽车零件的主力——德尔福汽车系统公司(Delphi Automotive Systems)作为分支独立出去这一做法,标志着通用汽车长期所奉行的精益生产理念、分包/转包制、模块化组装以及外包给尚未加入工会、独立的零部件供应商制度已进入"高潮"阶段。同样,它也可以被视为通用汽车对这些制度所引发的工人抗议行动的一次回应。因此,早年工人(通过斗争)所获得的来之不易的成

---

① David McNally, *Global Slump: The Economics and Politics of Crisis and Resistance* (Oakland: PM Press, 2011), 36; Simon Mohun, "Aggregate Capital Productivity in the U.S. Economy, 1964 – 2001," *Cambridge Journal of Economics* 33, no. 5 (2009): 1023 – 46, quoted in McNally, *Global Slump*, 48.
② Sylvia A. Allegretto, "The State of Working America's Wealth, 2011," *Economic Policy Institute Briefing Paper* 292, March 23, 2011; Emmanuel Saez, "Striking It Richer: The Evolution of Top Incomes in the United States (updated with 2009 and 2010 Estimates)," available at http://elsa.berkeley.edu/~saez/saez – UStopincomes – 2010.pdf (accessed January 10, 2014).
③ Vincent Mosco and Catherine McKercher, *The Laboring of Communication* (Lanham, Md.: Lexington, 2008).
④ Harvey, *Enigma of Capital*, 12. See also Doug Henwood, interview, "Austerity in the Face of Weakness," *The Real News*, August 26, 2010, available at http://therealnews.com/t2/index.php?option=com_content&task=view&id=31&Itemid=74&jumival=5518 (accessed January 10, 2014).
⑤ Rattner, *Overhaul*, 184, 247.
⑥ "How Many Auto Workers Are in Your State?", *USA Today*, December 4, 2008, available at at http://usatoday30.usatoday.com/money/autos/2008 – 12 – 04 – auto – workers – by – state_n.htm (accessed January 10, 2014).
⑦ Bill Vlasic, Hiroko Tabuchi, and Charles Duhigg, "An American Model for Tech Jobs?", *New York Times*, August 5, 2012 (with maps).

果正在流失,令人痛心。越来越少的汽车工人居住在底特律的工会镇,或者,他们也越来越少地成为曾一度无比风光的全美汽车工人联合会的一分子。随着全美汽车工人联合会会员数量的大幅下降,该联合会权力遭到削弱,全盘科层化,并不断向资方妥协,进一步损害汽车工人的协商权力。对此,汽车企业强化了工人们在谈判过程中就薪金待遇、福利、工作安全、退休金以及公司劳动纪律等方面所被迫达成的妥协①。1990年代,通用汽车公司高级管理人员孤注一掷,推出"油老虎"运动型多用途车。此举导致利润率的飙升,似乎暂时证实了这一战略的正确性。然而,在新世纪初,汽车生产能力过剩的问题已在全球范围内反复出现②。中国的汽车生产③与销售却一路火爆,中国的汽车生产商将大量汽车出口至发展中国家。随着汽车全球销售量升至史上最高(2011年7 500万台),北美、日本特别是西欧的高成本生产商却相继遭到重创④。销售量呈两位数地下降,这已成通用汽车的(市场)常态;而汽油价格的猛涨彻底终结了通用汽车的运动型多用途车的市场战略。甚至在2008年金融危机出现之前,通用汽车曾醉心于"诱因计划",例如采用现金返还或打折等方式,以此维持其生产线的正常运转⑤。

经济衰退的来临向我们展示了政治优先是如何影响汽车制造的。通用汽车高层管理人员毕恭毕敬地来到华盛顿。某私募股权行业高层史蒂文·拉特勒(Steven Rattner)成为联邦救助美国通用汽车(以及克莱斯勒汽车公司)的人选。他曾对外大放厥词:"对汽车行业施以援手是美国政府为数不多的可称为成功的救助之举。底特律真是走运"⑥。他的这番结论毫无根据。通用汽车得到联邦政府总计500亿美元救助资金的承诺⑦。这一"受到(政府)控制的破产局面"(controlled bankruptcy)使得通用汽车在联邦政府的操控下关闭20家工厂,裁员数万人,取消数十年的工作规则,推广不雇佣工会会员的工作标准,剥夺工人的罢工权,消除工人医疗保险这样的"遗留成本",缩减加入全美汽车工人

---

① Gregg Shotwell, *Autoworkers under the Gun: A Shop-Floor View of the End of the American Dream* (Chicago: Haymarket, 2011),7-66,quote at 19.
② 另一例子是,丰田、本田以及尼桑等日本汽车制造商的海外生产不断增加,与此同时,国内工厂闲置率持续上升,请参见 Chester Dawson, "For Toyota, Patriotism and Profits May Not Mix," *Wall Street Journal*, November 29,2011.
③ 外界预测,中国汽车产量将在2013年首次超过欧洲,具体请参见 Peter Marsh, Chris Bryant, and Richard Milne, "Milestone for China Car Output," *Financial Times*, January 2,2013.
④ Keith Bradsher, "Cheap Chinese Cars Make Valuable Gains in Emerging Markets," *New York Times*, July 6,2012; John Reed, "Car Industry Grows to Record Size Despite Challenging Year," *Financial Times*, December 19,2011; Li Fangfang, "Auto Industry Roars into Life," *ChinaWatch*, China Daily, November 30,2011. 截至2013年,全球预计将生产8 240万台轿车与轻型货车,具体请参见 Peter Marsh, "U. S. and China Look to Drive Car Industry," *Financial Times*, January 2,2013.
⑤ Rattner, *Overhaul*,16.
⑥ Rattner, *Overhaul*,13.
⑦ Neil Barofsky, *Bailout: An Inside Account of How Washington Abandoned Main Street While Rescuing Wall Street* (New York: Free Press,2012),177.

联合会的工人数量至 5 000 名左右①。(福特汽车公司尚未破产,却利用这一契机关闭工厂,与工人重新签订合同)。

只有根深蒂固的特权阶级才敢称这一切为"成功"。尼尔·巴若夫斯基(Neil Barofsky)稍后指出,同时向银行业提供数万亿美元救助的联邦政府人员"始终如一地"奉行一种"双重标准"②。看起来,汽车工人(而非银行家们)可以随随便便地被打发走或被放弃。拉特勒独断地拒绝了他称之为"全美汽车工人联合会的极端条款,根据该项条款,所有下岗工人可以获得他们日常工资的 95% 作为赔偿金"③,他的团队抱有一种他颇为赞赏的"坚定的资本主义视角"。在拉特勒恣意任性的臆想里,雇员与退休人员"应当分担痛苦"④。成立工会的汽车工人在争取美国(工人)生活标准的问题上曾扮演着极为重要的历史角色,以至于当政府重拳打压汽车工人时,导致"工人阶级状况的恶化"⑤。

一面是美国路面上行使的车辆平均使用年限已达历史新高,平均 11.4 年;另一面则是通用汽车在破产后的两年后,大肆庆祝其在美国本土的销售额的复苏。通用汽车在北美的装配工厂的数量从 2006 年的 23 家减少到 17 家。这些工厂实行全天候的三班倒工作制,通用汽车指望着它们助其增加 18% 的市场份额⑥。

通用汽车的精简措施从多个方面向我们提供了很好的一课。工薪阶层的消费力不断下降,而企业在网络体系与服务上的投资一路飙升,与之相伴的,还有提高生产率的自动化技术。金融危机后,美国经济维持着与衰退前几乎同样水平的增长率,可工作机会减少了 700 万。实际上,2001 年至 2011 年这段时期在过去 80 年间是极为特殊的,因为就业率下降,而生产率上升⑦(2011 年,就业开支[employment spending]只增长了 2%,相较之下,在硬件与软件上的商业开支则增长 26%⑧)。在边缘地区,自动化的更新周期,特别是他们陷入与中产阶级职业相关的"知识工作"中时,激发了经济学家保罗·克鲁格曼(Paul Krugman)对英国卢德分子的同情之心,后者曾在 19 世纪伊始激烈地反抗资本对

---

① Stein, *Pivotal Decade*, 299; Shotwell, *Autoworkers*, 175.
② Barofsky, *Bailout*, 175, 179.
③ Rattner, *Overhaul*, 29, see also 68.
④ Rattner, *Overhaul*, 53, 57.
⑤ Shotwell, *Autoworkers*, 175; Lee Sustar, Afterword, in Shotwell, *Autoworkers*, 230.
⑥ Robert Wright, "GM Plants at Full Tilt to Feed U. S. Car Demand," *Financial Times*, October 1, 2013. Chris Woodyard, "Autoworkers Pushed to Limit as Many Plants Max Out," *USA Today*, May 23, 2012; Bill Vlasic and Jack Ewing, "After a Loss, GM Plans Fast Action in Europe," *New York Times*, August 3, 2012; Jeff Bennett, "GM Offers Free Car – Care to Bolster U. S. Sales," *Wall Street Journal*, June 7, 2013; Bill Vlasic, "Car Sales Climb Sharply in Strong Start to 2013," *New York Times*, February 2, 2013.
⑦ Paul Krugman, "Sympathy for the Luddites," *New York Times*, June 14, 2013; International Labor Organization, *World of Work Report* 2013, available at http://www.ilo.org/global/research/global–reports/world–of–work/lang—en/index.htm (accessed January 10, 2014).
⑧ Rattner, *Overhaul*, 53, 57.

羊毛工业的技术入侵①。《金融时报》引用"损毁工作的技术"②来描述这一局面;麻省理工学院经济学家埃里克-布林约尔松(Erik Brynjolfsson)与安德鲁·麦卡菲(Andrew McAfee)也承认,以计算机为基础对技术工种进行自动化改造,将直接导致净裁员人数的上升③。2014年,谷歌董事长埃里克·施密特(Eric Schmidt)在达沃斯召开世界经济论坛前夕向外界确认,此前自动化技术无法覆盖到的工种当前也岌岌可危了④。

2010年企业利润占美国国民收入的比例达到有史以来最高,在2011年初这一份额依然居高不下。同样,2013年,通用汽车在北美地区利润率的增长势头强劲迅猛⑤。相反,用于支付工人工资和薪金的那部分国民收入降到最低;即便把工人工资与福利加在一起,2010年的总数也是自1965年以来最低值,且仍处于下跌状态中⑥。

与之相比,据《金融时报》报道,欧洲各国"并没有那么果断坚决地着手处理过剩生产能力的问题"⑦,以至于欧洲汽车制造工厂的产能利用率太低而无法维持运转、获取利润。2012年,欧洲现有的汽车产业在满足既有的消费需求的基础上,每年完全可以多生产1 000万台汽车,这一情况到了2013年有所恶化⑧。历经价格大战与狂跌不止的销售额后,欧洲汽车市场陷入困境。部分制造商尚能维持运营,还有部分制造商则难以为继。2013年夏末,欧洲汽车销量自1990年以来跌至最低⑨。正如《金融时报》一直强调,欧洲民众对汽车需求的减弱"暴露了汽车行业长期存在的过剩生产能力的痼疾。与美国不同,2008年金融风波后这一问题因为政治势力与工会对关闭工厂的抵制,非但没有得到解决反而愈演愈烈"⑩。菲亚特首席执行官塞尔吉奥·马尔乔内(Sergio Marchionne)也许会埋怨,相关措施必须实施,企业合并也势在必行⑪。欧洲的各大汽车高管或许会催促欧洲各国政府以中间人身份对工厂实行关停并转。然而,1 130万名汽车工人(占在岗员工总数的5.3%)的抵制行为在大面积失业的情形下表明,缩减产能行为(capacity cut-

---

① Paul Krugman, "Sympathy for the Luddites," *New York Times*, June 14, 2013. 数十年前,前诺贝尔经济学奖得主曾重点考察过这一议题,具体请参见 Wassily W. Leontieff, "Technological Advance, Economic Growth, and the Distribution of Income," *Population and Development Review* 9 no. 3 (September 1983):407 – 8.
② "The Lex Column," *Financial Times*, August 10, 2010.
③ Erik Brynjolfsson and Andrew McAfee, *Race against the Machine* (Digital Frontier Press, 2011). E-book.
④ John Gapper and Richard Waters, "Google Chief Warns of IT Threat," *Financial Times*, January 24, 2014.
⑤ Nathan Bomey, "Strong North American Sales Propels GM to $1.2 Billion Profit", *Detroit Free Press*, July 25, 2013. Available at http://www.freep.com/article/20130725/BUSINESS0101/307250080/General-Motors-earnings (accessed January 10, 2014).
⑥ Floyd Norris, "As Corporate Profits Rise, Workers' Income Declines," *New York Times*, August 6, 2011.
⑦ Wright, "GM Plants at Full Tilt."
⑧ Henry Foy, "EU Car Sales Lowest since 1993," *Financial Times*, June 19, 2013.
⑨ Henry Foy and Chris Bryant, "European Car Sales at Lowest Level since 1990," *Financial Times*, September 18, 2013.
⑩ John Reed, "Car Industry's Resistance to Change Comes Home to Roost," *Financial Times*, June 7, 2012.
⑪ Bernard Simon and John Reed, "European Carmakers Must Consolidate, Says Fiat Chief," *Financial Times*, January 12, 2012.

backs)依然与"政治密切相关"①。

然而,在大西洋的另一边,制造业生产背后的政治风云却呈现出另一个迥异的景象。国家出台的政策对加入工会的汽车工人而言,无异于一记重拳(并无利好消息)。在此之后,右翼资本家沉瀣一气,联合要求立法,将密歇根州这一美国历史上产业集体谈判的中心转变成"劳动权利"州②。在此情境下,我们必须把网络驱动的企业重组(additional cycles of)视为更大的反动的现代化战略的一部分。

根据报道,"一辆现代轿车"早已化身为"车轮上的计算机",包含数百种电子控制系统(2011年地震摧毁了一家专业生产计算机芯片的日本工厂,这是"对全球汽车产业的一次持久且严重的打击")③。美国汽车行业的高管雇佣数以百计的软件开发商,对汽车进行更高程度的数字化开发,以区别市面上(其他国家或地区生产的)汽车产品④。同时,正如福特汽车首席执行官比尔·福特(Bill Ford)老谋深算地指出,"全球经济停滞"(global gridlock)问题将导致"智能交通系统"的普遍建立⑤。在城市、州和联邦政府的慷慨相助下,诸如瓦泽(Waze,2013年被谷歌收购)、优步科技或苹果等新兴或现有的公司正将传感器、移动电话和数据分析服务应用到交通系统上⑥。通过给汽车配置无线技术从而共享网络的方式,旨在(至少在理论层面)保障行驶在装有传感器的公路上的汽车能够躲开愈发严重的交通堵塞。除了车载导航系统,数字化汽车将配置更多电子设备,无论是无线热点还是声控信息系统。这样,在路况较差的情况下,驾驶者依然能够自娱自乐⑦。然而,《金融时报》报道,汽车黑客"正成为严重的威胁"⑧。2013年,自走车(无人驾驶汽车)已在美国三个州获批投入生产⑨。

---

① Henry Foy and Chris Bryant, "Battered and Bruised Sector Holds Breath over Signs of Growth," *Financial Times*, June 17, 2013; Chris Bryant, "Pressure Rises on Carmakers as Sales in Europe Hit the Skids," *Financial Times*, March 20, 2013.

② Anthony Riedel, "Know Your Rights: Michigan's Right to Work Law," *Freedom@Work*, July 2, 2013, available at http://www.nrtw.org/en/blog/know – your – rights – michigan – right – work – 03212013 (accessed January 10, 2014).

③ Andrew Pollack and Steve Lohr, "The Chip That Powers Cars," *New York Times*, April 28, 2011. 也请参见 "Jonathan Soble, "Tsunami Takes Its Toll on Toyota," *Financial Times*, June 11 – 12, 2011.

④ Jaclyn Trop, "Tired of Silicon Valley? Try Motor City," *New York Times*, July 1, 2013.

⑤ Daniel Thomas and John Reed, "Ford Head Warns Rise to 4bn Cars Risks World Gridlock," *Financial Times*, February 27, 2012. 2013年,福特公司增强其北美制造基地的生产能力,具体请参见 Mike Ramsey, "Ford to Add 200,000 Vehicles to 2013 North American Output", *Wall Street Journal*, May 22, 2013.

⑥ Shira Ovide, "Tapping 'Big Data' to Fill Potholes," *Wall Street Journal*, June 12, 2012.

⑦ Chris Nuttall, "Welcome to the Real Infobahn," interview with Bill Ford, *Financial Times*, October 25, 2011; Thomas and Reed, "Ford Head Warns"; John Reed, "Visions of Mobility in the Megacity," Special Report: The Future of the Car, *Financial Times*, September 13, 2011; John Reed, "Carmakers Weaving on Information Superhighway," *Financial Times*, July 25, 2011.

⑧ Chris Bryant, "High – Tech Cars under Threat from Hackers on Information Super – highway," *Financial Times*, March 24, 2013.

⑨ Claire Cain Miller and Matthew L. Wald, "Self – Driving Cars for Testing Are Supported by U. S.," *New York Times*, May 31, 2013.

这一项目还涉及更为庞大的基础设施的改造工程,不仅包括数字化计量的公路的修建与电力网的改造,还与机器通讯的问题有关(M2M,有时又被称为"物联网")。机器通讯所需组件(传感器、智能卡以及用于在移动网络中接发数据的无线电子设备)的成本在2012年已经下降至每单位10美元不到,其应用前景不可小觑。现在,"智能"垃圾桶可以发出信号,要求垃圾处理公司前来收取垃圾;冰箱能够发出指令,要求更换新的奶瓶用纸板;小汽车可以传达加油或更换备用件的信息,甚至通知保险公司某一司机已经超速①。机器通讯的狂热分子幻想着一个价值万亿的市场,而高科技制造企业开始为美国通用电气提出的"工业互联网"理念大唱赞歌②。传感器成本的下降(思科企业评估,到2020年,将产生500亿美元的收支[operating]),与企业数据分析系统的建立(通用汽车计划于2013年底之前在其硅谷研发基地新增千余名数据专家),意味着汽车产业发展正在向海量、多样、随时连线的机器通讯与数据流转型。无论是喷气发动机、其他工业设备,还是冰箱、洗衣机或电视机(都在实现这一转型)③。实时全数据(All-data-all-the-time)已成为口头禅,犹如人们在每一天的每一个时间节点上(工作中、在街上或家里)生产数据一般④。

于是,一个新的平台即将对未来的市场参与者开放:谁来提供专业软件与服务,从而向这一新兴的工业互联网领域注入能量?要拓展资本的覆盖范围,使资本进入教育、文化遗产、政府服务、医药和生物科技这类的商品开发项目(我们将在第三部分进行具体分析)中,前提在于网络基础设施的现代化与升级。数字设备供应商、系统集成商、云服务供应商以及数据分析企业从四面八方涌进(工业互联网)这一领域。例如,微软与丰田达成战略合作意向,丰田使用微软公司的云服务软件,以整合客户家庭终端或移动设备与其电动汽车之间的信息传递。这样,丰田车的司机可以远程启动暖气设备或检测汽车的电量,或在电费较为便宜的非繁忙时段给电动汽车充电。日本丰田首席执行官向顾客提供了一种他自认为颇具吸引力的选择,即每日清晨,客户能够与其汽车进行"对话",这一服务涵盖了不少于170个可使用云服务的国家或地区⑤。

通用汽车对其"新"网络战略(这让人想起了它在1980年代舍本逐利地贯彻实施而到了1990年代极力避免的战略)颇有些洋洋自得,尽管它看起来并不那么在意。董事长兼首席执行官丹·阿克森(Dan Akerson)2013年向外界宣布,"如今,汽车产业价值链的

---

① Jane Bird, "'Internet of Things' Breaks through $10 Barrier," *Financial Times*, February 27, 2012.
② Peter C. Evans and Marco Annunziata, "Industrial Internet: Pushing the Boundaries of Minds and Machines," GE publication, November 26, 2012. 也请参见 John Koten, "A Revolution in the Making," (report: "Manufacturing"), *Wall Street Journal*, June 11, 2013.
③ Richard Waters, "GE Creates a Platform Path for the 'Internet of Things'," *Financial Times*, June 20, 2013.
④ 关于这一发展的精辟论述请参见 Mark Andrejevic, "Defining the Sensor Society," *Television and New Media*, 即出。
⑤ April Dembosky and John Reed, "Microsoft and Toyota to Build Car Interface," *Financial Times*, April 7, 2011.

每一环节都联入计算机网络,并且相互连接。这意味着从设计到展厅(每一部分都在网络之中)"。"这是任何公司(不仅仅是汽车制造商)在 21 世纪取得商业成功的原因:你必须拥有信息技术的核心竞争力。你必须拥有信息技术,掌控这门技术;如果你没有,你只能眼睁睁地看着其他企业突发奇想,遥遥领先,或遭遇发展瓶颈(例如财务危机)"①。阿克森在通用汽车新的数据中心所举行的开幕仪式上说出了上面这番话。这个数据中心是通用汽车用来改进其运营模式的四所新的研发基地之一,由此又增加了更多内部从事信息技术的雇员②。

尽管如此,提高美国普通人每况愈下的生活标准的愿景依然遥遥无期。工资钳制现象早已屡见不鲜,以至于奥巴马政府值得自我炫耀的政绩仅仅是在救助汽车工业过程中保住了成千上万的工人的饭碗(工资待遇并不好)③。然而,高薪稳定、有福利和退休金保障的工会工作(union jobs)亦岌岌可危;与此同时,人们越来越难找到一份带薪工作。美国工会所代表的工人的比例,降至 20 世纪初以来最低水平。因为通胀缘故,2012 年末美国工资中位数相比于 2000 年,回落了 8 个百分点④;人均实际可支配收入在过去 5 年间平均每年缩减 0.4%——这是 1964 年开始搜集这些数据以来的最低纪录⑤。在通用汽车获政府救助并再次盈利的这段时间,底特律这个数十年间象征着美国工人阶级权力的城市申请破产⑥。对此,联邦政府无动于衷、保持缄默。

在 1979 年至 1982 年联邦储备银行所实施的财政紧缩方案的刺激下,网络驱动的生产体系与劳动过程的重组导致了长期的工资水平压滞。这反过来拖垮了消费者需求,后者正是推进以债务为基础的金融体系的若干动力之一。

---

① Melissa Burden,"GM to Invest ﹩258M in Milford Twp. Data Center,"*Detroit News*,May 14,2013.
② Alex Luft,"General Motors Announces Fourth Information Technology Center in Chandler,Arizona,"*GM Authority*,March 7,2013.
③ Bill Vlasic,Hiroko Tabuchi,and Charles Duhigg,"An American Model for Tech Jobs?",*New York Times*,August 5,2012.
④ Robert Reich,"Consumption Drops,Unemployment Rises,and DC Politicians Are Clueless:Here's Why," February 25,2013,available at www. truth - out. org/news/item/14771 (accessed January 10,2014).
⑤ Spencer Jakab,"Income Sinkhole Hurts Consumer Spending,"*Wall Street Journal*,March 29,2013.
⑥ Monica Davey,"Financial Crisis Just a Symptom of Detroit Woes,"*New York Times*,July 9,2013;Michael A. Fletcher,"Detroit Files Largest Municipal Bankruptcy in U. S. history,"*Washington Post*,July 18,2013,available at:http://www.washingtonpost. com/business/economy/2013/07/18/a8db3f0e - efe6 - 11e2 - bed3 - b9b6fe264871 _ story. html (accessed January 10,2014).

第 3 章
网络化的金融化

金融化意味着在 1970 年代经济危机的背景下数字资本主义崛起的另一面向。信息处理设备与软件并入金融系统。国内,金融系统作为阶级权力的工具发挥作用;国际上,它作为资本主义扩张与帝国控制的支点进行运作。然而,网络支持的金融化再次处于自相矛盾的势头(contradictory momentum)中:与其认为它是稳定积累的工具,毋宁视其为危机的负载者。

多方动力推进金融化发展。其中之一便是,遭遇工资钳制的数百万工人不得不仰赖借贷这一方式满足其即期消费以及住房、汽车、教育与医疗等其他消费的欲望。另一推动力则是跨国制造商、连锁零售企业、农业综合企业以及服务供应商的发展战略导致财政的不断膨胀。它们的投资与运营成本要求多币种结算,服从于各国或各地区不同的税务管辖权,放弃那些需要管理的利润。外商直接投资改变了全球消费、储蓄与贸易的模式,引发了国家之间的金融失衡现象。这些失衡冲击了自二战以来就已实施的固定汇率制度。1970 年代初固定汇率制不断增强,随后尼克松政府放弃固定汇率制(实行黄金与美元比价的自由浮动)。"无限的管理能力"[1]使美国成为生机勃勃的全球资本主义的金融指挥家。如今这一能力备受质疑,充满不确定因素。利率、汇率、国际收支经常项目顺差的变动以及主权债务已成烫手山芋。与此同时,流动资本(俗称"热钱")跨越边境涌入国内,寻求即时回报。因此,金融化战略的启动,折射出深层次的发展动向,而非反映出银行家的贪婪这么简单[2]。

---

[1] Leo Panitch and Sam Gindin, *The Making of Global Capitalism* (London: Verso, 2012), 79.
[2] Panitch and Gindin, *Making of Global Capitalism*; John Bellamy Foster and Fred Magdoff, *The Great Financial Crisis: Causes and Consequences* (New York: Monthly Review, 2009); Geoff Mann, "Colletti's Credit Crunch," *New Left Review* 56 (March/April 2009): 121 – 24; David Harvey, "Is This Really the End of Neoliberalism?", *Counterpunch*, March 13/15, 2009.

1983年，齐斯·哈默林克(Cees Hamelink)指出，金融化也代表一种与新的信息技术合流的趋势①。生机盎然的网络系统激活了金融化发展，后者也仰仗于网络化技术；2008年，金融服务企业成为美国第二大信息通信技术的需求源②(467亿美元，占美国非农行业在信息通讯技术设备与软件上的年度开销总数的18.4%③)。本章接下来旨在梳理(金融化与信息通信技术之间)这一复杂的关系，并阐释网络化的金融化发展如何把压力源再次引入资本主义危机趋势之中。

二战结束后的二十余年间，是整个20世纪里美国金融系统发展最为稳定的时期。新政改革通过打碎整个金融系统的方式，拯救了该系统并强化其运行能力：投资银行的股票与债券发行、保险条款的制定、商业银行的储蓄与借贷业务、房地产交易，以及经纪人的股票与债券交易在结构上全部被分割开，互不连属。与华尔街银行以及银行系统走得很近的，是美国财政部与联邦储备银行。这些机构或部门，与国际性的机构相互联结。促成这些机构间稳固联系的机制包括：(1)固定汇率机制，这是1944年在布雷顿森林成立的国际货币基金组织的44个成员国共同设定的产物；(2)关税及贸易总协定，1947年出台相关政策，鼓吹投资自由化；(3)国际复兴开发银行(简称"世界银行")，向欠发达国家或地区的战略性/营利性的发展项目提供或发放贷款；(4)美国财政部与联邦储备银行，同美国贸易伙伴(例如伦敦市)的中央银行和私营金融体系之间结成紧密关系。国内，美国大银行在"黄金时代"中狠赚一把，也不忘与其他个别国家保持紧密合作的关系。在相当长的一段时间里，美国充当着协调者、担保人与动态的全球资本主义体系的主要受益方这三重角色④。

1960年代中期，经济压力与紧张(stresses and strains)开始产生衍生效应(ramifying)⑤。美国主导的重建西欧与日本资本主义的工程，虽然用于防御苏联与中国，却产生了悖论性的后果，即再次引发资本主义国家之间的竞争。这给以利润为导向的企业发展战略带来极大的压力，并凸显了美国对额外的投资渠道与市场契机的诉求。对此，美国主要采取了(首先向西欧)提高外商直接投资的措施。跨国企业在国外藏匿了大量资

---

① Cees J. Hamelink, *Finance and Information: A Study of Converging Interests* (Norwood, N.J.: Ablex, 1983).
② U.S. Census Bureau News, "Census Bureau Reports 11 Percent Increase in U.S. Business Spending on Information and Communication Technology in 2008," May 20, 2010, CB10-71; World Information Technology Services Alliance, "Digital Planet 2008, Executive Summary," 3.
③ U.S. Census Bureau, "Information and Communication Technology Survey," available at www.census.gov/econ/ict (accessed January 10, 2014).
④ Gindin and Panitch, *Making of Global Capitalism*; Leo Panitch and Sam Gindin, "Finance and American Empire," in *American Empire and the Political Economy of Global Finance*, ed. Leo Panitch and Martijn Konings (New York: Palgrave, 2009), 19; Stephen A. Marglin and Juliet B. Schor, eds., *The Golden Age of Capitalism: Reinterpreting the Postwar Experience* (Oxford: Clarendon, 1991).
⑤ Fred L. Block, *The Origins of International Economic Disorder: A Study of United States International Monetary Policy from World War II to the Present* (Berkeley: University of California Press, 1977).

产货币,以符合自身的会计与税收战略,或遵循当地关于外商投资的法律。由此出现的大批量"欧洲美元",给中央银行与公司财务主管带来挑战。

同样,美国的战略举措导致了国际金融失衡现象。美国设有海外军事基地的群岛一律奉行美国的"钳制"苏联与中国社会主义的政策。向其他国家派遣数万支军队,开支庞大;当钳制政策升级为全面战争时,美元的流出更为严重。1971年越南战争中,美国海外军费净开支已超过美国国际收支逆差[1]。

一项与美国高度相关的政策再次撕裂了(既存的)国际金融体系。从1940年代启动的马歇尔计划开始,美国便借助其他国家都难以望其项背的国内市场,以此为政治机制(经济需求的来源),积极投身于西欧与东亚地区的资本主义重建工作中。随着美国商业与消费者增加了对海外制造的产品的购买量,美国的经常账户赤字在不知不觉中悄然扩大,于是"无国籍美元"(stateless dollars)如潮水一般涌入它的贸易伙伴国。

这些外在刺激合力形成的压力,尤其是越战(庞大的)军费开销与1971年石油输出国组织疯狂提高原油价格,最终导致金融秩序瞬间崩溃。尼克松政府废除了美元的金本位制,转而实行浮动汇率制。这一举措缓解了压力,却造成了金融体系的不稳定状态,令人难以捉摸。当通胀现象更明显时,大投资家们主张应当以它们的金融资产的安全为优先。被卡特总统任命为美联储银行行长的保罗·沃尔克(Paul Volcker)上浮利率19个百分点,以满足大投资家的需求。这项有意为之的"休克疗法"迫使美国进入财政紧缩局面,失业率一路攀升,高达两位数[2]。

美国的财政紧缩方案,以及对阶级力量的重新制衡[3],最终体现在实际工资的停滞上;这反而刺激了普通家庭的信贷需求。酒店、石油公司以及零售商在20世纪上半叶发放了专用(special-purpose)信用卡。然而,到了1950年代和1960年代,银行大力推行信用卡,将之打造为最普遍的支付手段。其中,美国银行与同业银行扮演着推手的角色,它们纷纷向每个普通家庭邮寄信用卡,试图建立自身的国内(也逐步转向国际)信用体系。1978年,1.1万家银行可以签发信用卡,用户数高达上千万[4]。尽管如此,信用卡仍然没有成为普遍的支付手段,1984年信用卡消费只占消费者总支出的很小一部分(6%)。但是,根据科尔塔达的叙述,到2000年,"每个普通家庭的消费总支出的20%都将是由刷

---

[1] Judith Stein, *Pivotal Decade: How the United States Traded Factories for Services in the Seventies* (New Haven, Conn.: Yale University Press, 2010), 41.
[2] Panitch and Gindin, *Making of Global Capitalism*, 168.
[3] Panitch and Gindin, *Making of Global Capitalism*, 170–71.
[4] Lewis Mandell, *The Credit Card Industry: A History* (Boston: Twayne, 1990), xiv.

(信用)卡完成的"①。2011 年,美国消费者消费支出的一半已经由各种类型的信用卡支付②。信用卡手续费的总数十分惊人,"消费者购买习惯的信息,开始引发银行家与零售商对营销的兴趣"③。其他的金融产品也瞄准家庭市场,例如房屋净值贷款或基于抵押贷款的各类金融新产品④。

当强加给欠发达国家或地区的大额贷款成为负累时,美国国内居高不下的利率也波及国际金融体系。然而,美国各大银行、国际货币基金组织与世行完全不受债务危机所造成的灾难的影响,而债务危机正是它们亲投资者的政策所导致的。1980 年代,它们与欠发达国家或地区的统治精英里应外合(有时也剑拔弩张),化危机为契机,积极在贫穷国家推行"结构性调整",即激进的政策变革,以加强投资自由化与大规模推进国家资产私有化为目标⑤。由此导致的另一后果是,那些无法应对这些转变的第三世界人民口袋里的钱,以美元的形式源源不断地流入富裕的第一世界。

然而,价格波动,杠杆与风险都在增加。大公司急需加强金融稳定的工具,以帮助它们在购买对冲基金时能够抵御汇率波动或其他未知事件的影响。从金融体系的供给端来看,拥有企业股权的超大银行有了海量的投机资本的加持,不断革新其(金融)产品。日常贷款、抵押贷款、股票发行等产品被利润丰厚的有偿服务后来居上,例如现金管理、外汇、对冲基金、商业票据、定期存款、回购协议、企业或政府股票、债券和证券的交易等⑥。新成立且毫无章法的金融机构日渐膨胀:它们把那些吸纳了对冲基金、私募股权基金、退休基金与风险投资基金的"影子"机构招致麾下。为了符合自身的弹性与运营的自由度,大银行发明了"特殊投资工具",而这套工具无法合法地列入它们的总账目里。

这些好勇斗狠的银行高管们很早就反对加诸金融产业结构与金融业务上的各种限制。新政改革者对银行合并与利率都施以严格的限定,并且他们画出一条清晰的红线,以区别吸收存款的商业银行与主营证券发行的投资银行。第一国民城市银行前首席执行官李世同(Walter Wriston)1961 年在美国打破常规地启用可流通存单业务,并持续将定期存款折合成欧元计算⑦。许多银行步其后尘。

为了推出多样化且深入民心的支付机制,为了能够在不同国家或地区进行集资或配

---

① James W. Cortada, *The Digital Hand*, Volume 2: *How Computers Changed the Work of American Financial, Telecommunications, Media, and Entertainment Industries* (New York: Oxford University Press, 2006), 33, 61.
② "Cashed Out," The Lex Column, *Financial Times*, February 11, 2013.
③ Cortada, *Digital Hand*, vol. 2, 63.
④ David Harvey, *Enigma of Capital* (New York: Oxford University Press); Robert B. Reich, *After – Shock: The Next Economy and America's Future* (New York: Vintage, 2011); Charles H. Ferguson, *Predator Nation: Corporate Criminals, Political Corruption, and the Hijacking of America* (New York: Crown, 2012).
⑤ Vijay Prashad, *The Poorer Nations: Toward a Possible History of the Global South* (London: Verso, 2012).
⑥ Panitch and Gindin, *Making of Global Capitalism*, 174.
⑦ Jeff Madrick, *Age of Greed* (New York: Knopf, 2011), 16 – 19.

置资本,为了提供新的债权债务工具,为了加快资本流通的速度(当然首先是为了增加它们的收益),金融机构不得不扫除某些政治障碍。在1970年代至1990年代间,政治家认可了新的金融中介机构的合法性,放松了对现有机构的限制(或放任自流),这使得后者能够准入或重新准入那些尚未充分开发或预先被排除在外的市场。零敲碎打般的法制改革为全国范围内的电子资金转账、自动取款机网络、跨州银行业务办理以及那些能够认购公司债券、出售抵押贷款并能渗透至金融体系任何层面的(拥有企业股权的)大银行的出现铺平了道路①。在此情形下,紧要之处在于,套利交易、如银行数学家构想金融创新那样尽快研发新产品、自营业务交易,以及对每一阶层的消费者的每一交易收取高额费用的行为等一律日常化了。上述情况没有一例表明,支付与借贷机制已经丧失了其结构上的重要性。相反,这些根本性的功能湮没在代表大投资者(首当其冲的,应当是那些金融机构)利益的投机性交易活动之中。金融行业利润占企业利润总额的比例从1980年的15%猛涨至2006年27%②。然而,杠杆(银行可加以利用的借入资金的数量)与风险(尽管它经常被巧妙地遮掩起来)都在增加。

网络与软件驱动的产品或运营服务正好就成为这一全球性、高科技金融体系的基础设施。

据估算,1966年,金融行业整体(包括金融、保险与房地产)在计算机配置上所花费的成本占全国计算机配置总成本的17%,不及制造业投入总额的一半③。金融行业配置计算机系统,最初用于处理不断增加的支票,协调并控制储蓄与借贷业务④。如今,应用计算机的金融领域不断扩大。

1968年在美国国内13 600家商业银行里,大约有1 000家开始配备计算机,另外2 000家银行使用其他银行和独立的服务机构所提供的异地计算机业务。一些大银行、信用卡公司和独立供应商已开始向其他银行和企业客户推销专业的金融计算机服务。在银行内部之间,以及支持商业交易的支付机制内,正启动各类金融功能的自动化。然而,美国银行家协会得寸进尺,期待金融资本涵盖的范围能进一步扩大。

1968年美国银行家协会宣布,银行支行与它们的总部、联营银行与它们的控股公司、银行与它们的代理商行、银行与联邦储备银行以及其他政府机构、银行与它们的储户、借款人以及其他客户之间都需要有效的传播手段。该战略的成功有赖于"相关的通信设备

---

① Cortada, *Digital Hand*, vol. 2, 18.
② National Commission on the Causes of the Finzancial and Economic Crisis, *Financial Crisis Inquiry Report*, 2011, xvii. A larger increase in the proportion of profits claimed by financial institutions over this interval is given in Stein, *Pivotal Decade*, 296.
③ Dan Schiller, *Telematics and Government* (Norwood: Ablex, 1982), table 4, p. 24.
④ Cortada, *Digital Hand*, vol. 2, 60–73.

与服务的改善和发展"①。纽约清算所银行同业支付系统(CHIPS,1970 年建立)、环球银行金融电信协会(SWIFT,1973 年成立)以及大型信用卡网络的建立或形成,标志着电子金融业务的发展进入高峰阶段。1970 年代末,每天都有数百亿美元在这些系统间来回流动②。

1970 年,美国银行家协会在另一场诉讼中再一次指明,随着数据网络已成为金融行业的运营基础,"专门为银行业及其客户设计或定制的"服务应当成为优先考虑的发展战略③。特别是几家在国际上处于主导地位的超大银行(对这一服务)几近"痴迷",它们在网络技术的配置上花费过多。1980 年,美国大通银行在百余个国家或地区里使用网络技术以协调其金融业务。例如,它旗下的企业现金管理业务能够在西欧几乎任何一个国家(或以任何币种)检索到(retrieve)账户信息。诚如大通银行向外宣称的那般,这使得财务主管可以查阅到最新的账户信息变动情况,由此通过大通银行的网络实时划拨资金以"确保充分合理地利用资金"。大通的一位高管透露,"电信业已经进入爆炸式增长的时期",从而保证银行能够满足其跨国企业客户的需求④。

在美国几家大型商业与投资银行之中,大通并不是独一无二的。制造商汉诺威配备了分组交换的内部网络:1981 年,汉诺威与美国通用电话电子公司的远程登录网相互连接,向超过 30 个国家或地区的企业用户提供包括电子邮件在内的网络服务⑤。美国银行在国内 50 个州和 94 个国家或地区开展业务。从 1985 年开始,它便启动一项 5 年计划,耗资 50 亿美元建立全方位的信息技术与应用系统⑥。摩根·斯坦利在 1979 年至 1984 年间,将数据处理的预算提高了 5 倍,(除此之外)旨在建立供内部使用的自动交易分析与处理系统⑦。作为当之无愧的行业先锋与最重要的跨国金融服务公司,花旗银行在 1980 年已经在 94 个国家或地区建立分支机构。花旗通过卫星以及其他传播媒体与客户

---

① Federal Communications Commission, "In the Matter of Regulatory and Policy Problems Presented by the Interdependence of Computer and Communication Services and Facilities," CC Docket No. 16979, *American Bankers Association Comment*, March 4, 1968, 1, 2, 3, 23, in Dan Schiller, *Telematics and Government*, 28.
② Cortada, *Digital Hand*, vol. 2, 75.
③ FCC, "In the Matter of Establishment of Policies and Procedures for Consideration of Applications to Provide Specialized Common Carrier Services in the Domestic Public Point – to – Point Microwave Service," CC Docket No. 18920, Comment of American Banking Association October 12, 1970, 1525, in Dan Schiller, *Telematics and Government*, 45.
④ Letter from Kay Riddle, Vice President, Chase Manhattan Bank, to Richardson Preyer, Chairman, Subcommittee on Government Information and Individual Rights, Committee on Government Operations, U. S. House of Representatives, 96th Cong., 2d Sess., Hearings on International Data Flow, March 10, 13, 27, and April 21, 1980, 739 – 42, in Dan Schiller, *Telematics and Government*, 100 – 101.
⑤ Barry D. Wessler, "United States Public Packet Networks: An Update," *Telecommunication Journal* 47, no. 6 (1980), 374; "Electronic Mail Cuts Bank's Phone Dependence," *ComputerWorld*, June 29, 1981, 19, both in Dan Schiller, *Telematics and Government*, 54.
⑥ "Bank of America Rushes into the Information Age," *Business Week*, April 15, 1985, 110 – 12.
⑦ Marilyn A. Harris, "Morgan Stanley's High – Tech Boot Camp," *Business Week*, December 24, 1984, 79 – 82.

终端相连,并利用这些客户终端向它的商业用户提供金融信息与交易管理服务。花旗在产品研发上耗费巨大,并大量生产专用硬件与软件,从而"向客户提供最新的工具,与其他服务提供商相互区别"①。花旗银行断言,"保证准入"一个统一的计算机通讯网络的能力,"对那些打算提供国际金融中介服务的机构而言,在所有层面上一直都是最根本的(要素)"②。

越来越多的公司股票和债券交易开始通过庞大且广布的计算机网络完成。纽约证交所的成交额从1950年的5.25亿美元猛涨至1970年的29.4亿美元;到了1990年,交易额暴增至400亿美元,2004年达到3 670亿美元③。持有股票的美国人(占美国总人口数)的比例的增长态势,与国家出台的一系列破坏现有的退休计划、鼓吹私人养老金和401k账户的政策密不可分。(美国劳工部提供的资料显示:2012年,483 000个退休账户计划涵盖7 200万参与者④)。美国证券交易委员会批准电子交易,以实时监控证券价格并能在全国范围内完成实际交易;于是,交易的速度大大增加⑤。1971年全国证券交易商协会自动报价系统(纳斯达克,NASDAQ)的创建,再次推进了数字化重新整合的步伐⑥。纳斯达克与纽约证交所合作,1972年共同成立一家分支机构——证券行业自动化公司(SIAC)。该公司除了承担清算与结算职能外,还成功建立了服务于证交所290个成员行号的网络;这张网络以150万英里的载波电路为基础,载波电路由5颗陆地与3颗搭载卫星提供⑦。

网络集中于消费金融业务,部分拜苏格兰人约翰·谢泼德-巴伦(John Shepherd-Barron)所赐——1965年,他在洗澡时突然间想到自动柜员机的主意;两年后,伦敦北部的巴克莱银行让自动取款机正式投入使用(巴伦的同乡詹姆斯·古德菲勒[James Goodfellow]被视为加密的塑料卡与计算机化的个人识别编码技术的发明者)。在美国,自动取款机从1978年的7 700台⑧上升至2012年的40.9万台⑨。国际上,维萨信用卡的自动取款机网络(the Visa/Plus ATM network)在全球120个国家里拥有64.5万台自动取款

---

① Citicorp, *Annual Report* 1981, inside back cover.
② Citicorp, *Annual Report* 1981, inside front cover.
③ Cortada, *Digital Hand*, vol. 2, 155–56.
④ Gretchen Morgenson, "The Curtain Opens on 401(k) Fees," *New York Times*, June 3, 2012.
⑤ Cortada, *Digital Hand*, vol. 2, 158.
⑥ Cortada, *Digital Hand*, vol. 2, 169.
⑦ Statement of Vincent P. Moore Jr. in U. S. Senate, 95th Cong. , Committee on Commerce, Science, and Transportation, Subcommittee on Communications, Hearings on Domestic Telecommunications Common Carrier Policies, 1st Sess. , 21, March 22, 1977, Two Parts. Serial No. 95–42 (Washington, D. C. : GPO, 1977), 1048, in Dan Schiller, *Telematics and Government*, 64.
⑧ Hamelink, *Finance and Information*, 54.
⑨ Robin Sidel, "ATM's Fall Short on Disability Rule," *Wall Street Journal*, March 8, 2012.

机;整个世界都在吹嘘这种让人丢掉工作、总数约为两百万台的机器①。与此同时,电子交易对纸币的需求越来越小,英美两国的纸币数量开始大幅度减少;现金交易占总交易的比例从1999年的73%下降到2009年59%②。2010年,纽约人出租车收费的三分之一都是刷(信用)卡完成的③。

随着网上银行业务成为主流,电子支付的边界反而倒退了④。2011年4 400万美国家庭使用网上银行业务,这不仅产生了利润丰厚的手续费,也因为进行跨行在线支付的流程过于烦琐,反而使用户倾向于只选择一家网上银行⑤。电子支付手段不断翻新。正当数字化衰退接踵而至之时,信用卡公司联合谷歌、易趣等科技企业,共同推出移动终端的支付业务⑥。

整个1980年代,银行以平均每年19%的速度增加购买计算机设备、电信业务以及软件的预算⑦。用于分析与完成投资管理、债务管理、财务策划与外汇交易的数据库和各种工具,通过本地终端吸引了大量企业客户⑧。菲亚特并非唯一一家使用计算机处理现金管理业务的公司:1983年,菲亚特希望通过这种方式集中化管理共计540亿美元的现金流,进而"牢牢控制分布在55个国家的421家公司"⑨。花旗银行的罗伯特·怀特(Robert B. White)承认,"很难想象每天全世界所有银行的现金交易额度","绝大部分"的世界出口贸易"都以银行提供的贸易信贷的形式完成,这催生了一种完全依赖于世界电信媒体的国际金融交易行为"⑩。

在接下来的几十年里,(电信与金融业之间的)这种联结进一步加深。2006年,摩根大通集团号称自己拥有一支多达2万人的信息技术团队,每年的信息技术预算高达70亿美元。近年来,该集团花费巨资"打造面向机构投资者与对冲基金客户的尖端贸易平台"⑪。2008年金融危机爆发后,花旗集团雇佣2.5万名软件开发工程师,每年花费在信

---

① Visa credit card letter to cardholder, May 2012; Phil Davison, "Pioneer of ATM technology and Other Bank Innovations," *Financial Times*, May 29 – 30, 2010.
② Maija Palmer, "More Flash than Cash," *Financial Times*, March 21, 2012.
③ Binyamin Appelbaum, "As Plastic Reigns, Printing of Money Slows," *New York Times*, July 7, 2011.
④ Palmer, "More Flash than Cash".
⑤ Nelson D. Schwartz, "Online Banking Keeps Customers on Hook for Fees," *New York Times*, October 16, 2011.
⑥ Maija Palmer, "Racing to Make the Mobile Wallet Pay," *Financial Times*, December 1, 2011.
⑦ Joel Kurtzman, *The Death of Money* (Boston: Little, Brown, 1993), 26.
⑧ Citibank Electronic Banking and Cash Management Division, "Electronic Banking: An Executive's Guide" (New York: n. d. [1981?]).
⑨ "Clever Cash Management Revs Fiat's Finances," *Business Week*, April 30, 1984, 60.
⑩ Quoted in John M. Eger, "The Brussels Mandate: An Alliance for the Future of World Communications and Information Policy," address before the Conference on Transnational Data Regulation, Brussels, Belgium, February 9, 1978, 1 – 2.
⑪ Mara Der Hovanesian, "JP Morgan: The Bank of Technology," *Business Week*, June 19, 2006, available at http://www.businessweek.com/stories/2006 – 06 – 18/jpmorgan – the – bank – of – technology (accessed January 10, 2014).

息通信技术领域的资金据估计高达49亿美元,这还不包括运营费用①。此时(2010年),花旗集团26万名雇员有超过三分之二的人不在美国境内工作②,但母公司依然能够掌握海外巨额的现金收支情况(2011年可能高达5 000亿美元)③。(金融危机后)直到2011年的3年时间里,货币交易量狂涨21%,以至于外汇交易量平均每日4万亿美元④。由于财政部、美联储与世界顶级的国际银行构成美国金融复合体(financial complex),美元仍然是世界最主要的储备货币;核心工业产品(首先是石油)依旧以美元定价,以保证美国的货币政策能强势地影响其他国家⑤。

建设宏大的网络化的金融体系工程,将债务平摊给每一个社会机构,并以名目繁多的工具将之包装起来⑥。从1978年至2007年,美国金融机构所负债务总量增长了12倍:从3万亿美元飙升至36万亿美元⑦。美国政府出台的政策鼓励人们负债消费,并视其为政治上的权宜之计,以及于己有利的行为。于是,人们长期固守的节约与储蓄的习惯遭到侵蚀。然而,债务是潜在的火药桶。帕尼奇与因丁(Panitch and Gindin)曾着重指出,债务引发一连串危机的爆发。系统经理能够疏导1980年代第三世界的债务危机,他们也能够成功钳制1987年股票市场的闪电崩盘、1980年代末储蓄信贷危机、1997年亚洲金融危机以及稍后长期资本管理公司的倒台,甚至1999—2000年间互联网泡沫经济(等一系列危机的走势和局面)⑧。危机管理得以常态化,成为在更稳固基础上重建金融体系的无可替代的(救市)方案。

在2001—2007年里,美国的抵押贷款债务翻了一番,这6年上涨的幅度几可等同于前面所有年份的总和。数万亿美元被抵押,它建立在"房价将永远处于上升势头,即便抵押贷款者的债务不断增加,他们也不可能拖欠按揭"⑨这一信念基础之上。该信念反而成为金融体系中最薄弱的一环:2007年美国普通家庭、商业与政府(地方和联邦)所负债务总数大约占美国国内生产总值的350%⑩。大银行与影子银行铤而走险从事违法勾当,恶

---

① Francesco Guerrera,"Citigroup Ramps Up Tech Cuts,"*Financial Times*,May 22,2009.
② John Cassidy,"What Good Is Wall Street?",*New Yorker*,November 29,2010.
③ Helen Thomas and Jeremy Lemer,"US Groups Blame Tax as Cash Held Overseas Tops $500bn,"*Financial Times*,July 28,2011.
④ Jennifer Hughes,"Battle Lines Are Drawn in Changing Landscape,"*Financial Times*,October 3,2011.
⑤ Panitch and Gindin,*Making of Global Capitalism*.
⑥ Foster and Magdoff,*Great Financial Crisis*;Martin Wolf,"A Hard Slog in the Foot-hills of Debt,"*Financial Times*,March 14,2012.
⑦ National Commission on the Causes of the Financial and Economic Crisis,*Financial Crisis Inquiry Report*,2011,xvii;Stein,*Pivotal Decade*,296.
⑧ Panitch and Gindin,*Making of Global Capitalism*,247-71.
⑨ National Commission on the Causes of the Financial and Economic Crisis,*Financial Crisis Inquiry Report*,2011,7,6(quote).
⑩ Fred Magdoff and Michael D. Yates,*The ABCs of the Economic Crisis:What Working People Need to Know*(New York:Monthly Review,2009),76.

化了这一局面。部分银行不惜牺牲客户利益,挪用账户资金采取投机行为,其他一些大银行涉嫌操纵伦敦银行同业拆借利率(LIBOR),从而人为设定财务合约(无论是衍生金融投资工具还是抵押贷款产品)涉及的数万亿美元的利息费用[1]。据说还有银行(暗中)操控外汇市场[2]。评级机构不再独立于这些大银行之外,而是与它们的金主沆瀣一气,(违心地)将那些明显不可靠的证券、债券、股票评定为"可靠、高回报"[3]。2007年,当经济出现稍微放缓迹象,而不少抵押人无法继续支付按揭贷款时,这一过度金融杠杆化(over-leveraged)并充满欺骗性的金融体系开始崩塌。

随着全球金融的联系不断增强,网络支持的工具与产品已被投入使用,这使金融风险改头换面,并扩散至全世界。当美国的抵押担保证券市场某一不起眼的角落开始出现混乱局面时,网络即刻转而向外界展示了其致命的活力(death-ray pulse)[4]。雨果·雷迪斯(Hugo Radice)表示,"这一潜在的传染链可以触及全球金融最深的角落"[5]。杠杆(债务)成为这场火灾的燃料,直白地说,债务无处不在。此时,危机让全球金融体系摇摇欲坠、危如累卵。到底什么原因使得每一类的金融中介机构都能负债无数?无人知晓。当首要的信贷机制开始冻结,危机所波及的已经远不止金融领域。公司在日常运营过程中每天可以吸纳的由金融资产提供担保的隔夜贷款可至数十亿美元;不过,银行清楚为这些交易提供担保的金融资产实际上一文不名,它们也没有合理理由确认竞争对手的资产是否更加可靠,于是拒绝全部贷款申请[6]。尽管随后爆发的危机的许多细节还无法得知或比较模糊,但是系统经理已经无法阻止这场浩劫蔓延至全世界。

为了应对这场危机,美联储主导的央行向金融体系注入大量流动资金。在经济学家马丁·沃尔夫(Martin Wolf)看来,倘若它们没有这么做,"我们将毫无疑问地经历第二次经济大萧条"[7]。估算可能有所不同,但央行采取的干预行为无疑是前所未有的。《彭博市场月刊》的一则报道透露,美联储在2008年12月5日这一天就向银行系统私下输入1.2万亿美元,2009年3月美国央行投入7.7万亿美元旨在稳定局势[8]。这则报道所依

---

[1] David Enrich,"Fresh Charges Readied in Rate-Rigging Case," *Wall Street Journal*, June 18, 2013; Caroline Binham, Phillip Stafford, and Kara Scannell,"'Lord Libor' Trio Put ICAP at Heart of Rate-Rigging Scandal," *Financial Times*, September 26, 2013.
[2] Caroline Binham, John Aglionby, and Megan Murphy,"Swiss Probe UBS and Other Banks over Alleged Rigging of Forex Market," *Financial Times*, October 5/6, 2013.
[3] Ferguson, *Predator Nation*.
[4] International Monetary Fund,"How Linkages Fuel the Fire: The Transmission of Financial Stress from Advanced to Emerging Economies," in *World Economic Outlook*, April 2009, chapter 4.
[5] Hugo Radice,"The Next Banking Crisis," *The Bullet* 574 (November 28, 2011), 2.
[6] Mark Blyth, *Austerity: The History of a Dangerous Idea* (New York: Oxford University Press, 2013), 23-26.
[7] Martin Wolf,"America Owes a Lot to Bernanke," *Financial Times*, June 5, 2013.
[8] Bob Ivry, Bradley Keoun, and Phil Kuntz,"Secret Fed Loans Gave Banks $13 Billion Undisclosed to Congress," *Bloomberg Markets*, November 27, 2011, 1-2.

据的,是记者凭借《信息自由法案》而获得的档案。稍晚的另一则报道,来自于某位局内人提供的关于政府如何处理金融危机的资料。该报道声称,美国政府("救市")所投入的资金依然只多不少①。其他一些曝光的信息向外界披露,美联储已向全球14家央行(包括瑞士与韩国)注入高达5 800亿美元的流动资金②。在经济恢复时期(大概从2009年6月开始),美联储实施"量化宽松"政策,向美国金融体系额外提供2万亿美元的援助。

尽管金融危机由此受到钳制,但它造成了无法逆转的破坏。数百万的美国借贷者所欠房屋抵押贷款远超他们的抵押物之价值;数万亿美元的家庭财富瞬间灰飞烟灭,即便此前已有数百万抵押权人丧失抵押品赎回权(法院拍卖房屋),可大多数抵押权人依旧要面对房屋被没收的窘境③。房地产市场在2013年有所回暖,却仍未回到可保经济稳定的水平上。实际上,2013年房产价格的上升或许并非是经济再度复苏的迹象,而是对冲基金相互抬高房产价格(旨在投机性获利)策略的结果。同样,美国联邦储备银行采取的"量化宽松"宏观政策,也激活了股市投机行为,推动了"热钱"大量流向世界范围内高利息的投资领域。投资者保证金借款行为不断出现,美国大量发行市政债券,每一种现象都标示经济情势再度紧绷,令人困扰,尽管(或由于)银行利润再度出现通胀④。只有建诸投资与工作基础之上的经济全面复苏才能使当前的政治经济形势回归正常,当本书(英文版)付梓出版之时,还未出现任何真正意义上的经济复苏的迹象⑤。

三种后续趋势

第一种趋势是,高科技金融与缺乏行业担当的两种情况并存,并将一直存在。美国前劳工部部长罗伯特·里奇(Robert B. Reich)仔细地叙述了华尔街如何利用手中权势竭尽全力阻止重大变革的过程:"一有可能,金融界便迫不及待地向外宣称经济衰退已经过去,金融体系已经运转良好,并集中对议员进行游说以反对任何重大变革法案的通过。

---

① Neil Barofsky, *Bailout: An Inside Account of How Washington Abandoned Main Street While Rescuing Wall Street* (New York: Free Press, 2012).
② Neil Irwin, "Fed's Aid In '08 Crisis Stretched Worldwide," *New York Times*, February 24, 2014.
③ Shahien Nasiripour, "A Million a Year Still Face Foreclosure," *Financial Times*, April 4, 2012. 前不良资产救助计划(TARP)的特别监察长(Special Inspector General)巴霍夫斯基(Neil Barofsky)曾表示,联邦政府救市计划耗资"最高可至4.7万亿美元",可参见 Barofsky, Bailout, 162.
④ Floyd Norris, "Shades of 2007 Borrowing," *New York Times*, June 1, 2013; Gretchen Morgenson, "Quantity over Quality in Bank Profits," *New York Times*, June 2, 2013; Floyd Norris, "A Portent of Peril for Muni Boldholders," *New York Times*, June 7, 2013.
⑤ "To achieve a full recovery and healthy growth of the world economy will be a long and tortuous process," declared Chinese leader Xi Jinping in October 2013. James Pomfret and Randy Fabi, "China's Xi Sees 'Long and Tortuous' World Economic Recovery," *Reuters*, October 7, 2013, available at http://www.reuters.com/article/2013/10/07/us-asia-china-idUSBRE99609L20131007 (accessed January 10, 2014).

这样,那些潜藏的问题压根没有得到解决。"①里奇总结道,"因为'旧常态'让我们深陷困境,所以我们无法回到'正常'"②。

财政部高级官员依然满是高盛投资或华尔街其他银行的"毕业生"。出于共同的阶级利益,当然也躲不开银行强硬的游说压力,大量类似的投机性金融活动、机构设置以及那些导致金融危机的可怕动机,依然未受到任何影响③。监管政府救市计划的官员宣称,(这一计划)"早已被华尔街全权掌控,对它而言……('救市')无非是一个史无前例、涉及数万亿美元的游戏场所,他们可以恣意欺诈、从事自利交易"④。相反,"现状虽遭到极大破坏"⑤,但它依然存在。

第二种趋势是,政府采取一些改革措施⑥,可在"金融机构太庞大而不能倒闭"的名义下,大量金融资本依旧不受到政府规制的有效监管⑦。一项旨在遏制银行自营交易中明显腐败行为的政策(即《沃尔克规则》),(实施过程中)存在各种例外情况,哪怕在摩根集团声称旗下的伦敦雇员利用个人账户谋取私利从而蒙受50亿美元的损失之后⑧,(《沃尔克规则》)仍旧被推迟执行⑨。由银行说客起草、立法者批复的一系列法案,旨在恢复原状⑩,这样也就蓄意破坏了多德-弗兰克(Dodd-Frank)金融蜕变法案。货币市场基金、资产抵押债券与回购市场三方共同构成数万亿美元的"影子银行"复合体。该复合体非但没有受到任何规制,反而成为吉莉安·泰德(Gillian Tett)所说的美国金融体系的阿喀琉斯之踵(最薄弱环节)⑪。美国人可能以分期付款的方式偿还家庭债务⑫,但他们的信

---

① Reich, *After-Shock*, 8.
② Reich, *After-Shock*, 75.
③ Simon Johnson and James Kwak, *Thirteen Bankers* (New York: Pantheon, 2010); Brooke Masters, "Alert on 'Shadow Bank' Threat," *Financial Times*, March 15, 2012.
④ Barofsky, *Bailout*, 129, 132.
⑤ Barofsky, *Bailout*, 149, 160.
⑥ Brooke Masters, "Banks Are Short $566bn, Says Fitch Study," *Financial Times*, May 17, 2012, available at http://www.ft.com/intl/cms/s/0/d436e1ee-9fec-11e1-94ba-00144feabdc0.html#axzz1v7hZ9MyF (accessed January 10, 2014).
⑦ "当前银行业最显著的发展趋势是,银行业绩日渐下滑的同时,银行高管行为愈发放肆无耻",可参见,Jessie Eisinger, "How the U.S. Shelters and Subsidizes the Banking Industry," *New York Times*, June 30, 2011. 也可参见 Scott Patterson and Jean Eaglesham, "SEC Probes Rapid Trading," *Wall Street Journal*, March 23, 2012; 以及 Edward Wyatt, "S.E.C. Is Avoiding Tough Sanctions for Large Banks," *New York Times*, February 3, 2012; 还有 Sheila McNulty, "Speculators Return in Wake of Enron," *Financial Times*, December 2, 2011.
⑧ Shahien Nasiripour and Tom Braithwaite, "Fed Extends Volcker Rule Deadline," *Financial Times*, April 19, 2012, available at http://www.ft.com/intl/cms/s/0/ffc56a56-8a4d-11e1-93c9-00144feab49a.html#axzz1u7B83aRX (accessed January 10, 2014); William Watts, "U.S. Stock Futures Hit by J.P. Morgan," *Wall Street Journal*, May 11, 2012.
⑨ James B. Stewart, "Volcker Rule, Once Simple, Now Boggles," *New York Times*, October 22, 2011.
⑩ Barofsky, Bailout, 148; Eric Lipton and Ben Protess, "Banks' Lobbyists Help in Drafting Financial Bills," *New York Times*, May 24, 2013.
⑪ Gillian Tett, "The Achilles Heel of America's Financial System," *Financial Times*, July 31, 2012; Sebastian Mallaby, "Finance Must Escape the Shadows," *Financial Times*, August 1, 2012.
⑫ Gillian Tett, "Americans Are Now Ahead in Paying Down Their Debts," *Financial Times*, May 10, 2013.

用卡账单看起来越良好,他们的大学学费贷款(反而)越糟糕。2013 年,大学学费贷款共计 1 万亿美元,并且它与债务融资抵押贷款一样,处于金融资本的操控之下①。一旦美国财政部与美联储以实际行动确认那些至关重要的(金融)机构"太庞大而不能倒闭",向 25 所华尔街顶级公司提供的救助(2010 年高达 1 350 亿美元)即刻破了纪录②。第二种趋势表明,如若没有彻底且充满曲折地重新建构世界政治经济的话,那么这场危机不可能就此结束。第二次世界大战以降,美国不仅通过大型银行、美国联邦储备银行与财政部,更通过国际货币基金组织、世行及与之联盟的国际组织,俨然成为主导全球金融的权力集团。然而,1990 年代以及 2000 年年初,该体系不断面临挑战。巴西、俄罗斯、印度、中国与南非这些在国际上逐渐扩大影响力的国家,开始向国际货币基金组织与世行提出额外的投票权重与决策权等诉求③。上述 5 国被高盛(2001 年)命名为"金砖国家",当 5 个国家在 2008 年(正是金融危机爆发之时)举行系列会谈,并组建国际政治实体时,它们将金融家的幻想转变成政治现实。

2012 年,中国国家开发银行签署了用人民币结算的信贷协议,准备向印度、巴西、俄罗斯与南非注入人民币贷款;已经离任(担任高盛高级顾问一职)的前世行行长罗伯特·佐利克(Robert Zoellick)希望"金砖银行"能够被纳入以美国为中心的世行体系之中④。大量且有时还比较严重的分歧逐渐浮出水面:美国所提出的投资自由政策长期以来受到国际社会的尊崇,但如今它正备受抨击。抨击它的正是那些遭受着巴西总统迪尔玛·罗塞夫(Dilma Rousseff)所说的热钱"海啸"冲击的国家,而热钱"海啸"的出现,离不开美国和欧盟所奉行的极端宽松的货币政策⑤。于是,美元作为全球储备货币的独特地位开始受到争议:众多僵尸银行与一家负债累累的政府难道有利于全球资本的稳定? 2013 年 6 月,美国联邦储备委员会向外宣布计划削减新一轮量化宽松政策 2 万亿美元。由此,美国金融体系所承受的压力显而易见。该声明一出,即刻引发全球商品价格的大幅度下跌,更刺激印尼、印度、南非与巴西等国的"热钱"大量外流。这说明,全球经济在美国货币政策面前显得多么不堪一击⑥。出乎意料的是,美联储随后公开宣称,它将继续保持高

---

① Jessica Silver‑Greenberg and Catherine Rampell, "Sallie Mae Will Split as Loans Face Scrutiny," *New York Times*, May 30, 2013.
② Barofsky, *Bailout*, 217.
③ Alan Beattie, "An Exercise of Influence," *Financial Times*, April 3, 2012; James Fontanella‑Khan, "BRICs Call for More Power at IMF," *Financial Times*, March 30, 2012.
④ Henny Sender, "China Offers Other Brics Renmimbi Loans," *Financial Times*, March 8, 2012; James Lamont, "Zoellick Backs Creation of Brics Bank," *Financial Times*, April 2, 2012.
⑤ Joe Leahy, "Opponents to Free Capital Flows Seek to Sway IMF," *Financial Times*, May 7, 2012.
⑥ Nathaniel Popper, "Global Sell‑Off Shows Fed Reach beyond the U.S.," *New York Times*, June 21, 2013.

达850亿美元的每月资产采购力度①。危机管理依然是当今世界(首要)的议事日程,然而,全球资本主义体系的深度重构与之相伴相随,有时甚至以一种意想不到的方式重建全球资本主义体系。我将在第三部分阐释,这一矛盾重重的过程同样让网络化的传播与信息体系难承其重。

第三种趋势是,这场危机非但不会消失,相反将不断分叉,继续蔓延。债务没有消除:实际上,整个美国与西欧的债务都极大地增加了。可资本主义国家的障眼法,使得许多富裕国家所背负的债务在数字化衰退的初期从金融公司转嫁到政府身上②。资本家及其阶级联盟宣告没有其他办法拯救危机,于是它们提出"主权债务危机"这一说法——在我写书的过程中,希腊一直成为西方报章头条的主角,但西欧国家(美国紧随其后)启动财政紧缩方案,并将紧缩对象锁定在普通工人的生活水平上。这一政治攻击十分密集。在美国,对债权人友好的阶级斗争,假借"共度时艰"之名,狠狠地打击了住宅抵押贷款持有人,还有养老金、医疗、教育以及其他社会福利项目。尽管2013年紧缩"信条"作为一种经济理论备受质疑和抨击,但克鲁格曼这位批评家仍正确地指出,实际上,财政紧缩方案依然固若金汤③。随着本书最终完稿,拥有亿万身家的投资者正资助一场针对美国政府债务限额政策、精心算计的正面进攻,希望借此釜底抽薪,将社会支出与社会保障据为己有④。

很明显,金融业的网络化并非解决(危机)之道;数字化衰退仍将持续,网络化的金融化进程将失去控制、缺乏担当,一如银行网络投资再度兴盛⑤。花旗集团签署协议,要求美国国际商用机器公司(IBM)开发的超级电脑"华生"为其服务,并"重新思考与设定我们的客户与顾客同钱打交道的多种方式"⑥。摩根集团在信息技术上的年度开支攀升至2011年的85亿美元⑦;同年,据估计,对冲基金有可能额外花费20.9亿美元在信息技术的配置上⑧。反过来,金融业不断地向网络发展施加影响力。

---

① Patrick Jenkins, "Five Bitter Pills," *Financial Times*, September 13, 2013; Robin Harding, James Politi, and Michael Mackenzie, "Fed Blinks on Tapering of QE3," *Financial Times*, September 19, 2013.
② Wolf, "Hard Slog."
③ Paul Krugman, "The Big Shrug," *New York Times*, June 10, 2013; Lawrence Summers, "The Buck Does Not Stop with Reinhart and Rogoff," *Financial Times*, May 6, 2013; Robert Kuttner, *Debtors' Prison: The Politics of Austerity versus Possibility* (New York: Knopf, 2013).
④ Sheryl Gay Stolberg and Mike McIntire, "A Federal Budget Crisis Months in the Planning," *New York Times*, October 6, 2013.
⑤ Paul Taylor, "Bank Tech Expenditure Set to Rise," *Financial Times*, The Connected Business, September 18, 2013, available at http://http://www.ft.com/cms/s/0/33a6cde2-13af-11e3-9289-00144feabdc0.html#axzz2qfXFvI2L (accessed January 10, 2014).
⑥ Quoted in Robert Shrimsley, "A Supercomputer for Citigroup," *Financial Times*, March 8, 2012.
⑦ Francesco Guerrera and Justin Baer, "JPMorgan Cuts Trading Systems," *Financial Times*, February 16, 2011.
⑧ "Hedge Funds to Spend \$2.09 Billion on Information Technology in 2011," *Business Wire*, September 29, 2011, available at http://www.businesswire.com/news/home/20110929006008/en#.UtmoR2Tnb9k (accessed January 10, 2014).

这一点，2010年秋海伯尼亚公司（Hibernia）宣布将兴建一条新的横跨大西洋的海底电缆可为例证。1998年至2001年间，在互联网泡沫的高峰期共有7条新的电缆搭建完毕，跨大西洋海底电缆市场发展过度；随后，激烈的价格竞争与紧接其后的公司破产，导致价格的"奇观式"下跌，那些存活下来的网络运营者只能下调价格：2010年带宽价格"全球最低"。海伯尼亚公司的海底电缆是看起来厄运不断的电缆市场在过去近10年里投资兴建的第一条电缆。海伯尼亚银行的底气在哪？它预计（兴建的这条）"项目快线"（Project Express）电缆由于使用更加直接的物理通路，可以减少大约5毫秒的"回路延迟"（return-path latency）时间：例如，在纽约与伦敦之间的信息传递一来一回，就存在着"回路延迟"。这条电缆一旦建成，它可是大西洋两岸间最快的一条通路。对于普通用户而言，这样的边际增益毫无用处。然而，对于某一公司或集团而言，这可是（别人）无法超越的优势。某位分析师指出，"金融机构只求高速贸易，它们就是速度魔鬼；金融机构曾公开宣称，两个贸易地点之间的信息传送速度哪怕节省那么几毫秒，便可让它们获益匪浅，年进账数千万美元——所以，它们乐于花更多的资金兴建更快的信息传输通道"①。到2011年，对冲基金、证券交易所与超大银行的高频贸易占美国股权交易额的七成，约占欧洲股权交易额的三分之一②。对于那些能够负担此费用的公司而言，市场的投机倒把不再聚焦于对某家特定公司盈利能力的精确估算，而是充分开掘网络基础设施的创新发展的潜力。高盛、巴克莱、瑞士信贷与摩根士丹利已经建立了以算法为中心的贸易体系，旨在跟踪股票价格的细微变动，进而攫取每一分利润。"它们详细了解不同的证券交易所的（运营）情况，基于即期行情以及对（股票）过去表现的数据分析，试图预测每一只股票有可能在接下来的几分之一秒钟的价格走向"③。然后，它们自己签署买卖委托单。这些不受规制的电子领域的运行仰仗于高速网络④；某位分析师表示，地点很关键，服务器要尽可能地靠近这些交易所⑤。海伯尼亚公司计划重新铺设管

---

① "Hibernia Pulls Ahead in Trans-Atlantic Speed Race," *TeleGeography*, CommsUpdate, September 30, 2010, quoting TeleGeography Vice President of Research Tim Stronge.
② Scott Patterson, *Dark Pools: High Speed Traders, A. I. Bandits, and the Threat to the Global Financial System* (New York: Crown Business, 2012), 8.
③ Steve Kroft, "How Speed Traders Are Changing Wall Street," *Sixty Minutes*, CBS, October 10, 2010, available at http://www.cbsnews.com/news/how-speed-traders-are-changing-wall-street-07-10-2010 (accessed January 10, 2014).
④ Patterson, *Dark Pools*, 9.
⑤ "Slaves to the algorithm," Lex Column, *Financial Times*, July 13, 2011. 有趣之处在于，除去日本的亚洲其他地区，高频交易仅仅占股权交易额的5%，具体请参见 Jeremy Grant and Telis Demos, "Ultra-fast Traders Braced for Tough Curbs in Europe," *Financial Times*, October 14, 2011.

道,以获得更大的信息流动空间,从而为它的首选客户赢得优势①(然而,因为这一工程牵涉到它的承建商之一——中国设备提供商华为公司的安全问题,美国政府责成海伯尼亚银行暂停该计划)。纽约与芝加哥的大型商品交易所之间正在建设类似的超快信息传输通道,横跨北极地区的海底通道正在建设中,这样再次减少了东京与伦敦之间的"回路延迟"时间②。

逐渐地,算法交易不仅基于股市行情与收益表,随着它准入专用网络与交易所,便更依赖于社交网络用户与网络聊天室上传的数据③。2010 年 5 月 6 日(美国证券市场)出现了所谓的"闪电崩盘",计算机驱动的交易毫无缘由地使道琼斯指数重挫(9%):在短短几个小时内,美国股市损失(随后收回)1 万亿美元④。

到底发生了什么,直到 2013 年这一事件还依旧成谜。可这些网络化的技术创新有可能导致更大范围的功能紊乱,正如脸书以及其他公司将它们首次公开募股搞砸归咎于软件故障。然而,美国的规制部门并未启动改革措施⑤,以至于当骑士资本集团(2012 年占全美股票交易额的 11%)引进了一套全新却未经检验的高频系统并杀入股市后,又一次(系统)失灵再次使 148 家公司的股价大幅下跌。某位分析师写道,"现在是金融机构之间展开'高频军备竞赛'的年代,这些公司无所不用其极,它们对技术的开掘已逼近现有技术的极限,更把技术推向(使用的)极致"⑥。援引记者弗洛伊德·诺里斯(Floyd Norris)较为慎重的话,这般做法将导致"风险不断增加"⑦。网络化的金融业依然在谱写它们的乐章。

---

① "项目快线"作为海伯尼亚"全球金融网络"的组成部分,曾得到来自中国华为与英国全球海事系统成立 3 年的合资企业(全球最大的海底电缆敷设船运营商)所提供的 2.5 亿美元的资助,具体请参见"Hibernia Atlantic Achieves an Important Milestone for Project Express," *Business Wire*, January 5, 2011, available at http://unified - communications . tmcnet. com/news/2011/01/05/5225567. htm (accessed January 10, 2014).

② Rich Miller, "More Speed—at ﹩80,000 a Millisecond," *DataCenter Knowledge*, January 24, 2011, available at http://www.datacenterknowledge. com/archives/2011/01/24/more - speed - at - 80000 - a - millisecond (accessed January 10, 2014); Sebastian Anthony, "﹩1.5bn: The Cost of Cutting London - Tokyo Latency by 60 ms," *ExtremeTech*, March 20, 2012, available at http://www.extremetech. com/extreme/122989 - 1 - 5 - billion - the - cost - of - cutting - london - toyko - latency - by -60ms (accessed January 10, 2014); Andrea Thomer, "Climate Change as a Safe Bet: Beneficiaries and Implications of Trans - Arctic Submarine Cable Projects. (Champaign - Urbana: University of Illinois, unpublished paper, Fall 2013)"

③ Maureen O' Hara and David Easley, "The Next Big Crash Could Be Caused by 'Big Data'," *Financial Times*, May 21, 2013.

④ "Knight Capital," *The Lex Column*, *Financial Times*, August 5, 2012.

⑤ Telis Demos, "Traders Still Waiting for Measures to Prevent a Repeat of 2010's 'Flash Crash'," *Financial Times*, May 7, 2012.

⑥ Tracy Alloway, "Knight's Woes Shine Light on Succession of Wall St. Glitches," *Financial Times*, August 4/5, 2012.

⑦ Floyd Norris, "Strong and Fast, But No Time to Think," *New York Times*, August 3, 2012;也请参见 Jessica Silver - Greenberg and Ben Protess, "Trying to Stay Nimble, Knight Capital Stumbles," *New York Times*, August 3, 2012;以及 Arash Massoudi, "Software Glitch Leaves Brokerage Knight Nursing Loss of ﹩440m," *Financial Times*, August 3, 2012.

第 4 章
网络化的军事化

网络化重组的第三个维度军事化,发端于美国政府在展开所向披靡的军事与情报行动上的开销。数字资本主义被视为一种永久性的、普遍军事化的(pervasively militarized)社会形态。这并不是因为军费开支是晚近出现的情况。从二战结束前(美国空投)核弹摧毁日本,到杜鲁门总统决定出兵朝鲜这段时间,美国的政治经济角色已被重新设定为(后方)仓库,其中,信息通信技术的重要性逐步显现。两种动力共同推进了这一过程。第一种动力是资本及其盟友的政治反向行动,以增加政府开支而无需贯彻(罗斯福)新政这一福利国家改革措施:这些改革赋予那些隶属工会的劳动者以权力,并削减企业权力。第二种动力是跨国商业、政治与军事精英的(社会)动员,以在全球范围内激活一种美式和平(Pax Americana)。

为何美国领导人要规划国内的政治经济发展,以迎接永久战争?二战后,美国的战略重心即刻转移到与社会主义对抗的问题上,尽管这一"对抗"通常被委婉地表达为"钳制"。苏联首当其冲地成为美国钳制的对象,但很快欧洲、中国与朝鲜半岛甚至整个世界都被纳入钳制范围。

即便欧洲国家不似日德两国(在战争中)被彻底摧毁,可二战使主要的欧洲国家在经济上元气大伤,并改变了它们的政治和意识形态动态(dynamics)。它们已很难阻止亚非拉国家(彼时开始被称为"第三世界")走上民族自决的道路。数十年来,革命民族主义者在不同国家开展革命活动,旨在实现(当地)民族自决这一目标。当20世纪初,中美洲、加勒比海和菲律宾等地区或国家爆发民族解放运动时,美国频繁地进行军事干涉,以扼杀它们——这算是预演。然而,美国在战后所面对的挑战更加严峻。

以印度和巴西为代表的第三世界国家开始实施进口替代战略以及其他相关的经济政策,以求更为自主的发展。而其他的第三世界国家(例如1949年后的中国)实际上主动撤离了资本主义市场。在这一历史情境下,冷战不外乎是一场争夺对世界人民、国家与资源的管理权的竞赛。除美国之外,西欧是全世界最大规模和最主要的资产阶级所在地。为了将其战略网络覆盖至西欧,美国介入到拆分德国的过程中,驻扎军队,并建立北大西洋公约组织。在日本、韩国以及中国台湾这些位于苏联和中国左侧的国家和地区,美国专门派遣数万名士兵驻防于此。美国向许多亚非拉国家的独裁者或专制君主提供帮助和支持,而逼迫那些受到民众欢迎、有时甚至通过民主程序选举出来的领导者退位。从伊朗到危地马拉、从智利到印尼、从刚果到越南,美国以隐秘或公开、小规模或大规模、直接管理或扶植本地代理的方式,对这些国家进行军事干预。针对美国人民的美国政府宣传战略,将这些军事干预描述成维护民主的正义之举。商业媒体的同声一辞,确保主战派(无论是民主党还是共和党)理念能够统摄国内舆论。不存在预先注定的成功,也无理所当然的胜利。在从杜鲁门到里根以及此后的总统任期内,美国始终处于"作战"状态,以占领并重构世界政治经济版图,进而实现短期或长期的资本目标。

  为了这一目标,一个无所不包的机构体系(institutional circuitry)得以建立。该机构包括:国防部(旨在整合此前彼此互不连属的军事部门);国家安全委员会(作为超级执行机构,为战略议题提供分析、筹划与决策等服务);中央情报局与国家安全局(负责执行秘密行动,并雇佣人才、使用[尖端]创新科技,以开发高度机密的监控程序)。由此,军事部门变成一支常备(武装)力量,远远超出此前备受限制且临时组建的官方渠道。这一行政部门(Executive Branch)很快就成为美国迄今为止最具影响力的要素①。尽管不同机构之间还存在些许分歧,但总统与军事情报部门对世界(局势)以及美国在其中的位置抱有相同的假设。

  有了跨部电台咨询委员会(the Interdepartment Radio Advisory Committee)、国家通信系统(the National Communications System)与国家安全局等少为人知或完全机密的组织的辅佐,政府内部的电磁频谱分配或传播管理等民用职能被统一归并到行政部门进行集中管理。这与国家(政府机构)的重构亦步亦趋,美国公司也重新调整方向。自1940年代以降,军事科技创新与武器设计占据重要地位。那些尽可能地开发各种通信与信息硬件和软件的公司,接到大量的军事订单。于是,在与战争有关的商品链中,高科技产品的生产往往假借"国家安全"之名。

  战时补给成为一项庞大、多方位且盈利丰厚的产业,产业核心是信息与传播技术。这一发展并非开风气之先,而早已有先例可循。美国卷入一战期间,诚如美国电话电报公司首席执行官华特·吉福德(Walter Gifford)在对陆军工业学院(Army Industrial

---

① Gareth Porter, *Perils of Dominance: Imbalance of Power and the Road to War in Vietnam* (Berkeley: University of California Press, 2005).

College)的演讲中所述,"贝尔公司 90% 的研发工作都与战争有关"①。然而,二战结束后,军事继续渗透进国家的科学基础结构中,使后者聚焦于网络的升级换代工作上,从而整合先进传播技术的武器系统的开发,以及维系指挥、控制与情报等传统军事功能。在(美国)数字技术转型的早期(也是关键时期),所有主要的计算机项目有四分之三与这一军事研究计划密切相关。美国国际商用机器公司早期生产的所有计算机,要么全部要么部分受到军事部门的资助②。

军事化的项目驱动了微电子学、电子计算机、基础软件开发以及网络工事创新等领域的发展;网络工事创新脱胎于远程预警线与美国国际商用机器公司的半自动地面设施。1960 年代,随着约翰逊总统与国防部部长罗伯特·麦克纳马拉(Robert McNamara)使越南战争升级,军事化的网络逐渐服膺于越战作为"电子战争"这一目标③。正如军事战争游戏连同实际战争不定期地将世界推向灾难边缘④,这些(军事)幻想变得越发浮夸、自以为是。正是里根的"星球大战"计划(或曰"战略防御计划"⑤)促使武器开支跃进互联网时代。当今,网络战争计划的筹备与开发就耗资数十亿美元。网络战争这一"想入非非的实在论"(援引米尔斯的术语⑥)已经在军事行动与战略的框架内被建制化了。

然而,网络密集型军事即便摆脱了环绕其周围的历史趋势、冲突以及各种偶然性的影响,仍然没有作为直线规划项目发展壮大起来。我们可以看到,1960 年代末,压力不断增加。越战开销使财政危机积重难返。美国成功地重建德国和日本,引发了资本家之间激烈的竞争。美国的资本家在更多的产业领域内遭遇各种困境。彼时,第三世界的政治形势如日中天;越南人继续把美国逼入绝境,尽管付出惨重的代价,却向其他国家的民族解放运动提供一个全球性的示范标本。1960 年代的后半叶,美国国内也正经历着转型:不断升级的反战运动、激进的民权运动以及(1970 年代初)的民众反抗⑦。这场民众抗议,既有对工资与福利收益的诉求,也有对工厂民主化以及国内/外交政策的变革的殷殷期盼。

对此,政策制定者出台激进的措施,试图恢复原本有利可图的资本积累模式。首先,

---

① Walter S. Gifford, address before the Army War College, Washington, D. C., in *Addresses, Papers and Interviews of Walter S. Gifford*, vol. 2, October 13, 1928 – December 2, 1937. 由美国电话电报公司的信息部门编制, New York, 1937, 203.
② James W. Cortada, *The Digital Hand*, Volume 3: *How Computers Changed the Work of American Public Sector Industries* (New York: Oxford University Press, 2008), 54.
③ Michael T. Klare, *War without End* (New York: Vintage, 1972), 165 – 209.
④ The Cuban missile crisis is the most – well – known episode. However, see Jamie Doward, "How a NATO War Game Took the World to the Brink of Nuclear Disaster," *The Guardian*, November 2, 2013.
⑤ Vincent Mosco, *The Pay – Per Society* (Toronto: Garamond, 1989), 131 – 72.
⑥ C. Wright Mills, *The Sociological Imagination* (New York: Oxford University Press, 2000).
⑦ Aaron Brenner, Robert Brenner, and Cal Winslow, eds., *Rebel Rank and File: Labor Militancy and Revolt from Below during the Long 1970s* (New York: Verso, 2010).

他们开始直接抨击那些有限的社会福利计划,后者是在新政期间得以推广,并只在约翰逊总统的"伟大社会"口号下得到拓展。其次,它们大力宣扬军事机构主导的与网络有关的投资项目,并鼓吹这些项目是更为宏大的战略的一部分,即信息与传播将成为市场另一新的增长极。即便存在周期性的反复,上述两大趋势自此一直保持下来。一面是1980年代第三世界的民族自决运动遭遇挫折,1989至1992年社会主义阵营的坍塌;相应地,则是美国的军费开支暂时呈现下降倾向,可这个国家的基本方向却没有发生根本性的变化,"和平红利"(苏联解体后有人提出这一说法)压根没有成型,永久性的战时经济或由其掌舵的"国家安全国家"(national security state)依然存在。

然而,军事的网络化具体表现为持续的结构性转变,后者从数字化革命的初始阶段到衰退期一直贯穿始终(本书第三部分将具体分析这一当代走向)。首先,政府做出开放电信市场的决策,动摇了既有的结构,从而为军工企业协作建设网络设施奠定基础。这需要建立新的机制以打破为数不多的大公司的垄断,例如美国电话电报公司。其次,随着资本投资与政府补贴持续注入信息系统,武器制造的商品链转向以网络化的军备生产为中心。再次,尽管美国依然在全球范围开展其军事行动,但在老对手被新的"敌人"所替代后,美国军队的战略定位已经转变。最后但绝非最次要的一点,意识形态建构的过程逐渐变成对美国外交政策基本要素的有目的的讨论,展示给美国老百姓的战争,永远都是紧急状态下保卫人权的战争,颇具迷惑性。以上四个方面需要进一步加以讨论。

历史上,美国电信基础设施给军方出了一道难题,因为计划与动员工作要求同私营企业(而非如英、法或其他国家,与国家电信部门)协作。而在私营企业中,美国电话电报公司算是龙头老大。美国早已开始实行一项可行的调整方案。然而,行政部门决定开放网络系统与应用程序的近用与使用权,导致该难题具有某种新的显著性①。

整个1970年代,美国国防部一直反对联邦通讯委员会做出的关于开放美国电信市场、引入竞争机制的决定。不过,这一由积累驱动的自由化政策一开始却得到尼克松政府中一部分高层决策者的支持。它不仅被贯彻执行,还孕育了一大批新的信息通信技术提供商与网络运营商。这些公司反过来不断与军事机构签订合同,生产令人眼花缭乱的新式武器、情报以及命令与控制系统。然而,(电信的)自由化过程也使得国防部处心积虑与美国电话电报公司保持的亲密(合作)关系毫无用处。美国电话电报公司是一家垂直一体化的企业,它扮演着国家电信基础设置的网络管理员角色。1982年,司法部依据反托拉斯法案要求拆分美国电话电报公司。国防部殚精竭虑,试图扭转乾坤无果后,军权明显受到掣肘,不再(如过往)能随心所欲地干预政府决策。司法部拆分美国电话电报

---

① 我在专著《远程信息处理与政府》中使用大量篇幅讨论行政部门就电信政策而展开的动员行为,具体可参见 *Telematics and Government* (Norwood: Ablex, 1982)。

公司之举,验证了维贾·普拉沙德(Vijay Prashad)的如下观点:此时,"美国政府授权了对其自身经济的重创行为,以此重塑经济"①,从而给资本积累找到一个新的和改良过的立足点。美国政府的激进做法,令许多旁观者大为震惊:不仅资产阶级的盈利战略被置于那些全球最大的资本集团之前,适用于网络运营者的军事协作机制也需要重新制定。

1983年中将劳伦斯曾惊呼,1982年的这场拆分"向国防部提出了一个特定的问题",因为军方"过去数十年间都仰仗于美国电话电报公司的一体化管理与统一网络"。身为美国国防大学的校长,劳伦斯清晰地阐述这一令其无比困扰的问题:突然间"一家机构的首尾控制权就这么没了,它将危及效率"②。国家引入不同企业相互竞争的机制,并开放网络设备的市场,由此导致国家网络基础设施的碎片化。据宝琳·威尔逊(Bolling Wilson)的观察,网络基础设施的碎片化使我们必须找寻另一种代替方法,以"把相互分离的机构重新整合成一个即时回应、可靠的整体"③。可如何整合?

里根政府尝试解决这一难题,尽管该政府创建了国家安全电信咨询委员会(National Security Telecommunications Advisory Committee),以向政府提供电信产业发展的紧急应对措施的相关建议(例如1982年主张拆分美国电话电报公司)。国家安全电信咨询委员会由"位移阵矩"的高级管理人员所组成,代表了美国主要电信、计算机与信息处理企业的利益。一位军事分析家1983年撰文指出,国家安全电信咨询委员会的成立,使一个壮大的行业的"领头者有了共同的责任意识,即保持(该行业)的发展能力"④。在一个不断自由化的市场环境里,危机管理拉近了军事部门与公司基础设施运营商之间的距离。同样,它也刺激了政府机构内部的持续变革。

肯尼迪总统创建国家通信系统,从而保证了军方手握监控全国网络安全的主导权。1984年里根总统拓展了该系统,并在2003年将其并入新成立的(内阁级机构)国土安全部下设的信息分析和基础设施保护部门(Information Analysis and Infrastructure Protection Directorate)里。1990年代,当克林顿总统签署行政指令第13010号(Executive Order 13010,禁止中国攻击性武器弹药进口)与第63号《总统决策令》(Presidential Decision Directive,首次提出"信息安全"概念),从而批准"关键基础设施保护"政策时,(军方的)协作与监管的职能不仅更加明确,并得到强化。小布什政府2002年通过了《国土安全法》;该法案及其相关的联邦政策将国土安全部设定为"协调行动的中心,以维护那些保

---

① Vijay Prashad, *The Poorer Nations: A Possible History of the Global South* (London: Verso, 2012), 52.
② R. D. Lawrence, "Preface," in *AT&T Aftermath of Antitrust: Preserving Positive Command and Control*, ed. George H. Bolling (Washington, D.C.: National Defense University Press, 1983), xi.
③ Bolling, *AT&T*, 2.
④ Bolling, *AT&T*, 12.

卫我们国家关键性的基础设施的计算机系统"①。国土安全部的职责在于,帮助"在公共部门与私营机构之间建立有效关系"②。在这持续的组织变革背后,镇压性国家机器再次与企业经济对接,计算机网络攻防职能更为紧密地联系在一起③。

后"9·11"时代的社会动员,正是在看起来互不连属、去中心化的以互联网为基础的网络基础设施的背景下,有助于推进与扩大由上至下的协作趋势。2005年,160位代表美国企业最高层的首席执行官出席了商业圆桌会议,他们号召政府"加强互联网以及保障互联网健康发展的基础设施的建设"④。美国企业不仅容易受到恐怖分子的攻击,更往往成为受其他威胁(运营中断、敌对国家、黑客与心怀不满的雇员)的对象。2006年2月,国土安全部联合6大内阁级部门以及英特尔、微软、赛门铁克、威瑞信和其他企业,加上英国、澳大利亚、新西兰、加拿大政府的代表,首次共同进行了一场"全面网络安全演习"(网络风暴),以检验应对模拟的网络进攻的机制。与往常一样,这一以及其他相关的举措被解释为军方防御;当然也与往常一样,这一解释具有误导性。

一位深受经济学家约翰·肯尼斯·加尔布雷斯(John Kenneth Galbraith)影响的分析家指出,在里根政府的军事建设时期,美国国防部已成为"一种庞大的规划系统,它比非共产主义国家里任何经济实体都要庞大"⑤。国土安全部作为规划机构所具有的效率性值得商榷;但很明显,社会主义世界的衰落并未使它的经济功能有所减少:在其秩序之下继续巩固利润、产出与就业。"9·11"之后,美国军费开支的规模极大地扩展;罗克斯伯勒(Roxborough)认为,数字化衰退伊始,"美国的四大军种(海/陆/空/海军陆战队)每一支都强过其他国家的武装力量"⑥。

美国的军事政策开始偏重于小布什政府所说的"武力转型"。这一战略正式确立了军方对武器与情报能力的倚重,而武器与情报能力越发依靠网络系统与应用。负责网络与信息一体化的助理国防部长选择(对于企业而言)与网络中心运营工业联盟(Network

---

① U. S. Government Accountability Office, "Critical Infrastructure Protection: Department of Homeland Security Faces Challenges in Fulfilling Cybersecurity Responsibilities," May 26, 2005 (GAO05 – 434), available at http://www.gao.gov/products/GAO – 05 – 434 (accessed January 10, 2014).
② P. E. Auerswald, L. M. Branscomb, T. M. La Porte, and M. – K. Erwann, eds., Seeds of Disaster, *Roots of Response*: How Private Action Can Reduce Public Vulnerability (New York: Cambridge University Press, 2006), xv.
③ Jason Healey, *A Fierce Domain*: Conflict in Cyberspace, 1986 to 2012 (Vienna, Va.: Cyber Conflict Studies Association and the Atlantic Council, 2013), 36, 65.
④ Business Roundtable, "Essential Steps to Strengthen America's Cyber Terrorism Preparedness," available at http://web.archive.org/web/20080911120233/http://www.businessroundtable.org/pdf/20060622002CyberReconFinal6106.pdf (accessed January 30, 2014).
⑤ John Tirman, "The Defense Economy Debate," in *The Militarization of High Technology*, ed. John Tirman (Cambridge: Ballinger, 1984), 4.
⑥ Ian Roxborough, "Weary Titan, Assertive Hegemon: Military Strategy, Globalization, and U. S. Preponderance," in *The Paradox of a Global USA*, ed. B. Mazlish, N. Chanda, and K. Weisbode (Stanford: Stanford University Press, 2007), 123.

Centric Operations Industry Consortium)合作,以便主导这一过程。美国的军事网络升级为国防部与战略司令部的主要运营单位(a leading unit)。战略司令部 2002 年由航空司令部与战略司令部合并而来,这是美国空间武器化军事诉求的重要信号。战略司令部承担过好几项重要任务:全球打击、导弹防御一体化、信息战以及全球指挥、控制、通信、计算机、情报、监视和侦察。2007 年 3 月,战略司令部司令詹姆斯·卡特赖特(James E. Cartwright)将军就这些使命在国会面前作证:

> 网络空间已经成为实战领域,但它与海陆空有所不同……网络空间国家安全战略(National Strategy to Secure Cyberspace)将网络空间描述成我们国家的神经系统,对我们国家的经济和国土安全事关重大。该战略认为所有的联邦部门和机构、国家和地方政府、私营企业和组织以及个人都有责任提高网络安全性……要做到这一点,关键在于在所有的军事行动中整合网络空间的能力……战略司令部身负(在国防部之下)规划与指导网络防御之责,肩挑组织网络进攻以完成上级分配的任务之担……历史告诉我们,纯粹的防御姿势可能招致重大风险;"马奇诺防线"这一末端防御模式,倘若没有辅以更具进攻性的远洋战略,最终必将失败……假使我们把"战争原则"应用到网络领域,正如我们在海陆空等领域所做的那样,我们将意识到,增强我们与敌人主动交手的能力,尤其是阻止那些有损我们利益的行动,更有助于我们保卫国家[①]。

2010 年,战略司令部下设网络司令部,以进一步集中化管理与升级计算机网络化的军事行动。在第三部分,我将再次论述这一新的作战空间所发挥的职能。目前,(我们)有充分的理由相信,建设进攻型网络武器装备实际上已彻底成为当务之急。关于美国正致力于进攻型网络的建设的说法不时见诸媒体。例如,《纽约时报》的一篇文章指出,"中国与俄罗斯都已出台进攻型信息战的(战略)规划",并承认(似乎有点后见之明)"美国据传已经启动网络战计划"[②]。(就这一议题)一项 2007 年的研究报告更加具体细致(尽管在它的描述里,美国政府致力于网络战的规模并不大):军方的愿景是,耗资数百万美元、投入数万人力,旨在开发计算机病毒,以作为军事冲突中的有效武器[③]。当英国广播电台公开了一份 2003 年国防部的解密文件(即"信息行动路线图")时,它似乎向我们透

---

① Available at http://www.gpo.gov/fdsys/pkg/CHRG-110Shrg39441/html/CHRG-110shrg39441.htm (accessed March 4,2014).
② Mark Landler and John Markoff, "After Computer Siege in Estonia, War Fears Turn to Cyberspace," *New York Times*, May 29,2007.
③ Diffie Whitfield and Susan Landau, *Privacy on the Line: The Politics of Wiretapping and Encryption* (Cambridge, Mass.: MIT Press,2007),114.

露出"(美国军方的网络战)计划将产生深远影响"这一讯号。该份经过精心编纂的文件显示,"美国军方希望自身具备摧毁地球每一部电话、每一台联网计算机和每一种雷达系统的(军事)实力"①。到了 2014 年,当奥巴马总统提名海军中将迈克·罗杰斯(Michael S. Rogers)同时兼任国安局局长与美国网络司令部司令官两大要职时,"美国已订立详细完备的网络战规划"这一信息就已人所共知。据媒体报道,罗杰斯自 1980 年以来就已协助开发计算机网络攻击技术②。

迄今为止,美国在几十个国家里依然保留数百家主要军事基地:长期以来,美国军事行动一直放眼全球。然而,21 世纪伊始,美国的战略布局(force projection)正经历一场战略转向。苏联解体,中东石油、中国作为新的威胁开始崛起,以及俄罗斯仍是有核国家等事实,促使美国将军事行动的重心从西欧转向东欧、中东、中亚以及(奥巴马时期的)太平洋地区。奥巴马政府察觉到"中国崛起"所形成的"挑战",毫无吝惜地将战略重心放在东亚与东南亚地区③。

同样,美国全球兵力投送的实质性目标也发生转变。数十年来,它以反对社会主义国家与挫败民族自决运动为己任。当美国的战略重心如今几乎全部转向非国家(non-state)行动者所形成的"不对称的"威胁时,美国另一关键的目标在于,转移、钳制或遏制那些实际存在的资本主义国家的敌对方,或即将成为资本主义国家敌对势力的国家或地区。关于这一话题,我将在第三部分继续讨论。还要增加一点,美国在全球范围内的兵力投送能力的增强离不开网络技术的深入发展。

为了统合美国遍布全球的军事行动,美国重新建构了全球传播体系,行指挥、控制、通信与搜集情报之职。这些(新建的传播体系)除了拥有战略司令部的帮助外,还得到海陆空三军、不同情报部门以及国防信息系统局(Defense Information Systems Agency)的从旁协助与打理。国防信息系统局创建于 1991 年(时值冷战结束),以替代 1960 年成立的国防通讯总署(Defense Communications Agency)。国防信息系统局共有 7 000 至 8 000 名雇员——对比一下联邦通讯委员会共计 1 850 名工作人员的规模,国防信息系统局的人员规模十分庞大④。国防信息系统局下设多个分级机构。例如,国防频谱管理局(Defense Spectrum Organization)下属的战略规划处(Strategic Planning Office)的职责在于

---

① A. Brookes, "US Plans to 'Fight the Net' Revealed." *BBC News*, January 27, 2006, available at http://news.bbc.co.uk/2/hi/americas/4655196.stm (accessed January 10, 2014).
② David E. Sanger and Thom Shanker, "Obama Picks a Cyber Expert to Lead N. S. A.," *New York Times*, January 31, 2014. 这一时间表与希利(Healey)所提供的基本一致,具体可参见 Healey, Fierce Domain.
③ Peter Baker, "Panetta's Pentagon, without the Blank Check," *New York Times*, October 24, 2011; Elisabeth Bumiller, "U. S. to Sustain Military Power in the Pacific, Panetta Says," *New York Times*, October 24, 2011; Hillary Clinton, "America's Pacific Century," *Foreign Policy* 189 (November 2011):56 - 63.
④ L. R. Mayer, "Wired," *CapitalEye*, January 7, 2007.

"现在以及未来,保证美国军方能够访问全球任何频谱资源"①。长久以来,美国军方一直是世界上唯一一个能够最大范围地使用频谱资源的国家。国防部承认它之所以能操控大型武器系统与卫星,"原因在于它与其他国家已签订国际协定,准许国防部在其他国家内部使用特定的频谱资源"。并且,军方对频谱资源的使用规模"自1991年沙漠风暴行动以来呈指数级别扩大"②。据推测,战略规划处经由北大西洋公约组织频谱管理局这一鲜为人知的机构(主要负责安排美国在国外的频谱资源的使用),与欧洲各大盟国保持合作关系。

美国国防部于1999年提出的全球信息网格设想,被暂时定为一项耗时20年的建设项目。从组织层面来看,它包括了国防信息系统局、战略司令部与国防部下属的其他机构,以及军方和情报部门。全球信息网格的目标听上去令人振奋:它"计划把国防部所有的信息系统、部门和应用整合成一张无缝、可靠且安全的网络",由此"协助国防部完成自身的(结构性)转型,即更加网络化或'网络中心化'的战争方式,以及占据相对于敌手而言获取信息的优势"。所签订的合同里,大部分武器系统与传感器都"极度依赖"这一尚未完工的基础设施③。

为了实现全球信息网格设想,全球信息网格不仅要战胜各种组织性对手,还要把许多尚未经过检验的传播技术绑定在一起,这呈现了技术与行动两个层面上的不确定性:(例如)极度高频的通信卫星、软件无线电、采用升级的路由器与交换器(技术)的地基光纤网络,以及改良的密码学。2004年,美国政府问责处(Government Accountability Office)强调,建设全球信息网格已招致"巨大的挑战与风险";两年后,该机构出台了一份更具批判色彩的评估报告。然而,全球信息网格的预估成本从2004年约莫210亿美元(直到2010财年)奇观式地上升至2006年的340亿美元(直到2011年)。高昂的成本确保了全球信息网格完成其军事目标,它必将推动基于互联网技术的信息通信技术创新。国防部在2006年曾大放厥词,声称仅全球信息网格中的组成部分之一即海军及陆战队局域网,就构成了世界上最大型的企业局域网,后者向550个地点和成百上千名用户提供服务④。建造并管理这一耗资数十亿美元的战略项目所积累的经验,成为它的主要承包商电子数据系统公司(Electronic Data Systems)的"前车之鉴",后者在面对非税收补贴的客户时可以借鉴这些经验。于是,资本积累总是与经济不景气紧紧相连。

---

① Defense Information Systems Agency, available at http://www.disa.mil/dso/spo.html (accessed January 10,2014).
② U. S. Government Accountability Office, *Telecommunications: Comprehensive Review of U. S. Spectrum Management with Broad Stakeholder Involvement Is Needed* (GAO-03-277) (Washington, D. C. :GAO,2003),30.
③ U. S. Government Accountability Office, *DOD Management Approach and Processes Not Well-Suited to Support Development of Global Information Grid* (GAO-06-211) (Washington, D. C. :GAO,2006),1,3,4.
④ U. S. Government Accountability Office, *DOD Management Approach*,1,6.

尽管上述这些倡议(initiatives)格局宏大,它们却丝毫没有削弱信息与通信对于享有治外法权的美国军方的作用。基于卫星的全球定位系统被整合进美国武器系统以及电子战争战略中。设在欧洲、日本、澳大利亚、塞浦路斯、阿森松岛以及美国等国家或地区的对地传输的卫星监听站,控制着可能多达上百颗的专用卫星(specialized satellite),并传输来自地球每一个角落的数据流;在过去 40 年间,美国在间谍卫星上就花费了 2 000 亿美元,令人咋舌。位于弗吉尼亚州亚历山大市的美军广播电视台(American Forces Radio and Television Service)运营武装部队网络(Armed Forces Network),该网络拥有九个电视频道,并向驻扎在 177 个国家的所有海外军事设施以及军舰播送节目。美国的军事结构如此依赖卫星,以至于对(军事)设施的任何(哪怕微小)威胁(例如当中国在 2007 年使用电磁波"装扮"一颗卫星时[①]),都可能快速引发美国的太空军事化战略升级。总之,到了 2011 年,美国政府在信息通信技术上的开支大约是每年 800 亿美元,其中有一半(或超过一半)的开销来自军事与情报部门。这使得美国政府成为世界上最大的信息通信技术消费者,并毫无争议地"在私营企业里产生一种深远的连锁效应"[②]。

尽管美国军方的现代化网络令其他国家极为敬畏,它的杀伤力势不可挡,但吊诡之处在于,美国的军事实力依然没有达到全知全能的地步。伊拉克和阿富汗的重要战役,至多导致了高度不确定的后果。这使得形塑海外以及(尤其是)国内舆论的任务刻不容缓。战争宣传手段再次被使用,以掩盖(战争)政策对直接目标人群还有绝大部分美国人利益的损害。

值得称赞的是,主流学术媒体对战争的意识形态建构机制给予一定的关注。爱德华·赫曼(Edward Herman)引领一批激进派学者,致力于绝大部分记录并揭露宣传(机制)的学术工作[③]。批判学者姑且承认了媒体的首要位置,或许理所当然,不足为奇;然而不仅是商业化媒体,还有电视剧、好莱坞电影与游戏都被征用为军国主义的现役推手。实际上,诚如大卫·阿什德(David Altheide)所言,经历了"9·11"事件的美国,"恐惧已经成为一种娱乐,它蔓延在大众文化与新闻产品中,不仅能产生利润,更能使政治决策人通过宣传手段掌控受众"[④]。

这一镇压式的意识形态工作,不但行使具体的操控战略的职能(manipulative representational strategies),也承担精心构筑制度关系的责任——1994 年出台的《通信协助执

---

① William J. Broad and David E. Sanger, "Flexing Muscle, China Destroys Satellite in Test," *New York Times*, January 19, 2007. 2007 年 3 月两会期间,中国绕月探测工程总指挥栾恩杰向外透露,中国第一颗人造月球卫星已研制完成(译者注)。
② Sean Collins Walsh, "Federal Push for 'Cloud' Technology Faces Skepticism," *New York Times*, August 22, 2011.
③ For example, Edward S. Herman and Noam Chomsky, *Manufacturing Consent: The Political Economy of the Mass Media* (New York: Pantheon, 2002).
④ David L. Altheide, *Terrorism and the Politics of Fear* (Lanham, Md.: AltaMira, 2006), 2.

法法案》(Communications Assistance for Law Enforcement Act)使上述职能付诸实施。经联邦通讯委员会的(扩大)解释,《通信协助执法法案》保证美国所有新的网络基础设施(包括互联网)都具备监听功能。自二战以来,监控国际传播一直存在。美国国家安全局对国内电子通信进行无证监听的事实早已被披露——尽管《纽约时报》高层遵从小布什总统的指示,直到他赢得2004年选举(连任成功)后方才使压制一年的报道见诸报端①。2013年斯诺登的爆料,才让大众(真正)了解到美国监控项目的覆盖范围之广、程度之深。此前,斯诺登供职于国家安全局的一家顶级承包商。我将在第三部分继续讨论这一轰动的泄密事件。

长期以来,美国精心炮制的基本且永恒不变的舆论基调是,美国有权对其领导人所决定的国家或地区(随时随地)进行干预。这一帝国主义论调在过去数十年间得到充分体现。30余年前,美国伟大的历史学家威廉·阿普尔曼·威廉斯(William Appleman Williams)②曾撰文指出,"国家高度掌控信息(的流动),并利用这一能力以国家安全之名做出不少重大决策,或打造一种意识形态,其内容更加明确、修辞更加强调帝国主义的行为准则"。利用美国军事实力重塑其他国家的经济与文化的真实原因,在最近几十年里则成为讨论的禁忌话题。

因此,军事化的数字资本主义推动资本对政府开销形成一种持续的结构性依赖,反过来也拓展并重新调整了政府开销。美国军费预算按实值计算,自2001年"9·11"事件以来的10年间上涨67%,以至于它的年度开支等同于其他20个军事最强国的开支总和③,这不仅符合小布什政府背后的新保守主义集团所制定的发展规划,也与更为温和的奥巴马总统的施政纲领并无冲突。在武器系统上所投入财力的增长速度更快,从2001年至2010年翻了一番,由(原来的)626亿美元上升至1 358亿美元;仅在这十年里,美国花费万亿美元用于购买武器装备④。

然而,建造这样的军事巨物,无法中和危机趋势。《纽约时报》统计了美国政府应对"9·11"事件10年来所投入的资金,高达3.3万亿美元⑤。据斯蒂格勒兹与琳达·比尔姆斯(Linda Bilmes)在2008年的"保守"估计,美国对伊拉克与阿富汗战争所耗费的成本

---

① Jane Mayer, "A Secret Sharer," *New Yorker*, May 23, 2011, 54.
② William Appleman Williams, *Empire as a Way of Life* (Oxford: Oxford University Press, 1980), 197.
③ David E. Sanger, *Confront and Conceal* (New York: Crown, 2012), 417, 418, citing "Threatening a Sacred Cow," *The Economist*, February 10, 2011.
④ Christopher Drew, "Military Is Said to Make Progress in Modernizing," *New York Times*, October 28, 2011.
⑤ 这些资金用于国家安全维护、伊战与阿富汗战争,以及救助美国伤员的医疗费用,具体可参见 David E. Sanger, "The Price of Lost Chances," *New York Times*, September 11, 2011; Amanda Cox, "A 9/11 Tally: $3.3 Trillion," *New York Times*, September 11, 2011. 可与 Clifford A. Kiracofe 文章 "Wars Leave Crumbling Infrastructure at Home for US" 对照, *Information Clearing House*, April 10, 2012.

总计3万亿至5万亿美元,随后几年,他们调高了这一数字①。这是否意味着(美国)军事的过度扩张?美国财政收支不平衡、政治多变(politically unsettled)等问题,能否支撑这一重担?

  2013年,美国财政紧张的状况已经昭然若揭。已退休的国防部长罗伯特·盖茨(Robert Gates)在对北约盟国的一次演讲中曾有意暗示,它们将不得不承担战争所带来的财政开销②。据报道,法国总统奥朗德对美国"在马里战争中没有给予更多支持"的做法"耿耿于怀"③。在军费近十年间连连增长后,2011年美国军费开支下降了1.2%④。美国国内围绕如何以及多大程度上能够在经济萧条时期减少联邦政府开支的议题而闹得不可开交,这导致2013年美国军费的再度削减⑤。政治党派纷争这一局面的确影响了美国的全球军事战略⑥。对美国外交政策的其他批评,可能产生了(某种)连锁式的衍生效应(knock-on ramification):根据媒体报道,在民众反抗推翻穆巴拉克在埃及的专制统治后,美国并没有实施戴维·桑格(David E. Sanger)所说的"阿拉伯之春马歇尔计划"⑦(an Arab Spring Marshall Plan,即以收买的方式达到想要的结果)。面对这一残酷局面,美国的军事承包商只能寻求多元化策略,例如提高对发展中国家的武器销量,或关闭工厂⑧。

  一定程度上,我们难以估量军事的过度扩张所付出的实际成本,因为这其中包括遭受无人机空袭的平民,还有美国国内不断下降的生活水平与遭受侵蚀的民主自由。为了使军费预算"神圣不可侵犯",对国内社会福利计划的抨击,在经济层面上早已"被合法化"。如今,这一张力已临近崩溃;国内(政府)逐渐着手解决(以牺牲工人阶级为代价的)军事与经济政策并重所引发的社会冲突。

  一个叛乱的世界正在形成,在这个世界里,从巴西到土耳其、从南非到美国,各地的抗议行动此起彼伏。在这个世界里,南非的大部分地区正在严肃认真地寻求取代亲美资本主义制度、建设大众民主的途径;在这个世界里,尽管美国军费开支过于高昂,但对美

---

① Joseph E. Stiglitz, "The Price of 9/11," *Project Syndicate*, September 1, 2011; Joseph Stiglitz and Linda Bilmes, "There Will Be No Peace Dividend after Afghanistan," *Financial Times*, January 24, 2013.
② Steven Erlanger, "Shrinking Europe Military Spending Is Examined," *New York Times*, April 23, 2013.
③ Mark Landler and Peter Baker, "Extending a Hand Abroad, Obama Often Finds a Cold Shoulder," *New York Times*, June 19, 2013.
④ Stockholm International Peace Research Institute, "World Military Spending Levels Out after 13 Years of Increases, Says SIPRI," April 17, 2012, available at http://www.sipri.org/media/pressreleases/2012/17-april-2012-world-military-spending-levels-out-after-13-years-of-increases-says-sipri (accessed January 10, 2014).
⑤ David E. Sanger and Thom Shanker, "Cuts Give Obama Path to Create Leaner Military," *New York Times*, March 11, 2013; "Squeezing the Pentagon," *The Economist*, July 6, 2013, 26-27.
⑥ Thom Shanker, "Hagel Gives Dire Assessment of Choices He Expects Cuts to Force on the Pentagon," *New York Times*, August 1, 2013.
⑦ Sanger, *Confront and Conceal*, 421.
⑧ Dion Nissenbaum, "Military Contractors Change Tactics," *Wall Street Journal*, January 4, 2013.

国而言,这点开支还远远不够。军事化战略并非维护数字资本主义的一支和平力量,而更为深入地加剧了危机。

因此,投入数字化网络建设的庞杂资金,成为当前全球政治经济的突出特征。通过生产、金融与军事开支等方式,信息通信技术投资项目已是应对1970年代经济衰退的举足轻重的措施。这不仅改变了企业与军事行为,扩大了资本主义社会关系的范围,更导致资本主义危机趋势不断累积。现在我们知道,最终,信息通信技术投资的明线将资本主义引领到濒危点,例如2008年金融危机就转化成一场数字化衰退。那么,通信与信息产业如何解决其自身的难题呢?经过这些年,通信与信息处理行业已成为信息通信技术最大的需求部门。围绕数字化网络而展开的第四维度的变革意味着什么?看起来,它是否能够回复政治经济的增长活力?让我们转向这一充满活力的领域,来思考这一深化的结构化变革,它体现了数字化衰退的起步与发展。

第二部分
传播的重组

第 5 章
历史的序幕

　　资本应对1970年代经济危机时所采取的措施,推动了生产、金融与军费开支等领域的大范围变革。这段时期,网络连接性与协调(分散各地)工作的能力不断增加,企业利润战略也得到革新。我曾在1999年写道,"生产过剩与竞争导致精英不断更新市场体系,这已经不是第一次了;但信息与通信被寄予厚望,成为解决危机的关键因素,这却是史无前例的"[①]。或许,我们应当把结构转型的第四个维度放在崛起的数字资本主义的中心,即传播产业上(加以审视)。

　　疾风骤雨似的技术与制度性变革撼动了传播产业,以至于原本看上去固若金汤的商品链开始塌陷断裂,并进行调整重组。这并未带来一致性的增长,而是极度不平衡的发展:经济发展的活力与灾难并存。然而,即便在这样的漩涡之中,一些根深蒂固的制度性优先事项依然存在,并处于实际主导地位。现有的体制四分五裂后,开始重建。这样,它能够扩大并强化那些已获得的传统成果。要理解这一复杂过程,我们需要重新回到近期出现的历史趋势上。

　　到了1970年代,美国已经拥有了世界上(结构)最精细的消费者传播产业。它所肩负的制度性使命,清晰翔实:传播构成了市场建设过程的基石。市场建设发端于19世纪末,引导美国人养成固定的消费习惯,即只消费那些大公司生产的全国性品牌的产品。两大截然不同的利润战略保障了不同轮次的媒体发展,从全国性杂志和电话到音乐唱片、广播与电视:它们依靠面向广告商的营销业务,又或者面向消费者的直销或出租业务等方式,赚取利润,提供服务。这些彼此迥异的利润路径所取得商业性成功,也仰仗于长期以来政府的慷慨布施:无论是对版权和专利权的垄断,还是渠道占有或电磁频谱使用权。还有另一种完全不同、较为抽象却同样至关重要的成本投入战略:普通人总需要阅

---

① Dan Schiller, *How to Think about Information* (Urbana: University of Illinois Press, 2007), 36.

读报纸和书籍、听广播和唱片、打电话或看电影和电视节目,这些都是劳动,而且属于免费劳动(实则就是劳动力①)。

援引盖瑞·菲尔兹(Gary Fields)的术语②,作为进入新的赢利领域的跳板,传播产业在应对 1970 年代危机中所扮演的特殊角色是,支撑并保障范围更加广泛的"修补"工作,从而使资本能够更新积累进程。每隔一段时间,流行的传播习惯就会发生变化,从而与这个标榜政策逆转、技术突破、投资飙升、跨国化以及商业多元化的时代保持同步。以往企业各自统领独立市场(无论是电视、电话业务还是音乐唱片或新闻)的局面被打破,传播体制发展的空间不断扩大,但该空间再次复制了寻利行为。

这一过程既非自发,亦非自动。传播产业的市场建设属于复杂的历史过程,不是一个月或一年,而是横跨数十年。传播产业的转型起始于 1960 年代末,它以国家政策的激进与可持续修复为前提。如我在第一部分所强调的,没有哪个领域像(普拉沙德所挑拣出来专门进行论述的)传播与信息产业那般,"美国政府授权了对其自身经济的重创行为,以此重塑经济,并遵循德国社会学家桑巴特提出的原则,'置之死地而后生——毁灭中才能诞生新的创造性精神'"③。

美国政府将传播产业转变成一个庞大、多面的"建筑工地",它的总设计师正是资本。我在别处已经详细讨论过加速的商品化的复杂过程如何掌控传播、信息与文化(领域)④。简言之,国家向资本担保一定会扩大商业与利润最大化的范围,甚至不惜以摧毁既有的实践、打断既定的商品链为代价。资本能够合理地染指或侵犯那些条款所规定的非专属或习惯做法,创立和挪用公共基金;与此同时,国家强化了资本在信息与文化领域内的私有产权,从而合法化了(资本的这些)侵犯之举。大卫·哈维把这一种具有历史重要性的政治经济转型称为"剥夺式积累"⑤。网络基础设施经过彻底革新后,具有了更深、更广的连接性:它不仅体现了技术创新,更通过政策变革,蚕食了这一基础设施的制度性基础。

1970 年代,美国有两家历史悠久的大型企业引领网络现代化的变革潮流。在变革潮流的中心即电信与商业计算机领域,美国电话电报公司与国际商用机器公司近乎垄断了各自的专业化行业。难道它们只会运用为时甚久的权力来占领计算机通信市场,如同它

---

① 这一洞见可参见 Dallas W. Smythe, "Communications: Blindspot of Western Marxism," *Canadian Journal of Political and Social Theory* 1, no. 3 (Fall 1977): 1–27. 进一步讨论可参见 Dan Schiller, *Theorizing Communication: A History* (New York: Oxford University Press, 1996).
② Gary Fields, *Territories of Profit: Communications, Capitalist Development, and the Innovative Enterprises of G. F. Swift and Dell Computer* (Stanford: Stanford University Press, 2004).
③ Vijay Prashad, *The Poorer Nations* (New York: Verso, 2012), 52.
④ Dan Schiller, *How to Think about Information*, 39–48.
⑤ David Harvey, *The New Imperialism* (Oxford: Oxford University Press, 2003), 137–82.

们崛起时所采取的战略那般？许多国家持有不同看法①,例如巴西、法国和日本。法国的政策制定者试图将这两家美国巨型公司从"远程信息处理"（或计算机通信）市场中驱逐出去。法国本土的一份顶级调查报告支持了这项（政府）决策②。

然而,除了针对美国电话电报公司与国际商用机器公司而可能发起的（一系列）行动外,其他大型公司,既作为供应商又作为主要的网络用户,也纷纷挤入计算机通信市场。这其中包括埃克森美孚、通用电气、通用汽车、花旗公司和西尔斯,每家公司都购买了网络系统与服务③。它们的动机各不相同:花旗将金融服务与帮助盈利的计算机软硬件的高级网络接入系统捆绑一起;西尔斯在早期的商业性可视图文领域,与国际商用机器公司和哥伦比亚广播公司展开合作;埃克森美孚则执着于办公设备的购买;通用汽车引进电子数据系统,并启动了营销计算机服务;通用电气取代了军用电子承包商兼广播网络所有者美国无线电公司（RCA）。上述商业冒险行为并未完全成功,这一事实不如通信市场不断拓宽与多元化的情况更为重要。

新生的产品与服务市场的形成,也改变了整个大环境。我在其他著作中已经讨论过产业维度的变革;此处,我想着重阐述消费者的变化。新媒体（如录像带、激光唱片和影音光碟）销售与出租业务,以及播放这些新媒体的回放系统（的发展）,促生了新的生利行业。随着装配这些设备的劳动力受资本召唤而集合起来——不仅在美国还有日本、墨西哥、韩国和中国台湾④,相应地,商品链得以拓展。其他一些新生的竞争对手进入到既存的媒体产业的销售或零售终端,从而改变了贸易条件。譬如,图书出版行业在与巴诺书店（Barnes and Noble）主导的连锁书店、销售越来越多图书产品的沃尔玛进行竞争时,感到压力重重。音乐产业对淘儿唱片行（Tower Records）或沃尔玛这样日益集中化的销售渠道又爱又恨,而票务大师（Ticket master）则成为演唱会市场上的一支生力军。好莱坞电影与电视节目包装公司,在百视达公司的影碟租赁与沃尔玛的影音光碟业务中发现了一条通往消费者的新路径。百思买与环城百货（还有沃尔玛）等仓储式电器商城已统领电子产品硬件零售市场。专业公司开发、游乐场或套装软件产品所提供的视频游戏突然间闯入到这个舞台。在（电视）节目播出领域,有线或卫星电视系统逐渐取代那些可以免费接收的地面广播站;节目制作商为依靠广告生存、播出新闻、电视剧和体育节目的优质电视网建造了新的市场"窗口",而地面电视频道因为有了"上星"的优势,可以向观众打

---

① 丹尼尔·贝尔具体讨论这一问题,可参见其文章 "The Social Framework of the Information Society," chapter 9 in *The Computer Age: A Twenty - Year View*, ed. Michael L. Dertouzos and Joel Moses (Cambridge, Mass.: MIT Press, 1979).

② Pierre Nora and Alain Minc, *The Computerization of Society* (Cambridge, Mass.: MIT Press, 1980 [1978]).

③ Kevin Robins and Frank Webster, "Information as a Social Relation," *Intermedia* 8, no.4 (July 1980), 30.

④ Jefferson Cowie, *Capital Moves: RCA's Seventy - Year Quest for Cheap Labor* (Ithaca, N.Y.: Cornell University Press, 1999); Mari Castañeda, "The Development of the U.S. Advanced Digital Television System, 1987 - 1997: The Property Creation of New Media," PhD diss., University of California, San Diego, 2000.

包出售打包现有或新的电视网节目的每月观看权。有线电视网代表大广告商的利益,它以受众细分与目标受众市场的主要代理商身份,进入消费者杂志和直邮领域。

当这些变革横扫传播市场时,传播市场的领导者不会坐以待毙。1980 至 1990 年代,它们启动了大规模合并①与跨国化战略②。有了政府的积极支持,长期以来彼此互不联属的媒体行业从图书出版、电影制作到电视被整合(至少被聚合)成庞大的多媒体企业。政府机关批准了几家非美国公司吞并通信传播这一政治敏感行业的大量美国资产:福克斯电视台、索尼公司、西格拉姆(Seagram)、松下电器和贝塔斯曼,这同样是对过往政策的藐视。而雅达利、任天堂和索尼等公司在不断扩大的视频游戏机和游戏市场中,赢得一席之地③。美国市场与主导市场的企业在传播产业不断加速的跨国化发展过程中,相互依存④。在每一个细分市场内,一如其他产业的企业,传播企业忙不迭地提高准入门槛,以防止那些可能的竞争对手的出现。然而我们知晓,它们持续不断的并购行为与减少竞争的策略,并未推动它们平稳地成为寡头集团。相反,传播行业的主导资本在数字化熔炉中遭到破坏。发生了什么?如何理解这一非比寻常的变化情况?

在其中起作用的有三大因素。第一个针对现有体制的因素,源自于 1970 年左右启动的政治与监管政策的(系列)变革:计算机通信网络在与市场权力的现有中心保持一定距离的基础上,不受约束地发展;同时,与之相连的领域的快速商品化也被合法化。不断增加的投资资金流向能在短期内带来大量回报的网络系统以及媒体与信息服务领域⑤,是第二个因素。打破现有稳定局面的第三个因素则是像万维网这样的复杂系统;出乎意料的是,它成为重构传播通信商品链的通用平台。

与传统观点形成鲜明对比的是,我也在别处强调过⑥,对美国垄断的网络运营商及其主要的计算机厂家各自统领的那些行业,美国政府一直进行干预,并加以限制。由此导致美国电话电报公司与国际商用机器公司被迫处于守势。一直走跨国路线的国际商用机器公司面对反托拉斯压力时,不得不接纳那些在过去甚少关注的软件独立供应商(十年后,这一计算机巨头不仅把它的操作系统软件,更把已成为市场领头羊的个人电脑所需的微型电子线路的快速交付业务,悉数转包给独立供应商;这样,不利局面命中注定般

---

① Jack Banks, *Monopoly Television: MTV's Quest to Control the Music* (Boulder, Colo.: Westview, 1996); William M. Kunz, *Culture Conglomerates: Consolidation in the Motion Picture and Television Industries* (Lanham, Md.: Rowman and Littlefield, 2006).
② Edward Herman and Robert McChesney, *The Global Media* (Aldershot: Edward Elgar, 1997).
③ Steven Kline, Nick Dyer-Witheford, and Greg de Peuter, *Digital Play: The Interaction of Technology, Culture, and Marketing* (Montreal: McGill-Queen's University Press, 2003).
④ Schiller, *How To Think about Information*, 101–44.
⑤ Bell, "Social Framework," 182.
⑥ Dan Schiller, *Telematics and Government* (Norwood: Ablex, 1982); Dan Schiller, *Digital Capitalism: Networking the Global Market System* (Cambridge, Mass.: MIT Press, 1999).

地加剧了)。而另一巨头美国电话电报公司自 1920 年代以来一直关注国内市场的发展;如今,行政部门及其直接规制者联邦通讯委员会不断采取行动,提倡市场开放,在此情形下,它被迫让那些高科技的无执照营业者也能分到一杯羹。司法部发起了一场加长版的反托拉斯诉讼,最终导致该公司在 1982 年被拆分。

在"去规制化""自由化"的口号下,政府决策制定者创造了对信息处理设备与软件进行投资的各种机遇。联邦规制者与反托拉斯官员为高科技的网络产业的增长扫清道路。针对形塑了全国核心网络(责任心与非歧视)的公共服务部门的批评有所缓和,或者(在公共利益)受到损害的时候才会出现。当前,(资本)积累被赋予优先地位。地区性计算机网络、卫星、微波设备、语音留言系统以及相关仪器的专业供应商蜂拥进入市场①。越来越多的网络工具由计算机公司生产,而非美国电话电报公司的附属机构西电公司或其他电信供应商;并且,网络工具的买方不仅包括处于垄断地位的电信运营商,还有非运营商,后者购买网络工具以建造属于它们自己的"公司"网络。这些变化很快从美国国内市场的边缘聚集至中心地带。由此,企业与国家机构将战略眼光瞄向全球。

充满活力的新兴产业挤入现有的通信领域中。在 20 世纪的最后 25 年间,个人电脑已成为市场重组与文化习惯的中心点。台式机的处理与储存功能不断增强,保证能便携式使用,并兼容一部分媒体功能(例如游戏)。尽管国际商用机器公司与部分个人电脑兼容机生产商(还有规模小得多的苹果公司)主导着终端产品的销售,可微软与英特尔公司占据了个人电脑销售的绝大部分利润份额。微软提供的预包装的软件(磁盘操作系统[DOS]和文字处理软件[Word])依然能够应用于像莲花(Lotus)这样的外部软件公司②。个人电脑为产品发展创造了一个齐特林(Zittrain)所狂热赞美的"富有生产力的"平台:这是一条相对开放、包纳的赢利之路③。地区性网络在公司化美国的发展趋势中开始崛起,并更为有效地使用台式机④。

随着对网络的资本投资在 1970 年代末至 1990 年代初之间不断增长,五花八门的项目集中在数据通信这一日渐发展、不可小觑的产业上。然而,在国内和国际层面,在地方性和广域的网络环境中,出现了大量互不连属却明显是相互竞争的(disparate and typically rival)技术(发展)路径。1976 年开始,欧洲与其他政府的交通部颁布了一项有影响力的"X.25"标准。该标准是指国内层面上中央国家应当资助、国际层面上国际电信联盟

---

① Ronald A. Cass and John Haring, *International Trade in Telecommunications* (Washington, D. C. / Cambridge, Mass. : AEI Press / MIT Press, 1998) , 91 – 92,104.
② Martin Campbell – Kelly, *From Airline Reservations to Sonic the Hedgehog : A History of the Software Industry* (Cambridge, Mass. : MIT Press, 2003) .
③ Jonathan Zittrain, *The Future of the Internet and How to Stop It* (New Haven, Conn. : Yale, 2008) , 11 – 18.
④ Urs von Burg, *The Triumph of Ethernet : Technological Communities and the Battle for the LAN Standard* (Stanford, Calif. : Stanford University Press, 2001) .

(International Telecommunication Union)成员国应当合作共同建设专用数据网。而以拥有最大的国内计算机网络市场而沾沾自喜的美国却采取截然不同的路径。一些美国企业认同并践行了"X.25"标准;其他一些企业开发专有系统(国际商用机器公司为代表,还存在其他一些公司);另一些企业与大学的军事承包商的网络,则遵循1970年代中期所创立的初始的互联网标准(TCP/IP)。珍妮特·阿巴特(Janet Abbate)认为,"大型计算机设备的管理者,心仪那些能够(帮助他们)自主掌控网络性能的协议",而非有助于政府部门限制专有数据网范围的协议①。他们获得美国政府的支持。在国际电信联盟1988年召开的世界电报电话行政大会(World Administrative Telegraph and Telephone Conference)上,美国进行了大规模的游说行动。对此,国际电信联盟顾问理查德·希尔(Richard Hill)指明,联盟"深受私有化、自由化与业务融合这一轮愈发强劲的趋势的影响"②。诚如参加此次会议的美国代表团所中意的那般,"私人运营商可以光明正大地使用租用专线来提供包括数据服务在内的各项业务"③。随后,美国开放政府资助的互联网骨干网,许以商用,并在1990年代早期对其进行彻底的私有化改造。这也算是美国政府给互联网标准"添砖加瓦"了。随着企业用户加快脚步,推进原本互不连属的网络相互连接与协调,它们已经迫不及待地在它们的分支机构内/之间贯彻这一"开放的"互联网标准④(詹姆斯·科尔塔达阐明,自此,许多公司除了使用互联网之外,还运营数据通信网络⑤)。

从供应角度来看,历经15年的并购运动,骨干网与零售服务成为两家大型的网络运营商(魏瑞森通讯与重组的美国电话电报公司)的新业务;斯普林特(Sprint)、世纪连接(Century Link)、德国电信(T-Mobile)以及其他小型承运商则只能在它们的阴影下继续运营。从需求的角度来看,它们向主营银行、制造业、零售、能源与农业经济等业务的跨国企业网络客户提供服务。这些用户增建了较为全面的数据中心与网络连接,并与大型商业承运商签订合同,从而将它们的专有系统整合进承运商更为包容的基础设施之中。

与此同时,市场中商品化的相关因素,使现状失去平衡,并再度导向巨型发展模式。美国的规制者一改往常作风,主动介入现有的电视商品链中,例如,通过订阅费的方式,支持有线以及卫星电视系统里新的电视模式的发展。免费电视依然还是受到保护(不能随便染指)的市场,但是,广播电视台或广播电视网的所有者,如同它们的竞争对手康卡

---

① Janet Abbate, *Inventing the Internet* (Cambridge, Mass.: MIT Press, 1999), 159, 160.
② Richard Hill, *The New International Telecommunications Regulations and the Internet: A Commentary and Legislative History* (Zurich: Schulthess, 2013), 7.
③ Hill, *New International Telecommunications*, 8; William J. Drake, "WATTC 88: Restructuring the International Telecommunications Regulations," *Telecommunications Policy* 12, no. 3 (September 1988): 217–33; Peter Cowhey and Jonathan D. Aronson, "The ITU in Transition," *Telecommunications Policy* 15, no. 4 (August 1991): 298–310.
④ Zittrain, *Future of the Internet*, 28.
⑤ James W. Cortada, *Information and the Modern Corporation* (Cambridge, Mass.: MIT Press, 2011).

斯特（Comcast）与直播电视公司（DirecTV）一样，开始多元化发展；于是，电视服务供应商不仅要获得广告商的青睐，还要赢得订阅费。2012年，世界范围内超过8亿用户付费观看电视[1]；在美国，大概85%的电视用户付费订阅[2]。同样，在消费市场，美国在线（America Online）、CompuServe与非凡网络（Prodigy）都开通了非互联拨号上网业务，以保证用户可以在线访问电子邮件，以及交由外部供应商提供的专属内容。相应地，计算机网络在两种有影响力的隐喻框架下发展壮大：1990年前后戈尔所提出的"信息高速公路"法案、1992年有线电视集团大亨约翰·马龙（John Malone）所提供的"五百个电视频道"服务[3]。尽管信息高速公路与五百个电视频道系统依然许诺着可遇不可求的市场增长，但植根于个人流动性与商业电视的这两大隐喻，把新兴业务限制在可控的范围之内。彼时，鲜有人能够明白，像美国在线这样的商业机构所运营的"围墙花园"因为太过封闭、规模太小而无法实现新兴互联网公司的宏大愿景。恰如互联网机构（在这些雄心壮志的鼓舞下）疯狂涌现，有线电视与商业在线公司坚信它们拥有独一无二的价值。

产业领导者与生俱来就拥有这份自信，也无可厚非。他们相信，新的技术会发展到一定程度，可以有效地辅佐他们优先选择的利润战略，这一点已经在电视、激光唱片以及录影带等不同的发展路径中得到证实。他们认为，多媒体企业将吸收他们所选择的技术并能保证盈利，与此同时抛弃或边缘化其他的技术。时代华纳公司担心自己无法在拥有不可限量的利润前景的市场上分到一杯羹，直到2000年它才遵照这一逻辑，不料却犯下商业世界有史以来最昂贵的错误之一：它让充满抱负的美国在线接管公司，可这是一家市值被投机性投资过分抬高的企业，其专有的网络路径哪怕在彼时早已陈旧老朽[4]。然而，在（时代华纳公司的）狂妄自大之外，还存在一些因素：传播产业大本营无法完全预知互联网将如何让（现有的）媒体图景四分五裂。

我们所说的"互联网"并没有彻底撼动这个世界。在万维网出现的前十年，那些遵守互联网协议的公司内部网就已呈现出不可小觑的发展势头；像3Com公司和太阳微系统

---

[1] "IPTV Broadband Penetration Reaches 15 Percent, Growth Prospects are Patchy," *TeleGeography*, CommsUpdate, June 20, 2012.
[2] U.S. Government Accountability Office, "Video Marketplace: Competition is Evolving, and Government Reporting Should Be Re-Evaluated" (GAO-13-576), June 2013, available at http://www.gao.gov/products/GAO-13-576 (accessed January 10, 2014).
[3] L. J. Davis, *The Billionaire Shell Game* (New York: Doubleday, 1998), 150.
[4] Dan Schiller, "Internet Feeding Frenzy," *Le Monde diplomatique*, February 2000, available at http://mondediplo.com/2000/02/02schiller (accessed January 10, 2014); Robert W. McChesney, *Digital Disconnect: How Capitalism Is Turning the Internet against Democracy* (New York: New Press, 2013), 123-24.

公司这种专门的网络设备供应商发展迅猛①。在1980年代末至1990年代这一段被压缩的时期,更进一步的技术发展彻底地拓展了互联网彼此协作的特性:在美国国家科学基金会(National Science Foundation)的支持下,建立互联网骨干网(这是美国最基础的互联网设施,发展迅速),并对其进行私有化改造;废除保障国际协作系统的早期发展的非商业政策;发明万维网,将之作为可免费使用的软件向全球推广;考虑到美国与海外市场,落实并确立对关键的互联网资源(地址分配与网络标识符)的协调与管理行为;公开发布一款可以显示图片的网络浏览器。上述这一切都可跻身于重大创新行列中。这些创新没有一样是因受到资本自我发展的即时刺激而出现的;上述所有创新都取决于非市场因素,例如美国政府。哪怕从1990年代中期起,产业引入这些疾风骤雨式的变革,实属不易。但投资与商品化所形成的庞大循环,层层累积在这些变革之上。

我们需要更多的研究来关注互联网发展过程中的某些里程碑事件。马修·克雷恩(Matthew Crain)②厘清了网景浏览器上市以来网络广告服务的形成根源。网络广告服务本身就是一个复杂的现象。它得到风险资本家、对冲基金与投资银行的资金支持,具有公关、宣传与啦啦队新闻的特性,更获得美国行政部门的坚定支持。因此,另一波资本(投资)的条件成熟了:资本争先恐后地进入不断扩大的通信市场,以获得普及数字化服务的先发优势。随着互联网与相关的新媒体成为投资场所和市场实验田,现有的商品链开始更改路径,这一变更有时甚至是彻底而猛烈的。1999—2000年间互联网泡沫的出现打断(而不是压抑)了(商品链变更)这一过程。政府关于企业—商品网络发展的政策变化,以及大量资本寻找出口,共同导致了通信产业的激烈变革,并使其在一个扩大的基础上得到重构。

我们不应该高估这一重构过程所具有的理性色彩。它是一个狂暴的、偶然性的有时甚至是自相残杀的过程。然而,日复一日不断修订的重构规划里,依然不变的是资本获取利润的诉求。利润导向的通信系统围绕新兴的技术潜力与崭新或重新制造的商品而重新建立起来,市场关系得以解放,进而吸纳供应的其他形式。那些依靠网络连接才能使用的产品与服务,过去是物以稀为贵,如今它们涵盖的范围可谓史无前例,且仍然在不断扩大。网络服务与应用已跳脱出市场使用规模不断增长的台式机范畴,并开始涉足大

---

① 1983至1993年,相互连接的计算机网络的数量猛增至数万,具体可参见 Vinton Cerf,"How the Internet Came to Be,"in *The Online User's Encyclopedia*,by Bernard Aboba (Boston:Addison – Wesley,1993),5. 也可参见 E. Fleischman,*Boeing Computer Services*,"A Large Corporate User's View of IPng," Internet Engineering Task Force Network Working Group RFC 1687,August 1994;以及 Abbate,*Inventing the Internet*.

② Matthew Crain,"The Revolution Will Be Commercialized:Finance,Public Policy,and the Construction of Internet Advertising," PhD diss. ,University of Illinois,Urbana – Champaign,2013;也请参见 Matthew Crain,"Financial Markets and Online Advertising:Reevaluating the Dotcom Investment Bubble," *Information*,*Communications and Society* 17,no. 3 (2014):371 – 84. Available at http://dx. doi. org/10. 1080/1369118X. 2013. 869615 (accessed January 31,2014).

型机构所运营的彼此分离的专有网络,例如大学、政府机关和企业。这一始料未及的网桥(bridging)功能产生了强劲且(对于现有的商业媒体而言)富有侵犯性的网络效应。市场权力的现有节点遭到破坏,并以一种截然不同的方式进行重建。法学家吴修铭(Tim Wu)描述了这个周期性的现象,由此,垄断企业才能重申其特权:对现存的通信技术的挑战,催生了一种新的"主令开关"①。在这一或其他相似的描述里,先发优势战略、网络效应、重要专利、对销售渠道的掌控、垂直整合以及(相当重要的)国家政策扶持等因素,共同保障了少数市场领导者的联合。政治学家马修·辛德曼(Matthew Hindman)的研究区分了准入门槛和参与门槛,从而佐证了上述观点②。在互联网领域,准入门槛很低;建立一个网站是一件轻松、花不了多少钱的事情,数百人已经这么做了。然而,组织互联网自身经验的能力却是另外一回事。有效的市场参与的门槛逐月增高。据产业分析家估计,微软曾试图从多个层面赶上谷歌,其花费的成本高达每年 50 亿美元③。根据风评,苹果单单涉足数字地图这一应用领域,就已花费(每年)5 亿到 10 亿美元④。

这个联盟中,只有少数公司才能够玩得起。在我的同事麦克切斯尼的笔下,万维网被老练地形容为正在形成中的垄断资本,它掌握在 5 家拥有排他性与反民主权力的企业手中⑤。然而,亚马逊、谷歌、苹果、微软与脸书等企业不得不面对和处理各方压力、动力、激励、局限性及其身处其中的政治经济的发展趋势。此处,我需要强调互联网通信行业的商品链,而非垄断本身。

此前已有学者使用大家所熟知的数据通信工程参照模型,作为一种"启发式的论据"⑥。在接下来的章节中,我也借助这一用法,旨在探查构成当前互联网的各种商品链:需要设备运行并访问系统,设备被卖给网络运营商、商业用户与住宅客户;服务通常提供给用户,以产生有关受众(访问)行为以及用户访问网站记录的跟踪数据,这些数据都可以卖给广告商。内容和应用服务通过直接付费或订阅的方式,售卖或租赁给用户。

---

① Tim Wu, *The Master Switch: The Rise and Fall of Information Empires* (New York: Knopf, 2010).
② Matthew Hindman, *The Myth of Digital Democracy* (Princeton: Princeton University Press, 2008).
③ Steve Lohr, "Can These Guys Make You 'Bing'?" *New York Times*, Sunday Business, July 31, 2011.
④ Quentin Hardy, "Head to Head over Mobile Maps," *New York Times*, June 18, 2012.
⑤ McChesney, *Digital Disconnect*. 类似的却非批判性的观点,可参见 John Battelle, "The Internet Big Five By Product Strength," available at http://battelle.media.com/archives/2012/01/the-internet-big-five-by-product-strength.php (accessed January 10, 2014);以及 Farhad Manjoo, "The Great Tech War of 2012," *Fast Company*, October 17, 2011, available at http://www.fastcompany.com/1784824/great-tech-war-2012.
⑥ Sascha D. Meinrath, James W. Losey, and Victor W. Pickard, "Digital Feudalism: Enclosures and Erasures from Digital Rights Management to the Digital Divide," *CommLaw Conspectus* 19, no. 2 (2011):431. "互联网生态系统"这一替代性概念的相关论述,可参见 Internet Advertising Bureau, Hamilton Consultants, Inc., with Dr. John Deighton and Dr. John Quelch, authors, "Economic Value of the Advertising-Supported Internet Ecosystem" (Cambridge, Mass.: Hamilton Consultants), June 10, 2009, exhibits 1-1, 1-2, 1-3, pp. 10-11, 13, 14.

第 6 章
网络通信商品链

我先从网络与接入设备这一全面且具有可塑性的基础设施入手,谈论网络通信的商品链问题。各类服务与应用系统层层叠加,组成网络与接入设备的基础设施结构;其他中介机构,连同操作系统、浏览器、搜索引擎、社交网络以及内容的供应商提供技术支持[1]。在数字化衰退时期,重组的速度近乎疯狂,辐射范围很广,这表明资本正争先恐后地打开并试图占有那些高利润的"魔盒"。

网络

当代通信产业的零售端(即我们作为消费者所体验的经历)背后,正是庞大无比的电信基础设施。亚马逊 Kindle 通过与承运人的第三方支付连接这一"幕后协议",使得用户能够下载书籍以及其他文本资料;智能手机在(对大部分人而言)看不见的电线、网线与无线电频率的帮助下,带领我们走向脸书和新浪微博。实际上,虚拟空间借助那些空间上安排得井然有序的基础设施,牢牢固定在物质世界里。诚如安德鲁·布鲁姆(Andrew Blum)所言,"互联网的网络结构,与铁路或电话系统一样,都固定在真实的物理空间中"[2]。

---

[1] 商务部指出,"互联网中介商帮助(用户)能够访问、传输或搜索第三方所产生的数据,或者向第三方提供互联网服务。互联网中介包括网站、博客站点、社交媒体以及其他允许个人能够提供或上传在线信息的服务商。互联网中介提供的服务对于互联网的增长与重要性而言,不可或缺"。具体可参见 U. S. Department of Commerce, National Telecommunications and Information Administration, Notice of Inquiry, "Global Free Flow of Information on the Internet," in *Federal Register* 75, no. 188 (September 29, 2010): 60072, available at http://www.gpo.gov/fdsys/pkg/FR-2010-09-29/pdf/2010-24385.pdf (accessed January 10, 2014).

[2] Andrew Blum, *Tubes: A Journey to the Center of the Internet* (New York: HarperCollins, 2012), 9. 卡斯特提出这一关键性观点,具体请参见 *The Informational City: Information Technology, Economic Restructuring and the Urban-Regional Process* (Oxford: Basil Blackwell, 1989).

我讨论这些基础设施的第一个观点也与之类似：这些网络的范围及其信息传送能力（数据传送速率或有效的传输速度①）都有了质的增长。20 世纪末，网络传输速度的不断提升，推动人们对"遥观宇宙"②理念的狂热追求，"遥观宇宙"正以"无线带宽"为标志。然而，即便（网络传输速度）增加，网络信息传送能力的分布与定价依然受到地区、服务以及消费者类型的影响而呈现不平衡发展的局面。随着数据信息包与数据传输费用的爆炸式增长，体量大的网络建立起来，以容纳所有类型的讯息（无论是声音、影像、电子邮件还是其他应用）③。当网络现代化以势不可当的方式席卷各个领域时，每个领域中扩张与钳制、（供应）过剩与不足之间的平衡模式，也随之发生猛烈且短暂的变化。

1960 年，全世界 1.42 亿部有线电话中，超过五分之四的电话分布在美国和西欧。半个世纪过去（2013 年年底），超过 10 亿部陆上电话更为广泛地分布在世界各地，订阅固定宽带这一通用服务的用户数增长至 6.88 亿。然而，这一增长被（实际上从近四分之一世纪之前就已出现的）另一增长势头所超越，即 68 亿移动电话用户数，这其中包括 21 亿移动宽带用户数（富裕用户订阅多种服务）④。增长可称得上现象级；准入/使用范围的这些扩张，不仅创造了新的传播不平等现象，也与这些现象相伴相随。2010 年，非洲的部分地区有一半人口无法使用无线信号⑤；2013 年，45% 的巴西人（其中包括 80% 的最低收入人群）从未接触过互联网⑥。与此同时，2010 年 7 月，宽带用户数在全球范围内突破 5 亿大关；其中，亚洲用户数占总数的 41%，欧洲占 30%，北美占 26%⑦。总体说来，发展中国家或地区的互联网用户数占世界总用户数的份额，从 2006 年的 44% 增长至 2011 年 62%。数十亿的老百姓享受到新形式的电子连接；世界范围内多达四分之三的移动电话的用户，来自非经济合作与发展组织的富裕成员国⑧。然而，整体的发展模式再生产出了不均衡与不平等问题。一面是北美与西欧迈入第 3 代或第 4 代无线宽带技术（3G 和 LTE）时代，享受以此为标准的最新移动互联网业务；一面则是第 2 代无线宽带技术的非洲用户数持续增加⑨。按照计划，非洲对国际带宽的需求原定在 2012 年至 2019 年间以每年

---

① As is helpfully specified by Eli Noam, "Let Them Eat Cellphones: Why Mobile Wireless Is No Solution for Broadband," *Journal of Information Policy* 1 (2011): 470.
② George Gilder, *Telecosm: How Infinite Bandwidth Will Revolutionize Our World* (New York: Free Press, 2000).
③ International Telecommunication Union (ITU), *Trends in Telecommunications Reform* 2013: *Transnational Aspects of Regulation in a Networked Society* (Geneva: ITU, April 18, 2013), 4.
④ ITU, *Trends in Telecommunications Reform* 2013, 1.
⑤ ITU, *Monitoring the WSIS Targets*, *World Telecom/ICT Development Report* 2010 (Geneva: ITU, 2010), 14, table 1.2.
⑥ "45% of Brazilians Have Never Had Internet Access, Reports Finds," *TeleGeography*, CommsUpdate, June 24, 2013.
⑦ "Forging a True Global Connection—Broadband Passes 500 Million Subscribers," *Broadband Forum*, available at http://www.broadband-forum.org/news/download/pressreleases/2010/500Million.pdf (accessed January 10, 2014).
⑧ ITU, "The World in 2011 ICT Facts and Figures," available at http://www.itu.int/ITU-D/ict/facts/2011 (accessed January 10, 2014).
⑨ "The Beginning of the End for 2G," *TeleGeography*, CommsUpdate, February 5, 2014.

51%的速度增长(这超过其他地区),不过请注意,非洲54个国家对国际带宽的总体需求,还不如加拿大一个国家多①。

我的第二个观点是,资本开支增长的重复周期,导致了空间、社会与技术层面上网络适用范围的不断扩大。在1992年至2001年这一长达10年的过渡期,电信产业占美国所有新增投资总额的三分之一②。有研究指出,世界电信产业的资本支出从2010年至2011年增长了5.8%,总支出为3 110亿美元③。根据联邦通信委员会的报告,数字化衰退的前两年(2008—2009年),"无线部门占所有电信投资的三成有余,占信息/通信产业投资总额的四分之一,以及美国经济中总体投资额的2%"。2011年,美国无线运营商投资金额高达250亿美元④。2013年,中国(也是全球)最大的无线运营商中国移动一家计划投资305亿美元⑤。

因此,我的叙述就不仅仅只是偏重技术进步层面,还包括无节制使用投资资本层面。这反过来又以制度性政策的激进变革为基础。我将在接下来的章节里阐释,这反过来以制度性政策的激进修订为基础。在世界的大部分地方,(对技术的)投资大多来自国外。据威瑞森通讯公司的观察,外商直接投资"已经成为开放的经济体中电信产业发展的驱动力";1999—2001年互联网泡沫的高峰时期,发展中国家的电信领域仍然能够汲取3 310亿美元的投资,远高于其他任何行业⑥。2012年,约32%(该份额仍不断增长)的全球信息技术开支(高达3.86万亿美元)预计来自"新兴市场"⑦。这一增长与企业(尤其是跨国资本)的需求有关。部分增长源于那些总部如今设立在欠发达国家(主要是中国)的公司,这些公司的规模相当于世界上最大型的企业规模的五分之一。然而,更多的全球网络投资额内生于发达市场经济体内,用以加快本地网络现代化的速度。

我的第三个观点是,上述所描绘的蜕变过程,无论我们赋予它什么样的进步意义,它从未摆脱资本主义政治经济的矛盾性驱动力。这一具有元问题色彩的特征体现在许多方面。网络现代化起源于电信产业结构与政策的激烈且彻底的改革。这场改革由美国引发的一系列变革所组成。随后,美国将这些变革树立为新自由主义改革的模板,向全

---

① "Africa's international bandwidth growth to lead the world," *TeleGeography*, Comms Update, October 31, 2013.
② Judith Stein, *Pivotal Decade: How the United States Traded Factories for Services in the Seventies* (New Haven, Conn.: Yale University Press, 2010), 286.
③ "Global Telecoms CAPEX to Top USD311 Billion in 2011, Report Says," *TeleGeography*, CommsUpdate, November 9, 2011.
④ U. S. FCC, *In the Matter of Implementation of Section 6002(b) of the Omnibus Budget Reconciliation Act of 1993*, Sixteenth Report, WT Docket No. 11–186, March 19, 2013, 20.
⑤ "China Mobile Launches TD–LTE Tender," *TeleGeography*, CommsUpdate, June 25, 2013.
⑥ "Comments of Verizon and Verizon Wireless," before the Department of Commerce, Global Free Flow of Information on the Internet, December 6, 2010, 7–8, available at http://www.ntia.doc.gov/files/ntia/comments/100921457–0457–01/attachments/12%2006%2010%20VZ,%20VZW%20comments_Global%20Internet.pdf (accessed January 10, 2014).
⑦ Mary Lennighan, "Going Global," *Total Telecom*, May 2012, 7.

世界推广①。市场自由化首先将焦点放在1967年至1970年间所形成的系统性基础上，这标志着(民主党)约翰逊与(共和党)尼克松政府维持两党一致的承诺的形成。在与司法部签订同意判决书后，1984年美国电话电报公司被拆分；1996年，新的电信法案出台。两大事件将美国国内自由化进程推向顶峰。这些变革尽管对市场在位者帮助良多②，却摧毁了每一个细分市场中受到保护的垄断基础。一言以蔽之，正如我们在第一章所见，政治决策优先考虑的是来源多样、充满活力与(极具)扩张性的网络产业，而非美国电话电报公司的特殊利益。作为(彼时)世界上最大的资本机构，(美国电话电报公司)这个垂直与水平皆一体化的巨兽企业在一个更广阔的网络产业内部，被活生生地撕成碎片。这样，一个足够广泛而能容纳绝大部分资产阶级的"垄断行业"便取代了它③。

同样，网络市场自由化的外在驱动力，不仅需要彻底变革，更创造了诱人的投资机遇。西欧与日本采取了美国的政策模式，却体现了相当程度的自主性。然而，许多欠发达国家或地区的自由化进程，更像是全球经济政策的副产品，受其引诱甚至被强制执行(自由化)。其中一些国家或地区的自由化，发生在1980—1990年代之间毁灭性的债务危机时期，并得到国际货币基金组织、世界银行以及美国财政部强制执行的"结构性调整"战略的支持④。经济学家罗杰·诺尔(Roger G. Noll)承认，"电信产业或其他基础设施行业的新自由主义变革的推动力，一定程度上与它们的表现毫无关系"，而是与利用私有化以及其他相关变革进而深化"更大规模的新自由主义改革"的可能性相关⑤。然而，由此导致的不断扩大的网络投资，不仅极大地拓展了服务的覆盖面，更在欠发达国家或地区孕育出大量的资本主义承运商。

国内与海外连接性之间的界限若要更加疏松，市场自由化是前提条件。主要运营商在某个国家内建立多个(网络)"接入点"，然后通过直属的跨境网络将它们相互连接。总部设在印度的塔塔通信，在埃及、海湾地区以及印度的主要城市之间铺设电缆，意在打造一个全资的、覆盖全球的光纤电缆网络⑥。"第3水平"通信公司(Level 3 Communications)2011年收购环球电讯，可为另一例证。合并后的公司在三大洲所建造的光纤网络

---

① Dan Schiller, *Telematics and Government* (Norwood: Ablex, 1982); Schiller, Digital Capitalism.
② Patricia Aufderheide, *Communication Policy and the Public Interest: The Telecommunications Act of 1996* (New York: Guilford, 1999).
③ I borrow here from Christopher Hill, *From Reformation to Industrial Revolution* (Harmondsworth: Penguin, 1988).
④ 若要了解结构性调整的整体情况，请参见 Biplab Dasgupta, *Structural Adjustment, Global Trade and the New Political Economy of Development* (London: Zed, 1998)。
⑤ Roger G. Noll, "Telecommunications Reform in Developing Countries," in *Economic Policy Reform: The Second Stage*, ed. Anne O. Krueger (Chicago: University of Chicago Press, 2000), 199. 也请参见 David Harvey, *A Brief History of Neoliberalism* (New York: Oxford University Press, 2007); 以及 Dan Schiller, *Digital Capitalism: Networking the Global Market System* (Cambridge, Mass.: MIT Press, 1999) 里关于更宏观的新自由主义议程及其与网络的关系的论述。
⑥ "Tata Completes Round-the-World Cable Network Ring," *TeleGeography*, Comms Update, March 22, 2012.

与海底(光缆)系统相连,并向70个国家超过700个城市提供点对点服务。它的客户涵盖了各类组织用户:大公司(或"企业"),财富500强中至少40%的企业都成为它的用户;政府部门、成百上千的承运商、移动运营商,以及互联网服务提供商。新科传媒(Singapore Technologies Telemedia)是它的最大股东之一,这表现出亚洲地区的资本(试图)进入跨国体系与应用服务的强烈欲望①。1990年代以及2000年之后兴建海底电缆的热潮,导致产能扩充的质的飞跃(有时甚至是生产能力过剩②),哪怕世界上其他一些国家或地区(的技术需求)依然得不到满足。

随着陈旧过时的系统让位于新系统,商品化的新领域已经形成并推动市场增长,以及更广阔的经济领域所具有的繁荣与萧条活力直接转移至电信产业,那么,将追逐利润(的诉求)寄托在(网络)连接性上的做法,导致了现有的社会优先事项以及公共服务原则。

早期与互联网的连接,并没有太多考虑利润的问题;在由只关心军事项目的计算机科学家所组成的特定社区中,大学与非营利社区发挥着超乎寻常的作用。当互联网日益流行后,服务提供模式围绕赢利目标进行重置;仅在美国,实际上有数千家公司涌现出来,向家庭和商业用户提供(网络)接入服务。此外,用于搜集与传输大容量数据的骨干网设施要么可以从现有的专业公司手上购得(例如美国最大网路交换中心[UUNET]),要么直接由大型网络运营商建造。一家网络运营商扮演一个具有构成性影响的角色:世界通讯公司(WorldCom),它在一次令外界震惊的金融欺诈事件后逐渐衰败。在整个1990年代以及下一个十年的初期,那些最大型的网络运营商通过(向前)与互联网服务整合、(向后)与骨干网一体化等方式,避开了对其核心业务(打造连接性)的各种威胁,并拼命向新的网络设施的中心地带迈进。

面向消费者市场的互联网接入服务迅速被大型服务提供商所控制;大部分地区的消费者面对一种双头垄断局面,即有线电视服务与电信服务。2011年,全美有线宽带订户数量的86%,掌握在13家互联网服务提供商手上;这13家提供商都是由有线电视或电信公司向前整合而成的③。骨干网络服务甚至更加集中。世界的大部分地区都采用这一相同的整合模式。在印度,唯一一家最大的电信服务提供商(政府控股的企业BNSL)旗

---

① "3 Is the Magic Number: Level 3 Merges with Global Crossing in USD3bn Stockfor–Stock Deal", *TeleGeography*, CommsUpdate, April 12, 2011; "Level 3 Completes Global Crossing Acquisition", *TeleGeography*, CommsUpdate, October 5, 2011.
② Dan Schiller, *How to Think about Information* (Urbana: University of Illinois Press, 2007), 80–100.
③ U. S. FCC, Office of Engineering and Technology and Consumer and Governmental Affairs Bureau, "Measuring Broadband America," August 2, 2011, 3, available at at http://www.fcc.gov/measuring–broadband–america/#read (accessed January 10, 2014)

下的用户数,占全国宽带订户总数的58%①。再如中国,2010年,两大网络运营商的用户数占全球4.92亿宽带订户数的1/5,更在中国本土占尽优势,固若金汤②;七家骨干网络服务提供商(其中有三家主要的商业性互联网服务提供商)都面向全国市场③。

同样,无论是美国电话电报公司、德国电信还是中国电信,这些主要的承运商都是采取向前整合的方式进入移动服务领域,尽管它们必须面对来自各种独立的移动运营商的挑战,也不得不在有时数量较大的补贴金额等问题上与设备制造商协商。苹果手机一直存在商品溢价现象;当2012年第二季度美国电话电报公司苹果合约机用户数下降时,美国电话电报公司向苹果支付的补贴也相应下跌,而后者的利润实际上增长了④。这是诸多征兆的其中之一——不少作者也认为——即承运商的多元化发展不仅仅折射出它们(所拥有的)企业权力⑤。从拨号上网到以电信或电缆为基础的宽带接入,再到移动电话系统与无线网络热点,大型有线和电缆运营商成功地引进网络技术,并将之视为在竞争中求得生存的(制胜)法宝。它们的市场份额可能比较大,利润比较高,然而其行动自由依然受限。

围绕技术与政策而展开的变革意味着这些大型的承运商如今已成为最重要的(并非唯一)网络连接性的推动者。大量用于在互联网上传输数据的设备,被直接售卖给商业用户。每一种大型企业致力于建造或管理属于它们自己的所谓的"企业网络",往往具有国际规模;这些需求侧系统中,规模最大的网络足以与小国家的全国性网络相抗衡。企业网络化的程度(与规模)不断扩大。作为这些网络所使用的设备的最大供应商,思科在全球范围内与"5.2万家合作伙伴保持联系"⑥,并以此自鸣得意。

围绕互联网技术,网络基础设施被重新建造;与此同时,它们的供给方也与长达一个世纪的制造方剥离开来。互联网"管道"供应商并不是历史上占主导地位的公司,例如美国历史悠久的西电公司(Western Electric,如今已被并购在法国公司阿尔卡特—朗讯旗下⑦),而是像思科或华为这样的新兴企业;华为是一家中国公司,2012年它的雇员已高

---

① Tushar Tajane, "Top Five Internet Service Providers of India (as of 2010)," TechZoom.org, February 24, 2011, available at http://techzoom.org/top-5-internet-service-providers-of-india-as-of-2010 (accessed January 10, 2014).

② "Broadband Provider Rankings: The Rise and Rise of China," *TeleGeography*, Comms Update, July 28, 2010.

③ Henry L. Hu, "The Political Economy of Governing ISPs in China: Perspectives of Net Neutrality and Vertical Integration," *China Quarterly* 207 (September 2011): 523.

④ Thomas Gryta, "AT&T Gets a Boost from Increased Smartphone Use," *Wall Street Journal*, July 25, 2012.

⑤ David Carr, "Telecom's Big Players Hold Back the Future," *New York Times*, May 20, 2013.

⑥ Testimony of Mary Brown, Cisco Systems Inc., before the Subcommittee on Technology and Innovation, Committee on Science, Space, and Technology, U.S. House of Representatives, Hearing on "Avoiding the Spectrum Crunch: Growing the Wireless Economy through Innovation," April 18, 2012, 3.

⑦ 2012年7月,阿尔卡特市值接近2006年它收购朗讯科技公司所花成本的1/5,该公司市值继续缩水,并不得不进行裁员。详见Daniel Thomas, "Alcatel-Lucent to Cut 5,000 Jobs," *Financial Times*, July 27, 2012.

达14万名,其客户遍布全球140个国家①。随后,像戴尔、惠普这些服务器制造商、EMC等存储媒体制造商以及在移动基础设施市场上取得成功的老牌供应商(一马当先的应该是瑞典的大型企业爱立信)②,相继加入这支由新兴企业所组成的队伍。同样,上述公司介入其中的商品链,被重新规划后(尤其通过第三方承包商)进入中国,思科以这样的方式将其95%的制造业务外包出去③。

这一新兴系统的网络工程所具有的看似中立的技术特征,佐证了向互联网(时代)转型变革的合理性。出于互联网工程和运营的目的,不论是大型的电信企业还是需求侧企业网络,这些运营商都被归类为"自主系统";并且,那些协调关键性的互联网资源的机构所分配给运营商的自主系统的数字地址,成为在互联网上发送通信流的路由表的基础。网络的互操作性构成互联网,这些网络的数量已提高了两个数量级。世界范围内,已存在百余家有线电话网络;2007年,自主系统的数量已过万④。通常情况下,自主系统运营商之间私下达成协议,以协调它们的网络互连、定价以及路径安排;因此,自营交易(而非公开的关税)决定网络间的数据传输⑤。任何情况下,所有的互联网服务提供商都不会被平等对待。批发商(所谓的骨干网或第一级网络)的数量不会太多,只有一小撮;在美国,它们都是由美国电话电报公司、威瑞森、斯普林特(Sprint)以及第三级网络来运营。这些系统运营商建造或者重建它们的网络,以容纳成倍增长的数据流量;城市、企业、国家,还有数据中心和智能手机占主导地位的新兴结构,产生了这些数据流量⑥。然而,谁向谁支付多少费用等问题,并非通过透明公开的方式加以解决。我们很难假设,互联网定价与歧视性条款无关;我们也有充分的理由认为,(互联网定价)有可能比此前电信产业受到规制的时代下的电话服务定价,要更加不公平。

网络的社会责任的受蚀程度,远比生产率的调整与市场歧视严重。这也影响到一大批工会工人的生活水平。加入工会的电信产业工人1983年占全美工会工人总数的

---

① "The Company That Spooked the World," *The Economist*, August 4, 2012; 西蒙菲莎大学博士文韵关于华为公司的博士毕业论文有助于我们更了解该公司的发展情况。
② Rex Milne, "Ericsson Suffers as Sales of Older Networks Decline," *Financial Times*, July 19, 2012.
③ "Cisco to Cut Workforce by 15%, Sell Factory," *BusinessWorld*, July 19, 2011; Jeff Gaumgartner, "Foxconn Buys Cisco's Set-Top Factory," *LR Cable News Analysis*, July 18, 2011, available at www.lightreading.com/document.asp?doc_id=210080&site (accessed January 10, 2014).
④ Rick Kuhn, Kotikalapudi Sriram, and Doug Montgomery, "Border Gateway Protocol Security: Recommendations of the National Institute of Standards and Technology," NIST Special Publication 800-54, July 2007, 2-2.
⑤ Milton L. Mueller, *Networks and States: The Global Politics of Internet Governance* (Cambridge, Mass.: MIT Press, 2010), 226, 239. 要更详细地了解该议题,请参见 Laura DeNardis, *The Global War For Internet Governance* (New Haven, Conn.: Yale University Press, 2014). 要统计已登记在案的自主系统的数量与名称,请见 For a tally of registered autonomous system numbers and names, see ftp://ftp.arin.net/info/asn.txt (accessed March 9, 2014).
⑥ ITU, *Trends In Telecommunication Reform* 2013: *Transnational Aspects of Regulation in a Networked Society*, 4, available at http://www.itu.int/pub/D-REG-TTR.14-2013 (accessed January 10, 2014).

55%，到了1974年，该比例下降至27%①。简言之，美国电信承运商（电信、电缆与卫星公司）在2001至2011年10年间，裁掉近40万名工人。一旦成立实力强大的工会，承运商反而有时置劳资集体谈判协议于不顾：2011年，威瑞森20万名雇员中30%的工人属于工会成员②。使资本进入移动通信系统，的确向部分有线电视运营商提供了逃避承担这些高昂成本的法律责任的机会。美国电信工会（The Communications Workers of America）在二战后初期通过抗争，为贝尔系统内各个层面的工人成功争取到一份全国性合同；随着美国电话电报公司在法律强制下进行业务拆分，以及企业网络大量出现，美国电信工会感受到多家公司的深深恶意。2007年一位分析家总结道，"美国电信工会一直保有它的核心力量，并击退大多数严重的妥协行动；但如今，它四周几乎都是不承认工会的企业，它所身处的行业，不仅竞争力大，更对其劳动力毫不留情"③。2011年，威瑞森要求工人向公司让步，接受福利削减、付薪病休日，以及缴纳健康计划费用与退休金等措施，从而触发了四年以来全国最大的一次工人罢工活动④。因此，罢工主体不仅仅限于那些最终向工资压制制度低头的工会工人。

电信产业的自由化导致市场混乱可能性的日益增长。数十年间，尽管电信产业未得到充分发展，却仍属于发展稳定的行业。然而，市场自由化以及紧随其后的互联网商业化，导致投资蜂拥而至，并最终引发2001年前后行业的崩溃，与大量运营商的破产⑤。将网络从一个例外、受到重度规制的领域转变成另一逐利争名的产业，只会使网络产业更容易受到同样影响宏观政治经济发展的动力的摆布。2012年出现了海底电缆建设的另一波热潮，尽管"现有的海底电缆还有大量潜在性能尚未被充分开发"⑥。

数字化衰退要求这一行业实行非均衡定价策略。网络运营商面对选择性价格竞争；并且，随着消费者市场的日趋饱和，与金融危机的持续，语音服务和某些国家整体的增长率为负⑦。在经济合作与发展组织的富裕成员国里，运营商收入在2008至2009年间下

---

① Jeffrey Keefe and Rosemary Batt, "United States," in *Telecommunications: Restructuring Work and Employment Relations Worldwide*, ed. Harry Katz (Ithaca, N. Y.: Cornell University Press,1997),33 – 43.
② Anton Troianovski, "Verizon Pursues Tough Line on Labor," *Wall Street Journal*, July 13,2011.
③ Kim Moody, *U. S. Labor in Trouble and Transition* (London: Verso,2007),54.
④ Greg Bensinger and Spencer E. Ante, "Verizon Strike Turns Nasty," *Wall Street Journal*, August 9,2011;Steven Greenhouse, "Verizon Landline Unit at Heart of Strike," *New York Times*, August 11,2011.
⑤ Dan Schiller, "End of the Telecom Revolution," *Le Monde diplomatique*, August 2003,28 – 29;Dan Schiller, *How to Think about Information*,80 – 100.
⑥ "Submarine Cable Construction Continues Despite Untapped Potential Capacity," *TeleGeography*, CommsUpdate, April 18, 2012.
⑦ "Service Provider Revenue Growth Bounces Back in Q3," *TeleGeography*, Comms Update, November 17,2010;Jenna Wortham, "Data Networks Pose a Threat to Wireless," *New York Times*, May 16,2011.

跌 5%①。然而,大规模的网络运营商依然赚得盆满钵满。究其实,按照经济合作与发展组织的解释,它们的寡头垄断地位、捆绑式服务营销、长期(有效)合同,以及通信服务逐渐被(人们)视为日常必需的支出项目的事实,都能解释这一(利润增长)现象;这样,"那些试图节约日常开支的普通家庭就能在其他方面避免浪费,至少作为第一节流标准"②。

　　普通家庭的财产多寡,视乎数字化衰退如何改变本土经验而定。尤其在遭受(数字化衰退)严重打击的南欧地区,2011 年初的经济停滞与失业率,意味着消费者必须减少有关电信方面的支出;而移动通讯服务所产生的收入,与每位用户的平均收入都在锐减③(对此,欧洲监管者采取措施,例如削减移动数据漫游费——这曾经是承运商获取丰厚利润的来源,以刺激消费④)。在爱尔兰、希腊和西班牙等备受(数字化衰退)折磨的国家,网络运营商四处触礁。一面是爱尔兰的智能手机用户数依然保持增长势头⑤,另一面则是爱尔兰电信(Eircom)的破产——可谓该国历史上规模最大的一起企业破产案例⑥。当国有企业希腊电信(OTE)被迫向德国电信出售其一成的股份,以减少其庞大的国内债务后,希腊电信在 2012 年第一季度的收入与去年同期相比,下降了 5%;其固网电话业务下跌了近 12%,固定宽带业务下跌 2.3%。希腊电信要求旗下雇员接受工资削减计划,以保有现有工作⑦。2012 年,德国电信(在希腊电信中)的股份上升至 40%⑧。西班牙电信公司(Telefonica)对外宣布,出于保护股东红利之目的,它将裁员 20%;可两年后,这家承运商的用户数仍然只减不升⑨。在法国四家运营商之间展开激烈的价格战,促使本国市场领导者法国电信(France Telecom,27% 国家所有)不得不出售其股份,或考虑进行合资企业改造,甚至合并⑩。哪怕在美国,尽管有两家承运商维持赢利状态,可经济不景气使大约三分之一的美国家庭停掉了有线(电视)服务,这对于收入锐减的有线电视行业而言,

---

① Organisation for Economic Cooperation and Development (OECD), *Communications Outlook* 2011 (Washington: OECD, 2011), 1.
② OECD, *Communications Outlook* 2011, 1.
③ Andrew Parker, "Telecoms Operators Feel the Pressure," *Financial Times*, June 10, 2011.
④ Kevin J. O'Brien, "In Europe, a Move to Slash Phone Roaming Charges," *New York Times*, July 6, 2011.
⑤ "Vodafone Ireland Reports 48% of Users Now Own Smartphones," *TeleGeography*, CommsUpdate, February 8, 2013.
⑥ Robin Wigglesworth and Daniel Thomas, "Hutchison Whampoa Bids Euro2bn for Bankrupt Eircom," *Financial Times*, May 5/6, 2012.
⑦ Jack Ewing, "In Asset Sale, Greece to Give up 10% Stake in Telecom Company," *New York Times*, June 7, 2011; "OTE's Group EBITDA Up 6.2%, Greek Figure Down 5.5%," *TeleGeography*, CommsUpdate, May 10, 2012.
⑧ Cornelius Rahn, "Deutsche Telekom's Greek Ambitions End with Cash Crunch," *Bloomberg Business Week*, June 26, 2012, available at http://www.bloomberg.com/news/2012-06-25/deutsche-telekom-s-greek-ambitions-end-with-cash-crunch.html (accessed January 10, 2014).
⑨ Andrew Parker, "Telefonica to Cut Spanish Workforce by 20% but Vows to Increase Dividends," *Financial Times*, April 15, 2011; "Net Debt Cut but Writedowns and Domestic Woes Hit Telefonica," *TeleGeography*, CommsUpdate, February 28, 2013.
⑩ Daniel Thomas and James Boxell, "Merger Ruled Out as France Telecom Eyes Other Deals," *Financial Times*, July 26, 2012.

几近雪上加霜①。

第四大趋势是,随着网络服务与应用程序的发展,占领那些能带来丰厚利润的新的战略领域(这一经济行为)再次出现,这其中包括通信(产业)商品链所发生的令人眼花缭乱的变革。

作为资本主义全球化重要的非本质属性,国际电话业务量在过去20年里的复合年增长率为13%;据估计,2010年共通话4 130亿分钟。然而,1990年代末,人们早已经预见语音通讯的互联网应用服务的火爆前景②。国际语音(通讯)业务在2008年明显放缓,不仅因为经济不景气所致,还与讯佳普(Skype)这家创立于2003年随后在2011年被微软收购的互联网语音协议服务提供商有关。2008年至2010年间,讯佳普的使用量翻了三番,长达1 900亿分钟;2011年它对外宣称月用户数高达1.7亿人次③。讯佳普所产生的国际话务量,是世界上所有电话公司加在一起所产生的话务总量的两倍;于是,仅在5年内,讯佳普一跃成为世界上最大的跨境语音通讯供应商④。尽管讯佳普终结了一个庞大的产业,可它的收入依然不足为外人道,尤其与传统的跨境电话产业收入相比,更显得微不足道(2010年,前者是8.6亿美元,后者则高达830亿美元)⑤。付费用户只是讯佳普用户基数极小的一部分(2009年810万人)⑥。其他替代性的通讯应用程序也开始流行起来:2014年,即时通讯程序"有事吗"(WhatsApp)、脸书即时通(Facebook Messenger)、共鸣(Viber),以及移动视频通话应用"探戈"通讯(Tango)、谷歌群聊(Google Hangouts)与三星旗下的"聊天"应用(ChatOn),每一项应用都在谷歌市场(Google Play)的在线应用商店上被下载和安装逾亿次⑦。

讯佳普的经验很好理解:"当前,通信产业的大部分价值已限于基础连接性(业务)

---

① Bensinger and Ante, "Verizon Strike Turns Nasty"; Steven Greenhouse, "Verizon Landline Unit"; U. S. FCC, *Implementation of Section* 6002(*b*) *of the Omnibus Budget Reconciliation Act of* 1993, WT Docket No. 11 – 186, adopted March 19, 2013, 25 – 26.

② Dan Schiller, *Digital Capitalism*, 26.

③ Richard Waters, Maija Palmer, and Tim Bradshaw, "Knocking at the Door of Tech Heaven," *Financial Times*, May 11, 2011.

④ "Microsoft's Acquisition of Skype," *TeleGeography*, CommsUpdate, May 11, 2011; "International Long – Distance Slumps, While Skype Soars," *TeleGeography*, The Feed, January 6, 2011; Joe Nocera, "The Cloud Hanging over Skype," *New York Times*, September 5, 2009; David Gelles and Maija Palmer, "Skype Deal Stumbles over Software Row," *Financial Times*, September 17, 2009.

⑤ Waters, Palmer, and Bradshaw, "Knocking"; Paul Taylor, "Skype's Changing Traffic Growth," *Financial Times*, May 10, 2011.

⑥ Maija Palmer, "Valuation Adds to Bubble Fears," *Financial Times*, May 11, 2011; David Gelles, "Skype Begins Move to List on Nasdaq," *Financial Times*, August 10, 2010; "Skype's Share of the Long – Distance Pie on the Increase," *TeleGeography*, CommsUpdate, March 24, 2009.

⑦ "Skype Traffic Continues to Thrive," *TeleGeography*, CommsUpdate, January 15, 2014.

上","像谷歌、苹果、思科这些公司而非承运商向消费者提供"①即时通信、语音与视频通话,以及网络会议等(新)业务。在美国,投资在承运商只能获得个位数回报,而"像网飞(Netflix)、苹果等这些业务依赖于(承运商)网络的企业,它们的投资回报率则高出数倍"②。然而,由于(承运商的)网络依然对它们的运营起着至关重要的作用,因此,网络运营商下定决心扳回一城,扭转局势;更主要的原因还在于,虽然数字化衰退在2009年到达最低点③,可它们的基础设施依然需要花费巨资进行升级以容纳日益增长的数据流④。但是,还有不少因素交织在一起,阻碍网络运营商实现它们的雄心壮志,即在网络产业商品链上占领或至少能进入那些具有战略意义、高利润的领域。承运商要面对和处理的问题包括:时紧时松的规制⑤、加诸在每用户平均收入上的慢性压力,以及智能手机供应商与打破现有局面的网络应用程序所形成的强大竞争力。

谁来承担这新一轮的现代化周期的成本？它如何改变既有的贸易条件？对运营商而言,传送一条文字或语音信息所需成本微乎其微;可建立足够的网络连接(系统)以满足每月数十亿次的搜索请求的开销就不容小觑了。谷歌、亚马逊、苹果、脸书与微软都争先恐后地建造服务器群,那么,谁来负担大型服务器群之间激增的互联网内容的运输费用？据估计,这一基于云计算的流量将占2016年的网络总流量的三分之二(2011年已占总流量的三分之一);用户数、设备与传感器数量、下载应用程序的总量,以及流媒体内容数量都实现了高速增长⑥。

网络运营商竭尽全力,希望能充分利用它们所拥有的优势地位,例如将它们的业务捆绑销售;或重组网络商品链("纵向市场")从而实现多样化经营;或推进调整同依靠网络(才能维持运营的)服务提供商之间的贸易条件。因此,矛盾频生;并且,处于不同位置的竞争者或扩大或保有它们的地盘,于是,部分竞争行为转向政治领域。对这些行为,我将作简要评述。

许多承运商向消费者提供语音、电视与上网的打包服务,这被称为"三网融合"(triple

---

① Charles S. Golvin of Forrester Research, quoted in Jenna Wortham, "Data Networks Pose a Threat to Wireless," *New York Times*, May 16, 2011; Daniel Thomas and Tim Bradshaw, "Mobile Groups Face Off with 'Killer Text Apps,'" *Financial Times*, April 29, 2013; Daniel Thomas and Tim Bradshaw, "Rapid Rise of Chat Apps Slims SMS Cash Cow for Mobile Operators," *Financial Times*, April 29, 2013.
② "Data Prices," The Lex Column, *Financial Times*, June 19, 2012.
③ ITU, Confronting the Crisis: Its Impact on the ICT Industry (Geneva: ITU, February 2009), 11, 37 – 39, available at at http://www.itu.int/osg/csd/emerging_trends/crisis/report – low – res.pdf (accessed January 10, 2014).
④ Wortham, "Data Networks."
⑤ Kathrin Hille, "Chinese Telecoms Bow to Regulator," *Financial Times*, December 2, 2011, available at http://www.ft.com/intl/cms/s/0/1260a290 – 1cd3 – 11e1 – 8daf – 00144feabdc0.html#axzz1fZTPtYTu (accessed January 10, 2014) 向我们提供了一个有趣的个案。
⑥ ITU, *Trends In Telecommunications Reform* 2013, 3 – 4. On this see Vincent Mosco, *To the Cloud: Big Data in a Turbulent World* (Boulder, Colo.: Paradigm, 2014).

play)。倘若加入移动服务,分析家估计又会称之为"四网融合"(quadruple play)。电视市场是最令商家梦寐以求的战利品。威瑞森曾豪掷230亿美元,意在通过光缆使大都市地区的美国家庭与企业直接享受到3D电视、超高清电视、高清视频会议与多人(线上)游戏等业务;随后,它便放缓了这一扩张战略。威瑞森进军视频行业的势头一直持续到2014年;一面是它的光纤视频服务拥有530万用户,与此同时,它也向客户推销在线电视流媒体服务,并计划通过它的蜂窝网络推送视频①。2012年,电信运营商提供的交互式网络电视(IPTV)服务在世界范围内拥有6 700万订阅户②,这一数字大约占全球8.12亿付费电视用户的8%。有趣的是,提供电视服务(无论是交互式网络电视还是其他模式)的承运商(移动或电信运营商)三强分别是:美洲移动(AmericaMovil)、中国电信与俄罗斯电信(RostelCom)③;法国电信、德国电信与威瑞森则组成第二梯队。电视商品链依然充满活力,尤其在亚洲,在线视频服务的火爆证明了这一点;在线视频不仅包括YouTube、网飞,还包括中国的PPTV(现在应当包括优土、搜狐、爱奇艺、迅雷等)。2011年,PPTV的月活跃用户数高达1.05亿人次④。

威瑞森或美国电话电报公司等电信企业在迎合商业用户上所具有的传统实力,使它们拥有康卡斯特这些有线电视系统运营商所不具备的(竞争)优势,因为后者主要面向家庭用户市场⑤。然而,欧洲和美国大型的有线电视运营商采取进入企业服务市场并推广它们的三重业务战略等方式(试图扭转局势);到了2011年,世界范围内的有线电视运营商拥有超过1亿的宽带用户,以及6 500万视频订户⑥。随着有线电视与电信企业之间的竞争日趋白热化,康卡斯特这家美国最大的有线电视公司也一举成为美国最大的消费者互联网服务提供商。重要之处在于,康卡斯特不仅把它的资源整合进它的网络基础设施中(本书付梓出版时,它以450亿美元对时代华纳有线电视公司的收购案悬而未决),更耗资数十亿美元从通用电气手上收购美国国家广播环球公司(2011年联邦通讯委员签字批

---

① "Verizon Completes 1Gbps GPON Field Trial," *TeleGeography*, CommsUpdate, August 18, 2010; Brian X. Chen and Quentin Hardy, "Verizon Plans to Buy Intel Media Division to Expand Its Television Services," *New York Times*, January 22, 2014.

② "Key Subscribers Milestones Passed as Telcos and Cablecos Battle It Out," *TeleGeography*, CommsUpdate, September 21, 2011; "IPTV Broadband Penetration Reaches 15 Percent, Growth Prospects Are Patchy," *TeleGeography*, The Feed, June 20, 2012.

③ "Telco Pay – TV Subscribers Approaching 100 Million," *TeleGeography*, CommsUpdate January 23, 2012.

④ Pyungho Kim, "Internet Protocol TV in Perspective: A Matrix of Continuity and Innovation," *Television & New Media* 10, no. 6 (November 2009): 536–45; "Softbank Buys 35% Stake in Chinese Online TV Provider Synacast," *TeleGeography*, CommsUpdate, February 4, 2011.

⑤ 中国移动或美国威瑞森等市场领导者现有网络的规模与容量,以及资本支出(例如威瑞森2009年支出逾170亿美元,2010支出与前一年持平),都是任何一家有线电视公司无法比拟的。具体请参见Roger Cheng, "Wireless Carriers Sow Confusion Over 4G" *Wall Street Journal*, November 4, 2010。

⑥ "Key Subscriber Milestones," *TeleGeography*, June 20, 2012.

准),以此整合媒体内容①。当网络电视(OTT)业务开始搅动有线电视与电信公司现有的贸易条件时②,它们更无所不用其极,旨在掌控电视服务市场。

康卡斯特进军内容生产领域,只是网络运营商开发所谓的"垂直市场"的一个典型案例。它们以现有业务拓宽"垂直市场",从电视到机器通信,从金融到健康医疗,从公共设施服务到电子商务。③ 作为垂直市场的全球领导者,日本电话电报公司下属的多科莫公司(NTT DoCoMo)计划在2015年完成占公司总收入五分之一的创收目标,即100亿欧元④。东亚地区,承运商对应用程序的开发与推广令人印象最为深刻;不少承运商正在向应用服务提供商转型,旨在提供包括手机铃声与移动金融服务等在内的一切业务。

承运商也加快步伐,尝试使诸如谷歌、脸书、苹果、亚马逊与网飞这些互联网中介商为网络数据买单⑤。它们向规制者上书请愿,并声称,只有向中介商收取不同的费用,它们才能够提高投资基金,进而对其宽带网络进行现代化改造⑥。当然,它们也不忘向中介商示好:网络运营商若能优先选择并引导网络流量,不仅可以实现有利于自身利益的运营效率,也能向网络中介商(以一定价格)提供它们中意的传送模式。

这样的"服务质量"首创行为使承运商不得不面对规制政策长期以来坚守的原则。到2012年,只有两个国家(智利和荷兰⑦)通过完整的立法程序颁布法律,要求在互联网上传输数据包时必须遵守非歧视原则,有时被称为"网络中立"原则;但是,大部分欧洲与北美国家早已实现了毫无偏见地传送其他实体的数据流(这一目标)⑧。

总体而言,美国的网络运营商向各类互联网服务提供商不同程度地开放它们的网络系统,也没有给予它们的子公司或特定客户专属特权。然而,随着网络运营商日渐壮大,

---

① David Gelles and Andrew Edgeclife-Johnson, "Comcast Deal Set to Reshape Media Industry," *Financial Times*, January 20, 2011; Brian Stelter and Tim Arango, "Comcast Spends Big in Pressing for Merger," *New York Times*, September 27, 2010; David Pogue, "Cable TV in Pursuit of Mobility," *New York Times*, March 2, 2011; Cecilia King, "Comcast, Time Warner Cable Agree to Merge in $45 Billion Deal," *Washington Post*, February 12, 2014.

② Shalini Ramachandran and Thomas Gryta, "Telecoms Selling TV Have Bigger Impact on Cable Firms," *Wall Street Journal*, November 1, 2013.

③ Derek Baldwin, "Telecoms Seek Alternate Income from Global Internet Giants," Gulf-news. com, October 5, 2011, available at http://gulfnews.com/business/features/telecoms-seek-alternate-income-from-global-internet-giants-1.885011 (accessed January 10, 2014).

④ Mary Lennighan, "Vertically Challenged," *TotalTelecom*, May 2012, 13.

⑤ Andrew Parker, "Telecoms Groups in Push for Internet Shake-Up," *Financial Times*, April 27, 2011; Simon Kuper, "Le Self-Made Man: Xavier Niel," *Financial Times*, May 4-5, 2013.

⑥ Andrew Parker and Stanley Pignal, "Push to End 'Free Lunch' for Content Providers," *Financial Times*, February 14, 2011; Andrew Parker and Tim Bradshaw, "European Telecoms Groups Seeking to Shake-Up Content Charging Models," *Financial Times*, July 12, 2011; Andrew Parker and Stanley Pignal, "EU Warned on Broadband Targets," *Financial Times*, July 14, 2011; Amy Graham, "How Carriers Will Make Money (from you) on 4G," CNN. com, November 10, 2011.

⑦ "Upper House Ratifies Dutch Net Neutrality Law," *TeleGeography*, CommsUpdate, May 10, 2012.

⑧ 关于美国情况,请参见 FCC 10 201, GN Docket 09-191, WC Docket 07-52, "In the Matter of Preserving the Open Internet Broadband Industry Practices," report and order released December 23, 2010.

并向前整合进入内容与应用程序领域,它们也求助于规制者和法院,希望获得授权,能在网络传送数据时进行区别对待。

于是,美国的有线电视公司与电信承运商提起系列诉讼,耗时数年。美国的政策规制者似乎没有从19世纪铁路时代的经验中吸取教训,反而变本加厉:不仅拒绝对互联网服务进行重新归类,坚持将其置于通用的承运商规则范围之内;而且,他们从法律层面区分了有线电视、电话网和移动网络。无疑,这番区分埋下了(打破现有稳定局面)隐患。移动系统可以更加随心所欲地采取歧视性措施,保护自己的商业利益①。法院裁定,因为联邦通信委员会没有将互联网服务归在"电信"领域,所以针对一般承运商的非歧视性条款不适用于承运商传输互联网数据这一情况。威瑞森无线起诉联邦通信委员会,认为委员会对网络中立性的处理没有上心,且违反了言论自由原则:威瑞森无线认为其应当比网飞等公司能以更符合自身利益的方式提供旗下的视频服务②。2014年1月,威瑞森赢得这场官司③。法庭认定,联邦通信委员会事实上对比原定计划更多的互联网中介机构拥有规制权限④:因而问题不在于委员会权限范围,而在于委员会如何配置这一监管权力。联邦通信委员会很少进行特定坚决的干预行为,承运商与网飞、谷歌等互联网公司就贸易条件展开的协商行为,都有可能遮蔽那些不为人所知的、主张民主且负责任的互联网通讯的诉求⑤。

根据胡亨利(Henry L. Hu)的看法,中国的政策制定根本不考虑"网络中立性的某些价值",因为七大骨干网络服务商与许多地方网络服务商处在无远弗届、复杂(却不完备)的政府审查系统之中⑥。然而,在中国要实现网络连接的统一性这一贸易条件,并非易

---

① Sascha D. Meinrath, James W. Losey, and Victor W. Pickard, "Digital Feudalism: Enclosures and Erasures from Digital Rights Management to the Digital Divide," *CommLaw Conspectus* 19, no. 2 (2011), 435–37.
② Marguerite Reardon, "Verizon to FCC: Free Speech Trumps Net Neutrality Rules," *C/Net*, July 3, 2012, available at http://news.cnet.com/8301-13578_3-57465695-38/verizon-to-fcc-free-speech-trumps-net-neutrality-rules (accessed January 10, 2014); Steve Musil, "Senate Confirms Tom Wheeler as FCC's New Chairman," *C/Net*, October 29, 2013, available at http://news.cnet.com/8301-1035_3-57609923-94/senate-confirms-tom-wheeler-as-fccs-new-chairman (accessed January 10, 2014).
③ Sam Gustin, "'Net Neutrality' Ruling Paves the Way For Internet 'Fast Lanes,'" *Time*, January 15, 2014; and, 关于法庭裁决的范围,请登录 http://www.cadc.uscourts.gov/internet/opinions.nsf/3AF8B4D938CDEEA685257C6000532062/$file/1355-1474943.pdf (accessed February 1, 2014).
④ Marvin Ammori, "Is the Internet Closing?" *Weekly Wonk*, January 16, 2014, available at http://weeklywonk.newamerica.net/articles/net-neutrality/ (accessed February 2, 2014); Edward Wyatt, "Industry and Congress Await the F.C.C. Chairman's Next Moves on Internet Rules," *New York Times*, February 10, 2014.
⑤ Edward Wyatt and Noam Cohen, "Comcast and Netflix Reach Deal on Service," *New York Times*, February 24, 2014.
⑥ Henry L. Hu, "The Political Economy of Governing ISPs in China: Perspectives of Net Neutrality and Vertical Integration," *China Quarterly* 207 (September 2011): 523–40, at 538 and 539. 要了解不同形式的技术监控,请参见"China," in *Access Controlled: The Shaping of Power, Rights, and Rule in Cyberspace*, ed. Ronald Deibert, John Palfrey, Rafal Rohozinski, and Jonathan Zittrain, 449–87 (Cambridge, Mass.: MIT Press, 2010). 将言论自由与国家审查置于由社会阶级关系所结构化的社会里加以考察,可参见赵月枝, *Communication in China* (Lanham, Md.: Rowman and Littlefield, 2008).

事,因为国有网络运营商、OTT服务提供商与作为竞争对手的国家有关部门之间的利益纷争(短时期内)无法得到解决①。

整个西欧,围绕数据传输条件而展开的论争却呈现另一种面貌。西欧排名前五的网络内容提供商全都是美国公司。像德国电信、法国电信与西班牙电信公司完全可以将非歧视条款视为不公平待遇而大加鞭挞,因为它让谷歌、脸书及其附属公司占尽便宜,并使欧洲进一步地依赖美国信息、媒体与文化产业(所提供的产品)②。到了2013年,这一情况促使法国(以及欧洲议会)颁布"第二条款";原本旨在保护法国音乐与电影制作产业的文化例外政策,如今也要进行修订,以适用于数字媒体行业③。

因此,基础设施建设与基本的网络连接服务依然至关重要,只是有关数据传输的贸易条件(被称为"媒体融合"时期的1980与1990年代的实践基础)仍旧处于变化不定的状态之中。安德鲁·奥德泽科(Andrew Odlyzko)指出,基本问题在于"服务提供商对社会所信赖的数据(比特)拥有多大程度的控制权"④。随着各自为政的中介商逐渐渗透到国家机构中进而寻求市场优势,政治干预肯定还将继续存在。而当移动网络流量的疯狂增长再次使论争聚焦于智能手机与平板电脑,这一议题又呈现出另外一种维度⑤。

苹果在手机市场上所取得的非凡成绩,极大地瓦解了与移动服务基础设施相连的商品链。实际上,苹果手机从整体上改变了网络政治经济情势。智能手机与平板电脑广泛的普及程度使得数据而非语音成为移动服务的中流砥柱⑥。无线基础设施已经迈向第三以及第四代⑦。不同的技术标准分别得到不同的制造商与网络运营商的支持⑧。并且,从一种技术标准跨入下一种技术标准(进行技术升级),必将导致产业的更新换代。国际市场纷争更加剧了这一趋势。中国试图建立一种本土性的技术标准,当前围绕中国移动与华为公司的崛起、印度用户数最多的承运商巴帝电信(Bharti Airtel),以及计划采用中国

---

① Hu, "Political Economy," 538, 540; "China Mobile Blames Rivals, OTT Products for Slip in Profits," *TeleGeography*, CommsUpdate, October 22, 2013. 关于中国言论自由的社会特征,以及与社会网络和其他数字服务相关的中间立场的其他文献,请参见期刊 Javnost 专辑 "Communication and the Class Divide in China," *Javnost* 19, no. 2 (2012), available at http://javnost-thepublic.org/issue/2012/2 (accessed January 10, 2014).
② "Net Neutrality," The Lex Column, *Financial Times*, January 5, 2011.
③ Peter Aspden, "Europe Casts Hollywood as the Bad-Guy," *Financial Times*, May 11/12, 2013; Hugh Carnegy, "France Touches on Idea of iTax for Tablets to Help Fund the Arts," *Financial Times*, May 14, 2013; David Jolly, "A Tax to Shore Up French Culture," *International Herald Tribune*, May 15, 2013.
④ Andrew Odlyzko, "Network Neutrality, Search Neutrality, and the Never-Ending Conflict between Efficiency and Fairness in Markets," *Review of Network Economics* 8, no. 1 (March 2009): 41.
⑤ 有线系统运营商与网络电视视频服务之间产生的富有政治意味的争斗及其个案,请参见 Thomas Catan and Amy Schatz, "U.S. Probes Cable for Limits on Net Video," *Wall Street Journal*, June 13, 2012.
⑥ Jenna Wortham, "Cellphones Now Used More for Data Than for Calls," *New York Times*, May 13, 2010.
⑦ "14% of Wireless Subs Connected to 3G Networks," *TeleGeography*, CommsUpdate, December 3, 2010.
⑧ Maija Palmer and Chris Nuttall, "Intel Succumbs to Evolution of 4G," *Financial Times*, August 17, 2010.

移动技术标准的日本软银企业(Softbank),该目标得以复兴①。

此处,更有效地运用频谱资源的需求成为重要因素。移动设备之间海量数据的传递引发关于频谱资源可用性的尖锐问题。部分美国学者认为,主要通过未经授权的频谱服务而实现的频率共用,在向移动宽带转型过程中发挥着关键性的作用②。排他性的许可经营制度所导致的效率低下现象(即慢性浪费,例如许多频段资源要么尚未使用要么未充分加以利用③),常被作为论据,用以佐证(频谱)配置政策需要进行全面修订。艾里·诺姆(Eli Noam)坚称,由于缺乏根本性的(政策)变革,频谱资源的短缺有可能成为阻碍发展的因素④。

于是,时任联邦通信委员会主席在2011年宣称:"从全球范围来看,思科企业从2009到2015年,对频谱资源的需求增长了60倍"⑤。同年另一位分析家指出:"对于规制者而言,频谱(资源)是当前的头号议程",尤其在2012至2013年间,它成为政策制定者的当务之急⑥。那么,用以扩张高利润的移动宽带市场的频谱资源应当如何分配?

一种回应是,提供免费的全国性无线网络⑦。倘若强势的市场行动者依据现有体制已经阻碍了资本的总体积累(一如拆分前的美国电话电报公司那样)这一事实,要求进行体制改革,那么有可能实现(全国性无线网络)战略。然而,直到最近,另一种方向的改革措施得以确立。1950年代在知识界处于边缘地带的观点⑧,即支持建立频谱资源的产权制度,反倒在近期有可能被合法化。美国从1994年开始,频谱拍卖取代了此前公共服务的各种形式;在接下来的十年里,拍卖制度扩展至全球的大部分地区。当然,拍卖制度赋予那些能够动用大笔资金的个体或企业以特权,让它们享有开发频谱资源的独家(却有限的)权利。联邦通信委员会在2008年的拍卖产生190亿美元的交易额,购买主体均为美国无线承运商⑨。为了获得梦寐以求的频谱资源而展开的"厮杀",导致移动承运商、谷歌和微软这样的互联网中介商以及消费电子产品企业形成暂时联盟,共同对抗现有的电

---

① Owen Fletcher, "Cell Shackles Crumble," *Wall Street Journal*, July 12, 2011.
② Meinrath, Losey, and Pickard, "Digital Feudalism," 435 – 37; Michael Calabrese, "Solving the 'Spectrum Crunch': Unlicensed Spectrum on a High – Fiber Diet," Time Warner Cable Research Program on Digital Communications Report Series, Fall 2013, available at http://twcresearchprogram.com (accessed January 10, 2014).
③ 请参见 Meinrath, Losey, and Pickard, "Digital Feudalism," 435.
④ Eli, "Let Them Eat Cellphones".
⑤ FCC Chairman Julius Genachowski, Remarks as Prepared for Delivery, "The Cloud: Unleashing Global Opportunities," Aspen IDEA Project, Brussels, Belgium, March 24, 2011, 3.
⑥ Ian Kemp, "Spectrum Spats," *TotalTelecom*, September 2011, 1.
⑦ Cecilia King, "Tech, Telecom Giants Take Sides as FCC Proposes Large Public WiFi Networks," *Washington Post*, February 3, 2013; Michael Calabrese, "Why the Feds Should Promote Wi – Fi Everywhere," slate.com, February 8, 2013.
⑧ Ronald Coase, "The Federal Communications Commission," *Journal of Law and Economics* 2, no. 2 (1959): 1 – 40.
⑨ Executive Office of the President, Council of Economic Advisors, "The Economic Benefits of New Spectrum for Wireless Broadband," February 2012, 18, 5.

视台与所谓的"公共安全"申索人(大部分来自警察与执法部门)①。但是,在苹果取得令人嫉恨的成功后,那些大型互联网中介商同承运商,都试图借助未经授权的频谱资源作为改变双方贸易条件的可能方式而展开竞争。与此同时,《中产阶级税收减免和增加就业 2012 法案》(the Middle‑Class Tax Relief and Job Creation Act of 2012)批准美国联邦通信委员会可以举办额外的拍卖活动②。

移动(媒体)的使用趋势导致对频谱资源的争夺与日俱增。语音电话不是不赚钱;在微信或苹果简讯服务(iMessenger)使(传统的)手机短信服务相形见绌之前,后者还是有利可图的(短信服务曾实现跨越式增长,美国无线电话用户在 2009 年 6 月至 2010 年之间发送文字短信共计 173 万亿条)③。可随着智能手机的成倍增长,数据流量很明显成为重要的增长节点。2009 年,文本信息、电子邮件、视频流、音乐以及其他数据服务超过移动电话语音服务④;2012 年,全世界排名前 1% 的移动电话用户所消耗的流量不及(通过智能手机、平板电脑与笔记本电脑无线上网所产生的)无线数据吞吐量的一半⑤。工程升级速度与手机基站的增长密度远远不够(2012 年仅在美国就有 26 万座基站⑥)。美国电话电报公司眼睁睁地看着移动数据在自己的网络里以令人惊愕的速度增长:从 2007 年至 2009 年共增长 5 000%⑦。

对此,美国承运商将频谱资源锁定在最有利的频段上,从而树立另一种它们所希望的准入门槛。2010 到 2013 年间,美国电话电报公司展开了一系列的频谱购买与报价协商活动,意在收购德国电信公司(T‑Mobile)⑧;此举将它的频谱拥有量提高 60%,并主要集中在苹果手机客户聚集的都市地区。然而,此项交易却被美国政府叫停。讽刺之处在

---

① Jonathan Spalter, "Should Some of Broadcasters' Spectrum Be Auctioned Off to Wireless Carriers?" *Wall Street Journal*, November 15, 2011; Amy Schatz, "Fight for Airwaves Set to Continue," *Wall Street Journal*, November 23, 2011. 同样,以第四代无线宽带技术为基础的系统,也提出有关频谱资源的诉求,后者此前大多专供卫星通信使用,请参见 Paul Taylor, "LightSquared Wins Waiver on 4G network," *Financial Times*, January 27, 2011.
② "Summary of the Middle Class Tax Relief and Job Creation Act of 2012," U. S. Senate Committee on Finance, available at http://www.finance.senate.gov/newsroom/chairman/release/?id=c42a8c8a‑52ad‑44af‑86b2‑4695aaff5378 (accessed January 10, 2014).
③ Cecilia Kang, "For Telecoms, Success Rests in Mobile Web Access," *Washington Post*, March 22, 2011.
④ Wortham, "Cellphones."
⑤ Kevin J. O'Brien, "Top 1% of Mobile Users Consume Half of World's Bandwidth, and Gap Is Growing," *New York Times*, January 6, 2012.
⑥ Noam, "Let Them Eat Cellphones."
⑦ Kevin J. O'Brien, "Getting What You Pay for on the Mobile Internet," *New York Times*, April 18, 2010.
⑧ Amy Schatz, "AT&T Is Set Back on Qualcomm Proposal," *Wall Street Journal*, August 10, 2011; Andrew Parker and Paul Taylor, "Spectrum at the Heart of AT&T's Audacious Move," *Financial Times*, March 22, 2011; "AT&T Buys Spectrum," The Lex Column, *Financial Times*, December 21, 2010; Associated Press, "Merger and Acquisitions in Telecoms, at a Glance," Boston.com, July 12, 2013.

于,美国电话电报公司不得不把自己的频谱资源转让给德国电信,以退出交易①。威瑞森无线与几家主要的有线电视集团联合进行市场营销,借此它获得市值36亿美元的频谱资源,并从美国蜂窝(U. S. Cellular)下属的一家子公司手上收购美国53个县的频谱资源②。美国第三大移动网络斯普林特获得对科维公司(Clearwire,无线宽带业务零售商)的全面控制权,旨在提升其频谱资产的价值,正如斯普林特被日本软银收购(意在提升后者的市值)③。美国最大的两家移动承运商充分开发其拥有的无可匹敌的频谱资源,不仅试图巩固它们的市场地位,也是为了向其客户推销含有月度使用上限的流量套餐④。

网络运营商采用一种互为补充的无线技术,迫不及待地开发另一种频谱带宽。1980年代中期,美国联邦通信委员会批准了此前未经许可的频谱;1990年代中期,这些频谱资源被整合进无线网络(Wi-Fi networks);2011年,成千上万或免费或付费的无线热点散布在144个国家的公共建筑、酒店、商厦、咖啡厅、饭店以及其他场所⑤。无线上网技术也被用于受到资助的(网络)连接业务。甚至在苹果手机出现之前,电信与有线运营商也能接入无线网络;2007年之前,美国、西欧与日本现有的部分移动承运商成为商业(无线)热点的顶级运营商⑥。美国电话电报公司2008年斥巨资(2.75亿美元)收购(网络)热点提供商中转企业(Wayport)后,一举成为大型(无线网络)运营商⑦。2010年至2013年,中国移动建造了据说是世界上最大的、由承运商主导的无线网络,共包含600万个接入点⑧;在中国东海的另一边,日本的移动承运商凯迪迪爱(KDDI)株式会社计划将它的无线热点增加10倍,总数达10万。在美国,5家最大的有线电视运营商共同建造了一张拥

---

① Gerrit Weismann and Helen Thomas, "Berlin Fears Grow over T-Mobile's US disposal," *Financial Times*, December 2, 2011.
② Brian Stelter, "With Verizon's $3.6 Billion Deal, Cable and Wireless Inch Closer," *New York Times*, November 3, 2011; "Verizon Strikes Deal to Acquire AWS Spectrum from US Cellular Affiliate," TeleGeography, CommsUpdate October 29, 2013.
③ Paul Taylor, "Sprint Investors Vote for SoftBank Takeover," *Financial Times*, June 26, 2013.
④ Peter Svensson, Associated Press, "Data Caps," *Denver Post*, July 6, 2011; "French Telcos Consider Capping 'Unlimited' Web Access," *TeleGeography*, CommsUpdate, August 22, 2011; Anton Troianovski and Thomas Gryta, "Verizon Overhauls Wireless Plans," *Wall Street Journal*, June 13, 2012.
⑤ Thanks to Ethan D. Schiller for some of the sources used in this paragraph. JiWire Global WiFiFinder, available at http://v4.jiwire.com/search-hotspot-locations.htm (accessed January 10, 2014).
⑥ "Broadband Wireless Exchange's 'Top Ten' Wi-Fi Hotspot Operators," available at http://www.bbwexchange.com/top10_wi-fi_hotspot_operators.asp (accessed January 10, 2014).
⑦ Glen Fleishman, "AT&T Now Biggest Hotspot Provider with Wayport Buy," Arstechnica, November 6, 2008, available at http://arstechnica.com/uncategorized/2008/11/atampt-becomes-worlds-largest-wifi-hotspot-provider-with-wayport-acquisition (accessed January 10, 2014).
⑧ "China Mobile Taps WiFi to Break Bandwidth Bottleneck," *TeleGeography*, Comms Update, June 28, 2013.

有 5 万热点的(无线)网络①。上述举动并非仅仅在未来的竞争中先下手为强,顾客对智能手机尤其是平板电脑的普遍接受,对承运商的移动网络造成很大的(流量)负担,承运商无非将这一负担转嫁到无线网络上②。

移动业务极大地减少了一个多世纪以来所形成的传统本地与长途(拨号)电话业务。但是,无线网络的发展经验告诉我们,这并未阻止有线网络承运商成为无线业务中的佼佼者。然而,发达市场经济体的移动承运商却难以在亚非拉地区吸引更多的无线网络用户③。这造成另一重要的趋势:世界的无线网络用户数不断增加,可总部设在富裕国家的网络承运商所拥有的用户数却在减少。

一个诱发因素在于,全球迈入无线网络时代,是速度不断加快的过程,如同 1999 至 2000 年互联网泡沫兴起那般。那些总部设在欠发达国家的网络运营商借此能够抓住有利时机(发展壮大)。对北美尤其是欧洲运营商来说,更严重的危机来自于它们在企业兼并与收购以及频谱资源(购买)上所投入的巨额资金。到了 2012 年,第四代频谱拍卖已经让法国运营商耗费 38 亿欧元,意大利运营商 39 亿欧元,德国运营商 44 亿欧元,以及西班牙运营商 16 亿欧元④。据估计,欧洲各大电信公司在 2012 年共负债 2 720 亿欧元,从 2000 年到 2012 年,它们的已注销资产合计约 1 340 亿欧元⑤。当然,现在数字化衰退已经降临。2011 年的一项商务咨询表明,四分之三的电信企业"因为拓展技术基础设施或进行融资收购而欠下累累债务"⑥,这都需承担一定的风险。倘若经济不景气导致(企业)收入缩水、营运利润减少,那么这些债务将有可能成为累赘,压垮企业⑦。遭受重创的欧洲地区,那些占主导地位的运营商希望通过变卖"非核心"资产等方式寻求解脱。西班牙电信公司因背负 570 亿欧元债务而苦苦挣扎,分析家认准它肯定以打折的价格出售了它拥有的近一半中国联通 10% 的所有权股份⑧。2014 年中期,欧洲的网络运营商依然身

---

① Tarmo Verki, "Public Wi‑Fi Hotspots to Grow 4‑fold by 2015; Study," *Reuters*, November 8, 2011, available at http://www.reuters.com/article/2011/11/09/us‑internet‑hotspots‑idUSTRE7A801W20111109 (accessed January 10, 2014); Paul Taylor, "Five Cable Operators to Join Up WiFi Networks," *Financial Times*, May 22, 2012; WBA Industry Report 2011, available at http://www.wballiance.com/resource‑centre/global‑developments‑wifi‑report.html (accessed January 10, 2014).
② Calabrese, "Solving the 'Spectrum Crunch,'" 5.
③ 具体请参见 Chiehyu Li and Bincy Ninan, New America Foundation, "An International Comparison of Cell Phone Plans and Prices," October 14, 2010, available at http://oti.newamerica.net/publications/policy/an_international_comparison_of_cell_phone_plans_and_prices (accessed January 10, 2014).
④ Daniel Thomas and Paul Taylor, "4G Upgrade Signals Threat and Opportunity," *Financial Times*, February 25/26, 2012.
⑤ Daniel Thomas, "European Operators Ready to Talk Mergers," *Financial Times*, June 19, 2012.
⑥ AlixPartners, in Daniel Thomas, "Study Points to Telecoms Default Risks," *Financial Times*, September 19, 2011.
⑦ "Leading Telcos' Stellar Performance," *ScreenAfrica*, November 29, 2011, available at http://www.screenafrica.com/page/news/industry/1112343 (accessed January 10, 2014).
⑧ Daniel Thomas, "Sawiris Targets Telecoms Buyouts," *Financial Times*, June 13, 2012.

处巨额债务的重压之下①。

一项显著的差异逐渐消逝。在2008年全球市值排名前十的电信公司中,有两家即中国移动与美洲移动(卡洛斯·斯利姆[Carlos Slim]在拉丁美洲的无线集团)的总部分别设在中国和墨西哥。这个原本就不平衡的跷跷板游戏仍将继续。中国移动在2011年拥有的6.11亿国内用户数到了2013年增至7亿。彼时,中国移动已成为拥有最高市值的承运商②。2010年,美洲移动在18个国家拥有2.17亿用户,并且该公司以29万千米的光纤网络为筹码,进入互联网与付费电视服务领域③。美洲移动的资本投资预算高达100亿美元,它希望到2014年自己已经庞大的用户群体能再增加一亿新用户④。2012年,它开始扩张其跨国运营业务,例如收购两家落后的欧洲企业的股份⑤。同样,香港的和记黄埔集团(Hutchison Whampoa)在欧洲拥有价值不菲的网络财产——当爱尔兰电信公司濒临破产时,它甚至竞价收购⑥。埃及电信亿万富翁那古布·萨维里斯(Naguib Sawiris)再次指望能够持有那些"业绩不佳"的欧洲网络运营商的股份⑦。

所以,网络服务所覆盖的地理范围发生了变化。随着全球移动电话的数量跃升至60亿部,尼日利亚、埃及、南非、印度与中国的新用户数持续增长⑧。2008年,南非移动(MTN)成为非洲最大的移动运营商,向17个非洲国家与少数中东国家的5 300万用户提供服务。三年后,它的用户数翻了三番,已逾1.5亿⑨。印度最大的移动公司巴帝电信在2011年已成为全球第五大电信运营商,在19个国家拥有超过2.2亿的顾客⑩。随着2012年进军卢旺达市场,它在非洲的网络业务已覆盖17个国家⑪。英国的沃达丰公司(Vodafone)在许多欠发达国家发展业务,并拥有中国运营商的少量所有权股份。但这是

---

① Daniel Thomas, "Europeans Telecoms Revenue Fall Accelerates," *Financial Times*, November 25, 2013.
② "China Mobile reports 1Q results," TeleGeography, CommsUpdate, May 3, 2011; Owen Fletcher, "Cell Shackles Crumble," *Wall Street Journal*, July 12, 2011; "iPhone, You Never Do," The Lex Column, *Financial Times*, September 12, 2013. 截至2014年,中国移动对外宣称用户数已达7.67亿,具体请参见"China Mobile Flexes 3G Muscles As Market Expands 78.8%," *TeleGeography*, CommsUpdate, January 21, 2014.
③ Adam Thomson, "Buzz in the Air as AMX Comes of Age," *Financial Times*, November 23, 2010.
④ Adam Thomson, "America Movil Aims for Extra 100m Mobile Users by 2014," *Financial Times*, November 19, 2010.
⑤ Haig Simonian and Eric Frey, "America Movil Buys into Telekom Austria," *Financial Times*, June 16/17, 2012; Robert Armstrong and Stuart Kirk, "America Movil," Lex in Depth, *Financial Times*, February 22, 2013.
⑥ Robin Wigglesworth and Daniel Thomas, "Hutchison Whampoa Bids Euros2bn for Bankrupt Eircom," *Financial Times*, May 5/6, 2012.
⑦ Daniel Thomas, "Sawiris Targets Telecoms Buyouts," *Financial Times*, June 13, 2012.
⑧ Daniel Obi, "Africom Deepens Insight on Global Telecom Brands on Africa," *Business Day*, November 15, 2011, available at http://mobileentertainmentafrica.com/news-2/africom-deepens-insight-on-global-telecom-brands-on-africa (accessed January 10, 2014).
⑨ Andrew Parker, "Upwardly Mobile," *Financial Times*, February 11, 2008; "MTN Group Notches 150 Million Subscribers," *TeleGeography*, CommsUpdate, June 24, 2011.
⑩ Mary Watkins, "Bharti Seeks to Streamline Operations with Integration of African Units," *Financial Times*, June 28, 2011.
⑪ "Airtel Launches Rwanda's Third Mobile Network," *TeleGeography*, CommsUpdate, April 2, 2012.

例外情况。大多数总部设在欧洲与美国的大型网络运营商要么从这些高增长地区撤离，要么尚未买进（该地区承运商的）股份。危机动态，杂糅着经济民族主义情结、各不相同的技术标准以及企业新贵所展现的商业头脑，限制了（欧美大型网络运营商的）选择。当威瑞森承诺出资1 300亿美元买下沃达丰在美国的无线分公司的45%股份时，它其实是在拿自己的国内市场做赌注①。

有趣的是，在个人的网络使用模式上，也是南方国家影响北方国家。高端的数据应用服务的目标受众是一群不把价格当回事的人，它与快速增长的语音和短信的低端服务相辅相成，但（所谓的南方影响北方）不仅限于此。同样，欠发达国家流行的预付费业务模式在数字资本主义的中心地带广为流行：2010年，美国每五个新的无线网络用户中只有三个采用预付费模式，到了2011年，预付费用户占总用户数的四分之一②。相较之下，在巴西，82%的移动用户（2011年年底，2.42亿用户中有1.91亿）使用预付费模式③。到2012年，部分智能手机服务提供商也开始推行预付费业务模式。不论在孟买，还是在洛杉矶和伦敦，预付费服务模式不仅吸引低收入用户，也将中等收入群体纳至麾下。借此，知名的承运商可以提前将它的用户绑定在一份为期两年的合约上。使用模式的变化，不只是营销方式的重置这么简单。

然而，对网络连接性的掌控，依然是唯一的竞争因素，因为网络通信商品链的其他环节也各自拥有重要的战略意义。在网络重构这一主导性过程中，网络设备发挥着重要作用。在乔布斯担任苹果公司首席执行官的最后几年——甚至在2007年发布第一代苹果手机之前，当他计划使用未经许可的无线网络以摆脱对现有承运商的依赖时——乔布斯就已经深刻意识到这一可能性④。相反，自苹果手机投放市场以来，苹果公司不断与无线网络合作方讨价还价，试图保证贸易条件能够更有利于己方⑤。接下来，我将更加直接地讨论网络设备。

---

① Ryan Knutson, Thomas Gryta, and Sam Schechner, "Verizon – Vodafone Impact: 'Colossal,'" *Wall Street Journal*, August 30, 2013; "Can You Hear Me Now?" The Lex Column, *Financial Times*, September 6, 2013; "Verizon Bonds," The Lex Column, *Financial Times*, September 12, 2013.
② New Millenium Research Council, "Major Milestone for U. S. Cell Phone Consumers: Prepaid to Account for 1 out of 4 Wireless Subscriptions by End of 2011," July 29, 2011.
③ "Brazil mobile base tops 242. 2m at end – 2011, Anatel says," *TeleGeography*, Comms Update January 17, 2012.
④ Nancy Gohring, "Jobs Wanted Own Network with Unlicensed Spectrum," *Computerworld*, November 15, 2011; and Chris Davies, "Jobs Schemed Apple WiFi Carrier Plot for Original iPhone," available at www. slashgear. com/jobs – schemed – apple – Wi – Fi – carrier – plot – for – original – iphone – 16195619 (accessed January 10, 2014).
⑤ 我的观点与Cheol Gi Bae保持一致，请参见"The Transformation of Wireless Telecommunications Policies in Korea: The Interplay between Technology, State, Industry, and Users," July 5, 2012, 手稿由作者保存; Brian X. Chen, Nick Wingfield, James Kanter, and Kevin J. O'Brien, "Europe Weighs iPhone Sale Deals with Carriers for Antitrust Abuse," *New York Times*, March 21, 2013.

设备

网络现代化的建设重在接入设备的研发。智能手机与平板电脑尤其对网络商品链的重组产生重大影响。为了占有高利润的魔盒,大型互联网中介商确定战略需求:要么售卖自己的移动设备,要么以其他方式与移动设备制造商联盟。

设备成倍增长:电视机与硬盘录像机、个人电脑、游戏机、机顶盒、数字音频播放器(MP3 players)、智能手机、平板电脑、电子阅读器、全球定位装置与可穿戴电子设备。许多设备或"平台"内置宽带互联网连接功能,以增强它们的"性能"。市场参与者积极寻求市场优势,例如向每一硬件都植入它自己或合作方的操作系统、浏览器与服务,并将它们与专有的数据中心相连以存储在"云端"。2013 年,四大市场领导者各自提供了或多或少经过紧密整合的"生态系统"所需的构成性要素①。在这凝聚力之下,却是潜流暗涌的变革。

2009 年,全球范围内大概有 2.1 亿台电视机上市,而年销售增长率却下跌 2.5%。2010 年,销售额大幅上扬,共 2.47 亿台②,与此同时,消费者热衷于将他们的显像管电视替换成平板屏幕。不过,销售额的增长主要源于电视机价格的下调③。这并非人们经常援引的学习曲线就能完全解释的:包括大尺寸液晶电视与采用发光二极管的平板技术在内的电视机,都供大于求,而越来越多的人选择在电脑或移动设备上观看电视节目。

数字化衰退时期消费者支出的紧缩,伴随着供应商之间激烈的竞争。不出所料,降价开始(尽管降价幅度并不算大),并且一直持续到电视机销售额再度下滑的 2013 年④。立体电视、超高清、2010 年占全球电视总销售额五分之一⑤的互联网电视等一系列技术创新,依然未能阻挡制造商的下行颓势。早在模拟信号时期就已主导电视制造业的日本公司,如今不得不将地盘拱手交给那些凭借数字平板电脑而崛起的韩国与中国台湾企业。一面是乐金与三星电视销量在 2012 年保持坚挺⑥,另一面却是具有传奇色彩的索尼电视销量连续八年遭遇下滑。索尼集团一直深受产业长期生产过剩的困扰,为此它不得

---

① Paul Taylor and Richard Waters,"Purchase Offers Platform for Consolidation of Hardware and Software Makers,"*Financial Times*,August 17,2011.
② Marconi/Pacific Viewpoint,"Television Manufacturing Wars of Today and Industry Battles of Tomorrow," March 2010;Chris Nuttall,"TV Makers Seek to Return 3D Revolution,"*Financial Times*,January 8 - 9,2011.
③ Marconi/Pacific Viewpoint,"Television Manufacturing";Reuters,"Samsung Faces Weak Outlook on Flat Screens and TVs,"*New York Times*,October 6,2010.
④ "Slow TV Sales to Spur LCD Panel Oversupply,"Cens. com,September 28,2010;Hiroko Tabuchi,"TV Prices Still Falling,Sony's Profit Drops 8.6%,"*New York Times*,February 3,2011;Brian X. Chen and Nick Wingfield,"TV Makers Drift to Next Big Thing,"*New York Times*,January 6,2014.
⑤ Nuttall,"TV Makers."
⑥ "Asian Electronics,"The Lex Column,*Financial Times*,July 26,2012.

不关闭旗下八家电视工厂中的四家,裁员一万人,变卖其纽约总部,以及将生产外包给更低成本的供应商;尽管如此,索尼在 2013 年开始盈利的原因却是日本政府的金融政策所导致的日元贬值①。日立、夏普、东芝和松下集团也向外宣布其财务亏损情况,裁员并降低生产量②。在中国,电视市场依旧欣欣向荣,不过,价格还是根本因素。索尼与松下在中国的电视机降价幅度高达三分之一,因为它们的销量仅为国产企业创维数码电视机销量的六分之一。创维、海信电器与 TCL 集团推出的低端产品与小型电视,成为增长最快的细分市场,一如中国拥有世界上最大的平板电视国内市场③。而百度、阿里巴巴与小米计划进入"智能电视"市场④,也说明中国企业在高端市场亦有作为。当苹果有可能把电视引入其标杆性的"生态系统"时,投机行为仍将持续⑤。

智能电视是一亮点。能够上网和使用网络应用程序的电视机销量大火,得益于微软体感(Kinect)控制器(2012 年在全球卖出 1 600 万台)的面世,以及网飞公司主导的在线电视与电影流媒体业务的走红。配置网络浏览器、无线上网以及应用商店功能的大尺寸高清电视,造就了新的竞争前沿态势,引发有时并非透明的市场动态⑥。

游戏机起初只是作为专业平台,销量强劲,跃身为市场佼佼者。随后它将触摸屏与手势姿势整合进游戏玩法之中,让游戏的幻想世界显得更加逼真,并将游戏经验上传至网上分享。开发费用一路飙升,让规模较小的公司完全吃不消;1990 年代,设计一款游戏机的成本大约在 5 万至 40 万美元之间;但到 2010 年这一数字猛涨至 2 000 万美元,并需要约 100 名开发者⑦。育碧(Ubisoft)和电子艺界(Electronic Arts)等大型游戏发行方,与华纳兄弟或暴雪公司(Activision Blizzard)这些腰缠万贯的集团展开竞争,都想收回因开

---

① Jonathan Soble,"Sony Warns of Grim Picture for TVs",*Financial Times*,December 21,2010;Jay Alabaster,"Sony Says It Lost ＄6.4 Billion Last Year,over Twice Earlier Forecast," *ComputerWorld*,April 10,2012,available at http://www.computerworld.com/s/article/9226018/Sony_says_it_lost_6.4_billion_last_fiscal_year_over_twice_earlier _forecast(accessed January 10,2014);Jonathan Soble,"Sony Faces Pressure to Pull Plug on TVs," *Financial Times*,August 17,2011;Jonathan Soble,"Sony's TV Woes Spur Losses of ＄1.2bn," *Financial Times*,November 3,2011;Jonathan Soble,"Sony Signals Strategy Shift by Halving TV Sales Target," *Financial Times*,November 5 – 6,2011;Jonathan Soble,"Sony Unveils Return to Profit," *Financial Times*,May 10,2013.

② Jonathan Soble,"Panasonic Warns It Faces Loss of ＄5.3bn," *Financial Times*,November 1,2011;Jonathan Soble, "Sony's TV Woes Spur Losses of ＄1.2bn," *Financial Times*,November 3,2011;Jonathan Soble,"Japanese Pioneers Turn Down the Volume," *Financial Times*,November 3,2011;Jennifer Thompson and Sarah Mishkin,"Japanese Tech Groups Join the Big TV Switch – Off," *Financial Times*,October 8,2013.

③ Mariko Yasu,"Foreign Makers Tune in to China's TV Market," *Bloomberg Business Week*,August 12,2010.

④ Thompson and Mishkin,"Japanese Tech Groups."

⑤ Tim Bradshaw,"Apple Falls Short of Revolutionary in TV," *Financial Times*,November 29,2013.

⑥ David Gelles and Paul Taylor,"Deal Secures Place in US Viewers' Homes," *Financial Times*,August 17,2011;Daisuke Wakabayashi,"Sony TV Unit Seeks Path to Profitability," *Wall Street Journal*,November 27 – 28,2010;Nuttall,"TV Makers";Chen and Wingfield,"TV Makers Drift."

⑦ Robert Cyran and Agnes T. Crane,"Ante Is Rising in Game Industry," *New York Times*,November 15,2010;Ian Sherr, "Developers Defeat Rising Game Costs," *Wall Street Journal*,June 11,2013.

发全球热门游戏而提前投下的巨额资金。有时它们能收回成本。《决胜时刻:现代战争3》(Call of Duty:Modern Warfare 3)在美国、加拿大和英国发行的第一天,就已经卖出650万份,不仅营收四亿美元,更创下产业新纪录①。

游戏机生产商必须面对它每一代升级的游戏设备必经的繁荣—萧条周期现象。任天堂2006年11月推出低价位动作感应游戏机Wii,随后其竞争对手相继开发出令人印象深刻的仿制品——例如微软生产的体感控制器,强化了其第二代家用游戏主机(Xbox 360)的性能②,于是Wii的销量暴跌。为此,任天堂大力推广立体模型,可仍然无法挽救其2012年不断下滑的销售额③。微软宣布与媒体集团达成一系列交易,从而保证订购的游戏玩家能够通过Xbox网络(Xbox Live)观看更多的电视节目④。截至2011年中,动作感应游戏机Wii(的销量)在家庭视频游戏市场中再次居于首位,共卖出8 600万台;可微软第二代家用游戏主机与索尼第三代游戏主机(PS3)各自的销售量都有5 000万台。微软第二代家用游戏主机的销量继续增长,2012年全球已安装用户数高达6 600万;并且,微软公司制定战略,试图将其游戏机打造成(每个家庭)客厅的枢纽设备⑤。

七年过后,微软和索尼才相继推出自己的新游戏机产品⑥。但在这个过渡时期,市场行情已经发生变化⑦。游戏玩家"转战"平板电脑和智能手机,让游戏机制造商承受巨大的利润损失,即使在线销售与订阅数不断增长也无济于事。活跃的在线游戏用户数在2007年至2010年间从2 200万上升到9 300万,并还将继续增长⑧。一项针对索尼第三

---

① Ben Fritz, "Video Game Sales Rise Only 1% in October," *Los Angeles Times*, November 12,2011, available at http://articles.latimes.com/2011/nov/12/business/la-fi-ct-game-sales-20111112 (accessed January 10,2014); "Service Record Call of Duty on Top," *Financial Times*, November 12-13,2011.
② Chris Nuttall, "Kinect Controller Helps Xbox Sales Overtake Flagging Wii," *Financial Times*, December 8,2010.
③ Jonathan Soble, "Nintendo Set to Unveil 3D Console," *Financial Times*, February 26-27,2011; Mark Hachman, "Nintendo, Sony to Suffer in 2012 as Console Market Plunges," *PC Magazine*, April 30,2012, available at http://www.pcmag.com/article2/ 0,2817,2403787,00.asp? google_editors_picks = true (accessed January 10,2014).
④ Nick Wingfield and Brian Stelter, "Xbox Live Challenges Cable Box," *New York Times*, December 5,2011.
⑤ Chris Nuttall, "Life Inside the Video Game," *Financial Times*, June 10,2011; Nick Wingfield and Daisuke Wakabayashi, "Next Wii to Play Off the Tablet Craze," *Wall Street Journal*, June 8,2011; Associated Press, "Nintendo Sinks to Loss in April-December Period on Strong Yen, Weak Sales of 3DS and Wii," *Washington Post*, January 26,2012; "Microsoft and Xbox," The Lex Column, *Financial Times*, March 28,2012.
⑥ Ian Sherr, "'Sonic' Gets a Second Chance," and accompanying graphic titled "State of Play," *Wall Street Journal*, June 7, 2012; Nick Wingfield, "Next Xbox Will Face New Array of Rivals," *New York Times*, May 22,2013; "A Game Controller, and More," *New York Times*, June 13,2013; Ian Sherr and Drew FitzGerald, "New Xbox One Moves Beyond Games," *Wall Street Journal*, May 22,2013; Daisuke Wakabayashi, "Nintendo Resists the Lure of Mobile Games," *Wall Street Journal*, June 12,2013; Ian Sherr and Daisuke Wakabayashi, "Xbox One to Launch at $499," *Wall Street Journal*, June 11,2013; Ian Sherr, "Microsoft Angers Gamers," *Wall Street Journal*, June 12,2013; Barney Jopson and Andrea Felsted, "Retailers Seek Gaming Bonanza," *Financial Times*, November 21,2013.
⑦ Nick Wingfield, "New Consoles on the Way, but Gaming Isn't the Same," *New York Times*, November 11,2013.
⑧ Jonathan Soble, "Sony Loses Face over Theft of PS3 Data," *Financial Times*, April 28,2011; Ben Fritz, "Video Game Sales Rise Only 1% in October," *Los Angeles Times*, November 12,2011, available at http://articles.latimes.com/2011/nov/12/business/la-fi-ct-game-sales-20111112 (accessed January 10,2014).

代游戏主机使用者的调查显示,线上与线下游戏时间加起来几乎占用户时间的一半;数字化视频光盘与蓝光视频、视频点播以及下载的电影和电视节目所花费的时间占用户时间的40%,网络音乐与社交媒体则占剩余的10%①。在微软体感控制器上市后第六天(价格150美元)的销量冲破8 000万台后,微软启动一项计划以拓展其使用范围;它与25大行业将近200家企业合作,推出包括医疗卫生、教育、汽车与广告在内的各项业务②。同样,微软新一代家用游戏主机(Xbox One)与索尼第四代游戏主机(PlayStation 4)延续了微软将游戏机改造成多功能媒体平台的战略。这一战略为它们带来巨额利润:2013年圣诞季,微软与索尼在北美推出产品的24小时内分别卖出100万台游戏机③。

另一类专业设备备受赞誉,普及率迅速上升。历经30年的发展与不断的商业倒闭,电子书阅读器的价格开始飙升,并且人们可以获得成百上千的电子书,于是,电子书阅读器的市场临爆点终于来临。在中国,汉王与盛大两家主要的供应商占据五分之四的市场份额(2011年,共计六亿电子书在市场上流通),像当当这样的企业也准备进军该市场④。在美国,亚马逊先声夺人,抢占优势,而索尼与巴诺书店(Barnes & Noble)广受好评的运营模式尽管得到微软的技术支持,却屡屡败下阵来。在数字化衰退席卷而来之后,电子书阅读器的销量反而强劲上扬;2011年上半年美国有一千万人在使用电子书阅读器⑤。2011年圣诞季,电子书阅读器跻身为热销产品,以至于截至2012年1月,美国20%的成年人人手一台阅读器⑥。它的走俏,与数字化电子书的易获取性密不可分;2010至2011年,美国电子书在销量上打败有声读物,并逐渐逼近纸质书销量⑦。

然而,日渐增长的电子书销量尚不足以解释图书整体销量在2011年为何整体下降2.5%⑧。大型实体零售商的崛起给出版商的传统经营模式带来巨大压力,如今随着亚马

---

① Soble, "Sony Loses Face."
② Chris Nuttall, "Microsoft Eyes Broader Use of Game Controller," *Financial Times*, October 31, 2011, available at http://www.ft.com/cms/s/2/21a337ca-0303-11e1-899a-00144feabdc0.html#axzz1cM1B1AdG (accessed January 10, 2014).
③ Mike Snider, "Sony Sells More than 1 Million PlayStation 4s," *USA Today*, November 17, 2013, available at http://www.usatoday.com/story/tech/gaming/2013/11/17/sony-sells-1-million-playstation-4s/3618217 (accessed January 10, 2014); Hannah Kuchler and Richard Waters, "Xbox and Cloud Help Microsoft Ease Fears", *Financial Times*, January 24, 2014.
④ "China's E-Book Market Heats Up", *Seeking Alpha*, January 3, 2012, available at http://seekingalpha.com/article/317149-china-s-e-book-market-heats-up (accessed January 10, 2014).
⑤ "E-Books Open Up," The Lex Column, *Financial Times*, September 3-4, 2011.
⑥ David Sarno, "Tablet, E-Reader Ownership Jumps to 19% in the US over the Holidays," *Los Angeles Times*, January 23, 2012, available at http://latimesblogs.latimes.com/technology/2012/01/tablet-e-reader-ownership-in-us-jumps-to-20-over-the-holidays.html (accessed January 10, 2014).
⑦ Claire Cain Miller, "E-Books Top Hardcovers at Amazon", *New York Times*, July 20, 2010; Julie Bosman, "E-Readers under Christmas Trees May Help E-Books Take Root," *New York Times*, December 24, 2010; Andrew Edgecliffe-Johnson, "E-Books Overtake Print Sales in US," *Financial Times*, April 15, 2011.
⑧ Andrew Edgecliffe-Johnson, "Amazon's Electronic Book Sales Beat Print," *Financial Times*, May 20, 2011.

逊掌握电子书的定价大权,出版商度日维艰①。面对此番情势,不少出版商选择与苹果合作,后者也有意向出版行业引进"代理模式"以保证出版商重新获得定价权,与此同时以苹果平板电脑牵制亚马逊电子书阅读器②。但在2012年4月,美国司法部以商业共谋之名,起诉五家出版商与苹果公司。一年后,所有的出版商选择和解,只有苹果公司(甚至在一位联邦法官裁定它曾密谋提高电子书的价格③后)依然不屈不挠,不断上诉④。当前,市面上销售的平板电脑,来自多家供应商,而它们所聚集的关于读者阅读习惯与方式的数据成为各供应商梦寐以求的商品⑤。

向多媒体平板电脑的技术转型,离不开网络连接性的升级换代;与电子书不同,在线轻松看电影与视频(甚至彩色杂志)或玩游戏,对带宽的要求很高。亚马逊以及巴诺书店都资助了无线网络的兴建,以降低消费者成本,并使第三和第四代无线网络承运商及其昂贵的数据流量包因无人问津而逐渐被市场淘汰⑥。

在向网络服务转型的过程中,台式机应当是第一个被广泛采用的多功能平台。然而,2000年后笔记本电脑的流行,撼动了台式机的中心地位。2010年全球范围内,包括笔记本电脑在内的个人电脑的出货量增长至3.5亿台⑦,可接下来的两年里,全球个人电脑出货速度开始放缓⑧。截至2013年年底,全球个人电脑出货量已经连续七个季度下跌⑨。2013年个人电脑的主要生产厂家是联想、惠普、戴尔以及宏基。2005年中国企业联想电脑完成对美国国际商用机器公司个人电脑事业部的收购;此后虽然出现些许的销量下滑,但凭借其国内市场的优势,联想再次成为个人电脑的顶级制造商:2009至2010年,中国的销量增长21%,几乎占联想总收入的一半。然而,中国个人电脑市场的繁荣只

---

① Andre Schiffrin, *Words and Money* (London: Verso, 2010), 105.
② David Gelles and Andrew Edgecliffe-Johnson, "Publishers Sued over E-Book Price 'Collusion'," *Financial Times*, April 12, 2012.
③ David Streitfeld, "E-Book Ruling Gives Amazon an Advantage," *New York Times*, July 11, 2013.
④ Julie Bosman, "Apple Negotiator Defends Tactics in an E-Book Trial," *New York Times*, June 14, 2013.
⑤ David Streitfeld, "As New Services Track Habits, the E-Books Are Reading You," *New York Times*, December 25, 2013.
⑥ Matt Hamblen, "Why the Kindle Fire and Nook Tablet are Wi-Fi Only", *ComputerWorld*, November 9, 2011.
⑦ Figures from Joseph Mann, "Apple iPad Surge Hits PC Shipments," *Financial Times*, January 13, 2011; compare "Gartner Says Worldwide PC Shipments to Increase 19 Percent in 2010 with Growth Slowing in Second Half of the Year," *Financial Times*, August 31, 2010.
⑧ Richard Waters, "Strength of Microsoft Sales Eases Wall St. Fears," *Financial Times*, October 29, 2010; Mary Watkins, "Tablets Start to Cause Side Effects for PCs," *Financial Times*, October 15, 2010; Chris Nuttall, "Computing's Old Guard Faces a Tough Year," *Financial Times*, December 31, 2010; Verne G. Kopytoff and Laurie J. Flynn, "PC Makers Are Seeing a Slowdown," *New York Times*, May 18, 2011; Joseph Menn, "Modest Profit for Microsoft as PC Sales Slow," *Financial Times*, October 21, 2011; Sarah Mishkin and Chris Nuttall, "PC Makers Face Tough Fight to Reignite Sales," *Financial Times*, July 16, 2012.
⑨ Scott Martin, "PC Market in 2013 Notches Worst Decline in History," *USA Today*, January 9, 2014, available at http://www.usatoday.com/story/tech/2014/01/09/pc-market-in-2013-notches-worst-decline-in-history/4394409 (accessed February 3, 2014).

是例外情况①。随着数字化衰退的来临,联想相继与日本电气组建合资公司、在巴西和德国开展一系列的收购行动,进而反超惠普,戴尔大幅削减其预期收益并着手进行企业重组;与此同时,惠普几乎退出个人电脑市场。随后平板电脑的大举入侵,上述公司原本微薄的利润更是雪上加霜②。

在消费者钟情于高端移动设备的初期,最大受益者当属苹果公司。在乔布斯离世后,苹果平板电脑的成功被人津津乐道,成为他个人传奇经历及其公司令人震惊的再度崛起的重要组成部分。苹果公司创立后25年即新世纪之交,业绩依然一路跌跌撞撞,与时代脱节,哪怕在它的传统优势领域即台式机市场上,也是如此:2001年苹果对外宣称营收54亿美元,亏损2 500万美元。然而在同一年,苹果公司来势汹汹,准备大干一场、反败为胜,甚至七年之后在数字化衰退的初期,也抵挡不住它成功的脚步。2010年,苹果获得650亿美元的收入,净收益140亿美元③;截至2013财政年度,收入与净收益分别增长至1 710亿美元与370亿美元,令人望洋兴叹④。乔布斯的苹果公司能够大肆进账,与它推出的在市场上取得轰动性成功的移动设备三件套密不可分:即2001年10月推出的苹果音乐播放器、2007年的苹果手机与2010年的平板电脑。2011年11月,苹果卖出三亿多台音乐播放器,在如今不断缩水的全美MP3播放器市场中的份额高达78%⑤。以苹果手机为代表的智能手机不仅具有音乐播放器的原有功能,更大举吞噬前者的市场销售额。苹果手机销量直线上升,从2010年的4 700万台上涨至2012年的1.36亿台,2013年销量持续飙升:苹果手机为苹果公司带来的收益占总收入的一半⑥。2011年,世界范围内的智能手机销量以绝对优势首次超过台式机:4.72亿台与3.53亿台⑦。2013年,内

---

① Lorraine Luk, "PC Maker Lenovo Posts 44% Gain in Profit," *Wall Street Journal*, November 11, 2010.

② Richard Waters, "Dell Cuts Revenue Outlook amid Dwindling Consumer Confidence," *Financial Times*, August 17, 2011; Joseph Menn, "HP Shares Plunge as Investors Take Fright at Scale and Timing of Revamp," *Financial Times*, August 20–21, 2011; Justin Scheck and Joann S. Lublin, "Investors Rebel against H–P Plan," *Wall Street Journal*, August 20–21, 2011; Richard Waters, "Tech Scramble Turns Sector on Its Head," *Financial Times*, August 20–21, 2011; Paul Taylor and Richard Waters, "Purchase Offers Platform for Consolidation of Hardware and Software Makers," *Financial Times*, August 17, 2011; Richard Waters, "Whitman Warns of Long HP Recovery," *Financial Times*, June 7, 2012; Kathrin Hille, "Lenovo in Talks as It Seeks Global Smartphone Expansion," *Financial Times*, June 5, 2013; Eric Pfanner, "Mobile Devices Overtake PC Sales at Lenovo," *New York Times*, August 16, 2013.

③ John Ashcroft, "Apple in the Digital Age from the iPod to the iPad," http://pro manchesterceo. typepad. com/files/apple–case–study–2011. pdf, table 16. 1, p. 21.

④ Apple, Inc., "Earnings Releases FY 2013," available at http://investor. apple. com/results. cfm (accessed February 3, 2014).

⑤ Chris Nuttall, "iPod Sales Melt Away but Apple Still Leads a Flagging Field," *Financial Times*, November 4, 2011.

⑥ Joseph Menn, "Apple iPad Sales Fail to Hit Forecasts," FT. com, October 10, 2010; Lorraine Luk and Yukari Iwatani Kane, "Apple Readies New iPhone," *Wall Street Journal*, July 7, 2011; Tim Bradshaw, "Apple Falls Victim to Its Own Success," *Financial Times*, January 25, 2013.

⑦ Richard Waters, "Mobilised against Mobile," *Financial Times*, May 25, 2012.

置上网功能的智能手机销量也超过入门级别的"功能手机"①。正如联想成为全球最大的台式机生产商,也要面对深受生产过剩困扰的不断缩水的市场,如今苹果所卖出的智能手机与平板电脑比个人电脑还多②。然而,它所占领的这一块至关重要的市场,也逐渐受到三星公司的蚕食:2013年第三季度,三星手机在全球智能手机市场上的份额为35%(苹果只占13.4%,尽管其利润更高)③。远远被苹果和三星甩在身后位居第三的是中国的设备供应商华为企业。

平板电脑则是另一现象级的电子产品(2010年,这一售价高的产品共卖出1 500万台,2013年更高达7 100万台),它与同属于苹果公司、重获新生的笔记本电脑争夺市场份额,并成为该公司仅次于苹果手机的第二大收入来源④。2011年底,如果把平板电脑归入个人电脑,那么苹果公司则是世界排名第一的个人电脑生产商⑤。随着2013年出货量的持续增加,消费者在平板电脑上的花销也相应激增⑥。

其他的消费性电子产品生产商被迫出局。在苹果平板电脑从一开始就占据全球平板电脑市场份额的60%至70%,以及苹果公司极力满足消费者需求⑦等情况下,三星和亚马逊等供应商想出一系列对策"狙击"苹果:例如亚马逊推出的Kindle Fire平板电脑就主打低价、性能偏少等功能。正是平板电脑所引发的轰动性市场效应,最终让谷歌与微软也按捺不住,2012年它们相继推出自己的平板电脑(Nexus 7与Surface),打破此前奉行的以软件开发为中心的发展战略⑧。

苹果凭借其产品成功地从大型网络运营商手里分得一杯羹,但所有这一切都发生在数字化衰退的背景下。2011年苹果推出第二代平板电脑,即刻催生了市值数十亿美元的第一代平板电脑二手市场。这一市场的规范化(如同此前二手唱片或数字化视频光盘那样),即二手平板电脑没有进入地方商店,而是在易趣(eBay)、无线电器材公司(Radio

---

① Daniel Thomas, "Smartphone Sales Outstrip Basic Devices for the First Time," *Financial Times*, August 15, 2013.
② Pfanner, "Mobile Devices"; Claire Cain Miller and David Gelles, "After Big Bet, Google to Sell Motorola Unit," *New York Times*, January 30, 2014.
③ Eric Pfanner, "Smartphone Leaders, Samsung and Apple, Settle In at Top," *New York Times*, October 30, 2013.
④ Charles Duhigg and Keith Bradsher, "How U.S. Lost Out on iPhone Work," *New York Times*, January 22, 2011; Nuttall, "iPod Sales"; Josh Lowensohn, " Apple's 2013 by the Numbers," C/Net, October 28, 2013, available at http://news.cnet.com/8301 - 13579_3 - 57609686 - 37/apples - 2013 - by - the - numbers - 150m - iphones - 71m - ipads (accessed February 3, 2014).
⑤ Paul McDougall, "Apple Now Top PC Maker, Report Says," *Information Week*, January 31, 2012.
⑥ Mary Watkins "Tablet Demand Set to Bolster IT Spending," *Financial Times*, March 31, 2011; Tim Bradshaw, "Tablets Drive Growth as PC Sales and Upgrades Slow," *Financial Times*, June 25, 2013; Brian X. Chen, "iPhone Sales Set Record For Quarter: 51 Million," *New York Times*, January 28, 2014.
⑦ Joseph Menn, "iPhone and Mac Sales Help Apple Profits Soar," *Financial Times*, April 21, 2011; "iPad 2 suppliers," The Lex Column, *Financial Times*, March 7, 2011; Ian Sherr, "Tablet War Is an Apple Rout," *Wall Street Journal*, August 12, 2011; Nick Wingfield and Nick Bilton, "The Race in Tablets Heats Up," *New York Times*, July 16, 2012.
⑧ Chris Nuttall and Sarah Mishkin, "Software Titans Enter the Physical World," *Financial Times*, August 10, 2012.

Shack）以及百思买（Best Buy）等大型零售商系统中售卖①,正是危机持续的标志。新型平板电脑和智能手机的市场开始向中国和印度等低收入国家扩张;苹果将这些国家视为利润增长的核心市场并且积极培育②。

　　苹果凭借移动设备所取得的爆发式成功,改变了数字化世界的构造板块。它代表了一种克鲁格曼（Paul Krugman）所说的"没有生产的利润"战略③。苹果公司将生产环节（无论是零部件生产还是最后组装）大部分外包给东亚地区的供应商。苹果手机商品链构成如下:9 个国家至少有 156 家企业生产零部件,最终由位于中国深圳的工厂工人完成组装;他们都是低收入、紧张不堪的年轻工人④。苹果公司最大的承包商是台企鸿海科技集团——全球第十大工厂,生产全球 40% 的消费性电子设备,并在中国大陆经营大型工厂（鸿海集团还在不断扩张,不仅在巴西设厂,更向索尼买下墨西哥厂,并购索尼斯洛伐克厂）⑤。为了不让鸿海独享利益,苹果将它的生产业务越来越多地外包给第二家台湾公司和硕联合科技股份有限公司⑥。在美国本土,苹果直接雇佣大约 4.3 万名雇员,相比于殚精竭虑为其海外承包商工作的 70 万工人而言⑦,这只是小数目。苹果公司的雇员主要从事软件开发与工业设计等工作,这些白领体现出苹果工人区别于其他工人的特质,以此设立市场价格标准。

　　2004 年前后,苹果就已将其时髦的电子设备作为撬棍,试图撬开通信商品链。随着苹果成功地将音乐播放器、手机与平板电脑插入其中,它也将这些产品"绑定"⑧在音乐软件（iTunes）上——这是苹果推出的销售音乐和其他试听商品的独家业务。这反过来刺激苹果的竞争者群起仿效,它们都试图建立自己的数字化领地,进而"可以设置规则,以掌

---

① April Dembosky,"iPad 2 Boosts Second – Hand Sales,"*Financial Times*,March 12 – 13,2011.
② Kathrin Hille,"Apple Achieves Cult Status with iPad 2 in China,"*Financial Times*,August 8,2011;Tim Bradshaw and Sarah Mishkin,"Apple Seals China Mobile Deal,"*Financial Times*,December 23,2013;Saritha Rai,"Cost of Cool In India? An iPhone,"*New York Times*,January 13,2014.
③ Paul Krugman,"Profits without Production,"*New York Times*,June 20,2013.
④ 邱凌川曾研究这些工人的传播实践及其潜能,请参见 Qiu,*Working – Class Network Society*（Cambridge,Mass.:MIT Press,2009）。关于中国信息技术与电子产业制造工人的研究,请参见 Yu Hong,*Labor,Class Formation,and China's Informationized Policy of Economic Development*（Lanham,Md.:Lexington,2011）。
⑤ Duhigg and Bradsher,"How U. S. Lost Out";Yuqing Xing and Neal Detert,"How the iPhone Widens the United States Trade Deficit with the People's Republic of China,"Asian Development Bank Institute,Working Paper No. 257,December 2010;"Employment:Defending Jobs,"*The Economist*,September 12,2011,available at http://www.economist.com/blogs/dailychart/2011/09/employment（accessed January 10,2014）;Ben Bland and Sarah Mishkin,"Foxconn Feels Strain of Staff Shortages,"*Financial Times*,October 8,2013;Malcolm Moore,"Apple's Child Labour Issues Worsen,"The Telegraph,February 15,2011,available at http://www.telegraph.co.uk/technology/apple/8324867/Apples – child – labour – issues – worsen.html（accessed January 10,2014）;Apple Inc.,"Apple Supplier Responsibility 2011 Progress Report,"available at http://www.apple.com/supplier responsibility（accessed October 10,2011）.
⑥ Sarah Mishkin,"Pegatron Takes a Bite out of Hon Hai's Apple,"*Financial Times*,May 15,2013.
⑦ Duhigg and Bradsher,"How U. S. Lost Out."
⑧ Jonathan Zittrain,*The Future of the Internet and How To Stop It*（New Haven,Conn.:Yale University Press,2008）.

控或限定与互联网其他部分的连接权限"①。操作系统、媒体商店以及流行的应用程序成为这场激烈的市场战役的关键。对此,苹果最主要的竞争对手谷歌将它的平板电脑手机业务外包给华硕与乐金集团,直接收购其设备制造商摩托罗拉移动公司(Motorola Mobility)②。当微软2013年收购诺基亚旗下日渐式微的手机制造商③时,它加固了这一并购趋势。移动市场的竞争优势紧紧围绕供应商将软件和业务嵌入实体设备的能力而展开。这一能力不仅是垂直整合的目标,更是供应商寻求专利地位的目的。摩托罗拉移动公司之于谷歌的吸引力,来自于前者拥有的1.7万项专利;两年后,当谷歌把摩托罗拉卖给联想时,它保留了大部分专利④。

在刚才的个案中,专利权可以从外部其他公司购买,或者通过公司内部的研发项目获得。2011年谷歌在研发项目上投入近50亿美元,2013年达到75亿美元(尽管这只是移动技术开发成本中的一部分⑤)。它的竞争对手微软拥有2.6万项美国与国际专利,还有3.6万项尚待确认;尽管这样,它的研发投入更多:2011年花费90亿美元⑥。2011年三星公司对外宣称,来年它将投入93亿美元的研发资金⑦。相较之下,2011年苹果的研发资金仅为24亿美元⑧、亚马逊⑨与脸书的投入更少。谷歌首席法务官大卫·德拉蒙德(David Drummond)2011年撰文指出,根据现有的法律解释,一部智能手机可能涉及25万种专利权⑩。

随着供应商试图围攻或抵抗竞争对手,不难预见,移动设备市场的专利之战必将打响⑪。谷歌不仅买下摩托罗拉移动,更从美国国际商用机器公司手里购得千项专利权,并帮助宏达国际电子股份有限公司与苹果展开专利战。苹果与微软合作,耗费45亿美元

---

① "A Virtual Counter–Revolution," *The Economist*, September 4, 2010.
② Amir Efrati, "Google Targets Amazon with Cloud Services," *Wall Street Journal*, June 29, 2012.
③ Charles Arthur, "Nokia's Handset Business Bought by Microsoft for Euro 5.44bn," *The Guardian*, September 3, 2013, available at http://www.theguardian.com/technology/2013/sep/03/nokia–handset–bought–microsoft (accessed February 24, 2014).
④ Paul Taylor and Richard Waters, "Google in $12.5bn Motorola Phone Deal," *Financial Times*, August 16, 2011; Richard Waters, "Search Group Puts Faith in Numbers," *Financial Times*, August 17, 2011; Miller and Gelles, "After Big Bet."
⑤ Google Inc., U.S. SEC Form 10–Q, June 30, 2011, 30, available at http://www.sec.gov/Archives/edgar/data/1288776/000119312511199078/d10q.htm (accessed January 10, 2014).
⑥ Microsoft Inc., SEC Form 10–K:9, July 28, 2011, available at http://www.sec.gov/Archives/edgar/data/789019/000119312511200680/d10k.htm (accessed January 10, 2014).
⑦ Kendra Srivastava, "Samsung to Spend $9.3 Billion on R&D," *Mobiledia*, August 30, 2011.
⑧ Apple Inc., U.S. SEC Form 10–K, September 24, 2011, 7, available at http://www.sec.gov/Archives/edgar/data/320193/000119312511282113/d220209d10k.htm (accessed January 10, 2014)
⑨ 过去几年,亚马逊花费十亿美元用于营销、技术研发与内容产制上,并且这些成本还将不断增长,请参见Amazon.com Inc., SEC 10–Q:19–21, July 27, 2011, available at http://phx.corporate–ir.net/phoenix.zhtml?c=97664&p=irol–reportsother (accessed March 10, 2014).
⑩ Steve Lohr, "A Bull Market in Tech Patents," *New York Times*, August 17, 2011.
⑪ "Google and HP," The Lex Column, *Financial Times*, August 20–21, 2011.

购买专利,共同瓜分这家破产的加拿大电信设备制造商北电网络(Nortel)。苹果利用这些专利,狙击它在智能手机和平板电脑市场上的对手和供应商的商业盗用行为。当移动设备成为新的市场支点,那么这场专利"军备竞赛"(例如苹果和三星在十个国家相继卷入 50 场纠纷)则代表一种构成性的特质(formative feature)①。同理,谷歌与三星至多保持一种谨慎合作的关系。谷歌廉价抛售其生产部门,并与三星达成一项全球专利授权协议,即盖乐世(Galaxy)手机可以运行各种定制款的谷歌安卓系统②。然而,三星一直试图摆脱对安卓系统的依赖,因此它自己开发了一款操作系统,并在 2014 年推出内置这一系统的智能手表③。

  在数字化衰退时期,移动连接的地理范围与移动设备的预期影响,都冲破了此前的限制。制造商的低价、非贴牌的生产模式(谷歌的大部分安卓软件就是如此),以及承运商推出的预付费业务,都刺激了移动设备的扩张发展。2009 年手机的季度出货量下降,可到了 2010 年年中,出货量一定程度地回升:2010 年每一季度出货量超过三亿台。然而,价格压力严重影响到供应商的利润空间④。无品牌手机重创五大手机供应商所拥有的市场,后者的市场份额从 2009 年的 83% 下降到 2010 年的 67%⑤。截至 2013 年,市面上流通的手机有五分之四使用安卓系统⑥。两家曾在早期的手机市场呼风唤雨的企业如今却落魄不堪。诺基亚的高端手机市场遭遇苹果和三星的无情蚕食,而它的低端产品又不敌那些无品牌手机。面对此情此景,诺基亚 2012 年推出一款售价仅为 45 美元的手机⑦(翌年,诺基亚将其手机业务卖给微软)。同样,黑莓手机一面遭受苹果和三星的挤压,另一面不得不与低价安卓手机展开竞争。2013 年,它对外宣布公司亏损 10 亿美元,

---

① Andreas Udo de Haes, "Samsung Seeks Ban of iPhone and iPad in The Netherlands," *ComputerWorld*, September 23, 2011, available at http://www.computerworld.com/s/article/9220230/Samsung_seeks_ban_of_iPhone_and_iPad_in_The_Netherlands (accessed January 10,2014); Associated Press, "Samsung vs. Apple War Set to Explode," September 23,2011, available at http://www.foxnews.com/scitech/2011/09/23/samsung-vs-apple-war-hits-high-gear (accessed January 10,2014); Richard Waters, "Cases with High Risks for All Sides," *Financial Times*, June 15,2012.
② Tim Bradshaw, "Google and Samsung Tied Closer Together with Global Patent Deal", *Financial Times*, January 27,2014.
③ Daniel Thomas, "Samsung Makes Break From Android Dependence," *Financial Times*, February 23,2014, available at http://www.ft.com/intl/cms/s/0/4073d516-9c7a-11e3-9360-00144feab7de.html?siteedition=intl#axzz2uFRgzdem (accessed February 24,2014).
④ Gustav Sandstrom, "Cellphone Vendors Face Price Pressure," *Wall Street Journal*, July 30,2010.
⑤ Gustav Sandstrom, "Low-Cost Chinese Cellphones Power Handset-Shipment Surge," *Wall Street Journal*, November 11, 2010.
⑥ Richard Waters, "Android's Momentum Eats into Apples and BlackBerrys," *Financial Times*, August 15,2013.
⑦ Mary Watkins, "Google's Android Dents Nokia Smartphone Dominance," *Financial Times*, Nov 11,2010; Andrew Parker and Andrew Ward, "Downwardly Mobile," *Financial Times*, February 25,2011; Chris Davies, "Nokia 1 Series Takes Web and Social Cheap for Next Billion," *Slashgear*, May 15,2012, available at: http://www.slashgear.com/nokia-1-series-takes-web-and-social-cheap-for-next-billion-15228279 (accessed January 10,2014).

并裁员 40%（共计 4.5 万名员工），试图自救①。换言之，"美国制造"的智能手机操作系统（苹果操作系统、安卓或微软视窗）所抢占的全球市场份额，从 2005 年的 5% 狂升至 2012 年的 88%。《金融时报》的一位专栏作家从地缘经济学的角度给描述这一变化的文章起了如下标题："欧洲在这场高风险的移动游戏中注定出局"②。

同样，一个饱和的市场也会带来其他问题。哪怕再成功的智能手机供应商也需要面对价格下调的问题。一面是苹果和三星的高端手机销量居高不下，尤其在作为它们全球最大市场的中国更是如此③；另一面则是"底特律和孟买这些地区的贫穷消费者的购买行为，将越来越成为额外增长的来源"④。为了迎合这些消费者，中国的制造商开始提供（有时向外出口）低价智能手机。联想、华为、宇龙和小米在中国的市场份额不可小觑，并且包括华为、联想在内的供应商，以及像魅族这样的小型公司也开始创建它们自己的应用商店⑤。2012 年，市场预估将卖出大概 3 亿台低端智能手机；同时，2012 至 2013 年售价在 200 美元以下的智能手机的全球销量份额将逐渐增加⑥。假若如预估那般，智能手机的市场飞速增长，那么这一增长主要来自贫穷国家——这也是"苹果将手机卖给中国移动（中国甚至全球迄今为止最大的移动承运商）的顾客"的决策具有战略意义的原因之一⑦。

随着无线设备日渐深入人们的日常生活（例如在 2013 年，四位美国司机里就有一位使用手机上网⑧），移动设备已成为不断扩大的工业转型的支点。智能手机与平板电脑在拥有数十亿潜在用户的基础上，为市场建设开辟了广阔的前景。无论主营唱片还是金融的公司，它们都围绕这些移动设备重构自身的商品链，并试图超越现有的市场份额。这

---

① "Tech, Tock, Tech, Tock," The Lex Column, *Financial Times*, June 5, 2012; Will Connors, "RIM Delays Phone, Shares Plunge 15%," *Wall Street Journal*, June 29, 2012; Richard Blackden, "Blackberry Job Cuts after $1bn Loss," *Financial Times*, September 21–22, 2013.
② John Gapper, "Europe Holds a Losing Hand in the High–Stakes Mobile Game," *Financial Times*, September 5, 2013.
③ 一项市场研究指出，2012 年第一季度，这些企业（包括三星）在中国市场上的手机销（1130 部手机）占中国手机总销量（3120 部手机）的 1/3，具体可参见 Paul Mozur, "China Vexes Smartphone Makers," *Wall Street Journal*, June 29, 2012。
④ "Smartphones," The Lex Column, *Financial Times*, January 8–9, 2011.
⑤ Tim Bradshaw and Sarah Mishkin, "China Joins Apple's Annual Ritual of the iPhone Launch," *Financial Times*, September 21–22, 2013; Tom Mitchell, Song Jung-a, and James Crabtree, "Apple Seeks Leap Forward in Biggest Market," *Financial Times*, September 12, 2013; Kathrin Hille, "Shake-out for China Mobile Makers," *Financial Times*, March 26, 2012; Kathrin Hille, "Smartphone Challenge from China," *Financial Times*, December 20, 2011; Paul Mozur, "China Vexes Smartphone Makers," *Wall Street Journal*, June 29, 2012; Kathrin Hille, "Lenovo in Talks as It Seeks Global Smartphone Expansion," *Financial Times*, June 5, 2013.
⑥ Robin Kwong, Chris Nuttall, and Paul Taylor, "Low-Tech Starts to Drive Growth in Smartphones," *Financial Times*, March 8, 2012; Mitchell, Song, and Crabtree, "Apple Seeks Leap Forward."
⑦ Associated Press, "Smart Phones Seen Tripling to 5.6 Billion by 2019," *USA Today*, November 11, 2013, available at http://www.usatoday.com/story/tech/2013/11/11/smartphones-forecast/3496169 (accessed January 10, 2014); Bradshaw and Mishkin, "Apple Seals China Mobile Deal."
⑧ Larry Copeland, "1 in 4 Surf Web While Behind Wheel," *USA Today*, November 12, 2013.

一点从亚马逊与台湾宏达国际电子股份有限公司签订合同开发新型号的智能手机就可见一斑。亚马逊此举希望新的系列产品"能够帮助其赢得更多消费者的忠诚度,尤其在人们越来越倾向于通过手机和平板电脑购物的情况下"①。

2011年全球范围内,掌上购物以及定位广告的相关领域的移动支付量高达860亿美元,用户数为1.4亿人②。根据理查德·沃特斯(Richard Waters)的观察,由于与不同的支付系统相连,"每一部智能手机都是一件完美工具,它能够将尚未成熟的欲望转化成即时性的满足感"③。在美国,包括威瑞森和美国电话电报公司在内的运营商,不得不与原本是其他领域的竞争对手展开竞争。谷歌、脸书、世行集团,以及维萨和万事达等信用卡公司,连同易趣的贝宝支付(PayPal),都试图打造自己的移动支付平台④。此番竞争不仅在国内,还延伸到国外。从日本到尼日利亚,从俄罗斯到墨西哥,各派资本都在争夺市场地位⑤。谷歌快人一步地面向美国商界推出"谷歌钱包"功能,尽管一开始该功能只向那些正好拥有三星4G手机(内嵌近场通信芯片)、使用斯普林特的美国网络,并拥有花旗银行万事达信用卡或谷歌签发的预付卡的用户开放⑥。这是变革的起因:美国市场依然落后于欧洲与东亚地区的市场,与此同时,可随时随地购物的美国市场正在向商业开放⑦。例如,苹果在2014年初正准备推出它的支付系统。

关于"哪个市场行动者能在这一商品链中优先占有高利润的魔盒"的问题,仅仅给出"上述涉猎范围广泛的集团"这个答案远远不够⑧。对于零售商而言,要激活消费者的点击购买行为也不是件容易的事。2010年年中,大部分美国零售商尚未优化其网站以激活

---

① Tim Bradshaw, Sarah Mishkin, and Barney Jopson, "Amazon in Mobile Venture with HTC," *Financial Times*, October 16, 2013.
② Jon Swartz, "Small Businesses Make Square Deals," *USA Today*, December 9, 2011.
③ Richard Waters, "Apple Set To Draw Battle Lines on Mobile Payments," *Financial Times*, January 30, 2014.
④ Martin Peers, "Phone Firms Make Mobile Payment Contact," *Wall Street Journal*, November 27–28, 2010; Tim Bradshaw and David Gelles, "Google Joins Payments Battle," *Financial Times*, February 17, 2011; Andrew Parker, "Groups Look at Apple and Google with Increasing Alarm," *Financial Times*, January 19, 2011.
⑤ Tom Standage, "Mobile Marvels," *The Economist*, a special report on telecoms in emerging markets, September 26, 2009; Parselelo Kantai, "Mobiles May Be Future of Banking," *Financial Times*, September 30, 2010; Suzanne Kapner, "Visa Steps Up Push into Mobile Banking," *Financial Times*, June 10, 2011. Late in 2013, Qatari telecoms group Ooredoo announced that it had more than one million mobile money customers in Qatar, Tunisia, and Indonesia. "Ooredoo Reaches 1m Mobile Money Customers," *TeleGeography*, CommsUpdate, November 6, 2013.
⑥ David Pogue, "No Cards, No Cash. Just a Phone," *New York Times*, September 22, 2011; Chris Nuttall, "Google Launches Wallet Service," *Financial Times*, September 20, 2011; "Google Wallet Opens for Business, Visa Gets On Board," *Los Angeles Times*, September 19, 2011, available at http://latimesblogs.latimes.com/technology/2011/09/google-wallet-opens-for-business-visa-gets-onboard.html (accessed January 10, 2014).
⑦ Lewis Dowling, "Telcos Can Use Prepaid Top-Ups to Break into M-Commerce—Study," *Total Telecom*, September 27, 2011, available at http://www.totaltele.com/view.aspx?ID=467935 (accessed January 10, 2014).
⑧ Maija Palmer, "Battle over Mobile Payments Intensifies," *Financial Times*, November 30, 2011, available at http://www.ft.com/intl/cms/s/2/cadb9bec-16cd-11e1-bc1d-00144feabdc0.html#axzz1fELZDNb1 (accessed January 10, 2014).

消费者的点击购买行为。实际上,美国排名前500的在线零售商中只有12%的网站可以在手机浏览器上访问①。以卫星定位技术为基础的定位广告(又被称为"地理围栏")②,选择那些流连于星巴克或百思买连锁分店的消费者为营销的目标受众。另外两家颇有商业野心的企业谷歌和苹果,则因为各自隐秘且富有侵略性的数据搜集计划被曝光而懊恼不已③。

苹果在其2012年的开发者大会上宣布,它将自主开发地图应用程序,以摆脱对谷歌地图应用的依赖。该声明证实,"手机地图应用的重要性不可小觑,以至于不能将开发权旁落他人之手"④(尽管苹果自己研发的地图应用程序普遍受到外界耻笑)。地理位置与日俱增的重要性也是谷歌2013年收购地图导航公司瓦泽(Waze)的原因⑤。网络中介商争先恐后地将数字地图置入手机商品链中,以满足它们至少三个目的:地方商业、定位广告以及移动支付。微软视窗系统联合诺基亚(2013年微软收购诺基亚手机业务),从而完成这项发展大计;谷歌则开发自己的安卓和地图应用程序;至于苹果,它有自己的操作系统,并与荷兰数字地图公司通腾(TomTom)签订协议⑥。

当移动设备侵入那些尚未完全与之配套或兼容的环境(高速公路与城市街道、教堂、医院和教室)中时,对此,人们显得束手无策,有时感觉不安全。同样,每年数亿台手机的销售量导致严重的环境问题,这一点理查德·马克斯韦尔(Richard Maxwell)与托比·米勒(Toby Miller)已有研究⑦。移动设备不但给窘迫不堪的能源供给造成更大的压力,并产生海量电子垃圾。那些电子废弃品的化学污染物会溶解到土壤里,也会被处理这些废品的人所吸收。

从资本的角度,更重要的问题在于,谁将从这些重构中的通信商品链中获益。任何

---

① Stephanie Clifford and Claire Cain Miller, "A Grip on Hand – Held Shopping," *New York Times*, April 16, 2011; Stephanie Clifford and Claire Cain Miller, "Tablet Apps with That Catalog Feel," *New York Times*, May 30, 2011.
② Jonathan Birchall, "Shoppers Get a Taste of Geographic Marketing," *Financial Times*, October 15, 2010.
③ Christian Sandvig and Dan Schiller, "Is Google's Spy – Fi about Privacy, or Something More?" *Huffington Post*, November 18, 2010, available at http://www.huffingtonpost.com/ christian – sandvig/is – googles – spyfi – about – pr_b_785015. html (accessed January 10, 2014). 在斯诺登事件产生前18个月,就已爆出安卓操作系统有可能用于搜集手机用户键盘输入的数据的新闻,请参见 Katherine Rushton, "Software on Android Phones 'Tracking Every Keystroke," The Telegraph, November 30, 2011, available at http://www.telegraph.co.uk/technology/mobile – phones/8927164/Software – on – Android – phones – tracking – every – key – stroke. html (accessed January 10, 2014).
④ Quentin Hardy, "Head to Head over Mobile Maps," *New York Times*, June 18, 2012.
⑤ Amir Efrati and Ben Vox Ruben, "Google Buys Startup Waze to Bolster Its Maps, Block Purchase by Rival," *Wall Street Journal*, June 12, 2013.
⑥ Matt Steinglass, "TomTom Repositions Itself with Apple Maps Tie – up," *Financial Times*, June 13, 2012.
⑦ Richard Maxwell and Toby Miller, *Greening the Media* (New York: Oxford University Press, 2012). 要简单的了解相关情况,请参见 Richard Maxwell and Toby Miller, "The Environment and Global Media and Communications Policy," in *The Handbook of Global Media and Communication Policy*, ed. R. Mansell and M. Raboy, 467 – 85 (London: Blackwell, 2011).

答案必须包括除了网络设备所占有的利润魔盒之外的另一类利润魔盒,即基于既有的基础设施而开发出来的应用程序与内容所占有的利润魔盒。

软件与应用程序

网络内容的生产过程,以及生产、利用与分享内容的网络工具的配置过程,不仅规模巨大,更具有社会复杂性。背后的动力多种多样:增加个人财富、公开发表个人作品和文集的私人动机;文化遗产组织与政府启动图书馆、档案馆与博物馆"大型数字化"战略的考量;非营利性和草根组织传播信息与通讯的目标;无论新旧、以赢利为目的的企业推动商品交换、为它们受版权保护的内容提供数字化"市场窗口"的诉求①。个体在网络上传内容的便利性,将网络转变成一个巨大的混杂物。截至 2011 年,共有 3.12 亿个网站;2013 年,谷歌能够搜索到 30 万亿网页②:多种形式、多种语言、多种变化。从"印刷"到"电子媒体"的进化不是单向度的转变,而是社会传播形式与信息的不规则的重组过程。如今,宣称某种社会身份似乎只需要你在网络上有规律地发表言论。既有的职业与劳动形式都发生变化,以保证言语具有数字化特征。

1990 年代,进入互联网领域就已成为互联网商业开发的前提条件。建立专属稳定的网络接入点是市场发展的主轴。由于万维网是围绕软件而建立起来的,因此谁能率先产生网络效应,谁就能赢得竞争优势:例如率先打造一个"任何人"都能进入的平台,因为看起来"每个人"都已经能进入其中。然而,市场成功不仅依靠(技术)创新,还需仰仗投资资本的使用权以及可持续性的商业推广。这一点,马修·克雷恩(Matthew Crain)已经指出③。

建造商品链的根本力量在于,它向外延伸,试图把握不同的关系与结构性联系。通过这些关系和联系,生产得以展开。依靠互联网的商品链包含几个功能性要素:操作系统软件与浏览器、搜索引擎、社交媒体以及在此之上的网络内容与应用程序。市场优势在哪?供应商不仅在各种利基市场里(与其他供应商)厮杀,还尝试借助它们的初始优势

---

① Katrina Fenlon, "Corporate Mass Digitization and Cultural Heritage: From Public Relations to Content Accumulation," unpublished research paper, Graduate School of Library and Information Science, University of Illinois at Urbana – Champaign, January 2014; Dan Schiller and ShinJoung Yeo, "*Powered by Google: Widening Access and Tightening Corporate Control*" (New York: Leonardo Electronic Almanac, forthcoming).

② Thomas O. Barnett, Covington and Burling LLP, Statement before Senate Judiciary Committee, Subcommittee on Antitrust, Competition Policy and Consumer Rights, *Hearing on Competition in Online Markets/Internet Search Issues*, September 21, 2011; April Dembosky and Richard Waters, "Desperately Seeking Data," *Financial Times*, January 19/20, 2013.

③ Matt Crain, "The Revolution Will Be Commercialized: Finance, Public Policy, and the Construction of Internet Advertising," PhD diss., University of Illinois, Urbana – Champaign, 2013.

打入其他领域,比如融合发展的产业或商品子链。一旦拥有庞大的用户群,供应商紧接着寻求利润渠道的多样化与扩大化,例如借助多功能的软件服务整合附加功能。抢先一步占有市场才是目的,并且攻防兼备。

罗伯特·麦克切斯尼(Robert McChesney)的研究让我们注意到那些使万维网技能与体验有机化的大型公司:谷歌、苹果、亚马逊、微软与脸书①。这些企业的市场导向各不相同,分别主打网络搜索与内容、硬件、电子商务、软件与社交媒体。但它们的利润战略经常相互融合,例如移动设备成为市场支点,媒体内容成为共享的必需品。

从行动研究公司(RIM)旗下的黑莓手机中吸取灵感,苹果将硬件紧密地整合进其专属的操作系统软件里,从而设立自己的模式。这不仅是苹果各种工业设计的契机,也使它"吸引到数量庞大的软件开发者进驻苹果应用商店——这是苹果公司在智能手机与平板电脑市场上所具有的优势"②。随着软件程序开发商与内容生产者涌入苹果操作系统的移动端③,公司成功跻身于媒体产业。现有的媒体公司通过表面看起来十分安全的销售渠道进行产品与内容交易,苹果抢夺了它们30%的产品与内容④。起初,这些公司松了一口气,随着形势的严峻它们变得愈发焦虑。经过重新调整的商品链让苹果及其软件开发商独占大部分利润,而其雇员的收入依然低下。

微软采取了截然不同的发展战略,再次显示它既有的实力。从1980年代开始,微软以它的桌面电脑操作系统为杠杆,主导个人电脑市场;1990年代末它继续将视窗系统与其网络浏览器捆绑在一起,借此奋力闯入万维网领域。直至最近,微软所占的逾80%的个人电脑操作系统市场份额为它带来了令人艳羡的利润。当前微软能否另辟蹊径,从而在智能手机和平板电脑市场上具有相对优势? 已经有好几种手机操作系统在市面上流通。其中,佼佼者当属苹果操作系统与谷歌的安卓系统。因此,微软试图成功地度过这一过渡期,进而迎头赶上。在苹果的移动设备及其专属的商业模式的重压下,微软首先与诺基亚手机业务结盟,随后直接收购后者⑤,凭借装有视窗系统的手机软件,微软扩大用户基础。随后它挤入平板电脑市场,并在意识到个人电脑的时代正在终结后,最终设

---

① Robert W. McChesney, *Digital Disconnect: How Capitalism Is Turning the Internet against Democracy* (New York: New Press,2013).
② Paul Taylor and Richard Waters, "Purchase Offers Platform for Consolidation of Hardware and Software Makers," *Financial Times*, August 17,2011.
③ Jessica E. Vascellaro, "Apps Developers Who Are Too Young to Drive," *Wall Street Journal*, June 18,2012; Richard Waters, "Android's Momentum Eats into Apples and BlackBerrys," *Financial Times*, August 15,2013.
④ Andrew Edgecliffe-Johnson, "Premium Content to Drive Tablets' Popularity," *Financial Times*, January 8-9,2011; David Gelles and Joseph Menn, "Publishers Anxious over Apple's Strategy," *Financial Times*, February 2,2011; Thomas Catan and Nathan Koppel, "Regulators Eye Apple Anew," *Wall Street Journal*, February 18,2011.
⑤ 2012年6月诺基亚市值已跌至十年前其高峰值的3成;十年前,它是全球手机供应商巨头,具体请参见 Daniel Thomas and Michael Stothard, "Nokia Plans Further 10,000 Job Cuts after Second Profit Warning," *Financial Times*, June 15,2012。

立了自己的平板电脑生产线①。微软对企业市场的把控,使它有底气击退一批在线的竞争者;然而,尽管微软的网络浏览器、备受好评的搜索引擎"必应"(Bing)及其"奢飞思"(Surface)平板电脑/个人电脑一体机取得市场成功,可巨大的成本投入依然没能使它在手机网络的重构过程中占据主导位置。

谷歌采取了第三条路径。谷歌凭借搜索引擎吸引海量的用户,并将他们源源不断地导向开放的万维网世界;它基本的赢利战略是,售卖广告以获得流入与流出网站的流量。谷歌将网站流量作为砝码,开发出众多颇受追捧的网络工具(主要是手机操作系统),并因此主导所有互联网功能。它投入资金保障其安卓操作系统的普及,拓展其广告网络并购买或认购一批应用程序与内容,从而试图对苹果公司形成包抄之势。谷歌网站要比它替用户搜索出来的网站更赚钱(它认为这一趋势仍将持续②),所以它毫无顾忌将旗下的所有网站都置于相关搜索结果的前列。2008年谷歌推出安卓系统以间接迎战苹果,此时移动设备在互联网市场的转型过程中如日中天;它准许宏达国际电子股份有限公司、摩托罗拉与三星等移动设备制造商免费安装自己的安卓系统。这些以及其他竞争者相继被苹果打败后,之所以能迅速并低成本地进入智能手机市场,原因在于它们免费试用谷歌的安卓系统。当智能手机普及,并占2010年全球手机销量的五分之一③、2013年的二分之一后,谷歌的战略取得成功。整体统计,安装安卓系统的智能手机生产商成为全球市场的主体;截至2010年,安装安卓系统的手机的全球销量总计6700万台,一举超过苹果手机④。三星凭借"盖乐世"型号智能手机,在2011年第三季度的全球销售业绩上完胜苹果,尽管它的利润率只是苹果的一半左右⑤。

那么谷歌呢?时任谷歌首席执行官的埃里克·施密特(Eric Schmidt)在2008年向(《纽约客》杂志记者)肯·奥莱塔(Ken Auletta)透露,移动设备仍有可能成为次焦点,因为"要维系这些平台,谷歌需要耗费更多资金,并向电话公司让出控制权"⑥。三年后,谷歌在世界范围内每天都激活55万台安装安卓系统的手机⑦。截至2012年,它的安卓软

---

① Paul Taylor,"RIM Pays Price of Failing to Lure Customers from Apple and Google," *Financial Times*, September 16, 2011; Richard Waters, "Mobilising against Mobile," *Financial Times*, May 25, 2012; Nick Wingfield, "Microsoft Is Expected to Introduce a Tablet," *New York Times*, June 16, 2012; Richard Waters, "Surface Tensions," *Financial Times*, June 23 – 24, 2012.

② Google, Inc., U.S. SEC 10 – Q, June 30, 2013, 33.

③ Gustav Sandstrom, "Low – Cost Chinese Cellphones Power Handset – Shipment Surge," *Wall Street Journal*, November 11, 2010.

④ Andrew Parker,"Google's Android Overtakes Nokia in Smartphone Race," *Financial Times*, February 1, 2011; Hiroko Tabuchi, "Japan Phone Makers See Opportunity in Android," *New York Times*, March 1, 2011.

⑤ Song Jung – a and Joseph Menn, "Samsung Takes Top Slot in Phone Sales," *Financial Times*, October 29 – 30, 2011.

⑥ Ken Auletta, *Googled: The End of the World as We Know It* (New York: Penguin, 2009), 294.

⑦ Anna Eppley, "The Man behind Google's Rise," *Wall Street Journal*, August 1, 2011.

件应用商店推出约 50 万种应用程序①,消费者下载应用程序数十亿次。2013 年下半年,安装苹果操作系统的移动设备约 7 亿台,相较之下,安装谷歌的安卓系统的移动设备则高达 10 亿台②。尽管如此,苹果在应用商店率先取得的成功依然帮助它占据应用商店销售总额的绝大部分(与谷歌游戏相比)。例如 2013 年苹果与谷歌的市场占比分别是 63%和 37%③。

如上所述,苹果成功建立了专属的生态系统,这诱使谷歌购买硬件设备以受其控制,例如 2012 年购买摩托罗拉旗下智能手机子公司。它的主要目的在于,垄断摩托罗拉的专利,借此保护自身产业发展;2014 年,谷歌所拥有的受法律保护的技术创新使它成为顶级的专利持有企业之一④。然而,为了使它的软件与硬件子公司生产的产品相协调,谷歌也提高它有可能提前实现的市场预期,即从那些正使用安卓操作系统的外部生产商中撤退。在这一点上,大韩民国的初期反应可为前车之鉴。在谷歌竞价收购摩托罗拉移动期间,韩国政府号召三星与乐金电子(分别是世界排名第二和第三的手机制造商)联合起来,旨在开发本土的手机操作系统从而摆脱对谷歌安卓系统的依赖⑤。三星继续与软件制造商英特尔、沃达丰、橘子系统(Orange)以及多科莫公司(这些都是顶级的手机企业)合作,力求制定出替换安卓系统的保险政策⑥。当谷歌打退堂鼓,把摩托罗拉卖给联想时,它希望能巩固与那些仍然依赖安卓系统的设备制造商(主要就是三星,它占全球安卓手机销量的四成⑦)的良好关系。

很快,安卓系统渗透到智能手机之外的领域里。2011 年秋,亚马逊与索尼各自宣布旗下平板电脑配置谷歌的操作系统软件。索尼计划优化其平板电脑配置,以让用户更好地体验索尼第四代游戏、唱片、电影,与此同时提供无线上网功能以连接其他的电子设备,譬如视频播放器与电视⑧。中国的联想集团在本土与苹果平板电脑展开竞争,控制成本的同时推出新型号的平板电脑,既能使用安卓又能兼容微软的视窗系统⑨。

---

① Jessica E. Vascellaro,"Developers to Apple:Promote Our Apps!",*Wall Street Journal*,June 13,2012.
② Tim Bradshaw and April Dembosky,"Apple keeps iPhone in the Upper Tier of the Market,"*Financial Times*,September 11,2013.
③ Tim Bradshaw,"Google Eats into Apple's app pile,"*Financial Times*,December 18,2013.
④ Richard Waters,"Google Races Higher in Patent League,"*Financial Times*,January 13,2014.
⑤ Christian Oliver,"S Korea to Develop Mobile Platform,"*Financial Times*,August 25,2011.
⑥ Financial Times Reporters,"Samsung Scrambles To Meet Chief's Reinvention Challenge,"*Financial Times*,January 28,2014.
⑦ Richard Waters,"Google Lifted on Android Optimism,"*Financial Times*,January 31,2014.
⑧ Jonathan Soble,"Sony to Challenge iPad with Tablet S,"*Financial Times*,September 16,2011,available at http://www.ft.com/intl/cms/s/2/4ad21130-e05c-11e0-ba12-00144feabdc0.html#axzz1YAWept1W (accessed January 10,2014).
⑨ Ben Worthen,Justin Scheck,and Gina Chon,"H-P Explores Quitting Computers as Profits Slide,"*Wall Street Journal*,August 19,2011;Joseph Menn,"HP Bosses Defend Strategy Shift after Shares Fall,"*ncial Times*,August 22,2011;Paul Taylor,"Lenovo to Throw Down iPad Gauntlet,"*Financial Times*,August 22,2011.

浏览器通常与操作系统绑定在一起,它成为竞争的另一领域。微软的浏览器迄今为止主导台式机;同时,谋智公司旗下的开源浏览器"火狐"异军突起,谷歌浏览器紧随其后。随着移动设备逐渐超越个人电脑成为主流,苹果开始宣称旗下浏览器在市场处于领先位置(例如2011年占五分之三的市场份额①)。随后,谷歌的安卓软件迅速取代了它,仅仅两年后,80%的已销售手机都使用安卓浏览器②。

"云存储"是影响手机市场的另一项技术③。大型互联网中介商围绕巨大的"服务器农场"重新调整其运营策略。"服务器农场"用于存储并向用户传送内容与应用程序④。英特尔公司曾有过统计,每600台智能手机与122台平板电脑需要额外增加一台服务器;于是,曾生产大部分服务器的惠普与戴尔公司受惠良多⑤。

大型数据中心成为更广泛地进行重建的基础设施的枢纽地带。客户可能会担心,将敏感的数据与软件储存在一个外部供应商那似乎不太安全,黑客攻击与服务器宕机更加剧着客户的担忧。然而,在成本与运营的层面上,云服务不断扩展。诚如我们所见,云服务正在产生巨大的网络流量。起决定作用的是,尽快建立传感器阵列与移动设备;移动设备的记忆与信息处理功能相对较弱,必须与日渐剧增的同步多种设备的用户需求以及互联网中介商旨在实现更好的控制、推进集中化供给的诉求相结合。

美国大型的数据中心服务提供商包括亚马逊、微软、谷歌、美国国际商用机器公司、威瑞森、全球服务托管云计算商(Rackspace)以及美国电话电报公司⑥。除了新泽西纽瓦克的数据中心外,苹果计划耗资十亿美元在北卡罗来纳州建立面积达50万平方英尺的数据中心⑦。脸书设在俄勒冈州中部的数据中心,大约有五个足球场那么大,并还将继续

---

① Peter Bright,"The End of an Era: Internet Explorer Drops below 50% of Web Usage,"*Ars Technica*,November 2,2011,available at http://arstechnica.com/microsoft/news/2011/11/the-end-of-an-era-internet-explorer-drops-below-50-percent-of-web-usage.ars(accessed January 10,2014).
② Richard Waters,"Android's Momentum Eats into Apples and BlackBerrys,"*Financial Times*,August 15,2013.
③ 关于云计算较早的入门读物,请参见 David Mitchell Smith,Daryl C. Plummer,and David W. Cearley,"The What,Why,and When of Cloud Computing,"Gartner Research ID Number G00168582,June 4,2009. 云计算的深入分析可参见 Vincent Mosco,*To the Cloud: Big Data in a Turbulent World*(Boulder,Colo.: Paradigm,2014).
④ "The concept of renting computing power goes back decades, to the days when companies would share space on a single mainframe with big spinning tape drives. The technology industry has matured to the point where there is now an emerging mass market for this rental model." Brad Stone and Ashlee Vance,"Companies Slowly Join Cloud-Computing,"*New York Times*,April 18,2010,available at http://www.nytimes.com/2010/04/19/technology/19cloud.html?_r=0(accessed January 10,2014).
⑤ Richard Waters and Chris Nuttall,"Cloud Computing Benefits Apple's Rivals,"*FT.com*,May 19,2011.
⑥ Stone and Vance,"Companies Slowly Join Cloud-Computing."一些不太知名却相对重要的企业也加入到这一市场竞争中;例如易昆尼克斯(Equinix)在全球37个国家里运营95家数据中心,请参见 "Equinix Expands to South America with Brazil Data Centre Purchase,"*TeleGeography*,CommsUpdate,February 23,2011.
⑦ The DataCenter Journal accords continuing coverage. Retrieved at www.datacenter journal.com.

扩建；该公司还将在北卡罗来纳州建立另一个与之媲美的机构①。俄勒冈和华盛顿以其低廉的土地价格与丰富的水能、风能，往往成为（互联网公司）首先考虑的地点：亚马逊、谷歌与微软都在西北各州拥有自己的数据中心②。数据中心的分布无论从国内还是国际的层面上，都显得不均衡。毫无疑问，美国的数据中心比任何一个国家都要多。发达国家整体上所占的高比例明显失衡。然而，美国国际商用机器公司计划在2014年年底跨越五大洲的13个国家建立40个数据中心；这一战略计划清楚地显示了数据中心的增长模式③。在本书的第三部分，我将分析向云计算的转型如何深刻影响美国的国际互联网政策；此处我只强调，云计算与互联网中介商的利润战略息息相关。

过去，自动配置的个人电脑是网络连接的枢纽；当前，个人电脑被支持移动设备的数据中心所替换。2008年全世界共有数十亿台个人电脑被使用，并且它们的销售量每年都有一亿台左右。不过，套用英特尔前首席技术官的话，云服务使个人电脑转变成一台"仅仅用于显示的设备而已"④。日复一日，消费者也从一种设备转向另一种设备；确保用户体验的延续性是竞争的关键，诚如谷歌2013年对外界所说的那样，"我们正在向一个动态的、多屏幕的环境转型"⑤。

互联网中介商再次显示出它们与众不同的实力，采取各不相同的战略以建立自己的云服务，但苹果的云服务（iCloud）最具代表性⑥。除了无与伦比的现金储备以及用历史事件图案装饰的品牌形象外，苹果还拥有两项令人生畏的资产：数亿台运行苹果操作系统软件的移动设备、全球范围内近乎同样规模的活跃信用卡用户⑦。在这些基础上，苹果云服务（2013年4月每天都有三亿人使用⑧）成为苹果气势汹汹地向各类媒体内容的分配领域进军的关键一步。作为世界上最大的电影零售商（占全球在线电影交易总额的一

---

① John Letzing, "Facebook Plants Roots in Central Oregon," *MarketWatch*, January 20, 2011. Retrieved at http://www.marketwatch.com/story/facebook – data – center – revitalizes – oregon – town – 2011 – 01 – 20 (accessed January 10, 2014).

② John Foley, "Signs Points to Amazon Data Center Expansion," *Information Week*, October 29, 2010, available at http://www.informationweek.com/services/hosted – applications/ signs – point – to – amazon – data – center – expans/ 228000376 (accessed January 10, 2014).

③ Quentin Hardy, "IBM Has Big Plans for Investments in the Cloud," *New York Times*, January 20, 2014.

④ Richard Waters and Chris Nuttall, "Cloud Threatens to End PC's Reign," *Financial Times*, June 11 – 12, 2011.

⑤ Google Inc., U.S. SEC 10 – Q, June 30, 2013, 33.

⑥ Miguel Helft, "Apple Unveils a 'Cloud' Storage Service for Music, Photos and Files," *New York Times*, June 7, 2011; Martin Peers, "Apple's Flashy Music Margins," *Wall Street Journal*, June 28, 2011.

⑦ Richard Waters, "Apple Races to Keep Users Firmly Wrapped in Its Cloud," *Financial Times*, June 9, 2011; Joseph Menn, "Apple's iPhone and iPad Apps Migrate to Mac," *Financial Times*, October 21, 2010; April Dembosky, "Facebook in Challenge to Apple with iPad App," *Financial Times*, October 11, 2011, available at http://www.ft.com/intl/cms/s/2/7b21838e – f38f – 11e0 – b98c – 00144feab49a.html#axzz1aQjfNW3O (accessed January 10, 2014); Andrew Ross Sorkin, "Suggestions for an Apple Shopping List," *New York Times*, July 31, 2012.

⑧ Tim Bradshaw, "Apple Investors Digest Cash Return but Hunger for Hardware," *Financial Times*, April 25, 2013.

半),苹果正加紧推行它的租赁模式①。

苹果的发展战略导致一种更不稳定的状态,而它的竞争对手——其他互联网中介商试图在面向消费者的内容与应用程序上与之相抗衡。由此导致的重构过程,吞噬了第三类市场行动者,即大型的多媒体企业。这些企业曾一度主导通信产业的政治经济发展,如今仍在帮助塑造重构过程的资本逻辑。

---

① Matthew Garrahan, "A Cloud up in the Air," *Financial Times*, August 1, 2011.

第 7 章
服务与应用程序

美国在线——时代华纳的分拆宣告了上一个千禧年的彻底终结,它也表明,现有的多媒体公司接管全新的数字系统与数字化业务的可能性烟消云散。相反,令这些多媒体巨头意外的是,他们不得不处于市场防守状态。抢占他们地盘的不仅包括宽带与移动互联网运营商,比如美国电话电报公司、威瑞森、康卡斯特,还包括资金充足的来自其他行业的竞争者与意料之外的"新贵":从早期的网景、雅虎(Yahoo!),再到后来的谷歌、苹果、亚马逊、微软(Microsoft)、脸书、网飞等[①]。

然而,并非只有这些媒体大亨被淘汰出局。根深蒂固的媒体集团可能陷入危机的事实,与众多批评分析家的预测不尽相同。本·巴格迪肯(Ben Bagdikian)从 1983 年开始写作,其有影响力的著作历经六次修订(最终修订版为 2000 年版)。在书中,他将"媒体垄断"(The Media Monopoly)描绘成不断巩固的权力节点。然而,以收入和利润这些传统的标准,或放在更加广泛的战略杠杆的背景下来衡量,21 世纪的前 20 年里,以谷歌、亚马逊、苹果和微软为首的互联网中介商纷纷追上甚至赶超新闻集团(News Corporation)、迪士尼(Disney)、维亚康姆(Viacom)、康卡斯特和时代华纳(Time-Warner)等传统的媒体巨头。不过,这一赶超的过程并非预示盈利机制的失效,反而表明信息和通信商品化的巨大延伸。为了实现这一目标,必须打破现有的贸易条件。

谷歌把导航服务作为"杠杆"。谷歌网站的网络流量巨大,它既作为把关人又逐步以主题终端的身份,通过提供各种内容获取高额利润。谷歌子公司 YouTube 占据网络视频流量的主要份额,截至 2013 年,它拥有十亿活跃用户[②]。除此之外,谷歌还运营谷歌地方

[①] Robert W. McChesney, *Digital Disconnect: How Capitalism Is Turning the Internet against Democracy* (New York: New Press, 2013); John Battelle, "The Internet Big Five by Product Strength," battellemedia.com, January 5, 2012.

[②] Tim Bradshaw, "YouTube Reaches 1bn User Milestone," *Financial Times*, March 22, 2013; Matthew Garrahan and Andrew Edgecliffe-Johnson, "YouTube Nears Subscription Service for Its Specialist Channels," *Financial Times*, May 6, 2013.

信息（Google Places）、谷歌新闻（Google News）、谷歌财经（Google Finance）和谷歌图书（Google Books）。同时，它的垂直搜索业务也使其能够准入旅游、购物和当地商业市场（包括地图、产品搜索、航班搜索）①。而由此产生的竞争对手的规模与业务范围值得注意。以谷歌涉及的其中一块业务"旅游信息"为例，截至2013年，它的对手猫途鹰（TripAdivisor）以21种语言运营30家网站②。

同样，苹果和脸书的发展有赖于被吸引到其网站上的用户；它们的盈利战略与谷歌不同，前者主要取决于用户在网站上做了什么。脸书推出或购买各种业务（例如收购Instagram）与内容。此外，它还与Zynga和Spotify等行外公司合作，以吸引用户浏览它们的网页并不失时机地向他们推送广告。苹果公司则通过应用商店向用户出售音乐、电影、书籍和游戏，并且通过云存储系统使用户能够访问这些内容。它还推出主打音乐流媒体的互联网电台服务。这些公司都不愿意看到流量集中在与自己无关的网站，因此它们不约而同地认为，提供媒介内容至关重要。

2008年，苹果手机正式发布，用户通过苹果的应用商店可以下载十万种应用程序；截至2011年底，苹果手机与平板电脑用户每月下载应用程序的次数高达十亿次。2008年至2013年底，苹果应用商店的总收入为214亿美元，而程序开发商从中赚取150亿美元③。2013年初，苹果每季度从音乐、电影和应用程序上获得的收入可达24亿美元④。短短五年间，苹果的在线运营模式已根深蒂固。苹果的应用商店可谓傲视群雄，共售卖65万种应用程序⑤，尽管它要面对谷歌等对手的激烈竞争。根据美国联邦通信委员会的报告，苹果主要的应用程序不仅包括导航和社交软件，还涉及新闻资讯应用、游戏、定位服务、图片共享、音乐视频软件和网络语音电话业务等内容。报告中还提到，"除此之外，第三方应用软件开发商还依照特殊用户、兴趣、癖好以及产业量身打造了数以千计的利基应用程序"⑥。2013年年底，全世界范围内27亿网络用户下

---

① Thomas O. Barnett, Covington & Burling LLP, "The Power of Google: Serving Consumers or Threatening Competition?" Statement before Senate Judiciary Committee, Subcommittee on Antitrust, Competition Policy and Consumer Rights, Hearing on Competition in Online Markets/Internet Search Issues, September 21, 2011, 5, available at http://www.gpo.gov/fdsys/pkg/CHRG-112shrg71471/html/CHRG-112shrg71471.htm (accessed January 10, 2014); Claire Cain Miller "As Web Search Goes Mobile, Apps Chip at Google's Lead," *New York Times*, April 4, 2013.

② Roger Blitz, "TripAdvisor's Anger at Google Incursion," *Financial Times*, April 1, 2013.

③ Tim Bradshaw, "Android Hits 10bn to Narrow App Gap with Apple," *Financial Times*, December 7, 2011; Dennis K. Berman, "Tin Pan Valley: The Coming Shakeout for App Makers," *Wall Street Journal*, June 13, 2012. 也请参见 Chris Nuttall, "Apple and Microsoft Wrestle with App Issues," *Financial Times*, June 11, 2012; Shaun Nichols, "Apple: Wow, Thanks for the $10bn-a-year App Store," *The Register*, January 7, 2014, available at http://www.theregister.co.uk/2014/01/07/apple_app_store_10bn_2013 (accessed February 3, 2014).

④ Tim Bradshaw, "Apple Investors Digest Cash Return but Hunger for Hardware," *Financial Times*, April 25, 2013

⑤ Jessica E. Vascellaro, "Developers to Apple: Promote Our Apps!" *Wall Street Journal*, June 13, 2012.

⑥ U.S. FCC 11 103, WT Docket No. 10-133, "Annual Report and Analysis of Competitive Market Conditions with Respect to Mobile Wireless, Including Commercial Mobile Services," *Fifteenth Report*, June 27, 2011, 21.

载应用程序的次数超过 750 亿①。

除了风险投资和出售股份外,所有通信产业与媒体还有三种资金来源:第一,直接支付,包括服务费、订阅费、网站授权许可费以及租赁费;第二,形式不断更新的广告;第三,非商业资助,包括政府或慈善基金以及自愿捐款。这三类资金来源以多种方式组合,在此基础上,通信系统得以建立或重建。面向在互联网上实现融合的每一条商品链的每一个环节,公司根据上述三种可能的营收模式重新规划战略,并重新调整运营方式。"新""旧"媒体之间的连接,加上互联网特定业务与应用程序具有的发展前景,与同时期不同商业模式的演变紧密相关。

协商之后的转型

那些传统媒体巨头从未遭遇"互联网"的对抗,甚至被后者淘汰。这并非一次性的替换过程,而是一场复杂且充满协商的转型之交。媒体巨头不仅全权掌控人们听说读写的商品,更与新出现的竞争者即大型互联网中介商保持战略性的互动关系。竞争对手不可小觑,并且互联网企业往往占据上风,可合作程度有增无减。各类企业都坚信,可盈利的领域有可能扩大或至少会有所调整,因此,这些企业致力于重构通信与信息商品链,甚至不惜改变贸易条件。

2011 年底,在全美访问量排名前十的网站中,只有维基百科既不依靠广告收入,也不依靠消费者直接支付而维持运营②。互联网业务的开展,必须以获得授权访问媒体集团受版权保护的内容与品牌为前提,而媒体集团也需要在数字化环境中获得更多利润③。正如一位分析家所说:"音乐、电影和电视之于互联网播放器而言,如同琴凳之于钢琴,不可分割"④。

争夺市场地位的战役愈演愈烈。在 2012 至 2013 年间,几大互联网公司联合它们的非营利性同盟组成了庞大的政治力量,有效地阻止针对在线版权的严格立法,而后者正由多媒体集团一举推动⑤。然而,随着新兴的互联网公司与现存的媒体企业达成协议,同

---

① ITU, *Trends in Telecommunications Reform* 2013, 3.
② "comScore Media Metrix Ranks Top 50 U. S. Web Properties for December 2011," comScore. com, January 23, 2012.
③ Jin Kim, "The Institutionalization of YouTube: From User – Generated Content to Professionally Generated Content," *Media, Culture and Society* 34, no. 1 (2012):53 – 67.
④ Patrick Zelnik, "A Universal – EMI Merger Could Rescue the Music Business," *Financial Times*, July 17, 2012.
⑤ Erica Orden and Geoffrey A. Fowler, "Hollywood Loses SOPA Story," *Wall Street Journal*, January 19, 2012. 2013 年末,国会议员发起第三次立法行动启动,以支持国安局监控行动,具体请参见 "Chair of Senate Intelligence Committee Says CISPA Sister Bill is in the Works," RT, September 25, 2013, available at http://rt.com/usa/feinstein – cispa – cyber – security – 342 (accessed January 10, 2014).

化的趋势毋庸置疑①。

媒体集团通过大量的市场窗口为不同的媒介产品建立不同的收入来源,互联网中介商却没有这么做。苹果、谷歌和微软的赢利情况令外界哗然:2012年,它们的营业利润率都在40%上下浮动②。媒体企业或网络运营商虽然利润不菲,但相较于互联网中介商,可算小巫见大巫。不过,互联网公司的利润与限定的细分市场密不可分。微软每年从个人电脑软件销售中赚取400亿美元;苹果的收入主要源自设备;亚马逊基本依赖电子商务;脸书在其计划书中直言其85%的收入源于广告③;谷歌95%的收入均来自广告,并得到单一形式的赞助④。倘若媒体集团需要向前整合进入数字业务领域,那么互联网中介商需要使它们的收入来源多样化⑤。对特定行业的评估,有助于我们对接下来的趋势有更清晰的认识。

五大跨国集团在20世纪下半叶相继吞并了美国数家图书出版公司(这一巨人仍在增长:国家批准贝塔斯曼旗下的兰登书屋[Random House]与皮尔松[Pearson]下属的企鹅出版集团[Penguin]合并,由此产生世界上最大的普通版图书出版商)⑥。这些集团的子公司发售少数可靠的畅销书作家的精装本或平装本图书,以此主导美国与欧洲图书贸易市场。然而,自从巴诺书店与博得斯(Borders)或沃尔玛这样的连锁大卖场主宰了图书零售市场以来,图书出版商的市场优势一去不复返。1995年,出版商又遭遇亚马逊网站的大举进攻。这家互联网零售商以诱人低价(起初每个季度都在亏损,旨在扩大市场份额)与免税的销售优势将本已处于困境的独立书店逼上绝路;与此同时,亚马逊的市场策略对连锁店和集团出版商造成巨大冲击。亚马逊借助其创新的电子零售渠道,重构了图书商品链;然而,亚马逊在图书出版行业依然属于"混血儿",直到2007年它推出电子书阅读器,这是因为在此之前它依然依赖传统的物流配送,将印刷术或唱片送到消费者手上。亚马逊全球公共政策副总裁保罗·米泽纳(Paul Misener)2010年向国会小组委员会透露,亚马逊每年在出口货运上的花费就高达10亿美元,平均每周的航运费用20万美

---

① Brooks Barnes,"Web Deals Cheer Hollywood, Despite Drop in Moviegoers," *New York Times*, February 24, 2012, available at http://www.nytimes.com/2012/02/25/business/media/web-deals-cheer-hollywood-despite-a-drop-in-moviegoers.html? google_editors_picks = true (accessed January 10, 2014).

② Richard Waters,"Profits May Elude Mobile Challengers," *Financial Times*, May 30, 2012, available at http://www.ft.com/intl/cms/s/0/2f3b764e-aa75-11e1-9331-00144feabdc0.html#axzz1wOsWPq5T (accessed January 10, 2014).

③ Facebook, Inc., Form S-1 Registration Statement with the U. S. Securities and Exchange Commission, February 1, 2012.

④ Google, Inc. 2011 10-K Report to the SEC, 10.

⑤ Robert Budden and Robert Cookson,"Search for Fresh Revenue Stream: Google Looks to Beat Music Rivals," *Financial Times*, February 23-24, 2013.

⑥ Julie Bosman,"Penguin and Random House Merge, Saying Change Will Come Slowly," *New York Times*, July 1, 2013, available at http://www.nytimes.com/2013/07/02/business/media/merger-of-penguin-and-random-house-is-completed.html? emc = eta1 (accessed January 10, 2104).

元。此外,他还补充一点:"美国邮政(The USPS)是我们为客户提供的服务中不可分割的一部分……网上购物实际上增加了对实体物流的需求"[①],而实体物流基本上只有通过美国邮政系统才能完成。

当电子书最终受到消费者欢迎,一切尘埃落定。斯蒂格·拉森(Stieg Larsson)的千禧年三部曲取得现象级的成功,紧随其后,亚马逊电子书的销售额在 2010 年 4 月至 6 月间,超过该网站精装本实体书的销量[②]。同年,亚马逊电子书的销售额高达 8.78 亿美元,占图书交易总额的 6.4%[③]。然而,这一改变并非命中注定,毕竟,前 30 年间电子书的销售业绩并不令人满意,甚至被视为"错误的开始"。推动电子书获得市场成功的因素之一是出版商优先采用了图书出版的数字化技术,本世纪初,绝大多数商业出版的书籍已经数字化了[④]。第二大诱因来自谷歌。谷歌掠取了图书馆与图书馆员代为管理的数百万的学术公共资源,此举加速了文化资源的大规模数字化进程[⑤]。美国联邦法官否决了谷歌与出版商以及作者之间的贸易条件,这仅仅终止了谷歌的数字图书扫描计划(可 1 500 万册图书已经扫描完毕),却没有剥夺它的这一权利[⑥]。2013 年,谷歌和出版商达成协议后,它在与作者之间的法律纠纷中最终胜诉,轰动一时;这再次为谷歌的文化商品化战略铺平道路[⑦]。

价廉物美的电子书阅读器的普及构成第三个因素。亚马逊推出的阅读器大获成功,

---

① Statement of Paul Misener, vice president for Global Public Policy, Amazon.com, Hearing before the Senate Committee on Homeland Security and Government Affairs, Subcommittee on Financial Management, Government Information, Federal Services, and International Security; and before the House Committee on Oversight and Government Reform, Subcommittee on Federal Workforce, Postal Service, and District of Columbia, June 23, 2010, 2, available at http://www.gpo.gov/fdsys/pkg/CHRG-111shrg58037/pdf/CHRG-111shrg58037.pdf (accessed January 10, 2014).
② Claire Cain Miller, "E-Books Top Hardcovers at Amazon," *New York Times*, July 20, 2010; Colin Robinson, "The Trouble with Amazon," *The Nation*, August 2-9, 2010. The trend persisted, as Amazon divulged in 2011 that mystery author Michael Connelly was the seventh writer to sell more than one million Kindle books. Jeffrey A. Trachtenberg, "… As New One Is Opening," *Wall Street Journal*, July 20, 2011.
③ Kevin J. O'Brien, "European E-Book Sales Hampered by Tax Structure," *New York Times*, December 1, 2011. 关于这一过渡时期的具体描述请参见 John B. Thompson, *Merchants of Culture: The Publishing Business in the Twenty-First Century*, 2nd ed. (New York: Plume, 2012), 313-76. 汤姆森提供的数据更低,尽管这只是一部分美国贸易出版商的数据。
④ Thompson, *Merchants of Culture*, 326.
⑤ Robert Darnton, *The Case for Books* (New York: Public Affairs, 2009); Ken Auletta, *Googled: The End of the World as We Know It* (New York: Penguin, 2009); Robert Darnton, "Google and the Future of Books," *New York Review of Books* 56, no. 2 (February 12, 2009); Hiroko Tabuchi, "To Win, Beat the Apps," *New York Times*, September 26, 2009.
⑥ Miguel Helft, "Federal Judge Rejects Google's Negotiated Deal to Digitize Books," *New York Times*, March 23, 2011. 也请参见 an Schiller and ShinJoung Yeo, "Powered by Google: Widening Access and Tightening Corporate Control" (New York: Leonardo Electronic Almanac, forthcoming).
⑦ Mike Masnick, "Google Gets Total Victory over Authors Guild: Book Scanning Is Fair Use," *Techdirt*, November 14, 2013, available at http://www.techdirt.com/articles/20131114/09561525242/google-gets-total-victory-over-authors-guild-book-scanning-is-fair-use.shtml (accessed January 10, 2014); "Google Books Wins Case against Authors over Putting Books Online," The Guardian, November 14, 2013, available at http://www.theguardian.com/books/2013/nov/14/google-books-wins-case-authors-online (accessed January 10, 2014).

此举创建了与苹果公司竞争的专属电子销售渠道的最终环节。而亚马逊对流行的电子书的低价策略(低于出版商标价的一半有余),则是最终催化剂。这一"先发者策略"帮助亚马逊占据市场份额,带来大量市场份额的同时,对出版业造成巨大冲击①。截至2013年,市面上每卖出的四本印刷书中就有一本来自亚马逊,亚马逊"在图书贸易中拥有史无前例的市场主导权"②。

当前,贸易条件反而对现存的书商与出版商非常不利。随着电子书的普及,美国两大连锁书店之一博得斯不得不向出版商打白条③。当出版商拒绝后,博得斯濒临破产,不得已关闭上百家书店④。巴诺书店努力将自己重新打造成"一个提供图书下载、阅读设备和应用软件的销售平台"⑤,并且与微软合作推出独家电子阅读器(Nook)。然而,随着独立书店在过去20年间遭遇血洗⑥,如今甚至连美国最大的传统书店也在竞争中节节败退,2013年亏损连连上升⑦。

现存的出版商正疯狂地寻求出路,以脱离亚马逊的电子书低价模式带来的影响。正如他们所见,曾经畅销的平装版图书这一根深蒂固的传统贸易形式正在消退⑧。与此相较,亚马逊建立起自己的图书出版机构,截至2011年中,亚马逊宣称已拥有了六个独立的版权标记⑨。由于各类作者都找到绕过现存出版商而直接将作品呈现给读者的方法,自出版行业(Self-publishing)开始蓬勃发展。出版集团关闭部分仓库,将其办公空间向外出租,减少印刷量,并试图削减支付给作者的预付款。西蒙 & 舒斯特(Simon & Schuster)、美国企鹅集团(Penguin Group USA)、阿歇特出版集团(Hachette Book Group)联手打造了网站(Bookish.com),以打破亚马逊在图书出版与销售领域一家独大的局面,另起炉灶⑩。他们试图给电子书涨价,特别是畅销作家的畅销书,比如史蒂芬·金(Stephen King)和麦克·康纳利(Michael Connelly)的作品⑪。苹果也推出平板电脑,借此进军电子书市场。此举确认了出版商在绝境中力求将图书零售价格回调至亚马逊9.99美元标准

---

① Thompson, *Merchants of Culture*, 337–39, 368–76.
② David Streitfeld, "As Competition Wanes, Amazon Cuts Back Discounts," *New York Times*, July 5, 2013.
③ Julie Bosman "Struggling Borders to Meet with Publishers," *New York Times*, January 4, 2011.
④ Mike Spector, "Borders Forced to Close All Its Stores," *Wall Street Journal*, July 19, 2011.
⑤ Trachtenberg, "...As New One Is Opening."
⑥ Julie Bosman, "A Reading of Relief at Annual Book Show," *New York Times*, June 1, 2013.
⑦ Associated Press, "Barnes & Noble's Loss More than Doubles," *Wall Street Journal*, June 25, 2013.
⑧ Julie Bosman, "The Dog-Eared Paperback, Newly Endangered in an E-Book Age," *New York Times*, September 2, 2011.
⑨ Barney Jopson and Andrew Edgecliffe-Johnson, "Amazon Acquires 450 Children's Titles to Enhance Publishing Role," *Financial Times*, December 7, 2011.
⑩ Julie Bosman, "Publishers Make a Plan: A 'One Stop' Book Site," *New York Times*, May 7, 2011.
⑪ Jeffrey A. Trachtenberg, "E-Book Prices Prop Up Print Siblings," *Wall Street Journal*, September 12, 2011, available at http://online.wsj.com/article/SB10001424053111904875404576532353109995700.html (accessed January 10, 2014).

之上价位的决心。然而,欧洲和美国政府指控以苹果为核心的小集团在电子书市场上密谋限制价格竞争①。司法部紧随其后,指控苹果和五大出版商暗中勾结,实行贸易管制,"以提高电子书价格,对抗亚马逊"。几大出版商都选择和解,只有苹果在 2013 年 7 月被判有罪后还不依不饶,继续上诉②。讽刺的是,这场官司反而使亚马逊斩获渔翁之利,独占电子书市场。汤普森(Thompson)③强调指出,或许紧要之处在于,图书出版行业缺乏必要的物质基础,而通货紧缩将持续对图书出版行业造成冲击,必须重新稳定图书出版行业。

音乐行业情况如何?1980 年代至 1990 年代期间,几家跨国集团收购全球领先的唱片公司,最终造成了百代唱片(EMI)、华纳唱片(Warner Music)、环球唱片(Universal)和索尼音乐(Sony)四家公司掌控了全球四分之三的音乐市场。百代唱片随后被拆分,公司两块主体业务分别被环球和索尼收购,于是全球只剩下三家音乐集团。如同图书出版与电影行业,音乐产业内的同业联盟掌握定价大权,意在建构或重建从黑胶唱片到唱片专辑(每张专辑一般包含 12 首左右的歌曲)的音乐市场。该行业的发展战略都瞄准著名歌手与畅销歌曲。1999 年,近 3 000 张专辑中仅仅 88 张唱片的销量就占总销量的四分之一④。然而,音乐产业发展往往离不开全世界青年的主体或个性表达,因而它的衰落可以被视为寡头垄断的行业遭遇网络传播渠道与唱片数字化无情狙击的经典案例。

不是所有人都能买得起作为某种奢侈消费品的图书;与图书不同,唱片的普及率相当高。讽刺之处在于,正是这一普及性使音乐产业在网络环境下显得有些不堪一击。毕竟,一系列经过精巧设计的设备保证了听者能够免费下载或分享那些尚未得到授权的音乐。面对此情此景,音乐行业转而求助法律途径与技术手段,试图继续掌控受版权保护的音乐及其原有的商业模式⑤。但是,这些策略并未成功。1999 年起,唱片专辑的销量步入长时期下滑的轨道⑥。当史蒂夫·乔布斯推出苹果音乐播放软件并将之与旗下在市场上大获成功的移动设备,最终与云端相关联,由此推动数字音乐的收入开始增长时,老牌的音乐集团才集体松了一口气。而当流媒体音乐服务流行起来并向特定的唱片支付

---

① Reuters, "EU Commission in E-Books Antitrust Probe of 5 Publishers, Apple," December 6, 2011, available at http://www.reuters.com/article/2011/12/06/eu-ebooks-idUSB5E7N100H20111206 (accessed January 10, 2014); Brian X. Chen and Julie Bosman, "Trial on E-Book Price-Fixing Puts Apple in the Spotlight," *New York Times*, June 3, 2013.
② Julie Bosman, "Publishers Tell of Disputes with Apple on E-Book Prices," *New York Times*, June 6, 2013; Brian X. Chen and Julie Bosman, "Apple Loses Antitrust Case on E-Books," *New York Times*, July 11, 2013; David Streitfeld, "E-Book Ruling Gives Amazon an Advantage," July 11, 2013.
③ Thompson, *Merchants of Culture*, 368.
④ Charles C. Mann, "The Heavenly Jukebox," *Atlantic Monthly*, September 2000, 50, in Patrick Burkart and Tom McCourt, *Digital Music Wars: Ownership and Control of the Celestial Jukebox* (Lanham, Md.: Rowman and Littlefield, 2006).
⑤ Burkart and McCourt, *Digital Music Wars*.
⑥ Eduardo Porter, "The Perpetual War: Pirates and Creators," *New York Times*, February 5, 2010.

版税时，他们更加安心落意。不过，他们必须接受传统产业收入减少以及产业结构重新调整等事实。

苹果公司掌握其播放器商店几亿用户的信用卡数据，并向这些用户提供大量且不断增加的专利内容①。另外，如前所述，对于直接通过手机和平板电脑销售的所有订阅内容，苹果要求抽取30%的收入分成。尽管在反垄断法的压力下，苹果公司一定程度上放宽限制，准许杂志、报纸、音乐和视频的出版商享有更大的自由，直接在线售卖内容而无需通过其播放器软件②。然而，苹果很快又锻造出一条全新的在线音乐销售的子链。2011年，全球数字音乐收入约合52亿美元，苹果播放器的收入占了将近70%③。与此同时，唱片公司极不情愿地接受这样的音乐销售模式。这种模式建立在单曲而非完整专辑的销售基础上，对他们而言，它背后只是更为薄利的资本逻辑。

唱片公司从市场新入者那里获得的大量版税进一步缓解了其营业情况。用户可以通过三条途径向它们支付版税以获得授权使用音乐：要么通过"声破天"（Spotify）和"笛泽"（Deezer）这样的流媒体音乐服务平台直接支付；要么在"天狼星 XM"（Sirius XM）或是"潘多拉"音乐电台（Pandora）上借助"声交所"（SoundExchange）等版权组织进行间接支付④；或者通过苹果自己的网络电台进行支付。然而，部分流媒体服务商未来的财政状况并不乐观，因为尽管他们拥有上百万听众，但只有很小一部分属于付费用户，况且广告收益尚不足以弥补他们运营成本的差额⑤。唱片公司对于亚马逊在2011年秋季推出的低价位多媒体平板电脑"金读之光"（Kindle Fire）寄予厚望，希望亚马逊的这款电脑能够成为苹果平板电脑的有力竞争对手，以增加它们对抗苹果的砝码。脸书则构想出另一套替代方案，即增加某些特色功能，例如提示好友正在听的歌曲，并提供"声破天"或在线音乐网络博客（MOG）等流媒体服务音乐提供商的链接以方便用户下载歌曲⑥。而2011年年底正式进入市场的谷歌音乐将旗下下载商店同社交网站（Google +）捆绑起来：消费者可以购买谷歌音乐1300万首正版歌曲，用户好友可以免费收听，不过只能听一次。即便如此，未授权的资源共享依然存在，并成为一种普遍性的"规范"；据一份评估报告，2012

---

① "The Web's New Walls," *The Economist*, September 4, 2010; Richard Waters, "Media Will Be Forced to Play by the Internet's Rules," *FT. com*, March 9, 2011.
② Miguel Helft, "Apple Gives Publishers Sales Break," *New York Times*, June 10, 2011.
③ Matthew Garrahan, "GE Group Squares Up to Apple in iTunes Case," *Financial Times*, May 23, 2012, available at http://www.ft.com/intl/cms/s/0/5f34ca8c-a4ec-11e1-b421-00144feabdc0.html#axzz1vmWCk89W (accessed January 10, 2014).
④ Ben Sisario, "Royalties from Digital Radio Start to Carry Some Weight," *New York Times*, June 18, 2012.
⑤ Ben Sisario, "A Stream of Music, Not Revenue," *New York Times*, December 13, 2013.
⑥ Ben Sisario, "Facebook to Offer Path to Media," *New York Times*, September 19, 2011. 也请参见 April Dembosky, "Facebook Eyes Digital Stream of Revenue with Credits System" *Financial Times*, July 20, 2011.

年,未授权资源共享占据全年网络流量的四分之一①。尽管谷歌已经主动提出,它将改变搜索算法以减少盗版网站出现在搜索结果前列的可能性(此前,谷歌已经数次接到版权所有方撤下盗版网站链接的要求),但几大唱片公司仍持续向谷歌施压,迫使其终止在搜索结果中出现盗版网站链接的做法②。

1980至1990年代间,六大跨国集团收购美国主要的电影制片厂,以此牢牢把控全球的电影发行③。依靠影星、导演与热门电影,这些好莱坞巨头不仅成为全球最大也是最赚钱的产业的中心,更与大型的音乐、出版、游戏公司联手。在美国政府"体贴地"撤销针对交叉所有权的禁令后,电影公司迅速与美国电视产业整合④。卫星电视和有线电视分销服务的推广,为院线电影打开了一扇新的"窗户"(即二级市场)。随后,数字化视频光盘的到来则形成更大的冲击,它并未构成竞争威胁,而是迅速成为该行业唯一重要的收入来源。那么,互联网电影和视频能否打开一扇新的市场窗口?

相较于经常附属于它们的唱片公司,好莱坞巨头有效地躲避了线上的市场竞争:因为下载一部电影所花费的时间要远长于下载一首歌。但随着宽带的普及,盗版资源的分享也随之流行起来。当数字化衰退席卷而来,大的电影公司不仅要面对数字化视频光盘销量锐减的问题,并处理盗版资源泛滥的情况,更要与已取得巨大成功的网飞公司展开竞争。在此之前,网飞公司从在线订购与邮政快递相结合的混合式销售渠道(可与亚马逊相媲美)起步,成功建立了在线发行渠道。然而,在数字化衰退时期,网飞公司推出一项向订阅用户在线推送影视产品的业务;截至2013年秋,网飞宣称其在美国拥有3 100万流媒体用户以及400万国际用户⑤。包括几大互联网中介商在内的其他"闯入者"进一步(将网络市场的发展主流)集中在商业性的网络发行上。习惯于与连锁影院谈判的好莱坞,在1948年反垄断法案打破了好莱坞电影公司制作、发行与放映三位一体的格局后,

---

① Eduardo Porter, "The Perpetual War: Pirates and Creators," *New York Times*, February 5, 2012.
② Chloe Albanesius, "Google to Demote Sites with 'High Number' of Copyright Complaints," *PC Magazine*, August 10, 2012; Robert Budden and Robert Cookson, "Search for Fresh Revenue Stream: Google Looks to Beat Music Rivals," *Financial Times*, February 23 – 24, 2013.
③ Janet Wasko, *Hollywood in the Information Age: Beyond the Silver Screen* (London: Polity, 1994); Toby Miller, Nitin Govil, John McMurria, Richard Maxwell, and Ting Wang, *Global Hollywood* 2 (London: British Film Institute, 2005).
④ William Kunz, *Conglomerate Culture: Consolidation in the Motion Picture and Television Industries* (Lanham, Md.: Rowman and Littlefield, 2006).
⑤ Tim Arango and David Carr, "Netflix's Move onto the Web Stirs Rivalries," *New York Times*, November 25, 2010; Brian Stelter, "Netflix's Profit Rises amid a Rush to On – Demand," *New York Times*, April 26, 2011; Brian Stelter, "Netflix Partner Says Comcast 'Toll' Threatens Online Video Delivery," *New York Times*, Media Decoder, November 29, 2010; "Netflix to Stream Films and TV Abroad," *New York Times*, July 6, 2011; Amy Chozick, "Viacom Strikes an Extensive Deal with Amazon to Stream Children's Shows," *New York Times*, June 5, 2013; Agustino Fontevecchia, "Netflix Banks On 'House of Cards' and 'Orange Is the New Black' to Quadruple Its Profits," *Forbes*, October 21, 2013, available at http://www.forbes.com/sites/afontevecchia/2013/10/21/netflixs – awesome – shows – bring – in – more – subscribers – as – profits – quadruple – in – q3 (accessed January 10, 2014).

继续往前寻求新的增长渠道。三家好莱坞巨头甚至成功地建立起专属的线上服务平台"葫芦"(Hulu);尽管该网站盈利,但它还是给所有者带来战略规划的困扰①。

像图书、唱片和电影这样的收费媒体商品,网络售价非常低。普华永道在2012年曾预测,此轮商品的贬值将"拖慢"全球媒体收入的增长速度②。随着好莱坞电影制片厂的进一步萎缩,其利润"从微薄转变为零"③。然而,网络重构的过程甚至不限于这些收费的媒体产品而向外继续延伸。依赖广告的媒体也被卷入其中,首当其冲的当属电视媒体④。

大部分产业融合的最初设想最终取代了原有的电视次商品链。网络电视开始崛起,并成为一支破坏性的力量。于是,电视市场的领导者亦步亦趋,遵照电影产业同行的做法。网飞公司成为面向订户的跨国电视承办商;它开始购买与生产原创内容,并跟随亚马逊的做法,执行一整套行之有效的商业消费建议系统(比如:如果你喜欢X,那你有可能也喜欢Y)。葫芦则在网络电视业务上赚得盆满钵满,这部分归功于三大股东新闻集团、迪士尼和康卡斯特向其提供的电视节目独播权⑤。倘若谷歌优化其视频服务而能维系既有的广告收入,并与媒体公司合作为旗下不同的主题频道制作原创内容,那么,谷歌的视频网站(YouTube)极有可能成为一支不可小觑的市场力量⑥。视频媒体(Vimeo)以及其他的网络供应商的力量也不断壮大。

经历30年增长后⑦,有预言称,电视在全球广告支出中所占份额将于2013年达到顶峰,即便如此,电视媒体所具有的显著性却是无可争辩的⑧:越来越多的人正通过更多的途径,花更多的时间来收看更多的电视节目。七大媒体集团生产的电视节目总时长占美国国内总收视时间的95%,与之相对应的,则是它们在节目内容生产上所耗费的巨额资金(在2012年,时代华纳耗资46亿美元购买节目)⑨。当谷歌和苹果正考虑如何进军电

---

① "Hulu Attracts Wide Range of Initial Bids," *Financial Times*, May 25–26, 2013.
② Emily Steel, "Digital Drag Forecast on Media Growth," *Financial Times*, June 12, 2012.
③ Michael Cieply and Brooks Barnes, "The Incredible Shrinking Studio," *New York Times*, December 23, 2013.
④ Matt Richtel and Brian Stelter, "In the Living Room, Hooked on Pay TV," *New York Times*, August 23, 2010. 要了解基本情况,请参见 D. Lotz, *The Television Will Be Revolutionized* (New York: New York University Press, 2007).
⑤ Matthew Garrahan, "Hulu to Put Original TV Shows on Web," *Financial Times*, May 22, 2012. 背景资料请参见 Li and Andrew Edgecliffe-Johnson, "Hulu IPO Nears in Drive for Content," *Financial Times*, August 17, 2010; Jessca E. Vascellaro, "Disney's CEO Says Hulu Will Be Sold," *Wall Street Journal*, July 7, 2011; Jessica E. Vascellaro and Sam Schechner, "Hulu's Owners Weigh Cons of a Possible Sale of the Site," *Wall Street Journal*, June 27, 2011; Brian Stelter, "Hulu Owners Call Off Sale, Instead Pledging to Invest to Take on Rivals," *New York Times*, July 13, 2013.
⑥ Brooke Barnes, "Disney and YouTube Make a Video Deal," *New York Times*, November 8, 2011; Matthew Garrahan and Andrew Edgecliffe-Johnson, "YouTube Nears Subscription Service for Its Specialist Channels," *Financial Times*, May 6, 2013; Worth Paying For?" *The Economist*, May 11, 2013.
⑦ Emily Steel, "TV's Grip on Global Ad Spend Set to Slip," *Financial Times*, December 9, 2013.
⑧ Chris Nuttall, "TV Apps Tune Into Uniformity," *Financial Times*, September 4, 2011, available at http://www.ft.com/intl/cms/s/2/49627f14-d707-11e0-bc73-00144feabdc0.html #axzz1WvrPzPdx, accessed January 10, 2014).
⑨ "Intel and TV," The Lex Column, *Financial Times*, June 27, 2013. 但文章并未说明这一数据能否应用到专业电视节目或用户生成内容(或非职业人员制作的内容)。

视市场时①,维亚康姆宣布与亚马逊展开全面长期合作:亚马逊获得维亚康姆独家节目播映权后推出"金牌服务",让观众可以付费订阅数千小时的尼克国际儿童频道(Nickelodeon)的节目②。康卡斯特表示将通过推特等社交媒体推广它们的节目③。广播公司和有线电视公司在维护其自身既得利益的同时,与互联网中介商合作,将节目上传至台式电脑、智能电视、笔记本电脑、平板电脑以及智能手机等各种网络终端。电视公司和互联网企业正逐渐携手,为同一事业而奋斗。谷歌首席执行官施密特2011年受邀在英国最负盛名的电视产业会议上发言,本身已说明一切。

但目前还存在其他不确定的因素。网络运营商能否通过交互式网络电视成功进军电视市场?网络电视里,哪一种节目能获得成功?作为在全球市场中流通的商品,节目类型会有怎样的变化?专业制作的电视节目是否与大量的网络用户自制视频共存,还是这种混合会产生变革?随着用户产生关于自身收视习惯的市场数据,并通过数字视频录像机、平板电脑与在线服务回传至企业,那么究竟是谁在掌控这些数据(尽管数字化衰退时期家庭用户安装数字视频录像机的数量急剧减少,但在2008年,共有5 000万家庭安装数字视频录像机,其中五分之四的家庭来自北美④)?

或许关键之处在于,电视产业收益的主要模式正面临重构⑤。数十年来,商业电视的业务主要是向受众提供稳定的节目,依照广告商要求进行节目编排。然而,这条次商品链已出现多处破裂。网络上不仅充斥着大量的节目片段,并能随时随地地观看,电视售卖广告的独特模式已不适应网络生态。互联网企业、广告公司与广告商是否会以自动化广告购买交易与"程序化购买"等新形式,取代现有的电视广告销售的预付体系呢?⑥ 电

---

① Brian Stelter, "Google Said to Weigh Supplying TV Channels," *New York Times*, July 17, 2013; U. S. Government Accountability Office, "Video Marketplace: Competition Is Evolving, and Government Reporting Should Be Reevaluated," GAO – 13 – 576, June 2013, 6 – 7.
② Amy Chozick, "Viacom Strikes an Extensive Deal with Amazon to Stream Children's Shows," *New York Times*, June 5, 2013.
③ Brian Stelter, "Comcast Hopes to Promote TV Shows in Twitter Deal," *New York Times*, October 9, 2013, available at http://www.nytimes.com/2013/10/10/business/media/ through – twitter – partnership – comcast – hopes – to – encourage – tv – viewing.html?_r=0 (accessed January 10, 2014).
④ Michael Dinan, "Report: Global DVR Homes to Quadruple in Five Years," TMCnet Cable Spotlight, October 28, 2008, available at http://cable.tmcnet.com/topics/cable/articles/43825 – report – global – dvr – homes – quadruple – five – years.htm (accessed January 10, 2014); Tom Morrod, "Cox and Cisco Launch First US Cable Multi – Room DVR," *IHS Screen Digest*, June 16, 2010, available at http://www.screendigest.com/news/cox – and – cisco – launch – us – cables – first – multi – room – dvr/view.html (accessed January 10, 2014).
⑤ Brian Stelter, "The TV – Internet Nuptials," *New York Times*, January 10, 2011; Claire Cain Miller and Brian Stelter, "Google TV Announces Its Programming Partners, but the Top Networks Are Absent," *New York Times*, October 4, 2010; Joseph Menn, "Apple Ups the Ante in Digital TV Battle," *Financial Times*, September 2, 2010.
⑥ Suzanne Vranica, "WPP Automated Ad Buys to Include Latin America," *Wall Street Journal*, June 10, 2013; Emily Steel, "Algorithms Threaten to End 'Mad Men' Era," *Financial Times*, May 14, 2013.

视广告将如何被重构,哪家公司将占据最大份额①?

因此,在详细地分析每一特定的媒体产业所发生的变革后,我将直接转向关于广告行业的讨论。网络通信行业的创新与变革,依然着眼于广告商利益;这比任何其他一切都更好地诠释了以赢利为目的的通信产业如何更全面地体现了它的立基之本。赞助制度正经历一个多世纪以来最为彻底的一次现代化变革。

---

① Andrew Edgecliffe-Johnson, "Nielsen Revamps Online Ad Ratings to Find Campaigns That Hit Home," *Financial Times*, August 8, 2011.

第 8 章
赞助商制度的"复苏"

广告商憎恨空白。对于消费产品制造商及其营销与广告的附属机构而言,广告商被排除在外的业务范围,构成了一块复杂的文化空白区;因为这些领域阻止或拒绝它们的销售行为,又或对销售行为漠不关心。如果这样一个文化实践的领域越来越受欢迎,吸引营销人员所觊觎的大量受众并让他们更合理地安排自己多余的时间,那么这些领域的界限就会变得极具威胁性。广告商的原则是,无论何时何地,(广告要)到达那些最有需求的受众;该原则转化成一种将文化空白区转变成广告标识的诉求。相较于任何超越性的权利意志,维系资本运营的动力更有效地促成了这种趋势;也就是说,它根植于资本的需求:先将已生产的商品卖出去,然后再生产与再售卖,从而实现资本循环周期。这一商品流通过程任何一个环节被打断(不论是当地某一特定的公司或行业,还是席卷全球的),都将导致危机的出现。

作为包括产品与服务在内的商品的生产者,广告商需要日常且广泛的途径(保证其广告与产品)到达购买者。数字化衰退导致资本无法在有利可图的情况下售卖堆积如山的商品,从而强化了广告商对到达途径的需求。正如衰退推动消费品制造商更迫切地希望卖出商品,新兴的互联网服务瓦解了原有的广告与销售模式,同时预示需要建立更有效到达消费者的方式。因此,广告不仅继续存在,并不断深化其作为数字化服务行业主要财政来源的角色。

实际上,广告与营销人员现在所预言的那些关于人类自发活动的论调,按照 20 年前的标准几乎难以想象。正如一位资深分析家所言,必须认识到"购买的冲动无处不在",并且迅速改变的习惯正吸引数亿网络用户,当然,营销人员也应声而来[①]。那么,营销人

---

① Stuart Elliott, "The Impulse to Buy Can Start Anywhere," *New York Times*, December 20, 2010; Andrew Edgecliffe-Johnson, "PwC Foresees Big Changes in Advertising Landscape," *Financial Times*, June 14, 2011.

员如何将这一广袤无垠的开阔地带转化成电子商务的标识与渠道？

简言之,广告与营销人员重构广告与销售模式,赋予广告与销售以决定性角色,进而完成更广阔的通信行业的重建过程。它是一个复杂的、动态的且尚未完成的过程。

首先,除了万维网,广告行业也在贪得无厌地进行不平衡的全球化扩张。2008年数字化衰退来临时,全球百强广告公司的广告预算的五分之三都投放在美国以外的媒体。而百强里44家美国公司更有11家把超过一半的广告投在国外。这其中包括世界最大的广告商宝洁公司,当年投放媒体的广告费用将近100亿美元[1]。一部分的广告集团在特定的发展中国家和欠发达地区[2]疯狂地收购公司;在它们的支持下,消费品制造商和零售商不再死死盯住北美、西欧和日本这些长期受到广告商青睐的富裕地区。要重新激活销售,中国无疑是最佳选择。吸引它们的,是中国社会特权阶层或庞大的农民工群体所具有的不断增强的消费潜力;他们对国外跨国公司的产品[3]或中国本土制造的商品[4](有些已成"大品牌")来者不拒。因此,广告不再局限于外部强加的形式。电影《变形金刚3:月黑之时》中植入了中国四大国产品牌:美特斯邦威(服装)、联想(电脑)、TCL(平板电视)和伊利(牛奶);这一好莱坞创造的广告植入新形式拓展至中国市场。该广告战略旨在帮助这些中国品牌扩大国际知名度,并借助好莱坞的名气提升国内市场份额[5]。在此过程中,广告成为连接国内资本与跨国资本的桥梁。全球百强广告公司投放中国媒体的广告费用中,宝洁公司占据27%;尽管如此,仍存在足够的增长空间:毕竟,中国(广告公司)仅仅占全球百强广告公司总开支的3.4%[6]。有预计显示,中国的电子商务销售将持续快速增长;2013年,中国的电子商务销售额已达到1 930亿美元,是美国的一半,并有望在三到四年间超过美国的网络销售总额[7]。同样,俄罗斯和印度也是(跨国广告公司)投放越来越多广告的地区;巴西则被预言将很快取代英国成为全球第五大广告市场[8]。事实上,广告的跨国化进程(覆盖全球),而不仅仅局限于金砖四国的范围。以尼日利亚为例,2001至2010年间,投放在这个非洲国家的广告费用翻了五倍[9]。

不过,广告的跨国化扩张有选择性的,而非泽披全球。数字化衰退促使广告商更为

---

[1] Laurel Wentz and Bradley Johnson, "Top 100 Global Advertisers Heap Their Spending Abroad; Focused 62% of Budgets outside U. S. Last Year, with Much Going to China," *Advertising Age* 80, no. 40 (2009):1.
[2] 全球第三大广告集团阳狮集团在2013年前18个月进行多达25次收购行动,具体请参见 "Advertising," The Lex Column, *Financial Times*, July 19, 2013.
[3] Laurie Burkitt, "In China, Women Begin Splurging," *Wall Street Journal*, June 13, 2011.
[4] Kathrin Hille, "Big Companies Face Long Road to Recognition," *Financial Times*, May 19, 2011; Patti Waldmeir, "Chinese Wares Face Struggle for Acceptance," *Financial Times*, May 22, 2012.
[5] Kathrin Hille, "Chinese Brands Star in Hollywood Movie," *Financial Times*, July 20, 2011.
[6] Wentz and Johnson, "Top 100," 1.
[7] Duncan Robinson, "Online Stores Think Local to Grow Global," *Financial Times*, January 25 – 26, 2014.
[8] Tim Bradshaw, "European Ad Spend Off Target," *Financial Times*, June 19, 2012.
[9] "Nigeria's Mad Men," *The Economist*, April 30, 2011.

谨慎地选择目标。除了那些最具消费需求的受众与增长地区外,其他地区的广告投入将遭到无情的削减。投放至西班牙的广告费用在 2007 至 2012 年间紧缩了三分之一有余;希腊更是超过一半①(这有时被称为"避险"②)。因此,正如广告源源不断地流入高增长地区和媒体,同时它也逃离那些广告商认为已无利可图或已过时的文化实践地区。

这与流行无甚关联:雷蒙·威廉斯数十年前指出,某一特定节目或类型或媒体被证明所拥有的大量观众,并不足以确保它能持续地获得经济收入。广告商抛弃观众的原因无外乎后者的市场价值下降,或者存在其他途径可以更有效或更廉价地到达观众。即使脸书这一历史上扩张最为疯狂(用户超过 10 亿,年收入超过 60 亿美元)的文化服务提供商在 2013 年前,它的未来发展依然变幻莫测,这是因为它尚未为广告商打造一个固定的平台③。在一家社交网络异化其用户之前,能吸引多少广告?对广告商而言,从社交网络买广告版面还是建专属网页向用户提供"品牌内容"更有效呢?如何解释 2013 年底可口可乐在推特上的账号拥有两百万粉丝?一位记者认为:"本质上,广告商身处于这个仅仅持续一到两年的实验项目的中心地带"。最终,他们"将放慢速度,然后评估这一切是否有效"④。(截至 2014 年,当脸书庆祝成立十周年时,它正不辞辛劳地重新打造移动广告平台;社交网络攻苦食啖,试图重新聚焦于手机广告和社交网络;社交网络"从广告商手中拿钱,如同从婴儿手里抢糖果"⑤。)

随后发生的动荡令人头晕目眩。一方面,美国的电视肥皂剧、报纸和杂志,与实行紧缩政策的欧洲⑥电视公司一样,广告收入急剧下跌⑦。总而言之,投放电视的广告费用占全球广告支出的超高份额,在 30 年间将小幅下挫⑧。与此同时,营销人员将注意力纷纷转向稳定的新兴热点。商业卫星电视服务在中国和中东地区始终保持增长态势⑨。2014 年,若在全球收视率最高的电视转播赛事之一美国国家橄榄球联盟超级碗中播出一则 30 秒的商业广告,需要花费 400 万美元,创历史新高⑩。2008 至 2009 年的金融危机期间,印度的报纸发行总量增加 6%,而广告收入增长 13%;尽管截至 2012 年,情况看起来不再那

---

① Bradshaw,"European Ad."
② Jonathan Barnard,ZenithOptimedia,in Bradshaw,"European Ad."
③ Robert Cookson,"Facebook Fights to Stay Down with the Kids," *Financial Times*,May 17,2013.
④ "Twitter over \$40," The Lex Column, *Financial Times*, November 10,2013; also see David Carr, "Marrying Companies and Content," *New York Times*, November 11,2013.
⑤ Hannah Kuchler and Emily Steel, "Online Advertisers 'Like' Facebook's Attention to Detail," *Financial Times*, January 31,2014.
⑥ Ben Fenton,"Broadcasters Face Bleak Picture of Advertising Cuts," *Financial Times*,May 10,2011.
⑦ Andrew Edgecliffe-Johnson, "As the World Turns, Advertisers Tire of Soap Operas," *Financial Times*, April 21,2011; Martin Peers, "Mixed Ad Message from Newspapers," *Wall Street Journal*, July 29,2010.
⑧ Emily Steel,"TV's Grip on Global Ad Spend Set to Slip," *Financial Times*,December 9,2013.
⑨ Helga Tawil-Souri,"Arab Television in Academic Scholarship," *Sociology Compass* 2,no.5 (2008):1400–1415.
⑩ Emily Steel,"Super Bowl Advertising Goes into Overdrive," *Financial Times*,February 1–2,2014.

么乐观①。回到美国,"西班牙语"市场的走红,推动了西班牙语电视台收入的集体增长②。此外,随着相对富裕的婴儿潮代际即将退休,广告商和营销人员不得不将他们所蔑视的老年人群视为充满诱惑的目标群体③。

2008 年末至 2009 年间,广告支出总体出现下滑;随后开始一定程度的反弹④。2012 年,伦敦夏季奥运会、欧冠联赛和美国总统选举⑤三大事件的合力,使广告商普遍认为广告支出将有所增加⑥。2013 年,全球广告业务共计花费 5 000 亿美元⑦。

正是基于这一不平衡且令人担忧的变化,广告商加速了他们重组通信商品链的步伐。对他们而言,科技革命产生一些正面的、令人垂涎的影响。万维网尤其是移动网络,创造了近乎无尽的广告与营销机遇,并因此导致贸易条件逐渐向大广告商倾斜。同样,由于万维网遵照广告商对用户数据的需求而建立,因此它不仅拓宽更强化了广告商的销售行为。这些趋势具有某些衍生效应,它们对于覆盖面更广的通信体系而言,影响深远。

早在万维网普及之前,广告商和市场已经预见到新的互动媒体的发展未来一片光明⑧。数字化衰退来临之际,广告商已经积累了 50 余年的互联网经营经验。当然,不确定性仍然存在,阻碍发展的因素也在增加:例如,2013 年一项研究表明,数千次营销活动的网上投放广告超过一半因为技术原因、用户抵制或涉嫌欺诈⑨而导致网民无法看到。然而,数十亿美元资金正涌入互联网广告市场。截至 2010 年,互联网仅次于电视成为世界第二大广告媒体。我们很容易就能想见,"广告业务模式与营销文化……如今正渗透进科技领域"⑩。脸书在其 2012 年招股说明书中提及,这场(媒体)融合本质上尚未最终成型,并解释,"社交网络的广告是一次巨大的市场机遇,它方兴未艾,仍在演变"⑪。事实

---

① Laura Houston Santhanam and Tom Rosenstiel, "Why US Newspapers Suffer More Than Others," Pew Research Center's Project for Excellence in Journalism:2011 State of the News Media, available at http://stateofthemedia.org/2011/mobile – survey/international – newspaper – economics (accessed January 10,2014).
② Andrew Edgecliffe – Johnson, "Hispanic Dawn Breaks for US," Financial Times, October 21, 2010; Stuart Elliott and Tanzina Vega, "TV Steps Up Pitch to Hispanic Market," New York Times, May 18,2011.
③ Bill Carter and Tanzina Vega, "In Shift, Ads Try to Entice Over – 55 Set," New York Times, May 14,2011. 据罗伯特·莱克(Robert Reich)的观察,全美前 10% 的家庭消费占总开支的 40%,具体请参见 Robert B. Reich, After – Shock:The Next Economy and America's Future (New York:Vintage,2011),36.
④ Tim Bradshaw, "WPP Lifts Forecasts as Ad Spending Rebounds," Financial Times, August 25,2010;Tanzina Vega, "After Two Slow Years, an Industry Rebound Begins," New York Times, January 3,2011;David Gelles, "Networks Vie for ＄18bn Ad Contracts," Financial Times, May 20,2011.
⑤ Tim Bradshaw and Adam Jones, "WPP Shrugs Off Marketing 'Storm Clouds,'" Financial Times, August 25,2011.
⑥ "Ad Years and Good Years," The Lex Column, Financial Times, March 2,2012.
⑦ Suzanne Vranica, "WPP Automated Ad Buys to Include Latin America," Wall Street Journal, June 10,2013.
⑧ Vincent Mosco, Pushbutton Fantasies (Norwood, N. J:Ablex,1982);Kevin Robins and Frank Webster, "Cybernetic Capitalism"in The Political Economy of Information, ed. Vincent Mosco and Janet Wasko (Madison:University of Wisconsin Press,1988),44 – 75.
⑨ Suzanne Vranica, "The Case of the Invisible Web Ads," Wall Street Journal, June 12,2013.
⑩ Ashlee, Vance, "Are Social Networks Gonna Blow?" Bloomberg BusinessWeek, April 18 – 24,2011.
⑪ Facebook Inc., Form S – 1 Registration Statement with the U. S. Securities and Exchange Commission, February 1,2012,4.

上,围绕万维网的连接性,广告业正经历一场令人激动的变革,尤其当它从台式电脑扩展至移动设备时①。

广告商调整他们的互动形式以产生与获取受众个人信息的历史由来已久,例如直邮广告、九位数的邮政编码、按照人口学标准细分的人群以及条形码都是互联网出现之前广告商所采取的形式②。1990年代中期网景公司首发新股,从机制上更全面地推进了将上述数据信息与指定个体的其他数据相互绑定的广告业务③。马修·克雷恩关于1990年代销售业务如何受到万维网的重构的研究,正好揭示了这一过程④。新技术、新的网络中介商以及(或许是最关键的)一个持支持态度的联邦政府,共同推动了商业对个体的合法监视。于是,尼尔森对家庭所做的概率抽样并以此绘制受众与节目内容之间的动态关系的业务,让位于全新的受众商品模式:即用户跟踪数据,它不仅适用于谷歌和脸书的网络服务,也能为数字视频录像系统与有线电视系统运营商所用;它既服务于电视,又能应用到通过其他设备所获取的服务上⑤。在联邦政府的批准下,围绕小型文本文件、点击量以及再次流回数字服务提供商与广告商那里的用户数据,互联网得以重构。随着用户的日常生活越来越与网络基础设施绑定在一起,数据生成与抓取的技术和业务往往同用户的生活步伐保持一致,并随时监测后者的变化。跟踪受众的技术试图延伸至每一个前沿领域。向受众跟踪技术的转型,与广告商自身获取受众信息的能力的转变密不可分;广告商不再分别统计销售、金融、地区与人口的数据。独特的计算机签名(即"指纹识别")、搜索历史以及位置数据,保证互联网服务提供商和广告商能够实时获取用户全天浏览网页的信息,这些信息补足了他们通过个人电脑浏览器中的小型文本文件所获取的

---

① 我的观点取自于凡·汤沃林(Van Couvering),后者不是把沃勒斯坦的商品链而是迈克·波特(Michael Porter)的价值或供应链概念,应用于互联网上,具体请参见 Elizabeth Van Couvering, "The History of the Internet Search Engine,"博士论文尚未发表, University of London, 94; Elizabeth Van Couvering, "Navigational Media: The Political Economy of Online Traffic," in *The Political Economies of the Media*, by Dwayne Winseck and Dal Yong Jin (London: Bloomsbury, 2011), 183–200.
② Oscar H. Gandy Jr., "The Political Economy of Personal Information," in *The Handbook of Political Economy of Communications*, ed. J. Wasko, G. Murdock, and H. Sousa (Chichester: Wiley–Blackwell, 2011), 436–57; Oscar H. Gandy Jr., *The Panoptic Sort: A Political Economy of Personal Information* (Boulder, Colo.: Westview, 1993).
③ Dan Schiller, *Digital Capitalism* (Cambridge, Mass.: MIT: 1999); Matthew Crain, "The Revolution Will Be Commercialized: Finance, Public Policy, and the Construction of Internet Advertising," PhD diss., University of Illinois, Urbana–Champaign, 2013.
④ Crain, "Revolution." Also see Joseph Turow, *The Daily You* (New Haven, Conn.: Yale University Press, 2011).
⑤ Jeff Chester, *Digital Destiny: New Media and the Future of Democracy* (New York: New Press, 2007), 127–58. Tim Bradshaw, "Facebook to Tap Into Mobile Ads," *Financial Times*, February 6, 2012; Lori Andrews, "Facebook Is Using You," *New York Times*, February 5, 2012; Turow, *Daily You*; Ted Striphas, *The Late Age of Print: Everyday Book Culture From Consumerism to Control* (New York: Columbia University Press, 2009), confirmed by Alexandra Alter, "Your E-Book Is Reading You," *Wall Street Journal*, June 29, 2012.

数据①。

截至 2012 年,平均每次访问互联网就会催生出 56 次数据收集行为,仅在 18 个月内该次数急剧增长;这些数据随后进入电脑化的拍卖系统中,即"实时竞价交易","只要有用户访问某网页,该记录就会拍卖给竞价最高者"②。搜索广告和显示广告是增长最快的两类广告,即便在数字化衰退期,它们仍保持两位数的增长③。随着网络用户从一家网址浏览至另一家网址,卖家能够锁定特定用户从而定点地将广告推送给他们,这项突破性的技术被称为"重新定位"④。广告商殚精竭虑,力求掌握这门技术。同时,广告商坚持认为,由于传统媒体通常无法产生这类用户数据,因此它们需要另辟蹊径,以获得这些数据;或言之,传统媒体应当对广告商树立的网络标准"尽责"。

向用户数据的转型与媒体财政系统的运作机制,扞格不入。以往,广告收入的一部分⑤用于支付(一般是间接支付)内容制作的成本。当网络用户在不同网站之间浏览时,根本无法预测他们是否会停留在某网站哪怕一个小时(更不要说一晚上),那么,广告商为何还要承担这笔昂贵的程序编制费用?广告商更愿意在网络用户个体的上网过程中插入商业信息,这样,无论用户浏览什么网站,他们都能将广告推送给最有消费需求的受众。向用户数据的转型所产生的衍生效果尚不明朗;然而,这一转型毫无疑问将超越广告本身。

谷歌开发出重新定位技术为其带来巨大的商业成功,从中我们可以得出不少启示⑥。要想找到一家网站,正式的搜索功能必不可少。即便那些声名在外的网站也需要搜索引擎将大部分流量导向它们。搜索反过来构成一道网关(经常是一道特定的网关);通过它,广告商得以与用户相互连接:2009 年的一项调查显示,将近 88% 的用户倾向于点击搜索结果中排名前三的网站链接⑦。这一瓶颈反而使搜索引擎成为网络传播领域中广告商竞相争夺的魔盒。在美国,微软公司的必应成为雅虎和脸书的专属搜索供应商。尽管它被预装在超过 70% 的新电脑中,可它仍然不敌谷歌。世界范围内,谷歌在绝大部分地区的互联网搜索市场都处于领先地位,只有在中国、韩国、俄罗斯和日本等少数几个国

---

① Adam Tanner,"The Web Cookie Is Dying. Here's The Creepier Technology That Comes Next,"*Forbes*,June 17,2013. Available at http://www.forbes.com/sites/adamtanner/2013/06/17/the-web-cookie-is-dying-heres-the-creepier-technology-that-comes-next(accessed January 10,2014).
② Julia Angwin,"Online Tracking Heats Up,"*Wall Street Journal*,June 18,2012.
③ Emily Steel,"Big Pop Seen for Online Ads,"*Wall Street Journal*,June 8,2011.
④ Emily Steel,"Big Pop Seen for Online Ads,"*Wall Street Journal*,June 8,2011.
⑤ McChesney,*Digital Disconnect:How Capitalism Is Turning the Internet against Democracy*(New York:New Press,2013).
⑥ Van Couvering,"Navigational Media." ShinJoung Yeo,"Behind the Search Box:The Political Economy of the Global Search Engine Industry,"draft PhD diss.,University of Illinois at Urbana-Champaign,这篇博士论文让我们深化了关于搜索服务以及谷歌搜索服务的基本情况。
⑦ Barnett,Statement before Senate Judiciary Committee,Subcommittee on Antitrust,*Competition Policy and Consumer Rights*,4.

家,是谷歌的其他竞争对手占据上风。

毫无疑问,搜索过程在网络空间无处不在。通常情况下,搜索毫不起眼地嵌在其他网络业务中。苹果的移动搜索功能不叫"搜索"而叫"Siri",即声控的虚拟"助手"①。谷歌的执行总裁埃里克·施密特曾在2011年指出,脸书的提问功能展示了"大量的搜索和信息功能";同样,亚马逊、沃尔玛、易趣等购物网站"本质上也属于搜索引擎,只不过,它们聚焦于商品搜索,并在用户搜索出结果之后向它们提供购买的契机"②。施密特或许还应当提及基于图像的搜索引擎:易趣允许用户拍下汽车的照片然后上传,进而在易趣的汽车销售图像库中进行配对③。以上一切都是真实的,但施密特很有心计地弱化了谷歌的力量。

2011年8月,谷歌掌控了美国国内79%以及欧洲94%的网络搜索市场,它占有美国80%的付费搜索广告,在国外,这一数字更高,达到83%④。在移动搜索与搜索广告领域,谷歌的优势更加明显:2011年3月,谷歌斩获大约97%到98%的移动搜索与移动搜索广告收入⑤。2011与2012年,谷歌年收入分别为400亿和480亿美元;(毫无疑问,)谷歌主导了网络广告市场,2013年谷歌的广告收入占全球数字广告总收入的31%⑥。然而,谷歌对于网络广告的重要性已经不仅局限于其收入本身,因为它不仅在其搜索列表旁边添加广告,更通过发布商联盟(Ad Sense Network)在其他数千家网站上添加广告。谷歌正在网络广告领域中呼风唤雨,并且,它在整个万维网世界里传播广告。另外,谷歌直接与WPP集团、奥姆尼康(宏盟集团,Omnicom)、埃培智市场咨询(Interpublic)、哈瓦斯集团(Havas)、日本电通(Dentsu)和阳狮集团(Publicis)⑦等营销巨头进行竞争。2007年,谷歌斥资31亿美元,击败微软与雅虎⑧成功收购双击公司(DoubleClick),这一行为催生了谷歌誓将成为在线广告网站领导者的雄心壮志。自此以后(如果不是在此之前),广告对于谷歌的结构与发展战略至关重要,并再次引发深远的衍生效应。

那么谷歌的网页排名是如何计算出来的?这些排名如何产生?谷歌是否运用其网

---

① 2011年苹果推出语音服务,使用演员苏珊·班奈特(Susan Bennett)的声音向1亿用户播报搜索结果,具体请参见 Jessica Ravitz,"'I'm the Original Voice of Siri,'" CNN, October 4, 2013, available at http://www.cnn.com/2013/10/04/tech/mobile/bennett-siri-iphone-voice (accessed February 7, 2014).
② Eric Schmidt, Executive Chairman, Google Inc., Testimony before the Senate Committee on the Judiciary, Subcommittee on Antitrust, Competition Policy, and Consumer Rights, September 21, 2011, 3-4, available at http://searchengineland.com/figz/wp-content/seloads/2011/09/Eric-Schmidt-Testimony.pdf (accessed January 10, 2014).
③ Dembosky and Richard Waters, "Desperately Seeking Data," *Financial Times*, January 19/20, 2013.
④ Barnett, *Statement*, 5.
⑤ Barnett, *Statement*, 10.
⑥ Emily Steel, "Marketers Wary of Branching Out on Twitter," *Financial Times*, October 8, 2013.
⑦ "Merger Set to Create a Marketing Leviathan," *Financial Times*, July 29, 2013; Andrew Edgecliffe-Johnson and Emily Steel, "Investors Cool over $35bn Publicis-Omnicom Tie-Up," *Financial Times*, July 30, 2013.
⑧ Ken Auletta, *Googled: The End of the World as We Know It* (New York: Penguin, 2009), 174.

关权力以反竞争的方式引导用户？例如它（在搜索结果中）突出自己的附属网站（这一做法为其带来的广告收入占2013年年度广告总收入的三分之二①），或者（刻意）不强调其竞争对手的网站。

当然，这是一个专属秘密。执行总裁施密特侧重强调谷歌战略乐善好施的一面。他所说的"我们这个时代伟大的智识挑战"，指的就是不断吸引研发投资的谷歌。他继续指出，"从一开始，谷歌不断优化自身的搜索算法；迄今，这套算法涵盖200多个因子，用以评估网站质量与相关性"②。这的确令人印象深刻。2010年，谷歌至少进行了13 311次"精确评估，以检验新的算法是否优化搜索结果"，这些评估导致516次"被认为有益于用户的"算法改进③。施密特强调，谷歌的搜索科技"一直在改进"，秉持"向用户提供最有用的信息"理念，旨在真心实意地提供"科学的搜索结果"④。截至2013年，谷歌搜索业务的年度研发支出高达75亿美元，其搜索业务正在进行一次大的调整。

然而，构建谷歌导航业务的逻辑，牢牢限制了网页排名的算法，这套算法不仅倾向于谷歌自身不断增加的内容与目标网站，更向成千上万的广告商敞开大门，这才是它隐藏最深的商业机密。因此，谷歌在互联网搜索中所扮演的"守门人"角色成为一项敏感的政策议题：谷歌主导搜索市场的地位（以及它对广告费用的虹吸效应，若没有谷歌，这些广告开支便流向国内公司、欧洲或者其他地方⑤）是否意味着它应该作为公共设施而受到规制？⑥ 2011至2012年间，谷歌在三大洲遭遇反垄断调查⑦。美国联邦贸易委员会在2011年6月就谷歌潜在的反竞争垄断发出民事调查传票；同年9月，美国参议院举办听证会，确认谷歌的搜索结果是否存在偏向。然而，在2013与2014两年里，谷歌以极为优惠的条款同美国与欧洲的反垄断委员会达成和解，以确保不会颠覆谷歌"将受到赞助的

---

① Google Inc., "Google, Inc. Announces Third Quarter 2013 Results," Google.com, October 17, 2013.
② Eric Schmidt, "MacTaggart Lecture, MediaGuardian Edinburgh International Television Festival, August 26, 2011, available at http://www.theguardian.com/media/interactive/2011/aug/26/eric-schmidt-mactaggart-lecture-full-text (accessed January 10, 2014).
③ Schmidt, "MacTaggart Lecture", 3.
④ Schmidt, "MacTaggart Lecture".
⑤ Andre Schiffrin, *Words and Money* (London: Verso, 2010), 74; James Kantor, "Facing Antitrust Fights at Home, Google Tries to Avoid One in Europe," *New York Times*, February 21, 2011.
⑥ Barnett, Statement, 10. 谷歌董事会主席与前任首席执行官施密特承认，"搜索具有主观性，没有所谓'正确的'搜索结果。我们搜索的科学过程，向用户提供对他们而言最有用的信息"，具体请参见 Schmidt, Testimony, 7. 另一谷歌的维护者认为，"要定义搜索过程中什么因素可能是'中立'的，这简直不可能"，具体请参见 Susan A. Creighton, partner, Wilson Sonsini Goodrich and Rosati, P.C., Testimony before the U.S. Senate Committee on the Judiciary Subcommittee on Antitrust, Competition Policy and Consumer Rights, September 21, 2011, available at http://www.gpo.gov/fdsys/pkg/CHRG-112shrg71471/pdf/CHRG-112shrg71471.pdf (accessed January 10, 2014); 也请参见 Richard Sennett, "Real Progressives Believe in Breaking Up Google," *Financial Times*, June 29, 2013.
⑦ Alex Barker, "EU Warns Google to Change or Face Fines," *Financial Times*, May 22, 2012.

网站链接及其自身的购物服务优先放在有机的搜索结果之前"这一运作模式①。也许,正如《金融时报》社论所指出的,网络搜索近似于脸书的社交网络和苹果的应用商城等其他在线业务,既然它构建出一个"赢者通吃"的市场(即反竞争垄断),就应当承担着某种"准公共服务的责任"②。

这家搜索巨头卷入庞杂的商业关系网络中,由此产生其他一些重要的问题。无论谷歌的市场支配力如何强大,它也无法削弱网络搜索业务嵌入其中的商品链的政治经济态势。所有的商业网站具备足够的动机,来影响它们在谷歌搜索结果中的排名。整个网络搜索(优化)行业愈发倾向于满足广告商的诉求,即它们的网站一定要排在或靠近谷歌搜索列表第一页的前列。像安布思沛(iProspect)、布鲁斯克莱(Bruce Clay Inc)、现身(Increase Visibility)、搜索引擎优化(SEO Inc.)等企业都处于这个市场的顶端。市场游击战使谷歌与少部分搜索引擎同上述搜索优化公司成为对立面。双方均被卷入商品链中,后者不仅包括搜索企业,还有广告商、搜索优化公司、主营数据追踪业务的公司以及外部内容提供商。不论是否与谷歌同属一个阵营,它们合力推动以网络搜索结构化为中心的盈利战略的现代化进程。诸如网络科技与数据挖掘等内部专业知识,则成为(赢利的)关键之道;据报道,2006至2011年这五年间,社交网络分析软件的领导品牌美国国际商用机器公司曾花费110亿美元用于收购此类软件的制造商③。

搜索市场的竞争态势更为激烈,不失为一件好事;可竞争不会自己主动卷入(更不用说中和)这一冗长的商业关系链。紧要之处在于,它更不容许搜索这一核心的文化与信息工具,同争先恐后(进入搜索市场)的资本所具有的利己主义目标相脱离。必须制订更为激进的计划,以重新定位搜索工具的社会目的,才能确保其具有的民主责任。我们需要确立一系列新的代表形式与实践(迫使谷歌公开其搜索算法只是开始),以实现这一目的。

然而,谷歌的导航服务一直被绑定在不断更新、不断扩大的销售战略上。谷歌开始与宏盟集团(为数不多的广告代理巨头之一)合作,旨在打造一个全球体系,以更加方便地购买显示广告。谷歌向宏盟集团提供分析数据,保障后者能够将显示广告精确推送给目标受众,并评估它们的表现。谷歌的某位副总裁如此评价这一社会资源的重新调配:"我们已经把谷歌的工程消防水管对准显示广告"④。宏盟集团还与美国在线、雅虎和微软结成类似的合作关系。由于获得"持续访问"上述四大在线企业数据的权限,宏盟集团希望"能更为持久、精确地将广告推送给向汽车购买者或体育粉丝等不同的统计人群;不

---

① Alex Barker and Richard Waters, "Google Deal Ends Antitrust Fight," *Financial Times*, February 6, 2014.
② "Google Settlement Is Not the Last Word" (editorial), *Financial Times*, February 6, 2014.
③ Philip Delves Broughton, "Brave New Networked World," *Financial Times*, July 19, 2011.
④ Neal Mohan, in Emily Steel, "Google Wins Omnicom as Ally," *Wall Street Journal*, July 15, 2010.

同的媒体所有者看待这些人群的方式也有所不同"①。为了阻止谷歌侵入数字广告行业，宏盟集团的全球竞争对手 WPP 与阳狮集团相继制定了可与之抗衡的发展战略；在接下来的部分我将讨论这些战略所导致的一些衍生效应。

在线服务提供商的商业合作关系产生了深远的效应，正如它们的先驱对此前媒体的冲击那样。2006 年，谷歌斥资 16.5 亿美元收购视频网站 YouTube 组成电视部；该部一直根据广告商的要求不断调整（业务和结构）②。数百万用户着迷于 YouTube 上非专业制作的视频内容：那么广告商如何可能寄生于（YouTube 所提供的）这种服务上？宝洁公司的首席品牌官在 2010 年证实，其旗下推出的古风（Old Spice）系列男士古龙水的广告视频剪辑（无论是公司制作的广告片还是消费者恶搞的短片）在 YouTube 上的点击量已逾 1.4 亿次③。但是，由于广告是谷歌的支柱业务，它不可能停止其销售和营销战略的步伐；因此它不断雇佣专业人员组建营销团队④。2013 年，谷歌向旗下 YouTube、在线应用程序商店（GooglePlay）以及其他业务的用户宣布，他们的照片、档案、评论和排名等信息都有可能替广告商在广告中为其产品背书；该条款覆盖谷歌显示广告网络所服务的 200 多万家网站，近十亿用户浏览过这些网站的显示广告⑤。

谷歌再一次在所有商业网络中介商中脱颖而出，成为唯一赢家。曾经作为互联网服务提供商的美国在线如今正谋求向网络广告公司转型，这些广告可以直接连接到公司的数字新闻或娱乐节目，或者连接到毫无关系的网站⑥。亚马逊利用其搜集到的消费者电子商务数据，在网站上刊登自己或者亚马逊网络中其他网站的广告；有预测称，亚马逊 2013 年的广告总收入将高达 8 亿美元⑦。世界最大的营销企业、广告业巨头 WPP 与推特合作，以直接访问推特平台；这样，它便可以整合推特上的数据，并为其客户创建数据产品⑧。同样，推特的招股说明书也透露，它的五大顶级"数据合作方"为它带来四分之三的

---

① Tim Bradshaw, "Omnicom in Deals to Target Online Ads," *Financial Times*, March 10, 2011.
② Randall Stross, "YouTube Wants You to Sit and Stay Awhile," *New York Times*, May 28, 2010; Dan Schiller and Christian Sandvig, "Is YouTube the Successor to Television—or to LIFE Magazine?" *Huffington Post*, March 12, 2010, available at http://www.huffingtonpost.com/dan-schiller/is-youtube-the-successor_b_497198.html (accessed January 10, 2014).
③ Stuart Elliott, "Marketers Trade Tales about Getting to Know Facebook and Twitter," *New York Times*, October 15, 2010.
④ Richard Waters, "Ad Revenue Rise Overshadowed by Ballooning Costs at Google," *Financial Times*, April 15, 2011.
⑤ Claire Cain Miller, "Google to Sell Users' Endorsements," *New York Times*, October 11, 2013, available at http://www.nytimes.com/2013/10/12/technology/google-sets-plan-to-sell-users-endorsements.html?_r=0 (accessed January 10, 2014); Cecilia Kang, "Google to Put User Photos, Comments in Online Ads," *Washington Post*, October 11, 2013, available at http://articles.washingtonpost.com/2013-10-11/business/42926754_1_google-and-facebook-google-user-google-policy (accessed January 10, 2014).
⑥ Emily Steel, "AOL Aims for a Slice of TV Ad Pie," *Financial Times*, May 9, 2013.
⑦ Barney Jopson, "Amazon Set to Sell $800m of Ads as It Woos Business from Rivals," *Financial Times*, June 5, 2013.
⑧ Robert Cookson, "WPP and Twitter in Analytics Alliance," *Financial Times*, June 7, 2013.

数据授权收入①；此外，推特还宣布，它试图挖掘更多的用户数据，用以帮助在其他的移动应用程序或是网站上刊登广告②。脸书担心青少年有可能对它产生厌烦，于是不遗余力地向广告商提供数据以及消费者访问信息的接入点，比如，它放宽了针对青少年已然很宽松的隐私条款③。

这是一次复杂的转型过程，充斥着各种断裂与随之而来的不确定性。这一过程中，最重要的或许与移动设备有关。2012年，越来越多的中国人通过手机而非个人电脑来上网；不久，从印尼到北美，全球的其他地方紧跟这一趋势。该转变引发的战略调整，"远不止使业务适应新的小屏幕那么简单"④。

诚如我们所见，其中一种战略调整就是谷歌、微软、亚马逊纷纷从软件和服务提供商转型为硬件制造商，以应对苹果的发展之道。第二种调整是，网络公司实现收入来源多样化，例如推出各种业务，进而从广告、电子商务和直销等途径获得营收。然而，这些转型或调整的紧迫性反映出如下事实：尽管大力发展移动端业务，但从移动媒体获得的广告收入仍然不敌从传统台式机获得的收入（2011年，在美国，这一组对比数据为15亿美元与320亿美元；尽管到2013年，前一数据有大幅增长）。换言之，2011年移动互联网使用占全美所有媒体使用的10%，可前者仅仅吸引了不到1%的全美广告费用⑤。智能手机和平板电脑共同创造了一个拥有无限买家的广告市场，让广告商被新媒体团团包围，毫无其他选择；贸易条件明确地向赞助商倾斜，而远离媒体（不只是网络）。时代出版公司的改变，可被视为当前已经天翻地覆的大环境的一个缩影：时代出版公司长期奉行采编与经营分离的方针，即公司的编辑与商业部门之间互不干涉；然而，新任时代出版公司的首席执行官公开表示，公司的编辑部与广告部应当通力合作⑥。此外，"品牌内容"或"内容营销"业务不断增长；通过这些业务，美国国际商用机器公司、通用汽车、激浪（Mountain Dew）和道琼斯这些赞助企业能够直接生产和推出社论或娱乐节目⑦。

然而，对于广告商以及那些依赖他们的网络服务提供商而言，或许可识别的个人信息所具有的地位，才能引发最大的不确定性；而侵入性的网络监控（及其所获得的个人信息数据），正是广告商和网络服务提供商孜孜不倦谋求发展的基本动力。尽管美国总统

---

① Twitter Inc., Form S-1 Registration Statement, U.S. SEC, October 3, 2013.
② Hannah Kuchler, Tim Bradshaw, and Emily Steel, "Twitter Looks to Mine User Data to Help Sell Advertising on Other Sites," *Financial Times*, October 15, 2013.
③ Vindu Goel, "Facebook Eases Privacy Rules for Teenagers," *New York Times*, October 17, 2013; Hannah Kuchler, Tim Bradshaw, and Emily Steel, "Facebook Admits That Teens Are Losing Interest," *Financial Times*, November 1, 2013.
④ Tim Bradshaw and Richard Waters, "Big Tech Forced to Answer the Phone," *Financial Times*, August 8, 2012.
⑤ Richard Waters, "Roaming for a Revenue Revolution," *Financial Times*, August 9, 2012.
⑥ Joe Nocera, "The Fall of the Wall?" *New York Times*, November 2, 2013.
⑦ Stuart Elliott, "Brought to You by Mountain Dew," *New York Times*, April 26. 2013; Stuart Elliott, "Content Marketing Beckons to an Executive From a Digital Agency," *New York Times*, May 24, 2013.

候选人有可能试图忽视这个问题,但它始终都是一个政治烫手山芋。

隐私(无隐私)

任何一位美国总统候选人都有可能提出隐私滥用的问题,将之整合进一大堆选战议题中并(承诺将)采取补救措施,由此为自己的选情加分。然而,值得注意的是,2012 年,共和、民主两党候选人都没有这么做①。2013 年,《纽约时报》就此发表社论:"州议员已经厌倦了苦等国会(在未来某一天)通过立法全面保护隐私权,他们正亲自着手解决这些问题"②。

在网络世界里,数据追踪与挖掘具有地方色彩:2009 年,50 家访问量最大的网站中有 36 家网站在它们的"隐私"政策中声明,它们允许第三方的数据追踪。实际上,这完全剥夺了消费者哪怕受到限制的监督权利;而这些权利原本就被写入网站的隐私保护政策之中③。移动设备所具有的侵略性略有不同,因为它们并不依赖于小型软件(例如小型文本文件);这些软件曾作为台式电脑最重要的追踪工具,现在依然如此④。米格尔·赫尔夫特(Miguel Helft)指出:"如果你的口袋装着一部智能手机,那么你基本上是在替谷歌或苹果免费打工,帮助它们最终向你直接推送更多的广告"。这些手机被设置成某种传感器,它们能自动感应到附近的手机信号发射塔与无线网络,并搜集数据⑤。2009 年 7 月至 2010 年,德国电信记录并保存同一用户超过 35 组不同的经纬度位置,每天获取近 300 次阅读信息。在美国,网络运营商甚至不需要精确报告他们所收集的数据的类型⑥(现在知道,需要向政府安全机构报备)。有了社交网络、搜索服务、移动设备、传感器阵列与数据中心的加持,一个市值数十亿美元的行业不断壮大⑦,它旨在捕捉并分析"大数据"⑧以服务于营销目的。

---

① 2012 年总统大选的民主党团强调"互联网自由",本书第三部分将重点考察这一议题;而共和党团则大肆宣扬第四修正案,但仅从政府侵犯个体权利的角度。
② New York Times Editorial Board, "States Take on Privacy," November 2, 2013, available at http://www.nytimes.com/2013/11/03/opinion/sunday/states-take-on-privacy.html?_r=0 (accessed January 10, 2014).
③ Lawrence E. Strickling, Assistant Secretary for Communications and Information, NTIA, Testimony before the Committee on Commerce, Science, and Transportation, U.S. Senate, March 16, 2011.
④ 移动设备传输的定位数据,以及用户网络浏览的发展史,成为密集型发展战略着眼的目标,具体请参见 Richard Waters, "Roaming for a Revenue Revolution," *Financial Times*, August 9, 2012; Emily Steel, "Web Groups Seek New Profiles as Cookie Crumbles," *Financial Times*, September 20, 2013.
⑤ Miguel Helft, "Phone Data Used to Fill Digital Map," *New York Times*, April 26, 2011.
⑥ Noam Cohen, "It's Tracking Your Every Move and You May Not Even Know," *New York Times*, March 26, 2011.
⑦ Richard Waters, "A Binary Goldmine," *Financial Times*, May 6, 2011.
⑧ Joel Stein, "Data Mining: How Companies Now Know Everything about You," *Time*, March 10, 2011; Joseph Menn, "Virtually Insecure," *Financial Times*, July 29, 2010.

对隐私的担忧毫无意外地几乎与现象本身同时出现。主管通信及信息事务的商务部部长助理兼美国国家电信及信息委员会主管劳伦斯·斯特里克林（Lawrence Strickling）承认，"个人信息的大规模采集、分析与储存正成为互联网经济的核心；然而，这些类似的业务越来越让消费者感到不安，因为他们不清楚自己活动和交易的数据如何被搜集、使用和储存"。一连串的调查表明，在隐私遭到滥用这一问题上，美国人表示不满并保持高度警惕，但同时，他们对隐私滥用的真实情况也缺乏足够了解①。向智能手机和移动互联网的转型，加上不断延伸的跟踪设备和数据挖掘技术②，使得斯特里克林所说的"理解个人数据流的困难"将变得"更加严重"③。

刑事入侵和普通的商业实务之间的界限非常模糊。有关敏感的消费数据的窃取与转移等重磅消息，我们早已有所耳闻。在2011年4月，黑客窃取了60个国家7 700万索尼（PlayStation）在线游戏账户的姓名、用户、邮箱、密码甚至信用卡数据④。差不多同一时间，黑客突破艾司隆公司（Epsilon）的计算机安全网，盗取摩根大通公司、花旗银行和塔吉特百货（Target）等使用艾司隆电子邮件营销服务的公司的用户列表；同时，黑客获取了花旗银行20万信用卡持有者的个人信息⑤。2013年，类似的刑事入侵和数据窃取不断威胁消费者在线数据（的安全）⑥。另一方面，在苹果、微软、谷歌相继陷入泄露移动定位数据的丑闻之后，荷兰的通腾导航科技公司因私下向荷兰警方售卖其客户的行驶数据而不得不出面公开道歉⑦。甚至在脸书对外宣称加强其隐私管控之后，《华尔街日报》所做的一次调查却揭示，脸书许多受欢迎的应用程序仍然把识别数据转送给外面的广告商以及数据追踪公司的数据⑧。谷歌面临"在日常运营中"非法窃听的指控——涉嫌收集互联网用户数据并向用户推送广告⑨。一项声名在外的独立研究披露，最受欢迎的100家网站中，每家网站平均装有12个数据追踪器，每个月批准上百种不同的追踪系统进入其中（完成数据搜集工作）："这就意味当一位用户访问某家网站，可能有100台追踪设备在用户完全不知情的情况下记录下这次访问"。网上追踪正在从台式电脑的网络浏览器延伸至手

---

① Strickling, Testimony.
② Tanzina Vega, "Web Code Offers New Ways to See What Users Do Online," *New York Times*, October 11, 2010; Steve Lohr, "New Ways to Exploit Raw Data May Bring Surge of Innovation, a Study Says," *New York Times*, May 13, 2011.
③ Strickling, Testimony, 3.
④ "Online Reputations in the Dirt," *The Economist*, April 30, 2011.
⑤ Richard Waters, "Grand Theft Data," *Financial Times*, April 30 – May 1, 2011; Eric Dash, "Citi Data Theft Points Up a Nagging Problem," *New York Times*, June 10, 2011.
⑥ Hannah Kuchler, "Industries Hit by Leap in Hacking Attacks," *Financial Times*, January 14, 2014.
⑦ Maija Palmer, "TomTom Apologises to Customers after Selling Driving Data to Police," *Financial Times*, April 29, 2011.
⑧ Emily Steel and Geoffrey Fowler, "Facebook in Privacy Breach," *Wall Street Journal*, October 18, 2010; Miguel Helft and Jenna Wortham, "Facebook Bows to Pressure over Privacy," *New York Times*, May 27, 2010. For a similar exposure see Joseph Menn, "Virtually Insecure," *Financial Times*, July 29, 2010.
⑨ Claire Cain Miller, "Google Accused of 'Wiretapping' in Gmail Scans," *New York Times*, October 2, 2013.

机、平板电脑、电视、机顶盒、游戏机以及越来越多的汽车上①。那么,日常的企业监控与非法侵犯隐私的界限在哪里?2013 年 6 月,爱德华·斯诺登对外揭露重要的互联网中介商与美国国家安全局合作掌控了电子生活的"入口"(sluice)这一事实,将问题推向全球政治的维度;关于斯诺登事件等一系列衍生效应,我将在第三部分进行讨论。

此处,必须强调"隐私"并不能从概念上完全涵盖当前有关监控的问题。对此,雷蒙德·瓦克斯(Raymond Wacks)如是解释,"'隐私'这个概念太模糊、太笨拙,反而无法有效地分析问题"②。随着网络商品链"从根本上重新定义了数据收集、使用与分享的方式、地点与主体"③,个人信息的政治经济界限正在被打破。这些议题与其认为是个体和个人的,毋宁认为是政治经济层面的。

美国公司和政府机关试图生产出一块遮瑕补丁,以掩盖它们将不断增长的数据整合进积累和控制结构中的种种努力,并竭力平复用户对侵权的各种焦虑情绪。早在斯诺登事件发生之前,美国商务部联合联邦贸易委员会就已在摸索缓解大众恐慌的方法。商务部试图将行为和功能分为有利的与有害的两大类,并尝试建立一套实用的言辞与法律规范以帮助宣传这一区分,同时促使信誉良好的资方公开出面表示支持。强制执行的行为准则被称为"公平信息实务准则";这些准则成为商务部所提交的关于消费者数据的"动态隐私框架"的"核心内容"④。2012 年,奥巴马政府提出网络消费者隐私权益法案⑤。

政策制定者认为需要将政策规制和约束置于他们所说的"创新"(盈利的委婉表达)之下。美国商务部下属机构互联网政策任务组(Internet Policy Task Force)认为,隐私政策的制定必须以"创新蓬勃发展"⑥为前提。相较于美国商务部,美国联邦贸易委员会更为大胆,他们希望将所有的隐私政策都限制在"紧跟动态市场"⑦这一大框架下。微软的

---

① Ashkan Soltani, Testimony before U. S. Senate, Committee on Commerce, Science, and Transportation, Hearing on the State of Online Consumer Privacy, March 16, 2011, 4, available at http://www. gpo. gov/fdsys/pkg/CHRG – 112shrg73308/html/CHRG – 112shrg73308. htm (accessed January 10, 2014).

② Raymond Wacks, *Privacy: A Very Short Introduction* (Oxford: Oxford University Press, 2010), xi.

③ Erich Andersen, Deputy General Counsel, Microsoft Corporation, "The Need for a Comprehensive Approach to Protecting Consumer Privacy," Statement before the Committee on Commerce, Science, and Transportation, U. S. Senate, Hearing on the State of Online Consumer Privacy, March 16, 2011, 3, available at http://www. gpo. gov/fdsys/pkg/CHRG – 112shrg73308/html/CHRG – 112shrg73308. htm (accessed January 10, 2014).

④ Strickling, Testimony, 5, 6.

⑤ The White House, "We Can't Wait," February 23, 2012, available at at http://www . whitehouse. gov/the – press – office/2012/02/23/we – can – t – wait – obama – administration – unveils – blueprint – privacy – bill – rights (accessed January 10, 2014).

⑥ Department of Commerce, Internet Policy Task Force, Commercial Data Privacy and Innovation in the Internet Economy: A Dynamic Policy Framework December 16, 2010, iii, available at http://www. ntia. doc. gov/report/2010/commercial – data – privacy – and – innovation – internet – economy – dynamic – policy – framework (accessed January 10, 2014).

⑦ Federal Trade Commission, Preliminary Staff Report, "Protecting Consumer Privacy in an Era of Rapid Change: A Proposed Framework for Business and Policymakers," December 1, 2010, 3. Also, Edward Wyatt, "After Adding Online Privacy Protections, F. T. C. Chief Resigns," *New York Times*, February 1, 2013.

副法律顾问宣称:"行业和政府必须共同解决的问题在于,如何更好地保障消费者隐私,同时保障商业能够开发出更多的创新产品和服务"①。圆圈怎能变成正方形呢?

一位高级政府官员指出,"如果用户并不相信他们在网上的个人信息是安全的,那么,他们就不会接受新的互联网服务项目,或完全投身于互联网商业活动中"②。那些占主导地位的互联网资本借助关于消费者隐私的令人眩晕的政策话语,求助政府能够在可被接受的数据收集行为与必将招致惩处的违法行为之间划清界限。"信任"作为一种临时性的修辞,被大肆宣传。这一话语框架虽然精细,其(虚伪性)却被轰动一时的斯诺登事件完全曝光。然而,隐私政策框架的核心问题(即合法化现有的运作模式,以巩固在线广告与销售的新形式)还需要我们额外加以检视。

1890年,大法官路易斯·布兰戴斯(Louis Brandeis)在美国法律界首创隐私权的定义,即"独处的权利"③。相比那些尖锐的政治担忧,布兰戴斯的定义显得柔和许多;毕竟,早期的美国法律制定者出于担忧,试图阻止专制的行政权(对个人隐私)的侵害。布兰戴斯的概念不是直接指向那些武断的搜查和国家检查邮局信件等侵犯政治自由的行为④,而是提出潜在的技术——商业发展有可能挑战中产阶级的"内部感知力"(domestic sensibilities,例如摄像头)这一问题。"隐私"成为一种路径,意在将未来的侵犯行为置于规训式的法律谈判进程之下。

正如奥斯卡·甘地(Oscar Gandy)较早的理解⑤,或凯莉·A. 盖茨(Kelly A. Gates)和马克·安捷维克(Mark Andrejevic)所做的深入阐释⑥,布兰戴斯提出隐私权概念后的数十年间,一套个人信息识别与使用机制普遍建立起来。无线射频辨识系统(Radio frequency identification systems)、智能卡(smart cards)、生物识别技术、传感器和日常的商业和政府的监控系统先后被添加进这一机制中;与此同时,网络服务成为个人信息生成与抓取的轴心。一台商业情报的在线机器,即盖茨所说的"监控文化"⑦逐渐渗透进日常生活。

---

① Andersen, *Statement*, 3.
② Lawrence E. Strickling, Assistant Secretary of Commerce for Communications and Information, Keynote Remarks Before Global Internet Governance Academic Network, Washington, D. C., May 5, 2011, 1, available at http://news. dot - nxt. com.
③ Samuel D. Warren and Louis D. Brandeis, "The Right to Privacy," *Harvard Law Review* 4, no. 5 (December 15, 1890):193.
④ Richard R. John, *Spreading The News: The Postal System from Franklin to Morse* (Cambridge: Harvard University Press, 1995); Colin Agur, "Negotiated Order: The Fourth Amendment, Telephone Surveillance, and Social Interactions, 1878 - 1968," *Information and Culture* 48, no. 4 (October - December 2013):419 - 47.
⑤ Gandy, "Political Economy," 436 - 57; Oscar H. Gandy Jr., *The Panoptic Sort: A Political Economy of Personal Information* (Boulder, Colo.: Westview, 1993).
⑥ Kelly A. Gates, *Our Biometric Future: Facial Recognition Technology and the Culture of Surveillance* (New York: New York University Press, 2011); Mark Andrejevic, *Info - Glut: How Too Much Information Is Changing the Way We Think and Know* (New York: Rout - ledge, 2013).
⑦ Gates, *Our Biometric Future*.

因此，哪怕是布兰戴斯关于隐私权的松散定义，也显得过于繁琐。根据微软公司的埃里希·安德森（Erich Andersen）直截了当的解释，这是因为每天人们都在"不同的设备上生产出海量数据，这些数据揭示了关于用户兴趣的宝贵信息"；既然这样，隐私不可能再与"'独处'有关"。美国企业和美国政府日常运作形式的变化，使它们不再接受布兰戴斯的概念：需要从根本上修订布兰戴斯关于隐私权的特征描述。安德森代表微软提出，隐私应当涉及如下几个方面，例如"知晓什么数据正被收集、数据用于什么目的，以及选择数据收集和使用的方式并确保这些过程都是安全的"①。

然而，这恰好构成一组经过精心修饰的遁词。一面是大资本和美国政府坚持认为，个人必须让渡出在生活中任何独处的权利，另一面却是它们在制度上不负责任。它们告知人们不妨接受微软所提出的"透明、控制与安全"这一颇具机巧、含混不清的标准。至于谁去收集数据、收集哪一类信息等问题，就主要交给公司与国家机构来决定。相反，那些更宏观深远的政治经济方面的问题被裁减：与其认为问题是民主自由与责任能否以及如何在全知全能的国家与企业的监视下继续发扬光大，毋宁认为核心问题仅仅在于，如何定义并公开一项政策，它能够缓解这些行动者对合法性的担忧。营销与广告公司再一次打出（行业）自律的旗号——这本来就是该行业长期受到青睐（惯常使用）的策略②。相较之下，它们坚决反对联邦贸易委员会所发出的简单易行的全面"不跟踪"的号召（这不是委员会一贯的做法）；诚如联邦贸易委员会主席乔恩·雷布维茨（Jon Leibowitz）所言，委员会之所以发起"不跟踪"号召，原因在于"在美国消费者看来，隐私权自律成效不大"③。

关于这一话语，曾有过不少提议；在此，我们没有必要一一细究。2011年，沃尔玛强调指出，"隐私问题的解决方案"应当"有助于提升全球的互操作性（interoperability）"。这是因为不同国家现有的隐私权法案之间存在巨大的落差，尤其在美国和欧盟之间（差别明显），而且双方互相威胁要扩大这一差别④。沃尔玛曾表示，"随着行业着手处理隐私问题，许多公司不得不考虑全球因素，挑战也随之而来，不同国家的隐私政策各不相同"。

---

① Andersen, *Statement*, 4.
② John Montgomery, Chief Operating Officer, North America, GroupM Interaction, Testimony before the Senate Commerce, Science, and Transportation Commit-tee, Hearing on "The State of Online Consumer Privacy," March 16, 2011, available at http://www.gpo.gov/fdsys/pkg/CHRG-112shrg73308/html/CHRG-112shrg73308.htm (accessed January 10, 2014).
③ 具体请参考 Edward Wyatt and Tanzina Vega, "F. T. C. Plan Backs Option to Limit Tracking Online," *New York Times*, December 2, 2010. 值得赞扬的是，相较于其他联邦机构，联邦贸易委员会依然保持其警惕的规制者的角色，具体请参见 Edward Wyatt, "As Online Ads Look More Like News Articles, F. T. C. Warns against Deception," *New York Times*, December 5, 2013.
④ Kevin J. O'Brien, "Panel to Urge Europe to Bolster Data Rules," *New York Times*, May 16, 2011.

也许,在沃尔玛看来,美国有必要增加其有名无实的国内政策的严密性①。对此,另一个企业领导者通用电气随声附和,它极力主张"一项强有力的隐私政策对于提升消费者的信任感至关重要"。通用电气的业务范围遍及全球 100 多个国家;在此基础上,它响应倡导,希望能"在制定国际通行的隐私权标准上提出相关建议"。此外,通用电气强调自愿的行为准则,并与沃尔玛持相同意见,即若要建立合用的隐私权框架,美国必须改革自身的法律与实践②。渗透到美国本土的英荷出版商和信息服务企业里德·爱思唯尔集团(Reed Elsevier),采取较为强硬的态度:它反对不追踪机制以及消费者的"选择性退出"条款③,并要求商务部应当在其权限范围内有所作为,从而使"跨境的数据传输更加便利"。此外,它还主张,商务部"应该鼓励其他国家跟随美国的领导,并采取与美国相似的更为弹性的隐私政策"④。

以上都是站在企业的角度所得出的观点。商务部认为企业视角具有合理性,它因此认为"美国的消费者用户隐私政策将得益于一系列的立法行动,这些立法行动旨在建立更加明确的消费者与商家行动准则,与此同时保护创新与信息的自由流动,毕竟它们都是互联网的标志"⑤。对于公众而言,当前(隐私权政策)现状不透明、不负责任,并处处遭遇反对,因此需要改变这一切。2011 年,奥巴马政府宣布支持立法,旨在为消费者建立"隐私保护的基本原则";然而,关于"公平信息实务原则"应当是什么的讨论从未消停。同时,围绕实质性的、结构性的权力差距(即完全透明的公民身份与不透明的企业或政府机构)而展开的争论不断发酵,却只导致形式上的些许变化。

随后,斯诺登向《卫报》的重磅爆料,断然改变了这一图景。他呈交的档案资料被全球其他新闻媒体获得;这些档案向我们揭示了美国政府和企业如何沆瀣一气,在全球范围内有组织地违反人权⑥。美国政府和企业小心翼翼建造的隐私权政策框架被无情地击碎,从而将讨论重新引至一些根本性的政治原则问题上。

---

① Wal - Mart to NTIA, Re: Commercial Data Privacy and Innovation in *the Internet Economy*: *A Dynamic Policy Framework* (Docket # 101214614 - 0615 - 1), January 27, 2011, 1 available at http://www. ntia. doc. gov/files/ntia/comments/101214614 - 0614 - 01/attachments/ Walmart%20Comments. pdf (accessed January 10, 2014).
② GE mentioned the Electronic Communications Privacy Act in this context. Nuala O'Connor Kelly, Chief Privacy Leader and Senior Counsel, Information Governance, General Electric, to NTIA, Internet Policy Task Force, Re: Commercial Data Privacy and Innovation in *the Internet Economy*: *A Dynamic Policy Framework*, RIN 0660 - XA22, January 28, 2011, 1, 2, 3, 4, available at http://www. ntia. doc. gov/files/ntia/comments/101214614 - 0614 - 01/attachments/GE%20comment%20letter. pdf (accessed January 10, 2014).
③ Steven Manzo, Vice President, Government Affairs, Reed Elsevier Inc., to Secretary Gary Locke, NTIA, Comments on "Commercial Data Privacy and Innovation in the Internet Economy: A Dynamic Policy Framework," January 28, 2011, 1, 3, 8, available at http://www. ntia. doc. gov/files/ntia/comments/101214614 - 0614 - 01/attachments/Reed%20Else - vier%20Comments%20to%20Department%20of%20Commerce. pdf (accessed January 10, 2014).
④ Manzo, *Comments*, 9.
⑤ Strickling, *Testimony*, 6 (quotes).
⑥ 相关系列报道请参见《卫报》网站:http://www. theguardian. com/world/the - nsa - files。

在联合国大会上,明显是美国中情局监控的特定目标人物巴西总统迪尔玛·罗塞夫(Dilma Rousseff)曾愤怒地回应:"在隐私权不受到保护的情况下,我们无法享受到真正的言论与观点自由,也因此更不会建立有效的民主制度"①。倘若某人遭到监控,对他而言,言论自由危机重重。然而,罗塞夫的抗议引发一系列相关问题:美国能够掌握全世界人民以及不同民族的传播行为,这究竟意味着什么? 言论自由、隐私权等与民主相关的权利能否既属于个体,又属于全社会呢?

的确,某种传统观点认为,只有在社会有能力包容其成员表达的所有观点时,言论自由才有可能达到最佳的状态②。隐私权利必须具备与言论自由同等的有机性。除非社会能够保障所有人免于监控的权利,否则民主社会必然遭到侵害。因此,我们如果只是借助强调不能侵犯个体权利的隐私权概念来理解当前的互联网营销,远远不够。我们所面对的问题,并非是对某些特定的不幸人群的偶然袭击,而是资本对人类互动所留下的无处不在的数据痕迹的全面占有。如今威胁民主与公民自由的,不仅是滥用的行政权力,还有利用个人信息的大文化企业。所以,当全社会必须选择退出时,(若要真正地保护隐私权,维系责任感,那么)仅仅提出一项消费者"选择性退出"条款作为解决之道,实在令人愕异。

官方的隐私政策和在线广告的发展进程,抢先阻止了这一解决办法的出台,并将解决之道引向其他方向。很明显,白色空间不断窄化、遭到削减,以保障销售商与间谍始终监视我们的生活。广告费用正迅速地流向其他领域:在广告流行后不到 20 年,互联网已经成为美国第二大广告媒体;投放互联网的广告费用占全美总广告预算的 20%,金额高达 310 亿美元(仅次于电视媒体,后者的广告费用占总预算的 38%),并始终保持快速增长的态势。哪怕在数字化衰退期,搜索与显示广告的花费依然保持两位数的增长③。2012 至 2013 年,投放至台式电脑以及(特别是)移动设备领域的广告数

---

① 援引自 Julian Borger, "Brazilian President: US Surveillance 'A Breach of International Law,'" *The Guardian*, September 24,2013, available at http://www.theguardian.com/world/ 2013/sep/24/brazil – president – un – speech – nsa – surveillance (accessed January 10,2014).

② 本·斯科特(Ben Scott)重新论述了这一社会 – 法治思潮传统,并梳理 1930 年代美国新闻工作者历史,具体请参见 Dale Benjamin Scott, "Labor's New Deal for Journalism: The Newspaper Guild in the 1930s," PhD diss., University of Illinois at Urbana – Champaign,2009.

③ Emily Steel, "Big Pop Seen for Online Ads," *Wall Street Journal*, June 8,2011;"Q3 '11 Internet Advertising Revenues up 22% from Year Ago, Climb to Nearly $7.9 Billion, According to IAB and PwC," November 30,2011, available at http://www.iab.net/about_the _iab/recent_press_releases/press_release_archive/press_release/pr – 113011 (accessed January 10,2014).

量急剧增长；2012年总广告费用增加了3.5%，2013年又增长了3.9%①。

关于个人信息的争论并非一次性的，而是一场持久战；在这场战役中，大广告商、网络运营商、互联网中介商以及媒体巨头，与民意构成对立双方。在过去六个月里，斯诺登细水长流的爆料最终使我们越来越确定，美国军事—情报复合体已经安装了一款无所不包、不受管辖的网络系统。例如，谁曾想到游戏"愤怒的小鸟"（由芬兰软件公司罗维奥[Rovio]推出的此款游戏，截至2014年在全球范围内已经被下载17亿余次）的玩家数据已经被美国国家安全局窃取②？美国依然作为全球互联网经济的中心，它所面临的压力与日俱增；在美国本土，隐私权倡议者始终努力推进实施更为强势的"不追踪"条款，正如广告商"丝毫不妥协，坚决反对（现有局面的）改变，因为那样会极大地限制他们收集信息的行为"③。大的网络中介商寻求创建新的个人标识以取代小型文本文件，希望借此扭转局势。这场争斗如何发展，无可预知，正如现在一般。

最后一个问题让我们再次回到这些正在重组的通信商品链对于经济增长的贡献上。

---

① ZenithOptimedia, "ZenithOptimedia forecasts stable ad growth in 2013 will pave way for recovery in 2014 and 2015," September 30, 2013, available at http://www.zenith optimedia.com/zenithoptimedia-forecasts-stable-ad-growth-in-2013-will-pave-way-for recovery-in-2014-and-2015 (accessed January 10, 2014). ZenithOptimedia, "Global Ad-spend Set to Return to Pre-Financial Crisis Growth Rates," April 7, 2014, accessed at http://www.zenithoptimedia.com/global-adspend-set-to-return-to-pre-financial-crisis-growth-rates.
② James Ball, "Angry Birds Firm Calls for Industry to Respond to NSA Spying Revelations," *The Guardian*, January 28, 2014, available at http://www.theguardian.com/world/2014/jan/28/angry-birds-rovio-respond-nsa-spying-revelations (accessed February 6, 2014).
③ Richard Waters, "Google Eyes Cookie Alternatives in Effort to Give Users Greater Control," *Financial Times*, September 19, 2013.

第 9 章
衰退中的增长？

基于网络商品链的通信产业的转型，是否构成了我们在第一部分所检视的矛盾模式的例外情形？我们发现，网络所激活的制造业、金融和军工产业的重组，最终引发深层次的危机。美国的信息与通信行业是否形成一种不同的发展模式？这一行业在信息通信技术和软件上的投资力度，远高于制造业或银行业甚至其他任何行业：2011 年，投资规模高达 805 亿美元，占总投资的 28%[①]。这些花费（还包括进入其他国家市场的开支）是否意味着新的时空修复，以及市场扩张与经济增长的基础正在形成？还是恰恰相反，网络通信商品链的投资将收入与收益从传统媒体输送至新媒体，以实现平稳的总体增长态势？

官方数据显示，2007 年，美国信息产业总收入达 1.08 万亿美元，2011 年为 1.17 万亿美元[②]。信息产业实现适度增长——在数字化衰退期反而明显[③]。如果对通信产业重构过程做更详细的分析，有助于厘清这一问题。

数字化衰退的七年（2008—2014 年）里，广告收入先降后升、广告商投放广告的媒体平台发生改变、应用程序取代独立服务，以及人们使用与消费媒体的习惯也相应发生转变。西欧与北美地区数百万家庭遭遇经济困境，严重影响以收费为基础的通信消费；而中国、印度、巴西及其他地区（自诩为）"中产阶级"的数量的增长也难以抵消这部分损失。并且，非白人与全球南方几十亿人口的贫困化问题，亟待解决。因此，加速发展数字

---

① U. S. Census, 2011 Information and Communications Technology Survey, table 2a "ICT Expenditures and Percent Change for Companies with Employees by Major Industry Sector: 2011 and 2010 Revised," available at http://www.census.gov/econ/ict/xls/2011/full_report.html (accessed January 10, 2014).

② U. S. Census Bureau, Annual and Quarterly Services Report, January 29, 2013, table 1 "Estimated Revenue for Employer and Non-Employer Firms: 2007 through 2011," available at http://www.census.gov/services/index.html (accessed January 10, 2014).

③ 该部门雇员的数量同时下跌，年工资总额几近持平，具体请参见 U. S. Census Bureau, County Business Patterns, North American FactFinder, retrieved at http://www.census.gov/econ/cbp/index.html (accessed January 10, 2014)。

化、移动与社交网络服务,必须防止那些被遗弃以及花销减少的区域的进一步扩大。我们需要深化研究,才能理解这一复杂的历史拼贴图景;在接下来的部分我将着重讨论美国(信息通信产业)的发展趋势。

付费服务遭到沉重打击,尤其在遭遇经济下滑同时未经授权就能使用文化产品的现象盛行的地方(例如美国)。以音乐行业为例,巡回演唱会的收入锐减,"因为身无分文的消费者只能待在家里":2009 年,全球最卖座的 50 场演唱会门票收入总计 33.4 亿美元,2010 年只有 29.2 亿美元,跌幅达 12%;在北美地区,跌幅更高达 15%[1]。2012 年,全球唱片行业长期衰退的局面有所缓解,不过缓解幅度不大,只增长了 0.3%——这是自 1999 年以来第一次出现增长[2]。数字音乐下载占数字音乐行业总收入的七成;并且,据称音乐流媒体服务也经历强势增长。然而,未经授权的文件共享现象依然普遍[3]。同样的紧缩情况发生在电影产业:数字化视频光盘的销售量"暴跌";在此之前,它一直是好莱坞最大的收入来源;2011 年初,销量下滑 20%[4]。美国人在家庭影音娱乐(数字化视频光碟、蓝光光碟以及数字下载)方面的开销,从 2008 年的 210 亿美元下降至 2010 年的 188 亿美元[5],下降了约 20 亿美元。尽管未经授权在网络观看电影和电视节目的行为与日俱增,美国的电影票房收入却有所上升[6],2008 至 2012 年间增长 12%,2012 年票房总收入为 108 亿美元[7]。同样,图书出版行业也出现类似的发展不均衡、喜忧参半的现象。行业研究员阿尔伯特·格列柯(Albert Greco)曾预计,2015 年,纸质出版物的销售额将从 2008 年的 180 亿美元减少至 139 亿美元;他还指出,2015 年,电子图书的销售额将达到 36 亿美元[8]。这些数字发行的涨落,无法补足传统试听与出版市场每况愈下的收入。

通信服务业再次呈现出双面形象。在美国,房地产市场的萧条与经济危机体现为有

---

[1] Ethan Smith, "New Blow to Music as Concerts Fizzle," *Wall Street Journal*, December 30, 2010.
[2] Matthew Garrahan and Andrew Edgecliffe-Johnson, "Digital Distribution Fails to Offset Fall in DVD Sales," *Financial Times*, January 7, 2011; "IFPI Publishes Digital Music Report 2013," February 26, 2013, available at www.ifpi.org/content/section_resources/dmr2013.html (accessed January 10, 2014).
[3] Tim Bradshaw, "Party Is Over for Music Downloads," *Financial Times*, September 26, 2010; "IFPI Publishes Digital Music Report 2013," February 26, 2013 available at http://www.ft.com/cms/s/0/4b5a3c80-c998-11df-b3d6-00144feab49a.html#axzz2quInqFKk (accessed January 10, 2014).
[4] Matthew Garrahan, "Fall of 20% in Sales of DVDs Poses Challenge for Hollywood," *Financial Times*, May 3, 2011.
[5] Matthew Garrahan and Andrew Edgecliffe-Johnson, "Digital distribution fails to offset fall in DVD sales," *Financial Times*, January 7, 2011.
[6] Matthew Garrahan, "Fall of 20% in Sales of DVDs Poses Challenge for Hollywood," *Financial Times*, May 3, 2011.
[7] MPAA, Theatrical Market Statistics 2010, 3, 4; MPAA Theatrical Market Statistics 2011, 4; MPAA Theatrical Market Statistics 2012, 4. Available at http://www.mpaa.org (accessed January 10, 2014).
[8] Jeffrey A. Trachtenberg, "New Economics Rewrite Book Business," *Wall Street Journal*, August 29, 2011, available at http://online.wsj.com/news/articles/SB10001424053111904875404576532351102200460 (accessed January 10, 2014).

线电视和室内电话订户的急剧减少①。2010年第三季度,美国有线电视用户数减少将近75万,是30年来最大的一次降幅②。翌年,有线电视产业总算再次站稳脚跟;有线电视运营商开始依赖商业服务与宽带订阅以寻求增长③。然而,YouTube网站的短视频业务,以及网飞公司允许订户共享账户等措施,部分代替了原有的有线电视服务产品(还很廉价)。随着原有订户接受线上流媒体服务,订户退订现象持续存在。在过去六年半时间里,美国最大的有线电视运营商康卡斯特公司的视频订阅者不断流失,它不得不重新调整战略,以减少用户流失现象④。再来看看另一种接入设备。美国疾控中心的报告指出,2009年12月,平均每四个美国家庭拥有一部手机,这一转变与收入有关;2009年,生活在赤贫线以下的成年人有三分之一的家庭没有安装固话。在这一领域,产品替代情况也时有发生,例如用户从老式的"电话"转向免费(或几乎免费)的网络语音电话业务。近三年内,截至2012年下半年,约五分之二(38.2%)的美国家庭仅拥有无绳电话⑤。一面是电话语音业务正日渐向软件应用服务转型,原有产业价值逐步被蒸发;另一面则是移动与住宅宽带业务持续增长。

大部分广告商赞助的内容仍然保持某种中立。在网络上能轻易找到并顺利访问同样的(线下)内容;消费者携带清单购物的习惯虽然受到极大冲击,他们还是坚持这一习惯,而不是陷入冲动消费中——两方面合力导致了消费类杂志销量的下降;并且,自2008至2009年消费类杂志行业陷入低迷后再也没有恢复元气。《美国周刊》(*US Weekly*)、《明星》(*Star*)、《名利场》(*Vanity Fair*)、《奥普拉杂志》(*Oprah Magazine*)、《时尚》(*Cosmopolitan*)、《时代周刊》(*Time*)以及《人物》(*People*)等杂志销量相继经历明显的下滑;与此同时,它们的电子版(收入)也无法弥补付费用户的流失与广告收入每况愈下所导致的损失⑥。

报纸则是一个极端的例子:随着读者转向在线聚合器(例如谷歌和雅虎)和新闻网

---

① David Gelles and Andrew Edgecliffe - Johnson,"Americans Ditch TV in Move to Save Money," *Financial Times*, May 4, 2011; Brian Stelter,"Ownership of TV Sets Falls in U. S.," *New York Times*, May 3, 2011. 2011年9月,瑞士信贷(Credit - Suisse)分析师指出,5个美国人中有1个1天内就能取消有线或卫星电视订阅服务,具体请参见 Andrew Edgecliffe - Johnson and David Gelles,"Uncertain Outlook Drags on Advertising," *Financial Times*, September 24 - 25, 2011.
② Matthew Garrahan,"Viewers Pull Plug on Cable TV," *Financial Times*, November 18, 2010.
③ Brian Stelter,"Cable Is Holding Web TV at Bay, Earnings Show," *New York Times*, October 30, 2011;也请参见 Matt Jarzemsky,"Pay - TV Subscriber Losses Felt at Cablevision, Dish," *Wall Street Journal*, August 10, 2011.
④ Emily Steel,"Comcast Bucks Video Loss Trend," *Financial Times*, January 29, 2014.
⑤ Stephen J. Blumberg and Julian V. Luke,"Wireless Substitution: Early Release of Estimates from the National Health Interview Survey, July - December 2012," Centers for Disease Control, available at http://www.cdc.gov/nchs/data/nhis/earlyrelease/wireless201306.pdf (accessed January 10, 2014).
⑥ Russell Adams,"Magazine Sales Fall as Celebrity Titles Fade," *Wall Street Journal*, August 10, 2011; Christine Haughney,"Magazine Sales Decline on Newsstands by 10%," *New York Times*, August 8, 2012; Emily Steel,"Magazine Sales Suffer Sharp Fall in US," *Financial Times*, August 8, 2012.

站,以及广告商对报纸媒体的放弃,这一长期处于核心地位的传统媒体已遭遇灭顶之灾。尽管如此,由于小型的地方性报业集团拥有者紧紧瞄准小众市场,报业发展的未来反而存在变数。从2005至2011年,甘尼特集团报业分支(全国范围内拥有80余家社区报纸,与一份全国性大报《今日美国》)的利润率(包括利息、税、货币贬值、分期偿还等因素)从29.6%下滑至依然强劲的28.3%①。然而,报纸的新闻功能依然岌岌可危。②

可支配收入的减少直接影响(消费者对)媒体的消费选择与方式;同样,廉价的数字替代产品也影响了消费者的选择,尽管它们中的一些并不合法。由于通信商品链按照变革的商业模式进行重构,因此,整个行业在数字化衰退期保持适度增长态势。

毫无疑问,人们花在通信与媒体上的时间越来越多。一份官方评估指出,1996年,美国成年人平均在通信(不包括电信)上所花费的时间为3 297小时③,2007与2008年,平均为3 545小时(估计2009年会有小幅下降)④。在过去12年中,美国成年人与通信有关的活动时间每周增加逾60小时。家用互联网服务、移动服务、游戏和基本的有线电视收视行为均有所增长。换言之,顶级互联网公司所获取的利润建立在它们挪用大量无偿(通常不被承认)劳动力的基础之上⑤(这解释了自2009年第二季度也就是官方所认定的"恢复期"后连续九个季度,为何美国消费者在电视上的支出增长83%,电脑支出增长50%⑥,甚至在平板电脑和智能手机上的开支急速上升)。2012年,美国信息技术公司向投资者支付的股息首次超过其他行业⑦。

为了进一步说明增长的问题,我们必须将美国国内的发展趋势置于全球范围内(即跨越美国国境)。1995至2010年间,经济合作与发展组织的34个成员国中,大部分国家

---

① Miriam Gottfried,"Warren Buffett's Cut – Price Community Spirit for Newspapers," *Wall Street Journal*, June 23 – 24, 2012.
② Pew Research Center, Project for Excellence in Journalism, "The State of the News Media 2013," available at http://stateofthemedia.org (accessed January 10,2014).
③ U. S. Department of Commerce, Statistical Abstract of the United States, table 1102, "Media Usage and Consumer Spending 1996 to 2005," available at http://www.census.gov/prod/2003pubs/02statab/infocom.pdf, p. 698, (accessed January 10,2014).
④ U. S. Department of Commerce, Statistical Abstract of the United States, table 1130, "Media Usage and Consumer Spending 2003 to 2009," available at http://www.census.gov/prod/2011pubs/11statab/infocomm.pdf, p. 711 (accessed January 10,2014).
⑤ ShinJoung Yeo, "The Mirage of Silicon Valley: Laboring in the Age of the 'New' Economy," presentation, Union for Democratic Communication, San Francisco, November 1,2013; ShinJoung Yeo, "Behind the Search Box: The Political Economy of the Global Search Engine Industry," draft PhD diss., University of Illinois at Urbana – Champaign,2013.
⑥ Conor Dougherty, "Holding Off on a Haircut To to Buy a New Car," *Wall Street Journal*,25 November 25,2011. 2008年,全美媒体消费总额上升2.3%,高达8826千亿美元,具体请参见Stephanie Clifford,"A Look Ahead at the Money in the Communications Industry," *New York Times*, August 4,2009.
⑦ Floyd Norris, "Technology Dividends Outpacing All Others," *New York Times*, January 12,2013.

移动与宽带互联网服务的增长导致通信设备与服务成为增长最快的家庭支出项目①。尽管传统媒体的利润一路下滑，但可以肯定的是，这一规模才是衡量（行业）真正增长的准确标准。

当然，年复一年，这些数字起落不定，尤其在数字化衰退期更加明显。根据世界信息技术和服务协会（其计算出来的统计数据同经济合作与发展组织以及美国人口普查局皆有所不同）的统计，在这场危机之前，全球范围内消费者的总开支，占全球信息通信技术总消费 2.7 万亿美元的 29%。由于缺少对移动数据服务的要求，世界信息技术和服务协会 2010 年曾预测，在移动数据服务的需求增长的刺激下，截至 2013 年，消费者开支将占空前扩张的全球市场（4.5 万亿美元）的三分之一②。无论如何，全球信息通信技术的花费实际上在 2009 年减少 1 080 亿美元，降幅达 3%；以至于该产业的预期增长路线不得不向下偏离。然而，从长远来看，整体发展还是趋向增长。2013 年中，全球信息通信技术年度开支似乎将增长 4.2%，"超过关于世界经济平稳增长的预期"③。从智能手机到门锁、珠宝以及冰箱④等一系列设备的增长，推动了全球信息通信技术的开支的增加；据预测，截至 2020 年，拥有唯一 IP 地址的设备将呈现数量级增长⑤。

经济合作与发展组织在 2013 年 9 月出台的一份报告中，仍然预测"互联网经济正处于蓬勃发展阶段"⑥。2014 年的规划指出，全球消费将增长 3.8 万亿美元，增幅达 3.1%⑦。与此同时，通信与信息行业总体上呈增长态势；并且，无论是应用程序商店、云服务以及影音流服务，还是高端智能手机、搜索引擎、社交网络，这些个人化的产业细分市场展现了令人羡慕的强大的全球市场的规模。经济合作与发展组织在 2013 年 9 月的报告中强调，"网络经济已成为新的增长点，它有可能推动整个经济的发展。"⑧

---

① Organisation for Economic Cooperation and Development, "*The Future of the Internet Economy: A Statistical Profile*," June 2011 Update," 28.
② World Information Technology and Services and Alliance (WITSA), "Digital Planet 2010: Executive Summary," October 2010, p. 15, fig. 5, available at http://www.witsa.org/v2/media_center/pdf/DP2010_ExecSumm_Final_LoRes.pdf (accessed January 10, 2014).
③ Bede McCarthy, "IT Spending Expected to Grow by 4% amid Uncertain Climate," *Financial Times*, January 4, 2013.
④ Don Clark, "'Internet of Things' in Reach," *Wall Street Journal*, January 6, 2014.
⑤ Bob Violino, "'Digital Industrial Economy' Combines Physical World and Virtual," *Information Management* 8 (October 2013); "New Devices Drive Global Information Technology Spending," DenverPost.com, October 8, 2013.
⑥ Organisation for Economic Co-operation and Development, "The Internet Economy on the Rise: Progress since the Seoul Declaration," OECD Publishing, 2013, available at http://www.keepeek.com/Digital-Asset-Management/oecd/science-and-technology/the-internet-economy-on-the-rise_9789264201545-en#page3 (accessed January 10, 2014).
⑦ Quentin Hardy, "Growth Returns to Tech, but Profits Will Not Be So Easy," *New York Times*, January 6, 2014.
⑧ Organization for Economic Cooperation and Development, "The Internet Economy on the Rise: Progress since the Seoul Declaration" (OECD, September 2013), available at http://www.oecd.org/sti/ieconomy/internet-economy-on-the-rise.htm (accessed February 8, 2014).

倘若网络商品链构成一种罕见的盈利增长极,那么我们也许会问,这一增长(成果)由谁占有?它如何在世界体系内进行分配?

截至2013年,根据某贸易集团的预测,亚太地区的信息通信技术开支占全球总开支的份额只比美洲低3.5%:亚太地区份额为31.1%,美洲为34.6%[1]。而亚太地区国家的市场增长率则大幅超过北美和欧洲地区[2]。世界上没有哪一个国家或地区像中国那样,其信息产业发展充满无限活力。2013年初,中国工信部颁布宽带新国标,要求新建小区必须光纤入户;并提出"宽带中国"计划,争取在2015年实现光纤到户宽带用户达4 000万[3]。同年8月,国务院设立新标准,并预测在光纤与第三代和第四代无线网络上的额外投资将推动互联网消费"以每年至少30%的速度"增长[4]。中国国内电影市场,已超过日本成为世界第二大市场,有望在五年内成为世界第一[5]。

上述对不同国家通信市场变化的勾勒表明,向数字资本主义的历史演变依然继续,尚未终结。这也导引出更为尖锐的问题:哪些资本在哪些国家的支持下,最终占有增长的果实,尤其是那些最赚钱的细分市场?哪些公司(总部设在哪些国家)最有机会从(重构的通信商品链所生产的)产品和服务中获利?哪些或哪些公司的新产品将导致进一步的经济增长,且利润滚滚而来?

带着这些问题,我们进入研究的最后阶段。正如数字化衰退凸显了网络、设备、应用程序与服务产业的变革,它也激化了政治经济矛盾。本诺·泰施克(Benno Teschke)呼吁"资本主义发展的再政治化;这一再政治化的过程,不仅指社会关系的建制化过程充满争斗,且充满区域差异,它更是对资本主义发展历史过程一次激进的地缘政治化"[6]。泰施克关于现代欧洲资本主义的早期发展的洞见,用于形容当下的数字资本主义与数字化衰退,简直再合适不过了。旨在获得更多利润从而将网络系统与服务"圈养"起来的行为,在当前信息的地缘政治图景中,成为一项新的话题;信息的地缘政治以不断激化的斗争为标志;这些斗争主要围绕对境外网络以及基于这些网络而不断增长的产业的控制权而展开。

---

[1] WITSA, *Digital Planet* 2010, 14, Figure 3.
[2] WITSA, *Digital Planet* 2010, 14; Daniel Thomas, "Asian Groups Set the Pace in IT Investment," *Financial Times*, January 29, 2013; Andrew Edgecliffe-Johnson, "Brics Set to Eclipse Western Digital Appetite," *Financial Times*, June 5, 2013.
[3] "Fibre in New Homes to Be Compulsory," *TeleGeography*, CommsUpdate, January 16, 2013.
[4] "China Sets New Targets for Broadband," *TeleGeography*, CommsUpdate, August 19, 2013; "News Analysis: Broadband Blueprint to Facilitate China's Economic Restructuring," Xinhuanet. com, August 19, 2013, available at www.xinhuanet.com/english/indepth/2013-08/19/c_1326439 (accessed January 10, 2014).
[5] Michael Cieply, "U. S. Box Office Heroes Proving Mortal in China," *New York Times*, April 22, 2013.
[6] Benno Teschke, "The Fetish of Geopolitics," *New Left Review* 69 (May-June 2011):90.

第 10 章
奋力寻求增长

数字化衰退丝毫没有消退的迹象。某些地方的政府部门有时能够暂时钳制(但无法解决)这一危机。政治经济体制尽管痼疾重重,但依然运转如故,却从未发生凤凰涅槃式的变革。然而,尽管数字化衰退期不断延长,互联网设备、服务和应用程序已持续成为利润积累的新源泉。

哪家公司或哪些国家能建立并掌控这些令各方觊觎、拥有全新的竞争优势的中心? 互联网的连接性已融入全球政治经济(脉络),它催生出新的商品,转变国家政策,并重构普通人工作、娱乐和交流的方式。赢利以及重新增长的关键领域已岌岌可危。与此同时,其他力量跃跃欲试,试图把控政治经济整体发展的趋势,这在赛博空间①(主要是互联网)里不断引爆矛盾和冲突。

将这一不断展开的动态发展过程置于国际背景下,构成本书第三部分的核心内容。只有把互联网视为一块大陆(法国《世界外交论衡》月刊[*Le Monde diplomatique*]主编塞奇·哈里米[Serge Halimi]的观点),我们才能更加容易地理解正在重塑这一管辖区域的激烈的地缘政治。2013 至 2014 年冬季,现有的"全球互联网治理"的制度机制疑似垮塌。它可能如何转变、是否会被取代,一切都是未知数。但围绕这一问题,注定将进一步爆发各种冲突,因为互联网依然属于跨国资本主义积累战略的前沿阵地。本书付梓出版时,境外互联网的管控结构的制衡,正行走在刀刃上,这也是第三部分要说明的问题。

互联网的发展受一种持久的结构性差异的型塑。美国资本仰仗于其在通信和信息处理领域中长期所具有的影响力,加上资本的流动状态,能够即时调整自身的配置运作

---

① 相较于开放互联网,"赛博空间"(本书有时译作"网络空间")包含更大范围的计算机系统,例如使用工业控制流程或各种不同的私营网络。这是因为工业控制系统的运行实际上并非完全同企业信息网络分离。我将在下文交替使用这两个概念,具体请参见 Richard Waters, "Industrial Control Systems Offer Open Door to Cyber Attacks," *Financial Times*, July 27, 2012。

情况。快速梳理一下当前十年的发展便可了解国内外的情况。统领企业路由设备、搜索引擎、社交网络以及智能手机与其他消费电器领域的分别是思科、谷歌、脸书与推特,苹果和(与三星战略联盟的)谷歌。英特尔主导半导体市场,可随着台式个人电脑逐渐被移动设备所取代,它原有的市场份额相继被爱立信、华为以及另一家美国公司高通(Qual-Comm)瓜分。甲骨文在数据库行业独领风骚,也不得不在商业软件领域面对德国 SAP 公司的竞争;微软则主导企业台式电脑操作系统市场。在商用服务与主机电脑市场,美国国际商用电器公司的赢利局面似乎从未受到数字化衰退的影响;2012 年年中,这家市值千亿美元的公司的平均收益超过华尔街自 2005 年每季度的平均收益预期,或与之持平①。美国向来以拥有两家世界收入最高的电信运营商而自豪:美国电话电报公司与威瑞森②。提供跨国云服务的企业全部来自美国。全球排名前四的计算机服务与咨询公司中,有三家来自美国,分别为:美国国际商用电器公司、电子数据系统(2008 年被惠普收购)以及埃森哲(Accenture:排名第四的则是法国凯捷咨询公司[Cap Gemini])。同样,美国公司也拥有需求侧领导力(这一领域通常为人所忽视):无论是沃尔玛、通用电气还是亚马逊,美国企业在互联网系统与应用程序上的技术创新俨然成为全球行业标准③。上述领域与创新的关键——互联网地址系统以及与之相关的技术职能也完全在美国政府与公司的主导和掌控之下④。因此,美国公司不仅是早期采纳者,更远远走在互联网技术发展的前列,对互联网的持续发展发挥着无人能及的影响力。

需要强调,美国的互联网系统与服务不仅先发制人地占据本国市场,更占领多个跨国市场。2010 年,苹果手机抢先一步成为全球热门手机,成功击溃韩国和中国的保护主义壁垒;截至 2013 年,苹果播放器用户从原来的 1.6 亿猛增至 5.75 亿⑤。2010 年,讯佳普声称其免费互联网电话服务拥有 5.6 亿用户⑥,脸书共有 5 亿用户(三年后用户数增长一倍),微软 7.89 亿用户,雅虎 6.33 亿用户⑦。这些数据不仅参差不齐,还存在统计可信度的问题。然而,美国供应商在海外市场牢牢树立起行业老大的位置,已是不争之事实。

---

① Steve Lohr, "I. B. M. Posts a Strong Quarter Despite Softness in Revenue," *New York Times*, July 19, 2012.
② Total Telecom, "The Global 100," October 24, 2013, available at http://totaltele.com.
③ Catherine L. Mann with Jacob F. Kirkegaard, *Accelerating the Globalization of America: The Role for Information Technology* (Washington, D. C.: Institute for International Economics, June 2006), 1; James W. Cortada, *The Digital Hand*, 3 vols. (New York: Oxford University Press, 2004 – 2008); David Moschella, *Customer – Driven IT: How Users Are Shaping Technology Industry Growth* (Boston: Harvard Business School Press, 2003).
④ Laura DeNardis, *The Global War for Internet Governance* (New Haven, Conn.: Yale University Press, 2014).
⑤ Daniel Eran Dilger, "Apple Now Adding 500,000 iTunes Accounts Per Day," Apple Insider, June 13, 2013, available at http://appleinsider.com/articles/13/06/14/apple – now – adding – 500000 – new – itunes – accounts – per – day (accessed February 7, 2014).
⑥ David Gelles, "Skype Begins Move to List on Nasdaq," *Financial Times*, August 10, 2010; "Skype's Share of the Long – Distance Pie on the Increase," *TeleGeography*, Comms Update, March 24, 2009.
⑦ Richard Waters, "Facebook on Course to Reach 1bn Users," *Financial Times*, July 22, 2010.

土耳其有92%的网民访问过脸书,印度尼西亚为87%(相比之下,美国仅67%)①。全球9.44亿网民中大部分人都在使用谷歌(就以2010年6月为例)。借此,谷歌得以快速推行其安卓操作系统②。推特的发展更为迅猛:2013年,推特对外宣称,月平均用户数高达2.15亿,几乎分布在"每一个国家",其中四分之三的用户不在美国本土③。

美国资本在互联网连接技术的掌握与开发上具有先发优势,加上其流动状态,使它能够在数字设备、服务、软件与应用程序等多个跨国市场中令人折服地占据领先地位。据估计,2010年,美国在信息通讯技术领域的投资高达1.2万亿美元,超过中国、日本、英国与俄罗斯的总和。一半以上的全球信息通讯技术研发经费来自美国。因此,正如某份战略报告所强调:"三成以上的全球互联网总收入以及四成以上的净收入由美国占有"④。美国政经军界领导者早已下定决心,执意将这一精心培养的竞争力优势发挥至极致。

援引世界体系理论,资本主义发展的历史循环暴露出一个周期性的主导逻辑,即中心资本主义国家不断对边缘地带再生产其自身的排外性力量。几个世纪以来,这一过程始终存在,仅出现过几次不太重要的(力量均势)改变。所以,美国在全球数字系统和服务市场上的统治地位,或许可被视为这一根深蒂固的模式再次被固定下来吗?

不急于回答这一问题,因为许多现象混杂一起,难以辨识。一方面,美国互联网巨头已经发展壮大,难以撼动它们现有的地位;它们还成功地渗透进众多竞争对手的防线(甚至是国内市场)。另一方面,随着资本主义占领全球,互联网连接性已成为这一历史阶段的资本主义政治经济(发展)的先决条件。资本主义的持续扩张引发或决定着许多其他新的变化。变化之一是,跨国资本的构成呈现多样化。本书第一部分已经指出,外商的直接投资不断向外流动,它首先来自美国,随后来自西欧和日本,现在其他国家也加入进来⑤。2012年,以中国为首的发展中国家吸收的外商直接投资高于发达国家;不仅如此,以中国、巴西、俄罗斯、印度和南非为首的发展中国家的对外直接投资占全球对外直接投资总额的近三分之一⑥。这一情况的出现,部分源于持续的数字化衰退——当代世界的第二大特点。随着美国和西欧经济下滑,南南国家的商品链与贸易流通蓬勃发展。总部设在大城市的世界级跨国公司(截至2010年,全球五百强企业中仅有三分之一的总部设在美国)利用互联网,同那些有可能让它们赢利的供应商与客户相互连接。

---

① Waters,"Facebook on Course."
② Jessica F. Vascellaro,"Google Agonizes on Privacy as Ad World Vaults Ahead," *Wall Street Journal*, August 10,2010.
③ Twitter, Inc., Form S–1 before the U.S. Securities and Exchange Commission, Registration Statement 3, October 2013,1,22.
④ John D. Negroponte,Samuel J. Palmisano,and Adam Segal, *Defending an Open*, *Global*, *Secure*, *and Resilient Internet* (New York:Council on Foreign Relations, June 2013), Independent Task Force Report no.70, p.9.
⑤ 联合国贸易与发展委员会年度世界投资报告是关键性的数据来源。
⑥ UNCTAD, *World Investment Report* 2013 (New York and Geneva:United Nations,2013),2.

这一转变改写了全球互联网的拓扑结构。简而言之,一面是国际互联网容量在2013年增长33%(这是前十年有记录的增长最慢的数据),因此,美国作为互联网中心的重要性正逐渐弱化:截至2010年及其之后,新加坡、东京、香港、土耳其、肯尼亚和巴西正在成为区域中心;另一面则是跨区域的数据流动不断扩大,与此同时,越来越多的互联网连接不再经由美国"中转"[1]:亚洲与欧洲(欧洲已主导非洲的网络连接,并增加与亚洲之间的网络流量)正在成为全球网络连接的核心枢纽[2]。此外,还出现其他的路由方案,它们使全球百余家主干网承运商之间的城际网络连接更为多样化:伦敦-纽约之间网络连接的容量占跨大西洋网络连接总容量的份额从2005年的46%跌至2011年的30%[3]。一定程度上,网络容量的结构性变化折射出美国互联网中介商跨国化的发展趋势:当亚马逊2010年在新加坡建造数据中心,旨在保证亚洲和澳大利亚的用户(包括"亚洲客户,还有在该地区拥有诸多用户的欧洲公司"[4])享受到更快捷的云服务时,此举大大增加了东南亚地区的信息流量。然而,从好的方面来看,美国互联网中心地位的衰落反应出现在所谓的"行星资本主义"的政治经济发展情况。提供互联网设备、服务和应用程序的产业,其影响力不断扩大,涉及领域多元化。众多重要的供应商面向的分众化市场既包括日本和欧洲,还有韩国、墨西哥、印度、南非、中国等多个国家。互联网的商业用户的分布更加广泛。

境外互联网连接(这一领域)并非共识之地,亦非管控之下的积累场所,相反充满持续不断的政治争论,这明确预示未来将发生更加宽泛的变革。它尤其是全球"流动的空间"的具体体现,它如何建立起来、依照什么原则建立起来,将产生哪些衍生效应?珍妮特·阿巴特在1999年出版的一本研究互联网发展史的重要著作中总结认为:"随着互联网逐渐成为国际性资源,美国长期以来拥有的行政事务的权威无疑将受到越来越多的挑战"[5]。杰克·戈德史密斯(Jack Goldsmith)和吴修铭早在2006年就已指明加强国家监管的行动如何随着互联网进一步入侵国内经济和全球文化领域而不断升级[6]。国家对"近

---

[1] "The Global Internet is Decentralising," TeleGeography's Global Internet Geography, *TeleGeography*, September 14, 2011.

[2] "Europe Emerges as Global Internet Hub," *TeleGeography*, CommsUpdate, September 18, 2013; "Middle East Operators Plot a New Path to Europe," *TeleGeography*, CommsUpdate, October 2, 2013; "Asia's Connectivity Patterns Shift as Carriers Become Less Dependent on US," *TeleGeography*, CommsUpdate, October 17, 2013.

[3] Stan Beer, "Global Internet No Longer US Centric," *ITWire*, September 14, 2011, available at www.itwire.com/it-industry-news/market/49749-global-internet-no-longer-US-centric (accessed January 10, 2014).

[4] Aaron Ricadela, "Amazon Looks to Widen Lead in Cloud Computing," *Bloomberg Business Week*, April 28, 2010, available at http://www.businessweek.com/technology/content/apr2010/tc20100428_085106.htm (accessed January 10, 2014).

[5] Janet Abbate, *Inventing the Internet* (Cambridge, Mass.: MIT Press, 1999), 208.

[6] Jack Goldsmith and Tim Wu, *Who Controls The Internet? Illusions of a Borderless World* (New York: Oxford University Press, 2006).

用权"的"控制"力度持续增强,范围进一步扩大①。在美国,关于国家监管的认知不断强化。然而,该观点回避了另一深刻的政治经济学问题:"全球网络治理"的现有结构是否平衡? 或言之,境外互联网的管理是否有序,从而保证全球每一个体都能被平等对待? 与此相关还包括如下开放却棘手的问题:建立在互联网连接基础上的新兴商品是资本主义再次增长的关键,那么谁在设计这些商品并从中获利? 世界各国如何以及为何尝试重组机制,以整合与进一步发展境外互联网? 这些举措能否保障互联网的稳定发展,以实现资本主义积累? 还是这些举措将互联网转变成战场,资本之间的竞争愈演愈烈?(出于这一目的,我考虑的问题是,互联网最终能否转变成一个"超越资本"的真正民主的系统。)

虽然遭受金融危机的重创,美国仍在境外互联网领域里占据独特位置。或许没有一家"组织系统"能够全权主导全球网络治理,但正如劳拉·蒂娜迪斯(Laura DeNardis)所言②,运营管理、政策制定以及互联网技术标准的主导权,依然掌握在与美国国家权力密切相关的机构手中。数字系统与服务的尖端技术仍旧过于集中在美国的互联网公司。诚然,境外互联网最初源自于国际间协作理念③;然而,诚如我们所见,美国牢牢掌握网络协调机制与政策的最终话事权。尤其是高度集中的互联网域名与寻址系统,完全受制于一家美国实体机构,即互联网名称与数字地址分配机构(ICANN)。该机构需对美国行政部门履行合同规定的义务。

这一权力差异造就一种悖论性的脆弱局面。在数字化衰退持续存在的背景下,美国的政策制定者不得不奋力一搏,不仅寻求壮大资本利用互联网连接性的能力,更试图巩固和保卫他们独有的特权。随后,赤裸裸的冲突接踵而至。我们需要仔细审视这些冲突,例如回顾和梳理美国各行政部门所发起的一系列特别倡议。首先,我简要地将这些倡议(政策)置于境外通信的长时段历史中。接下来,我要回答互联网治理如何受到美国国家安全局监控事件曝光所产生的反弹效应的影响,最后我再回到更广泛的政治经济的转型这一议题上。

我们不可公式化地预设资本与国家之间保有一致性。自美国与法国大革命爆发后,国家时而成为冲突的舞台。在那里,普世性的法律以及名义上的民主政体这一修辞,常常同资本的特定利益与诉求发生碰撞。任何给定的个案的结果都不是预先注定的,原因

---

① Ronald Deibert, John Palfrey, Rafal Rohozinski, Jonathan Zittrain, eds., *Access Controlled: The Shaping of Power, Rights, and Rule in Cyberspace* (Cambridge, Mass.: MIT Press, 2010).
② "The Global War for Internet Governance: Dr. Laura DeNardis," June 13, 2013, available at http://www.youtube.com/watch?v=tpChBW-3yL0 (accessed January 10, 2014).
③ Ronda Hauben, "The Internet: On Its International Origins and Collaborative Vision (A Work in Progress)," *Amateur Computerist* 12, no. 2 (Spring 2004).

有三：国家管理者与多元化、有时相互对立的社会行动者一样，都相对独立地设想和实施计划；资本与其他社会阶级之间对立冲突；资本与资本之间也会产生矛盾。大多数情形下，资本既没有构成一块铁板也无法形成稳定的利益共同体，因为资本的普遍利益在于维系资本积累的首要地位，而它必定与特定资本追逐利润的特殊利益相冲突。所以，仅仅依靠理论，无法解释上述结果：要理解还有赖于历史特殊性。

网络无法消除或超越普世性的政治权利与特定社会利益集团之间的冲突或矛盾。实际上，这些矛盾或冲突在网络的催化下变本加厉。19世纪末，在西欧和北美的富裕国家建立起全面、高度整合的全国电信网；与此同时（历史学家的研究表明）大资本与国家携手铺设海底电缆网络，进而使殖民地和前殖民地牢牢地依附于自身[1]。因此，电信网络与帝国主义从一开始就交织在一起。二战后亚洲与非洲地区兴起的去殖民化运动导致（网络）连接仍主要局限于城市飞地与跨国线路。同时，全国性网络的管理与运营权则移交给政府。（当然，政府不得不与电信产业利益集团进行磋商，或经常顺从于后者。）同样，这些新成立的国家也希望能够在国际电信联盟这一组织中谋得一职（拥有话事权）。国际电信联盟曾是帝国主义国家（联盟）的产物：最初职权范围只覆盖电报行业，后来扩展至广播与有线电话产业。二战后，国际电信联盟并入联合国组织，成为联合国下设的专门机构。

尽管国际电信联盟仍优先考虑发达市场经济体与跨国资本的诉求，但它坚持在一国一票的基础上制定政策与出台规制。1960至1970年代，亚非拉国家所引领的国家中心主义运动曾暂时对既存的支配（与被支配）模式造成威胁，它们试图建立"国际信息新秩序"。然而，这一倡议不断招致反对，尤其在罗纳德·里根（Ronald Reagan）与玛格丽特·撒切尔（Margaret Thatcher）上台后，更引发英美两国的强力抵制。同时，在去殖民化运动的浪潮逐渐消退、统治集团的稳固以及与跨国资本之间的和解等背景下，许多亚非拉国家的阶级结构更加固化。重建世界信息秩序的可能性再次出现。只不过，这次重建，并非在全球南方国家争取民族自决的反帝国主义运动，而是在以重新整合跨国资本、实现全球精英合作为目标的镇压式"新自由主义"运动的推动下完成。普拉沙德曾令人信服地阐释了这段历史（historical arc）[2]。

---

[1] Daniel R. Headrick, *The Tentacles of Progress: Technology Transfer in the Age of Imperialism*, 1850-1940 (New York: Oxford University Press, 1988), 97-144; Daniel R. Headrick, *The Invisible Weapon: Telecommunications and International Politics* 1851-1945 (New York: Oxford University Press, 1991); Jill Hills, *The Struggle for Control of Global Communication: The Formative Century* (Urbana: University of Illinois Press, 2002); Jill Hills, *Telecommunications and Empire* (Urbana: University of Illinois Press, 2007); Dan Schiller, "Geopolitical-Economic Conflict and Network Infrastructures" *Chinese Journal of Communication* 4, no. 1 (2011): 90-107; Dwayne R. Winseck and Robert M. Pike, *Communication and Empire: Media, Markets, and Globalization*, 1860-1930 (Durham, N. C.: Duke University Press, 2007).

[2] Vijay Prashad, *The Poorer Nations: A Possible History of the Global South* (New York: Verso, 2012).

截至1980年代末、1990年代初,不知何故出现了重建境外"流动的空间"的机遇,对此,美国资本与行政部门都跃跃欲试①。自1970年代起,美国资助的自由化发展战略早已削弱了国家公共服务原则与网络多边监管职权;企业与商业重建这一基础设施的自由成为政策制定的首要考量。面对各种要求建立国际信息新秩序的呼声,1980年代的债务危机被用于制定私有化项目,随后私有化浪潮一浪高过一浪。十余个国家对电信网络进行私有化改造。1990年代,美国行政部门针对旧秩序采取一系列对策,例如使境外互联网制度化,并以此重击结构化的国家监管制度②。美国行政部门的这一做法往往以权利为名,因为后者具有某种意气风发的传教士一般的精神气质;但是,互联网连接所造就的巨大成功,实际上建立在国家权力与资本投资进入网络的基础之上;资本进入网络意在深化资本主义全球化进程。

一项影响深远的经济发展方案应当含有某些民主化措施。克林顿总统发布的全球电子商务框架,旨在禁止全球互联网关税、贸易壁垒、各种税收或内容管制等制度,从而建立一个全球性的电子自由贸易区③。资本可随心所欲地进驻各种商业项目,前景不可限量。克林顿时代,政府给予厚望的领域正是那些美国所主导的"电脑软件、娱乐产品(电影、视频、游戏和录音)、信息服务(数据库与在线报纸)、技术信息、产品许可、金融服务,以及专业服务(商务与技术咨询、会计、建筑设计、法律咨询、旅游服务等)"等一系列产业④。很大程度上,美国的国家权力成功地推动经济建设。我曾在1999年出版的著作中强调指出:"每个月都有新的应用程序面世,它们侵蚀现有的国家媒体结构和管控制度;彼时,主张强势的互联网多边监管与规制系统的反潮流尚未成型"⑤。回顾过往,这种结果显然不仅确证了美国在苏联解体后的"单极时代"所拥有的强大实力,更证实其他国家对网络的接受度,这些国家的阶级基础与国民经济历经巨大变革:它们包括俄罗斯,以及西欧与东亚国家,还有以中国为首的全球南方国家。

然而,"流动的空间"的重建工作围绕美国与其他国家之间根本的权力差异而展开,这一不平衡状态自然埋下冲突的火种。数字化衰退(前述的几种趋势导致数字化衰退,以及危机本身造成的难以管控的偶然性事件)增大了这种可能性。于是,原本备受争议

---

① Useful texts are: William J. Drake, "WATTC‐88: Restructuring the International Telecommunications Regulations," *Telecommunications Policy* 12, no. 3 (1988): 217‐33; Peter Cowhey and Jonathan D. Aronson, "The ITU in Transition," *Telecommunication Policy* 15, no. 4 (1991): 298‐310; Richard Hill, *The New International Telecommunication Regulations and the Internet: A Commentary and Legislative History* (Zurich: Schultess, 2013).

② Dan Schiller, *Telematics and Government* (Norwood, N. J.: Ablex, 1982); Dan Schiller, *Digital Capitalism* (Cambridge, Mass.: MIT Press, 1999), 71‐72.

③ Schiller, *Digital Capitalism*, 74‐75.

④ The White House, "The Framework for Global Electronic Commerce," July 1, 1997, in Schiller, *Digital Capitalism*, 88.

⑤ Schiller, *Digital Capitalism*, 75.

的网络普遍管辖原则如今成为日益严峻的内斗场所。美国习惯于将(对它的)这些挑战描述成暴政国家和卑劣的独裁者所进行的不正当、谋取私利的干预行动;可这都是错误的描述。除美国外,其他国家或地区对这些挑战持有不同的看法:它们更像某种推动力,谋求改变早已深刻影响境外互联网结构布局的"单边控制"局面。这一推动力,是否有部分源自于其他国家面对卷土重来的资本主义国家之间的竞争而优厚对待国内资本的诉求?当然,我们不能把这些诉求仅仅化约为推动力。因此,美国主导的互联网"流动的空间"的重建工作,尽管高奏凯歌,却导致越发激烈的反弹。

两种类型的地缘政治挑战,威胁了美国在境外互联网连接方面所享有的特权。随着国内通信空间围绕跨国互联网而得以重建,出现了第一种地缘政治挑战,即面对权力的强取豪夺而重建国家威权的努力。另一种挑战则瞄准了由美国所掌控的全球互联网治理的中心化机制。美国的众多对手或盟友国家试图重新平衡这一管辖权,从而削弱甚至取代美国的主导地位。上述两种挑战折射出异质性的利益与价值观。没有一种推动力是可以化约的;这些挑战激发美国作出复杂且影响深远的回应。

这些挑战还产生了某些示范效应。一方面,网络空间可根据不同的目标和优先事项而重新加以塑造,这一点越来越明显;另一方面,跨国资本为维系其数字化商品链的稳定性而焦虑重重。流动空间的碎片化不仅构成对互联网互操作性的各种限制,更引发真正的危险。在一个跨国资本仰仗全球网络连接标准的年代,当经济扩张建立在跨国商品化战略的基础之上时,众多国内以及低于国家水平的互联网结构的分裂,将造成致命的伤害。我们也不难想见境外互联网管辖权之间存在的潜在竞争;当美国的国际通信卫星(Interlsat)同更受限制的苏联全球卫星通信系统(InterSputnik)并存时,这些潜在的竞争不仅是发达帝国主义时期更是冷战时代的主旋律。还存在另一种选择:全球互联网的互操作性或可保留,但它一定建立在经过变革、不那么美国中心主义的政治经济的基础(即"联邦互联网")之上。

有些挑战甚至在数字化衰退到来之前就已存在;为了对抗这些挑战,小布什政府采取了一种名为"该死的鱼雷!全速前进!"的方法。美国在制定互联网政策时,似乎把全世界其他国家都视为多余(其他国家曾一度真的很多余)。然而,当其他国家(竟然还包括欧盟)坚持认为,所有国家(而非仅仅美国)的政府都应当在互联网政策与关键的互联网资源管理等方面拥有"平等的地位和责任"(尤其是唯一识别码这一决定互联网运作的关键系统)时①,小布什政府应对挑战而采取的应对方式所产生的政治孤立效应在2005年尤为明显。各种变革使当前的局面动荡不安;弥尔顿·穆烈(Milton Mueller)2010年曾指出,美国所享有的互联网特权已面临"一场持久的消耗战;在这场战役中,这些特权将

---

① Milton L. Mueller, *Networks and States: The Global Politics of Internet Governance* (Cambridge, Mass.: MIT Press, 2010), 77.

悉数被削弱"①。

奥巴马政府重新调整美国政策的代表形式,而丝毫不触动其根本目标,这是奥巴马政府总体战略评估的一部分。尽管时值美国总统换届选举,一项高调的行政部门调整计划却开始启动;此次调整涉及面更广、更多样化,旨在颁布相关政策以保证美国能够继续支配互联网连接,并如美国利益集团所保证的那般有效地利用这一主导权。然而,布什总统的好战与自辩姿态,被置换成对民主过程、人权和国际礼让原则充满敬意的修辞。"合作""集体责任""透明""多方利益主义"等字眼成为(奥巴马政府的)口号②。

没有人比奥巴马总统更热衷于宣扬美国将"帮助公民社会行动者搭建可靠、稳当、安全的言论与结社自由的平台"。奥巴马宣称:"我们鼓励全世界人民利用数字媒体表达观点、分享信息、监督选举、揭露腐败,以及组织社会与政治活动;我们谴责一切骚扰、不正当逮捕或暴力对待新媒体技术使用者的行为"。然而,奥巴马也有意强调,这些高尚的原则不应仅仅应用于个体:"我们同样要保护互联网服务提供商以及其他连接服务的提供商,因为他们经常成为牵涉中介商责任的法律制度的受害者,例如不得不承担审查合法言论的责任"③。2011年当奥巴马总统批准《网络空间国际战略》时,该文件再次确认美国政府根深蒂固的"愿景,即正常情况下,无论数据来自何方、流向何方,它应当在网络上自由流通"。④

(通过上述报告)奥巴马表明美国政府下定决心,将对关键的互联网资源与境外互联网进行管控。其主要目的之一在于,保障数据通过网络化的商品链能够自由流动,不受任何限制。出于同样的原因,个体人权与跨国赢利战略以及国家力量的监管混淆在一起(过去数十年皆是如此)。接下来的章节里,我将具体分析这一项目,并表明该项目不仅引发了内部矛盾和冲突,其脆弱程度更出人意料。

---

① Mueller, *Networks and States*, 78.
② 例如可参见 Joseph Mann, "US Unveils International Internet Strategy," *FT. com*, May 17, 2011; Helene Cooper, "U. S. Calls for Global Cybersecurity Strategy," *New York Times*, May 16, 2011, available at http://www.nytimes.com/2011/05/17/us/politics/17cyber.html?_r=0 (accessed January 10, 2014).
③ The White House "International Strategy for Cyberspace: Prosperity, Security, and Openness in a Networked World," May 2011, 23-24 (original emphasis), available at http://www.whitehouse.gov/sites/default/files/rss_viewer/international_strategy_for_cyberspace.pdf (accessed January 10, 2014).
④ White House, "International Strategy for Cyberspace," 24.

第 11 章
新的外交政策的必要措施

数字化衰退时期,美国行政部门出台的多项方案相互关联,从而形成较为松散的协调机制,以维护与支持美国政府出台的关于境外互联网的政策。时任美国国务卿的希拉里·克林顿(Hillary Clinton)在奥巴马政府《网络空间国际战略》的发布会上讲话,她提出的七大网络议题已构成"新外交政策的必要措施"①。自前国务卿希拉里2010年提出"互联网自由"概念起,国务院再次抛出人权议题,以尽绵力②。

国务院提出(互联网自由)这一与战略报告保持一致的方案,源于谷歌的前首席执行官埃里克·施密特加入奥巴马的竞选团队。谷歌作为搜索引擎巨头以国家审查与黑客入侵为名,在2010年1月决定关闭中国版搜索服务;谷歌"退华"决定是否请示过国务院尚未可知。这不是问题重点。根据一位身处高位的中国问题研究专家的看法,北京方面"怀疑……美国政府暗中支持谷歌煽动中国网民的反政府情绪";与此同时,美国的政策制定部门不失时机地揪住谷歌退出中国大陆这件事情不放③。谷歌"退华"决定刚一公布,几乎同时,一大堆阿谀奉承的公开讲话如潮水般涌现出来④。尼古拉斯·D.克里斯托弗(Nicholas D. Kristof)的言论定下基调:"谷歌决定起身反抗中国的网络迫害,此举振奋人心。"随后,《纽约时报》就此事发表社论称:"谷歌停止审查自己在中国的搜索引擎服

---

① In Cheryl Pellerin, "DOD Expands International Cyber Cooperation, Official Says," *American Forces Press Service*, April 10, 2012, available at http://www.defense.gov/News/NewsArticle.aspx?ID=67889 (accessed January 10, 2014).
② Elizabeth Dickinson, "Internet Freedom," *Foreign Policy*, January 21, 2010, available at http://www.foreignpolicy.com/articles/2010/01/21/internet_freedom (accessed February 8, 2014).
③ Wang Jisi, "Understanding Strategic Distrust: The Chinese Side," in Kenneth Lieberthal and Wang Jisi, "Addressing U.S. – China Strategic Distrust," John L. Thornton China Center Monograph Series no. 4, March 2012 (Washington, D.C.: Brookings Institution, 2012),12. 需要指出,除了搜索服务,谷歌没有退出中国的其他市场,例如通过其广告意识项目(Ad Sense programs)在中国所建立的广告市场。
④ 接下来的内容取自于 Dan Schiller and Christian Sandvig, "Google v. China: Principled, Brave, or Business as Usual?" *Huffington Post Tech*, April 5, 2010, available at http://www.huffingtonpost.com/dan-schiller/google-v-china-principled_b_524727.html (accessed January 10, 2014).

务,这真是有原则、有魄力的决定"①。谷歌公开宣称"退华"决定后的11天,国务卿希拉里开始广泛宣传"互联网自由"理念②。

言论自由权利既是社会同时也是个体实现民主自决的基础;许多社会和个体为了争取这项有可能被利用或被损害的权利而遭受迫害、履险蹈危。丽贝卡·麦金农(Rebecca MacKinnon)不失公允地批评了"互联网自由"概念;在她看来,"互联网自由"只是一个充斥着各种模糊且互相冲突的意义的大杂烩概念:它既包括一个开放的互联网结构设想,又包含公民利用互联网在政治统治下赢取自由、政府在互联网络与平台上奉行不干预政策,以及毫无障碍地连接上网等诉求③。然而,倘若有意将这些设想或诉求混杂在一起呢?倘若美国官方宣布支持"互联网自由"理念只是为了实现算计与操控的目的呢?

在过去很长时间,美国惯于利用人权议题作为其外交政策的砝码。最近有篇论著指出,随着美国(最迟)在19世纪末成为帝国主义国家,美国的宪政形态与实践经验悖论性地成为一种强制性模式,而非普遍接受的美国政体:"美国诉诸武力,以强迫其殖民地、保护领地和被征服的领土上的人们跟随它在宪法上的领导"④。在这一大背景下,"信息的自由流动"理念从20世纪初开始,一直成为美国外交政策的有效利器,并在去殖民化与冷战时期成为其政策的核心组成部分⑤。

"自由流动"论采用普世性的人权这一诱惑人却误导人的语言,实际上难掩其背后严峻的经济与战略利益的诉求。谷歌作为一家追逐利润的公司,在美国政府的话语里竟被置换成一位敢于向独裁国家发起反抗的有原则的自由战士。翌年,与美国情报机构预测相反⑥,突尼斯和埃及的民众利用手机以及脸书与推特等社交媒体组织抗议,先后推翻独裁政府;在这一背景下,谷歌作为斗士的论调显得更加理直气壮。如今,这些数字服务(公司)已得到美国政府的大力宣传,美国官方将它们单独罗列出来,认为它们应当成为

---

① Nicholas D. Kristof, "Google Takes a Stand," *New York Times*, January 14, 2010, available at http://www.nytimes.com/2010/01/14/opinion/14kristof.html?_r=0 (accessed January 10, 2014); "Google and China," editorial, *New York Times*, March 23, 2010, available at http://www.nytimes.com/2010/03/24/opinion/24wed2.html (accessed January 10, 2014).
② A video of Secretary Clinton's speech is available at http://www.youtube.com/watch?v=DbwiXRmzKi0 (accessed February 8, 2014).
③ Rebecca MacKinnon, *Consent of the Networked: The Worldwide Struggle for Internet Freedom* (New York: Basic, 2012), 187–88.
④ George Athan Billias, *American Constitutionalism Heard Round the World*, 1776–1989 (New York: New York University Press, 2009), 223.
⑤ Herbert I. Schiller, "Authentic National Development versus the Free Flow of Information," *Le Monde diplomatique*, December 1974.
⑥ David E. Sanger, *Confront and Conceal: Obama's Secret Wars and Surprising Use of American Power* (New York: Crown, 2012), 279–80.

那些复杂、有时持续时间较长并实际上有可能转化为民主革命的社会运动的替代品①。

自由流动理念曾数次服务于美国利益；然而，随着跨国网络化商品链从受限的媒体产业领域扩展至整体的政治经济环境，该理念的重要性有所改变，不断提升。与此同时，自由流动论与时俱进，从而保证在变动的历史环境中继续保持其有效性。

战后最初几十年间，自由流动论主要针对两类国家：一是从腐败的欧洲帝国中脱离出来独立建国的新兴国家，二是苏联以及其他共产主义国家。时值美国全球实力与声望的顶峰，美国行政部门有意将民主自决与资本主义发展模式混为一谈。此举最初旨在让美国新闻通讯社有充分理由进入封闭的外国市场，但如今它已扩大其范围，为美国媒体公司向全世界出口美国文化商品（例如新闻、电视节目、音乐和电影等）提供合法性②。这些媒体公司的背后是美国外商直接投资；而这些投资的典型代表是企业广告商：他们大肆宣传消费资本主义的自恋模式，而美国正是这一模式的全球中心。2012年5月，正值美国外商投资获准进入缅甸之际；对此，可口可乐公司首席执行官宣称："可口可乐的悠久历史一直与美国外交政策的历史交织在一起"③。1912年，可口可乐首次进入亚洲市场：菲律宾作为战利品被美国接管不到十年，可口可乐公司进驻菲律宾市场。可口可乐于1927年进入中国，1949年撤离中国大陆，因为中国革命驱逐了大部分外商企业；然而，1979年，美国前总统卡特全面恢复中美关系，可口可乐"立即取道香港向中国大陆输送两万箱软饮料"④。如今，许多人称这种举动为"软实力"⑤。

1970年代末至1980年代初，自由流动论的辐射范围再次扩大与延伸。除了继续为美国的文化出口战略奠基铺路，自由流动论逐渐应用在"跨境数据流"领域中。本书第一部分已经指出，网络化商品链迅速形成并不断扩展；它们得以运转，部分由于商业流程数据流所发挥的作用使然。公司配置计算机传递海量数据，却拒不履行国家司法管辖范围内的任何责任；针对这一现象的激烈争论常常遭人遗忘（有时甚至限制了公司配置计算

---

① Mary Beth Sheridan, "U. S. Warns against Blocking Social Media, Elevates Internet Freedom Policies," *Washington Post*, January 28, 2011, available at http://www.washingtonpost.com/wp-dyn/content/article/2011/01/28/AR2011012804554.html (accessed February 8, 2014); Vijay Prashad, *Arab Spring, Libyan Winter* (Oakland, Calif.: AK, 2012), 15, 22. 丽贝卡·麦金农指出这一点，请参见 MacKinnon, *Consent of the Networked*, 192.

② Schiller, "Authentic National Development"; Herbert I. Schiller, *Communication and Cultural Domination* (White Plains, N. Y.: International Arts & Sciences, 1976).

③ Muhtar Kent, 转引自 "Myanmar Is Next Real Thing for Coke," *Financial Times*, June 15, 2012.

④ "Myanmar Is Next Real Thing," 16

⑤ Joseph S. Nye Jr., *Soft Power: The Means to Success in World Politics* (New York: Public Affairs, 2005).

机的相关发展计划)①。此后,这些争论偶有余音,欧洲和其他国家在"数据保护"问题上的立法便是其中之一。围绕跨境数据流的争议最多涉及数千家网络,可这一争议的解决明显偏向跨国资本而非履行民主责任,并且,它帮助加速与扩大了公司重组跨国商品链的步伐。

几十年过去,互联网的出现预示了这一演进过程进入新阶段。互联网的建立,以大量"自主系统"为基础:网络运营者包括互联网服务零售供应商和批发供应商、企业及其他组织用户。本书已详细分析跨国企业对网络系统与应用程序的依赖程度,若无后者,全球商业营运和市场操作一分钟都难以维持下去。然而,这不仅意味着上一个时代的终点,更意味着资本积累新的前沿阵地的诞生。基钦(Kitchin)与道奇(Dodge)曾分析指出,随着人们的航空旅行、消费、家庭以及其他空间受到远程存储码所控制的"各种功能"的重组,软件正决定着人们日常生活的方方面面②。数字资本主义的政治经济的界限一次次往后退。笔者在第二部分已指出,所谓的"物联网"成为目标:公司网络系统与应用程序用于控制一系列的性能和日常生活;机器之间的互动成为日常。诚如基钦与道奇所详述,软件"正日渐使家用电器、手动工具、运动设备、医疗器械、娱乐物件以及儿童玩具等日常用品具有额外或新的性能"③。然而,这些日常用品并非自足型物体,而是互联网所激活的设备对象,它有赖于与远程服务器所进行的数据交换。

于是,自由流动论作为某种超常的规则再次出现:它不仅要保护某个特定的行业或羽翼尚未丰满的商业进程,更要保护整个网络化的商品链——如今,它牢牢控制着已经重组的跨国资本主义体系。

倘若美国的科技公司成功实现云计算,或许网络化的商品链将控制跨国资本主义的未来发展。有关云计算的愿景并不新鲜,1960 至 1970 年代所提出"时间共享"理念可视为当今云计算概念的雏形。然而,近来渐成主流的却是集中化的服务器群(即数据中心)的数据存储与应用程序(开发业务)。2011 年 3 月,美国联邦通信委员会主席格纳科斯奇(Genachowski)援引一家私人咨询公司的数据,对外宣称云计算已成为市值 680 亿美元的全球性产业,且每年以 17% 的惊人速度不断增长。他指出,云计算"能够实现其他技术无

---

① United Nations Centre on Transnational Corporations, "Transborder Data Flows: Access to the International On – line Data – base Market: A Technical Paper," ST/CTC/41 (New York: United Nations, 1983); Karl P. Sauvant, *International Transactions in Services: The Politics of Transborder Data Flows* (Boulder, Colo. : Westview, 1986); Herbert I. Schiller, *Who Knows: Information in the Age of the Fortune* 500 (Norwood, N. J. : Ablex, 1981); Herbert I. Schiller, *Information and the Crisis Economy* (Norwood, N. J. : Ablex, 1984); Eileen Marie Mahoney, "Negotiating New Information Technology and National Development: The Role of the Intergovernmental Bureau for Informatics," PhD diss. , Temple University, 1987.
② Rob Kitchin and Martin Dodge, *Code/Space: Software and Everyday Life* (Cambridge, Mass. : MIT Press, 2011).
③ Kitchin and Dodge, *Code/Space*, 47.

法实现的协作",因而有可能在"医疗、教育以及能源领域"开掘"新市场与新业务"①。本书第二部分已分析,把持这一趋势或前沿地带的均为美国大型互联网中介商,包括亚马逊、微软、美国国际商用机器公司、苹果、脸书以及谷歌(截至 2011 年,谷歌已拥有 30 余家数据中心)②。

境外互联网在跨国商业活动中的作用愈发重要,这再次强化自由流动政策的重要性。数不胜数的现有或未来盈利项目都以无限制的跨境数据流动为前提。举一个熟悉的例子——苹果音乐播放器:它服务消费者市场,却以"软件即服务"的形式准入商业市场,意义深远。

这一商品化进程的技术前沿不仅要求防守牢靠,更需要进攻果断。格纳思科奇坚持认为,"保护主义"政策,尤其是"针对国内数据中心的严苛要求",抑制了国家之间的数据流动,将"削弱云计算所带来的高效率与成本降低等优势"③。格纳思科奇及其他政策制定者认为,这些限制应当取消。

一如往常,美国国内政治经济的发展不断逼迫大公司尽力推进"取消限制"行动,这里的公司主要是指法律上认可的公司。在美国法律发展进程中,经过很长一段时间,公司才享有"人"的合法地位。然而,自 1970 年代以来,激烈的社会运动导致美国宪法第一修正案赋予公司的"权利"不断扩大④。实际上,2010 年当谷歌与中国的"冷战"占据新闻头条时,美国最高法院在"公民团结"(Citizens United)一案的判决中,裁定宪法第一修正案应保障公司享有无限额捐助竞选活动的权利⑤。翌年初,美国电话电报公司向最高法院提起诉讼(试图阻止联邦通信委员会公开相关文件,最后败诉),要求公司在享有言论自由权外,还应当享有个人隐私权⑥。这正是时任国务卿希拉里·克林顿在谷歌退华还不到两周后,不失时机地高调重申"互联网自由"话语时的美国国内氛围。

可问题不在于中国采取了技术成熟、完全有效的审查系统⑦。相反,谷歌退华事件服

---

① FCC Chairman Julius Genachowski, "The Cloud: Unleashing Global Opportunities," Aspen IDEA Project, Brussels, Belgium, March 24, 2011, p. 2, available at http://www.fcc.gov/document/chairman-calls-unleashing-global-opportunities-brussels-speech (accessed January 10, 2014).

② John Letzing, "Facebook Plants Roots in Central Oregon," *MarketWatch*, January 20, 2011, 2, available at http://www.marketwatch.com/story/facebook-data-center-revitalizes-oregon-town-2011-01-20 (accessed January 10, 2014).

③ Genachowski, "The Cloud," 7.

④ Schiller, *Who Knows*, 79-97; Laura Stein, *Speech Rights in America: The First Amendment, Democracy, and the Media* (Urbana: University of Illinois Press, 2006).

⑤ *Citizens United v. Federal Election Commission*, 558 U. S. 310 (2010); 要了解在选举期间围绕该议题而展开的讨论,请参见 John Nichols and Robert W. McChesney, *Dollarocracy: How the Money and Media Election Complex is Destroying America* (New York: Nation, 2013).

⑥ Adam Liptak, "Court Weighs Whether Corporations Have Personal Privacy Rights," *New York Times*, January 19, 2011, available at http://www.nytimes.com/2011/01/20/us/20privacy.html (accessed January 10, 2014).

⑦ Yuezhi Zhao, *Communication in China* (Lanham, Md.: Rowman and Littlefield, 2008).

膺于美国有意模糊个体人权与跨国企业的网络化商品链之间区别的目的。希拉里的公开演讲的独特性在于,她试图将谷歌这一私有化企业的各项作为等同于民主自决。她对外宣称:"我们支持一个保障全人类平等享有知识与思想的互联网公司"。她恬不知耻地将自己提出的"互联网自由"概念置于一众历史遗产之列,其中包括富兰克林·罗斯福1941年关于"四大自由"的演讲以及埃莉诺·罗斯福在二战后就"世界人权宣言"理念所做的演说[1]。

国务卿希拉里继续强调,世界上每个人都应享有连接自由,即"政府不应阻止人民与互联网、与网站或与彼此相互连接"[2]。此处的"连接自由"应当凌驾于政府政策和国家管辖权之上;看起来,它当之无愧地将美国政策置于民主与人权的阵营之中,似乎美国的战略利益与企业利润战略都被抛诸一边。这种修辞深嵌于美国政策话语里。2011年,美国总统亲自出面,领衔发声,宣称"确保信息自由流动对于美国与全球的经济繁荣……以及普遍权利的推进都具有核心意义"[3]。

美国国务院出台的互联网政策早已与整个90年代美国政府所奉行的淳朴思路渐行渐远;后者旨在赋予互联网以一种几乎内生性的(all-but-immanent)权力,进而将人类从辛劳工作中解放出来。希拉里发出警告,"这些新技术并非无条件地造福人类:现代信息网络及其支持的技术既可用于行善亦可用于作恶……技术固然具有开放政府信息与推进(政府工作)透明化的潜力,与此同时它有可能被政府所褫夺以镇压异见,剥夺人权"[4]。为了进一步说明这一点,她祭出其法宝:"有些国家已经竖起电子藩篱,阻止本国人民与世界其他地方的网络相互连接。他们将(某些)语词、名称或短语从搜索引擎的结果中删除。他们侵犯了那些发表非暴力政治言论的公民个体的隐私权"[5]。的确,她所言非虚,她提及的每一件事应受到关注,同样,这些事例向经过深思熟虑的美国政策提供了素材。美国的与众不同(例如更自由、更美好)作为一种假设,早已成为一种理所当然的想法,根本无需言说或加以证明。

国务卿希拉里提议,"互联网自由"不仅是赢取政治自由的必要工具,更有利于经济增长。这位前国务卿并未从跨国公司商品链的角度出发,而是有意地以撒哈拉沙漠以南地区的妇女企业家获得小型贷款以及孟加拉国的手机使用者学习英语等自力更生的故

---

[1] Hillary Rodham Clinton, "*Remarks on Internet Freedom*," *The Newseum*, Washington, D. C., U. S. Department of State, January 21, 2010, 2, available at http://www.foreign policy.com/articles/2010/01/21/internet_freedom (accessed January 10, 2014).

[2] Clinton, "*Internet Freedom*," 5.

[3] White House, "*International Strategy for Cyberspace*," 3. 另一种声音请参见 Genachowski, "The Cloud," 1.

[4] Clinton, "*Internet Freedom*," 2. This theme was explicated in Evgeny Morozov, *The Net Delusion: The Dark Side of Internet Freedom* (New York: Public Affairs, 2011).

[5] Clinton, "*Internet Freedom*," 3.

事为个案,来论及互联网的经济前景。希拉里援引半个世纪以前冷战时期将商业大众传媒视为发展工具的学者[这里尤指丹尼尔·勒纳(Daniel Lerner)等人]曾发表的带有种族中心主义色彩的傲慢言论,借此表示"与全球信息网络连接,如同驶入通往现代化的匝道"①。

美国国务院组织成立的"全球互联网自由工作组"是这一现代化工程的核心组成部分。希拉里进一步指出,"我们正敦促美国媒体公司先行一步,质疑或挑战外国政府对于审查与监视的要求"②。这句话直截了当地表明,就谷歌在华搜索业务问题上,无论行政部门与谷歌之间发生过什么,政府都将毫无隐晦地与美国资本这一前哨阵地展开协作,共同推进互联网政策。

2011 年,国务卿希拉里再次就同一主题高调发表演讲。这一次,她毫不窘迫地将埃及整合进美国的网络平台里,毕竟,埃及人民方才成功推翻一手由美国所培植的独裁政府。希拉里称"全世界几百万人实时"响应埃及人民的游行示威,似乎在线交流本身在一定程度上导致了腐败且威权的穆巴拉克政府的倒台;紧接着她沉着冷静地向外宣称,美国政府与响应埃及人民呼声的人们并肩作战,"你们不是孤军奋战,我们与你们同在"③。我们或许可以假设,总体而言,埃及人民并未被(美国所)接纳;美国也未找到足够的经济资源以换取它想要达到的结果④;然而,"连接自由"论所辐射的范围(以及所吸引的受众),远远超出埃及。

希拉里强调,美国将对那些无论出于何种原因拒绝美国关于境外互联网的发展计划的国家发起反击——这些国家与"恐怖分子及其代理人"有关。她声称那些"破坏了我们或其他社会信息自由流动的规则的国家,对我们的经济造成极大的威胁";进而她指出,美国"誓将保卫自己的网络"⑤(实际上,早在乔治·W·布什担任总统期间,美国国务院早已将支持翻墙技术的计划升级为具体行动⑥)。希拉里补充到:"监控与应对互联网自由受到的威胁已经成为我国外交人员和发展专家日常工作的一部分。他们以遍布全球的大使馆为基地,以推进互联网自由为己任。美国将为身处于受到压制的互联网环境中的人们继续提供帮助:帮助他们避开过滤机制,进而比审查者、骇客以及那些因他们的网

---

① Clinton, "Internet Freedom," 4; Daniel Lerner, *The Passing of Traditional Society: Modernizing the Middle East* (New York: Macmillan, 1958).
② Clinton, "Internet Freedom," 7.
③ Hillary Rodham Clinton, "Internet Rights and Wrongs: Choices and Challenges in a Networked World," George Washington University, February 15, 2011, 1, available at http://blogs.state.gov/stories/2011/02/15/internet-rights-and-wrongs-choices-and-challenges-networked-world (accessed January 10, 2014).
④ Sanger, Confront and Conceal, 302-3, 314-15.
⑤ Clinton, "Internet Freedom," 4 (emphasis added).
⑥ MacKinnon, *Consent of the Networked*, 188.

上言论而殴打或关押他们的网络恶棍更快一步获得消息"。① 至此,美国不再纸上谈兵,而将逢机立断,采取切实行动。②

希拉里夸下海口声称,美国国务院已斥资千万,在对抗"互联网压制"的多面行动中"支持新兴的技术人员与行动分子"③。可她并没有指出这一行动本身赤裸裸地践踏了国家主权。2011年6月,资深记者詹姆斯·格兰兹(James Glanz)和约翰·马科夫(John Markoff)刊发报道揭露了该事实。格兰兹与马科夫在一项战略计划中发现"奥巴马政府在全球范围内推广'影子'互联网与手机系统,旨在帮助那些政治异见者瓦解试图通过审查或关闭通信网络而使他们噤声的政府"——这让人不禁联想起冷战高潮期艾森豪威尔政府的秘密项目。美国持续在不同情境下推广其翻墙软件,除此之外,它还在阿富汗、朝鲜以及(据两位记者暗示)其他地方执行"秘密计划",用于改革与配备"秘密无线网络"。格兰兹与马科夫在文中隐晦地将几大事件串联起来,"国务卿希拉里使互联网自由成为一项标志性事业。美国国务院对此却抱以谨慎态度,它对互联网自由的支持仅仅限于为了全人类而推进言论自由与人权这一'事业',而非以颠覆独裁政府为目的"。④ 然而,该结论不够全面:他们没有提及互联网自由论的经济功能。

美国在"互联网自由"论上所投入的火力,远远不止将美国的外交政策与某一家公司的战略利益相结合这么简单。然而,谷歌同美国政府表面上所达成的一致,实则着眼于更广泛的战略利益,因此它才会持续受到关注。2011年初埃及革命爆发后不久,奥巴马总统向他的一位助理指出:"我真希望……那位谷歌人能成为埃及总统"。此处的"谷歌人"是指谷歌营销主管威尔·戈宁(Wael Ghonim),他曾在脸书上成立小组[在穆巴拉克政府的警力将哈立德·赛义德(Khaled Said)迫害致死后,他祭出"我们都是赛义德"的口号]以声援当时在埃及爆发的大型抗议活动。⑤ 正因为此,谷歌一直以自己与市民社会和人权为伍而自豪,积极向表面上投身于改善人权的组织提供资金支持,并加以利用。这些组织构成了一个影子网络,其成员龙蛇混杂,有原则的、愚昧的或串通一气的行动分子或学者充斥其间。谷歌旗下智库"谷歌理念"(Google Ideas)负责人杰瑞德·科恩(Jared Cohen)可被视为这些社会关系网络的绝佳代表,他的存在证明,非政府组织、基金会、常青藤高校联盟、政府机构、互联网公司与资本之间存在着非一般的关系。⑥ 杰瑞德·科恩毕业于斯坦福大学,随后与谷歌首席执行官埃里克·施密特合著出书;2006年,在康多莉

---

① Clinton, "Internet Rights and Wrongs," 6.
② MacKinnon, *Consent of the Networked*, 189–91, reviews some of these.
③ Clinton, "Internet Rights and Wrongs," 6.
④ James Glanz and John Markoff, "U. S. Underwrites Internet Detour around Censors," *New York Times*, June 12, 2011.
⑤ Sanger, *Confront and Conceal*, 297.
⑥ Scott Shane, "Groups to Help Online Activists in Authoritarian Countries," *New York Times*, June 12, 2012.

扎·赖斯（Condoleezza Rice）担任美国国务卿期间，效力于国务院思想库（Policy Planning Staff），之后在希拉里麾下担任要职。赖斯如是描绘科恩，"他利用在思想库的职员身份，将社交媒体整合进我们的外交手段中。几年后，当推特与脸书成为中东地区民主变革的催化剂时，他的做法开始奏效"①。科恩一直宣扬"网络连接使所有人受益"这一理念②。2013年末，斯诺登披露事件发生后，科恩领导下的"谷歌理念"发布新款软件，它能帮助某些国家人民规避政府审查与监督机制，从而实现言论自由；此举旨在修复因为斯诺登事件而对谷歌声誉造成的损害（颇有深意的是，该软件只适用于火狐和谷歌浏览器，而与微软浏览器不兼容）。③

相关政策的不断出台，轻松地将美国政府与企业连成一体，休戚相关。2012年7月4日，当谷歌旗下的搜索引擎网站邀请用户行动起来，保护互联网自由时，这种"腹语术"开始流行。谷歌美洲地区公共政策与政府事务部副总裁苏珊·莫林娜丽（Susan Molinari）在公司博客中宣称："我们才开始见证一个自由而开放的互联网能够为人民，以及为我们所珍视的自由能做些什么"。

美国国务院的论调在其他部门或机构引发广泛共鸣，其中包括被卷入到这场战事（它曾是现在依然是战事），并在网络空间布施权力的美国其他行政机构。它们共有的首要目标是，伴随着基于美国管控的境外互联网而相继建立新兴的利润增长点，企业数据流不应当受到任何限制。

---

① Condoleezza Rice, *No Higher Honor: A Memoir of My Years in Washington* (New York: Crown, 2011), 305.
② Eric Schmidt and Jared Cohen, *The New Digital Age: Reshaping the Future of People, Nations and Businesses* (New York: Knopf, 2013), 28.
③ Gerry Shih, "*Google Unveils Services Promoting Free Expression*," *Reuters*, October 22, 2013, available at http://uk.reuters.com/article/2013/10/22/google-tools-idUKL1N0IB25B20131022 (accessed January 10, 2014).

第12章
关注商业：美国商务部与互联网

互联网的出现导致美国的政策权威发生偏移。始建于新政时期的独立的联邦监管机构美国联邦通信委员会，自1934年起便开始对非政府网络系统的发展进行监管。1960至1970年代，联邦通信委员会出台的一系列决策对于商业推广数据分组交换业务，以及1990年代互联网的商业化进程而言至关重要。然而，为了符合大多数公司与贸易协会的要求而加快推广计算机通信的应用范围，联邦通信委员会悖论性地放弃原有的大部分管辖权。① 当互联网被美国军方机构拆解并融入美国网络基础设施的核心时，联邦通信委员会早前放弃管辖权的做法反而为行政部门重掌管理权铺平了道路。

以新政时期国会授权为令牌，美国联邦通信委员会在权力被大大削弱的情况下，重启关于是否应当对作为一种通信服务的互联网连接进行规制的讨论。② 与此同时，美国商务部国家电信与信息管理局（NTIA）一举成为互联网政策制定的核心机构。该机构组建于尼克松执政时期，其民主问责制的程度远不如联邦通信委员会，并且，美国前总统比尔·克林顿的顾问埃拉·麦格辛纳（Ira Magaziner）授予该机构以监督互联网之职。互联网爱好者倾向于以其他国家及其"越轨"之举为参照，高举民主透明化的胜利旗帜，但美国自身的规制系统对此类论调嗤之以鼻。一个掌握互联网生杀大权的政府部门，却完全与问责及其他普遍规则绝缘。然而，美国商务部而非其他行政部门掌权互联网制定，再次证明1970年代经济危机以来资本积累功能地位的不断提高。

美国商务部旗下并非只有国家电信与信息管理局负责网络空间事务。奥巴马上台后第一年，商务部组建内部跨机构组织"互联网政策任务组"，并对外宣称成立小组旨在

---

① Dan Schiller, *Telematics and Government* (Norwood, N. J. : Ablex, 1982).
② Susan Crawford, *Captive Audience* (New Haven, Conn. : Yale University Press, 2013), 51 – 62, 作者评论这段历史中新近发生的事件.

"启动我们的创新引擎"①。互联网政策工作小组的成员来自商务部下属的几大不同单位,职权范围非常广泛,并直接向商务部部长汇报工作。工作小组的首要之务是调查"全球互联网信息自由流动"情况②。

经济发展取代政治自由成为优先议题,工作小组积极鼓吹自己与2008年《互联网经济发展未来的首尔宣言》之间的延续性。这使小组的调查工作具有某种"国际礼让"的色彩,毕竟,由经合组织发起、经39个国家政府及欧共体联合通过的"首尔宣言"旨在呼吁各政府"维持一个能保障信息自由流动、研究、创新、企业与商业转型的开放环境"③。美国商务部对这一呼吁表示赞同,并将无限制的数据流动视为经济复苏计划的组成部分:"在网络空间自由高效地传播信息的能力,正是当代消费者、商业、政治与教育活动的重中之重。1999年至2007年间,美国经济在企业对消费者电子商务领域内收获逾五倍的增长"④。商务部惊叹这些增长"在经济低迷期也丝毫没有放缓的迹象",例如2008年,"百强网络零售商的销售额增长14.3%",与之相比,零售业总销售额下降0.9%⑤。

工作小组的调查意在"确定并检视加诸在互联网信息流动之上的各种限制对美国与全球商业的影响"⑥。这是一次影响深远的授权(调查)。严禁色情以及对知识产权的侵犯,政府过滤以及缺少操作上的透明度(无论是消费者保护还是威权主义的强加行为)等这些议题,都重新置放在经济政策的棱镜下被加以审视。然而,清查或总结现有的问题远远不够。首要问题在于,如何为新兴的网络技术以及利用其进行流通的商品,制定有效的政策。美国商务部已详细说明,未来施加给互联网的诸多限制将如何影响云计算业务。

一定程度上有赖于数据中心的商品化战略实际上成为(实施)以下进程的首要切入点:

> 全球可兹使用的云计算服务的兴起(无论是联网邮件、办公高效套件产品,还是透过云端实现的通用计算、存储和通信服务等)引发了一系列有关地区限制的新问题;有些国家对本国可使用的非实体云服务施加种种限制。通过用户数据的弹性定位与信息处理能力,云服务成功地实现规模经济与员工精简(等

---

① U. S. Commerce Department, "Commerce Secretary Locke Announces Public Review of Privacy Policy and Innovation in the Internet Economy, Launches Internet Policy Task Force," press release, April 21, 2010, available at http://www.ntia.doc.gov/press-release/2010/commerce-secretary-locke-announces-public-review-privacy-policy-and-innovation-in (accessed January 10, 2014).
② U. S. Department of Commerce, Docket No. 100921457 - 0457 - 01, "Global Free Flow of Information on the Internet," *Federal Register* 75, no.188 (September 29, 2010), 60068.
③ Department of Commerce, "Global Free Flow," 60069. 特别需要指出,中国没有在"首尔宣言"上签字.
④ Department of Commerce, "Global Free Flow," 60069.
⑤ Department of Commerce, "Global Free Flow," 60069.
⑥ Department of Commerce, "Global Free Flow," 60068.

目标)。通常情况下,互联网用户并不知晓他们正享受到的服务的精确位置,或在云环境中他们数据的地理位置。对这些位置,用户丝毫没有任何控制权①。

这段话有一点尚未曾提及,即云服务的另一个优势在于,云服务为虎作伥,协助美国政府展开涉及范围庞大的国际电子监控计划。

简要地回顾人们如何转向发展云服务这段历史,能更好地帮助我们解释为何云服务在美国商务部所开展的信息自由流动的调查中占据显著位置。

直接储存在个人电脑、电子书阅读器等设备上的服务与应用程序之间的交易,以及储存在附属网络上的交易,并非天方夜谭,也非趋时奉势。过去数十年间,电话通讯录这一超大号的纸质书早已成为放在橱柜上的快速查询工具;当然,电话公司也雇佣电话查号操作员,为呼叫方提供他们所需的电话号码。甚至在自助服务已成为主流(以至于此前的带薪工作转嫁到不收取任何报偿的订户身上)后,呼叫方仍可选择使用电话通讯录或通过联网设备在电子数据库里查找号码。直至数字化衰退时期的到来,"白页"(White Page)电话簿最终被彻底淘汰②。

体量大的基础设施与通用移动平台合二为一,以打破原有的旨在满足提供服务与应用程序之需的结构性平衡。软件程序与应用程序一直是分开销售给用户:用户在计算机设备中一般先装软件,然后下载并安装应用程序。然而,越来越多的供应商将软件与应用程序放在其网站上售卖,供用户按需购买。宽带互联网连接与多功能移动设备推动互联网中介商加快实施云计算战略的进程,以重新集中服务供给,并获得更多的专属控制权。③ 基于云计算的盈利战略有望大规模改变互联网商品链。

云服务的经济利益已不是秘密。商务部熟谙,云计算仅仅是附在数据中心提供的业务上的一个名称而已;最大的数据中心占地百万平方英尺,摆放各种服务器与相关设备④。不仅数字房地产信托公司(Digital Realty)、杜邦发布罗科技公司(DuPont Fabros)、核心地产(CoreSite)等房地产投资信托公司,英特尔、戴尔、美国国际商用机器公司、易安信(EMC)、希捷、惠普等信息技术供应商,还有艾默生电气、伊顿(Eaton)等建有属于自己

---

① Department of Commerce,"Global Free Flow,"60071.
② Patrick McGeehan,"White Pages May Go Way of Rotary - Dialed Phone,"*New York Times*,May 7,2010,available at http://www.nytimes.com/2010/05/08/nyregion/08verizon.html(accessed January 10,2014);Michael Palm,"Phoning It In:Self - Service,Telecommunications,and New Consumer Labor,"PhD diss.,New York University,2010.
③ Richard Waters,"Cloud Control,"*Financial Times*,March 26,2009;Richard Waters,"Tech Rivals in Cloud Computing Clash,"*Financial Times*,March 28 - 29,2009.
④ If the internet were a country,in one account,"it would be the planet's fifth - biggest consumer of power,ahead of India and Germany."Alex Roslin,"Dirty Data:The Internet's Giant Carbon Footprint,"*Montreal Gazette*,June 4,2011,available at http://alblogedup.blogspot.com/2012/06/dirty - data - internets - giant - carbon.html(accessed January 10,2014).

的高能耗电力系统的公司,都使用这些大型的服务器农场。① 2009 年,北美地区商业数据中心运营商创造的总收入为 57 亿美元,2011 年预计将增至 81 亿美元,这一增长在经济低迷的背景下可谓惊人。② 云服务供应商需要大量的硬盘驱动存储,这是希捷在泰国的工厂遭遇洪灾后,(营收)暂时遭受重创的原因。③

云计算的经济利益已从个人用户拓展至企业与政府。在美国总务管理局(General Services Administration)批准亚马逊网络服务(AWS)为政府部门的云服务供应商后,至 2010 年,亚马逊网络服务系统已服务于 20 家联邦机构。对此,亚马逊吹嘘,这一市场是"我们增长最快的客户细分市场之一"④。随后,联邦政府相继与谷歌、微软签订有关云服务的合同。⑤ 这些存放服务器的大型仓库还助力商业与金融行业的各项活动。在亚马逊网络服务系统的客户名单中,礼来(Eli Lilly)、辉瑞(Pfizer)、奥多比系统(Adobe Systems)与网飞赫然在列。⑥ 微软推出的云服务操作系统(Windows Azure)帮助开发可运行在其数据中心的各种应用程序;它宣称明尼苏达矿务与制造业公司(3M)与美联社为其客户。⑦

除房地产投资信托公司(租赁给内容与服务供应商)外,谷歌、苹果、微软、亚马逊、脸书、洛克希德·马丁(Lock-heed Martin)、机架空间(Rackspace)、威瑞森与美国国际商用机器公司等一众互联网公司都建有属于自己的数据中心。阿卡迈(Akamai)紧跟潮流,建造一整套流行的"内容发布网络",试图提升云服务性能。谷歌在美国乃至全球范围内,高瞻远瞩地设立十余所数据中心。杨信庄(ShinJoung Yeo;音译)发现,谷歌斥资数十亿美元建立大型数据中心,进而全面打通各个中心等做法,使其成为全球互联网基础设施最大的组成部分之一。⑧ 亚马逊很早便建立大规模的云服务设施:存储在亚马逊数据中

---

① Richard Waters and Chris Nuttall,"Apple's Rivals Benefit from the New Style of Computing,"*Financial Times*,May 19,2011.
② Anton Troianovski,"Storage Wars:Web Growth Sparks Data-Center Boom,"*Wall Street Journal*,July 7,2011.
③ Nick Bilton,"Thailand Floods Affect Cloud Computing,"*New York Times*,November 4,2011,available at http://bits.blogs.nytimes.com/2011/11/04/thailand-floods-will-affect-computer-makers-and-web-sites(accessed January 10,2014).
④ Dave Winer,"US Govt a Big User of Amazon Web Services,"December 28,2010,available at http://scripting.com/stories/2010/12/28/usGovtABigUserOfAmazonWebS.html(accessed January 10,2014).
⑤ 借由这一新的私有化行动,政府希望关闭现有两千余家数据中心中的八百家;1998 年只有 432 家数据中心,随后大幅增长。具体请参见 Steve Lohr,"U.S. to Close 800 Computer Data Centers,"*New York Times*,July 20,2011.
⑥ Aaron Ricadela,"Amazon Looks to Widen Lead in Cloud Computing,"*Bloomberg Business Week*,April 28,2010,available at http://www.businessweek.com/technology/content/apr2010/tc20100428_085106.htm(accessed January 10,2014).
⑦ Ricadela,"Amazon."
⑧ ShinJoung Yeo,"From Paper Mill to Google Data Center:The Role of Network Infrastructure and Digital Capitalism,"paper presented at the Annual Meeting of the International Association for Media and Communication Research Istanbul,Turkey,July 13-17,2011,5.

心的文档数量仅仅在 2011 年一年内增长近两倍,达到 7 620 亿份。① 据报道,2013 年 4 月,每天约有三亿人使用苹果云服务,较当年一月份同比增长 20%。②

关于云服务的隐喻说法可能有些牵强附会,但大型互联网中介商正在云服务领域抢滩占地——旨在建造覆盖面更广、更为通用的销售渠道,并将计算机信息处理能力应用于新项目,从而制定新的商品化策略。消费者云服务在本书第二部分已有提及③。然而,据一家咨询公司 2009 年估计,透过"云服务"实现的业务流程才是整个市场最大的组成部分④。并且,其紧要之处在于,美国供应商不仅在国内更在全球云服务供应中占据主导地位,实际上,他们主导"每一个细分市场"⑤。30 年前,笔者曾梳理过来自零售、银行、石油、制造等各行各业的大型公司如何自发组织起来并打破美国电话电报公司对美国电信业的垄断地位,进而诱使联邦通信委员会时断时续地开放网络设备与服务市场。⑥ 美国商务部所展开的关于互联网信息自由流动的调查,由于引发企业与贸易协会的批评,反而使一群既得利益者享有特权。若一并考虑,上述内容显示了资本利益的广度,正是代表这些资本,美国的行政部门才致力于解决那些被确定为关键性的政策问题。

其中,关键问题之一是要把商务部调查的重心同持续困扰媒介内容所有者的非专有、无授权的数据流动现象区分开来。由个体艺术家、工会以及来自美国与其他国家的各类公司[例如美国作曲家、作家与出版商协会(ASCAP)、美国导演工会(DGA)、教会音乐出版商协会(Church Music Publishers Association)、美国电影协会(MPAA)、全国运动汽车竞赛协会(NASCAR)、美国唱片业协会(RIAA)以及里德·爱思唯尔集团(Reed Elsevier)等]组成"版权联盟"。该联盟极力强调"版权法的实施并不妨碍信息的自由流动,反而促进信息流动……版权作品的生产与销售环节的大幅创新,直接与维系和保障销售这些作品的线上市场的行为密切相关"⑦。真正自由的文化,即超越并不限于以商品形式流通的作品,在网络空间毫无一席之地。"版权联盟"明确指出,"政策制定者强调信息的自

---

① Barney Jopson, "Nasa and Netflix among Users as Expansion Continues at Amazon Cloud Business," *Financial Times*, March 24 - 25, 2012.
② Tim Bradshaw, "Apple Investors Digest Cash Return but Hunger for Hardware," *Financial Times*, April 25, 2013.
③ 电视节目是这一混合型服务的重要组成部分,电视网的联盟使它们很快加入到云服务的竞争中。具体请参见 David Gelles, "Online Storage Seen as Curbing Piracy," *Financial Times*, June 9, 2011。
④ "Gartner Says Worldwide Cloud Services Revenue Will Grow 21.3 Percent in 2009," March 26, 2009, available at http://www.gartner.com/newsroom/id/920712 (accessed January 10, 2014).
⑤ Information Technology and Innovation Foundation, "How Much Will PRISM Cost U.S. Cloud Computing Providers?" August 5, 2013, available at http://mpictcenter.blogspot.com/2013/08/itif-how-much-will-prism-cost-us-cloud.html (accessed January 10, 2014).
⑥ Schiller, *Telematics and Government*.
⑦ Comments of the Copyright Alliance before the U.S. Department of Commerce, "In the Matter of Global Free Flow of Information on the Internet," Docket No. 100921457 - 0457 - 01, November 15, 2010, 7, 4; available at http://www.ntia.doc.gov/files/ntia/comments/100921457 - 0457 - 01/attachments/Copyright%20Alliance%20filing%20in%20Commerce%20NoI%20on%20free%20flow%20of%20information%202011%2015%2010.pdf (accessed January 10, 2014).

由流动不等同于被剥离了所有权的版权作品的流通,这一点至关重要"①。

美国商会所创建的国际知识产权中心,旨在协调成员在这一领域里的利益;该中心的立场更为尖锐:"内容侵权绝非受保护言论。那些欺诈消费者兜售假冒伪劣产品、或贩卖盗版产品的公司,它们传播的信息应被视为伪信息(misinformation),不可与互联网上流动的其他信息相提并论,并且,明智的公共政策不应给予前者以同等待遇"②。相较之下,美国电影协会的评论显得更加得体,却难掩其激进色彩:"在互联网上推行法治,进而推行知识产权绝不能与限制言论自由或信息流动相混淆";美国电影协会一直秉持信息自由流动的原则,它所采取的相关措施最早可追溯至二战结束后不久。三年后,法国出台"文化例外"政策,即主张电影、音乐等文化实践行为应当从贸易协定和商业机制中剥离出来;对此,美国电影协会先发制人,将所谓的"文化例外"比作赤裸裸的盗窃行径。无论是"文化例外"论还是盗窃行径,都抑制在线销售的市场发展。并且美国电影协会坚持认为,这两者如同那些试图监控文化产品在本土试听市场流向的国家所出台的政策一样,应当被降低到绝对最小值③。

知识产权的诸多限制实际上有助于信息的自由流动这一奇怪的观点(却在这一进程中形同通则),受到美国国际工商理事会(United States Council for International Business)的赞同;此举表明,这一观点并非媒体企业狭隘的一面之词。理事会成员"包括总部设在美国的国际企业与专业服务机构,横跨美国经济的各个领域,业务遍布世界各个区域"。它公开宣称"以用户为导向"。它寻求美国帮助以对抗"那些针对收集、使用或传播个人信息的限制行为,加密的监管举措,强加在方位或传感器信息上的限制,数字内容的定额分配制,以及其他限制性行为"。理事会将目标瞄向加诸在网络电话语音程序上的限制行为;这些限制行为似乎成为一种令人信服的论据(compelling argument),从而为进一步抵制那些旨在"妨碍企业获得全球平台的经济效应与效率"的国家所出台的政策提供合法性理由。而限制电信产业或相关的信息通信技术部门的外商直接投资的规定,应当予以放宽或取消。最后,也是最关键的,服务供应商不应当被迫在国内存储或处理数据,

---

① Copyright Alliance, "Global Free Flow," 11-12.
② David T. Hirschmann, Global Intellectual Property Center, to The Honorable Gary Locke, Secretary of Commerce, Re: Global Free Flow of Information on the Internet, November 15, 2010, 3, available at http://www.ntia.doc.gov/files/ntia/comments/100921457-0457-01/attachments/GIPC% 20Comments% 20 -% 20Free % 20Flow% 20of% 20Information% 20FRN.pdf (accessed January 10, 2014).
③ A. Robert Pisano, President, Motion Picture Association of America, to Office of the Secretary, U.S. Department of Commerce, Re: Global Free Flow of Information on the Internet, December 6, 2010: 2 (quote), 12, available at http://www.ntia.doc.gov/files/ ntia/comments/100921457-0457-01/attachments/international% 20filingMPAA.pdf (accessed January 10, 2014).

"(这实际上等于)要求本地投资,并将数据置于本地管辖范围内"①。

同样,技术美国(TechAmerica)协会将这些议题应用于资本领域。技术美国协会代表近1200家公司;它由美国电子协会(the American Electronics Association)、网络安全产业联盟(the Cyber Security Industry Alliance)、美国信息技术协会(the Information Technology Association of America)以及政府电子与信息技术协会(the Government Electronics and Information Technology Association)合并而成。在宣称"美国无疑是信息网络的创建、开发与使用领域的领头羊"后,技术美国协会随后抛出这么一句用词古怪的话:"在与互联网和电子商务相关的领域里,美国占领思维领导与公共政策发展的前沿地带"②。然而,技术美国协会凸显了美国(信息)自由流动政策中所存在的不可忽视的张力。美国联邦调查局呼吁应拓宽《通信协助执法法案》的权限范围,例如要求所有通信服务应当对美国执法部门保持透明,并随时可被后者拦截。这一呼吁可能诱使其他国家"将美国的规制权威视为可兹效仿的模板,而这些国家付出的沉重代价以及公民自由度方面与美国不相上下,甚至有过之而无不及"。简言之,颇有深意的是,技术美国协会敦促应尽快制定"保障信息在国内自由流动"的相关政策③。上述(以及下文提到的)批评与评论明显针对美国那些原本旨在严控互联网中介商的法例草案;经过长时期的抗争,议案屡遭驳回后以新的形式再度出现④。然而,有关美国国家安全局监控互联网流量的新闻报道及其评论,促使我们思考美国行政部门与互联网中介商之间是否展开了一场谨慎且隐蔽的讨论⑤。

技术美国协会对外单独强调保护云服务的需求。"随着云计算持续扩张,跨境数据量也随之增加。若在用户内容的管辖权问题上仍有争议,那么供应商很难在履行其法律义务以及展开全球技术运营的同时,还能保障其顾客权利"⑥。这一议题有可能波及互联网的互操作性;技术美国协会强调:"为保持互联网的全球运作,我们应当创建唯一的权

---

① United States Council for International Business, Response to Notice of Inquiry on Global Free Flow of Information on the Internet, December 6, 2010, available at http://www.ntia.doc.gov/files/ntia/comments/100921457 – 0457 – 01/attachments/final%20draft%20USCIB%20FREE%20FLOW%20OF%20INFO%20NOI.pdf (accessed January 10, 2014).

② TechAmerica Submission, Notice of Inquiry on Global Free Flow of Information on the Internet, December 6, 2010: 1 – 2.

③ TechAmerica Submission, Notice of Inquiry on Global Free Flow of Information on the Internet, December 6, 2010: 2 (root), 3 – 4 (law enforcement).

④ Useful documentation and commentary are provided in David Moon, Patrick Ruffini, and David Segal, eds., *Hacking Politics: How Geeks, Progressives, the Tea Party, Gamers, Anarchists and Suits Teamed Up to Defeat SOPA and Save the Internet* (New York: OR, 2013).

⑤ Dan Schiller, "Whose Internet?" *Le Monde diplomatique*, October 2013, available at http://mondediplo.com/2013/10/09surveillance (accessed January 10, 2014).

⑥ TechAmerica Submission, Notice of Inquiry on Global Free Flow of Information on the Internet, December 6, 2010, 7, available at http://www.ntia.doc.gov/files/ntia/comments/100921457 – 0457 – 01/attachments/TechAmericaResponse_DOCNOI_Global FreeFlowInformation_6Dec2010.FINALpdf.pdf (accessed January 10, 2014).

威性的根服务器,它能解析所有顶级域名①。此处"解析"是指向每一个网站分配独一无二的标志站点地址(identifier)。美国的互联网号码分配局(the Internet Assigned Numbers Authority)管理并持有这本权威的互联网地址簿。我们将在下文中看到,互联网号码分配局的职能不仅构成重要的权力点,更成为反对(政府)权力(运作)的闪点。

美国商业软件联盟(the Business Software Alliance)进一步拓宽这一进程的范围;商业软件联盟的成员包括奥多比、苹果、思科、戴尔、惠普、美国国际商用机器公司、英特尔、迈克菲(McAfee)、微软、西门子、赛贝斯(Sybase),以及赛门铁克(Symantec)等。商业软件联盟自诩为"全球商业软件产业及其硬件合作商的代言人……在80个国家致力于拓展软件市场"。该联盟强调其成员"代表世界上发展速度最快的行业之一",并着重指出2009年,软件行业已为美国创造370亿美元的国际收支顺差②。商业软件联盟指出,主张信息私有化的诉求一直是并仍然是流动空间的前提条件:"互联网的成功建诸知识产权的基础之上"。为了支持这一自圆其说的论调,联盟不惜援引1985年美国最高法院所做出的臭名昭彰且在历史上一直备受争议的判决:"制宪者有意使版权成为言论自由的发动机"③。

美国商业软件联盟再次提出诉求,主张彻底贯彻(信息)自由流动的准则,以适应网络技术所引发的重构进程:"随着软件产业加速转向云计算模式,由此顾客透过互联网体验软件与信息技术的性能,那么打破跨境数据流的藩篱成为当务之急。云计算经济学的核心组成在于,无论可用的计算资源在哪,用户都能够不受限地取用数据和工作量"。商业软件联盟详细阐述了这一战略要点:

> 云计算代表下一代计算形态,有赖于信息的自由流动……政府官员愈发认识到围绕数据传输所形成的不同(标准)的国际框架,已然造成云计算的准入障碍。美国、欧盟以及亚太经合组织各自拥有一套独立的彼此之间相互冲突的隐私与数据规制标准。政府应当形成统一的跨境数据流的规制标准,从而为云端的在线市场的发展进一步扫清障碍。④

同理,倘若无法形成统一的跨境数据流的规制标准,那么云服务的商业承诺将可能

---

① TechAmerica Submission, *Global Free Flow*, 2.
② Robert W. Holleyman, II, President and CEO, Business Software Alliance, to The Honorable Gary Locke, Secretary of Commerce, Re: Inquiry on the Global Free Flow of Information on the Internet, December 6, 2010, p. 1, 2, available at http://www.ntia.doc.gov/files/ntia/comments/100921457 - 0457 - 01/attachments/BSA% 20NOI% 20Submission% 20 - % 20Commerce% 20Global% 20Free% 20Flow% 20of% 20Information% 20FINAL% 20% 283% 29.pdf (accessed January 10, 2014).
③ *Harper & Row Publishers Inc. v. Nation Enters*, 471 U. S. 539 (1985), in Holleyman, "Re: Inquiry," 3.
④ Holleyman, "Re: Inquiry," 6 - 7.

无法实现。

微软公司以个体名义阐述了对上述议题的看法，而这些议题在它看来本应该首先由商务部提出："对数据中心以及其他计算机基础设施的空前投资，连同宽带网络（对生活和工作的）全面渗透，使人类迈向云计算时代。在云计算时代，各类复杂的应用程序与服务完全可通过互联网，远程提供给消费者与公司。然而，唯有信息与数据的自由流动，才能保障这些投资充分发挥效能"。软件巨头微软特别指明（可能）威胁（信息与数据自由流动）的三类限制："某一管辖范围内对内容与服务的"审查"以及其他直接限制"，"数据传输到其他管辖范围所受到的限制，对远程数据声称享有广泛的管辖权"①。

在审查议题上，微软是全球网络倡议（the Global Network Initiative）的共同创始者，公开支持"互联网自由"（它没有提到美国国务卿也同样使用这一术语）。该软件公司警告说，它每进入新市场时定会"考察（该地区）的言论自由与隐私是否受到侵害"；"倘若某一国家的风险评级显示过高，我们有必要削减对该国提供的服务项目，或重新考虑投资计划"②。随后谈及数据传送问题时，微软表示，"政府制定的隐私与数据安全政策"抑制了数据出口，束缚了商业发展。在微软看来，《欧盟数据保护指令》（the European Union Data Protection Directive）与其说是烦琐，毋宁是同声敌忾——"有些管辖区比欧盟更为严苛，几乎完全禁止特定数据的出口"，例如加拿大新斯科舍省与英属哥伦比亚省。其他国家的公共部门采购合同"往往要求数据必须存储于本地"。在总结对（信息与数据流动的）第二种限制的抗议后，微软解释称"全球范围内各地的数据保护要求连成一片，这导致经济负担加重，遵从成本上升，以及全球化企业投资的动力减弱"。因此，"供应商有可能被迫将数据储存在实施出口限制的本地管辖区，反而降低云计算的核心功效"③。这又是一项阻碍云计算利润最大化的潜在威胁。

实际上，"对政府管辖范围的不确定"造成微软云服务的第三重严重阻碍。部分国家宣称只有数据存储国享有司法管辖权；另一些国家则认为，倘若某些特定服务推广至本国，"或与数据相关的用户居住在本国"，那么它们就享有管辖权。还有一些国家"基于云计算供应商在本国开展业务"的事实，坚持要求管辖权。一旦"用户因担心数据被外国政府获取或适用于外国法律，而在使用线上服务问题上犹豫不决"时，这种"管辖权范围的不可预测性"有可能性引发云计算市场的衰落。微软以一种含糊其辞的语气补充到："潜

---

① Comments of Microsoft Corporation, before the United States Department of Commerce, Global Free Flow of Information on the Internet Notice of Inquiry, December 6, 2010: 1, available at http://www.ntia.doc.gov/files/ntia/comments/100921457 – 0457 – 01/attachments/Microsoft% 20 – % 20Comments% 20on% 20the% 20Free% 20Flow% 20of% 20Information% 20on% 20the% 20Internet% 20 – % 20Dec% 206% 202010.pdf (accessed January 10, 2014).

② Microsoft, "Global Free Flow," 2.

③ Microsoft, "Global Free Flow," 3 – 4.

在的海外云用户也对他们的数据存储于美国表示担忧,因为他们意识到美国政府能够依照《爱国者法案》自由获取用户信息"①。这一担忧确有先见之明,毕竟,美国国家安全局所实施的监控计划的曝光导致用户信息被美国政府获取的风险大大增加。

微软对外宣称,政府应发挥十分关键的作用,因为"私营部门无法单独解决数据管理框架各不相同所催生的问题"。并且,这些问题"只有随着云计算的普及才会日渐严峻"。政府间协作非常紧要。对此,微软敦促:"大西洋两岸政府(应当)同心一致,共同推进全球统一的管理框架,这样,才能为亚洲以及其他地区未来(就此问题)所达成的协商树立模板"②。这里的"模板"是指美国分别同大西洋与太平洋对岸的贸易伙伴所签署的一揽子贸易协定③。

谷歌因与中国政府的对峙而自带"光环",它用充满自利主义且沾沾自喜意味的术语评价商务部的行动:"保护并促进信息流动与言论的自由是谷歌的核心价值观"。④ 深入推进信息自由流动并抵制那些"妨碍与分裂互联网"的各项政策(在谷歌看来,这些政策不利于经济发展与就业机会的增长),将推动政府出台"一项多管齐下的战略"。例如,加诸信息流动之上的不公平或破坏性的限制必须登记在案并予以公开。违反现有贸易规则的国家应面临"适当惩处措施",应制定新的双边、区域或多边国际贸易协定,以推进透明化,并确保"互联网中介商的有效运行"。由于政府间组织"行动缓慢……并逐渐被那些不仅阻碍言论自由更偏袒政府控制的公司或民族企业的国家所控制"(美国好像就不是这样),因此,彻底贯彻(信息)自由流动政策,需要"各地产业、非政府组织与学术实体的通力协作,毕竟它们最有资格为全球互联网用户代言"。⑤ 然而,谷歌避而不谈上述组织是否代表用户利益而运作,反而继续表明自己的主要目标。

为了展现自己对高尚原则的坚持,谷歌同意美国对内政策也可能需要修改,断言"美国是互联网的诞生地,必须继续在负责任的网络管理上树立榜样,从而保证个人与公司能够享有数字信息的自由流动所带来的各种益处,并在此基础上寻求发展"⑥。谷歌向那些"保护本土公司的利益而不惜操控互联网"的国家(同样,美国好像就不这样做)大肆开火。它指出,二十多个政府"部分或完全屏蔽谷歌的网络业务,或要求限制性条款,以

---

① Microsoft,"Global Free Flow,"4.
② Microsoft,"Global Free Flow,"5–6.
③ ShinJoung Yeo,"Behind the Search Box:The Political Economy of the Global Search Engine Industry,"PhD diss. draft,University of Illinois at Urbana–Champaign,2014.
④ Google,Comments to the Department of Commerce,Notice of Inquiry on the Global Free Flow of Information on the Internet,1,available at http://www.ntia.doc.gov/files/ntia/comments/100921457–0457–01/attachments/Commerce-FreeExpressionNOI.pdf(accessed January 10,2014).
⑤ Google,"Comments,"2.
⑥ Google,"Comments,"3.

保证政府能够在其管辖范围内访问谷歌资源"。谷歌大量援引开放网络促进会(OpenNet Initiative)的研究结果,由此列出一长串"倒退发展"的(国家或政府)名单;开放网络促进会是加拿大、美国和英国顶级大学的研究者相互结成的合作组织①。尤其在中国,"一面是大部分美国互联网服务被拒之门外,或受到严格限制,另一面则是中国互联网企业提供相同的网络业务,尽管其中也含有不亚于(境外互联网公司所提供的)'攻击性信息'"。谷歌站在自己及其商业对手的立场上,引用《外交政策》刊登的一篇文章,强调指出,某些政府所批准的"山寨"网站正成为脸书、推特、雅虎旗下图片分享网站(Flickr)、谷歌旗下免费网络博客发布平台(Blogger)以及博客系统(WordPress)等社交网站的最大负担②。

谷歌毫不隐讳地将其全球商业计划作为优先考量的政策重心。随着网络流量的持续增长,全球互联网用户已经构成"庞大的新的用户基础,其面向的市场不仅包括电子邮件等互联网服务,还包括当前日渐通过互联网进行宣传、营销和销售的耐用品与服务市场"③。谷歌善于利用这一跨国性的消费群体,使自己成功跻身于"美国大型互联网公司"行列;根据某咨询公司的研究数据,这些公司的"收入有近一半来自美国境外"。例如,谷歌2010年第一季度总收入的53%来自美国境外市场,"谷歌过半的搜索行为发生在美国境外"④(上述数据不逊色于2013⑤)。

谷歌关于自身所扮演的(协助用户)访问互联网的中介者角色的描述,俨然一副超越各种利益的做派。谷歌宣称,每当政府限制其网络业务时,它"影响了所有利用谷歌进行交流、交易与宣传的商业组织与个人"。实际上,谷歌暗示"政府干涉所谓的互联网中介商时,(商业)业务中断尤为明显"。⑥ 这样的公司(谷歌身在其列)因其作为数字资本主义建设的推动者角色及其紧要性,而应当在(信息)自由流动政策的贯彻过程中享有特权地位。

由于其他政府的举措似乎动摇了谷歌在线盈利的境外基础,美国政府应立即采取行动,就互联网"交通规则"议题(与他国)展开谈判。这些规则除了包括政府透明度最大化,以及废除互联网服务的执照要求外,还主张应当"确保相关的网络业务无需接受本地投资或通过本地的基础设施便能向本地推广"。2007年启动谈判并最终签署的《韩美自由贸易协定》包含有关跨境信息流动的条款。按照谷歌的建议,这些条款应具有法律约

---

① Google,"Comments,"3–4.
② Google,"Comments,"8. The article was "Beijing's Foreign Internet Purge," Foreign Policy, January 15, 2010, available at http://www.foreignpolicy.com/articles/2010/01/14/chinas_foreign–internet_purge.
③ Google,"Comments,"5.
④ Google,"Comments,"5–6.
⑤ Google Inc., Form 10–Q, U.S. Securities and Exchange Commission, for the Quarterly Period Ended June 30, 2013, 36.
⑥ Google,"Comments,"7.

束力(而非属于附带条件),其适用范围应扩展至"所有电子信息流动"行为,并应整合进其他贸易协定中①。同样,谷歌公然反对联合国附属机构国际电信联盟等政府间组织或机构享有互联网政策制定的权限,稍后我将继续讨论这一点②。

代表电脑与视频游戏公司的娱乐软件协会(Entertainment Software Association)表示:"在某一管辖范围运行大型的服务器农场可能要比在另一个管辖范围获得更高的成本效益,或其他有关延迟性的考虑有可能导致(网络)处理功能更靠近消费者群体"。然而,这一"冗长的信息管控进路方法可能同时涉及多个管辖范围的法律"。视频游戏公司不得不直面这些互不连属的有关"法律强制访问、数据保留、数据安全、审查、国家安全及其他条件"的管控标准。娱乐软件协会以生动的个案证明部分国家之间的共谋行为,由此强调"相互冲突的隐私与信息安全的管理制度所导致的不确定性,有可能阻碍云计算服务的发展"。娱乐软件协会与谷歌观点一致,认为可以依循如下途径"拨乱反正":要么贯彻执行自由贸易协定,尤其是美国与韩国、哥伦比亚、巴拿马所签署的自由贸易协定;要么诉诸世界贸易组织成员此前依照《服务贸易总协定》所作出的承诺(《服务贸易总协定》:"可能已经赋予那些主要提供云服务与网络服务的公司以海外运营和访问互联网的权利,例如它们可以通过跨境运营,或者借助数据中心或东道国当地其他企业的运营等方式,来访问互联网")③。

互联网服务供应商、电子商务公司与贸易协会共同组成的互联网商业联盟表达了同样的担忧:它们反对那些"加诸收集、使用或传输个人数据、出口特定商品与服务,以及加密规则上的各种限制;加诸收集与使用本地信息上的各种限制,以及使用特定互联网应用程序所遭遇的各类限制等。所有这些限制行为都严重影响了全球贸易与投资"④。

计算机与通信行业协会(Computer and Communications Industry Association)公布了其大小公司会员所达成的共识。这些公司员工总数超过60万,年收入总和逾2 000亿美元。计算机与通信行业协会强调:"当我们讨论互联网信息的全球自由流动时,我们指的是价值数万亿美元的美国经济活动"。增强信息商品自由流动的首要性地位,将推动行政部

---

① Google, "Comments," 13 – 14. On this free trade agreement, see Martin Hart – Lands – berg, *Capitalist Globalization: Consequences, Resistance, and Alternatives* (New York: Monthly Review, 2013), pp. 90 – 130.

② Google, "Comments," 15.

③ Comments of the Entertainment Software Association before the U. S. Department of Commerce, in the Matter of the Notice of Inquiry on 'Global Free Flow of Information on the Internet,' December 6, 2010, 3, 7, available at http://www.ntia.doc.gov/files/ntia/comments/100921457 – 0457 – 01/attachments/Global% 20Flow% 20NOI% 20 – % 20ESA% 20comments% 2012 – 6 – 10% 20% 28FINAL% 29.pdf (accessed January 10, 2014).

④ Heidi Salow and Kate Lucente, Internet Commerce Coalition, to U. S. Department of Commerce, Re: Global Free Flow of Information on the Internet, December 6, 2010, 1, available at http://www.ntia.doc.gov/files/ntia/comments/100921457 – 0457 – 01/attachments/ ICC% 20Letter% 20to% 20DOC% 20re_% 20Free% 20Flow% 20of% 20Information% 20on % 20the% 20Global% 20Internet.pdf (accessed January 10, 2014).

门采取影响同样深远的措施。美国贸易代表应当基于贸易伙伴对信息歧视与互联网审查的控诉来进行贸易,因为"数字商品与服务是我们贸易政策的核心要素"。应当复兴世界贸易组织的多边框架与双边自由贸易协定①。美国国务院在面对40余个国家的"信息越轨"行为(计算机与通信行业协会单单挑出伊朗、中国和土耳其)时,应当加大资金投入力度,以支持全球网络倡议,以及在"互联网受限国家所推广的"类似的"突破网络审查技术的项目"②。

计算机与通信行业协会指出,"美国硬件、软件与服务公司所组成的特别小组在华盛顿聚首,共同讨论商务部《全球互联网信息自由流动》调查报告中的多项议题"③,暗示商务部可能正对美国网络公司所表达的片面担忧做出回应。这一贸易组织所透露的建议暗指各利益攸关方或许正围绕互联网治理等议题,形成一个脆弱且微妙的联盟:"为了在互联网治理领域有所成效,多方利益攸关者组织肩负起类似'全球互联网自由'(Global Internet Freedom)的使命,并从商业机构的跨国部门、非商业非政府组织以及专家学者队伍中吸收代表。多方利益攸关者组织决不能由部分民族国家主导,也不能将国家纳为成员。然而,来自同一国家或同一半球的公司或非政府组织也不能支配多方利益攸关者组织,这一点也很重要"④。不过,当我们考虑到如下事实,即现有的互联网治理的主要组织,其成员基本上来自经合组织成员国的公司(尤其是美国),那么上述建议实际上十分明显地扩大了既有的全球权力差距。

最后,计算机与通信行业协会再次提及技术美国协会、谷歌与微软曾相继提出的议题,以此作为总结:"我们必须承认,互联网自由应当先从自己国内开始实施。我们不鼓励网络审查与监控,以及内容封锁,或尽可能地改变网络内容呈现的优先顺序。如果不得不采取上述措施,它们必须保有时限、严格限制,并保证过程公开透明。最后,我们不能指定互联网中间商为执法机关。倘若美国无法维持一个自由开放的互联网空间,其他国家估计也不太能够做到"⑤。而随后曝光的美国政府大规模监控不同互联网用户群体的事件⑥,则不得不让我们思索,上述(计算机与通信行业协会)的声明,无非是试图修订

---

① Comments of Computer & Communications Industry Association [CCIA] before the Department of Commerce, In Re: Global Free Flow of Information on the Internet, December 6, 2010, 2, 22 – 3, available at http://www.ccianet.org/wp-content/uploads/library/NTIA%20Global%20Free%20Flow%20of%20Information%20Comments.pdf (accessed January 10, 2014).
② Comments of CCIA, 10.
③ Comments of CCIA, 21.
④ Comments of CCIA, 21.
⑤ Comments of CCIA, 23.
⑥ 了解大概情况,请参见 Glenn Greenwald, "As Europe Erupts over U.S. Spying, NSA Chief Says Government Must Stop Media," *The Guardian*, October 25, 2013, available at http://www.theguardian.com/commentisfree/2013/oct/25/europe-erupts-nsa-spying-chief-government (accessed January 10, 2014).

美国政府政策、经过加密的政治诉求,以防止造成不稳定局面的曝光事件的出现。

威瑞森对外宣称,它已斥资"数百亿美元",向财富1 000强公司的98%提供覆盖159个国家的全球网络协议服务(IP Services)。该公司随后发出声明,"美国政府的国际宣传机构应继续推广唯一的互操作性的全球互联网空间,它不受任何政府限制,后者往往干预或阻碍那些知情的消费者推进网络服务与内容的持续发展"。消费者实际上是否"知情"或许是一个需要严肃讨论的问题。然而,威瑞森继续重申,"数不胜数、各不相同的政策与国家运营标准"以及"特定国家"(在相关政策上所体现出的)不同程度的复杂性,不仅"威胁到全球互联网的完整性,还有可能减缓甚至阻碍重要网络协议服务在全球范围内的布局"。网络电话、开源发展项目,以及像威瑞森数据中心所提供的"公共、私有以及混合的云计算服务",可兹为证。因此,网络碎片化的趋势不仅威胁到威瑞森的盈利战略,如其他互联网中介商所言,还影响了威瑞森跨国客户的各个互联网中介商,因为"客户只需要从一家供应商那里获得一整套统一的服务"①。

威瑞森坚决反对互联网应当服膺于"20世纪铜线电话产业所遗留的规制范式",并试图抵制数十个国家禁止或限制网络电话应用程序的举措②。彼时,这数十个国家中,美国也赫然在列。国家公共设施委员会与美国联邦通信委员会(仍致力于推广其软弱无力的"网络中立性"理念)正在黑暗中摸索③。作为世界第二大网络运营商,威瑞森随后表示,"消费者保护条例与义务不应适用于运营商以商业客户为目标受众群而提供的跨境服务"④。威瑞森对外宣称,它很自豪自己能够正式投身于"《承诺、价值观与行为准则》"(Commitment and Value and Code of Conduct)所倡导的人权价值观的推广战略中"⑤。还需要做些什么才能进一步展示其美德?

易趣及其子公司贝宝的交易平台覆盖全球23个国家,它对外宣称其全球活跃用户已逾9 300万。如果加上其他专门市场,例如票务交易网站(StubHub)与其他分类广告网站,易趣的业务范围遍及千余个城市。易趣先于美国商务部采取干预行为,并自诩因为旨在保障"消费者与小型企业的赋权应当是美国政府的驱动原则"(这一理念)所以干预行为具有广泛基础。由此,消费者主权成为利器,用以驱使互联网中介商(尤其是易趣)追逐自身利益。易趣表示:"易趣坚定地认为,无论消费者身居何处,他们都享有以公平合理的价格购买合法产品或服务的基本权利"。易趣所有业务的25%"来自跨境贸易",

---

① Comments of Verizon and Verizon Wireless, before the Department of Commerce, Global Free Flow of Information on the Internet, December 6, 2010, 1, 2, available at http://www.ntia.doc.gov/files/ntia/comments/100921457 - 0457 - 01/attachments/12%2006%2010%20VZ,%20VZW%20comments_Global%20Internet.pdf (accessed January 10, 2014).
② Verizon, "Comments," 2, 4.
③ Verizon, "Comments," 19 - 20.
④ Verizon, "Comments," 5.
⑤ Verizon, "Comments," 10.

并且"我们预计跨境贸易在总业务量中所占份额还将持续增长"。然而,部分生产商采取"反消费者"战略,进而"抵制电子商务给零售市场所带来的日渐激烈的竞争"。例如,禁止分销商在网上售卖产品,要求电商必须同时经营实体店,预先确定制造商产品的最低价格等。"若没有政府的适当干预或指导",上述这些"不公平且反竞争的战略"将有可能继续存在①。

整个过程中,确保专属的数据流的自由流动的相关政策,无非代表了跨国资本的普遍诉求。诚然,倘若不考虑美国跨国资本所扮演的主导性角色,那么我们无法解释为何过去 20 余年间治外法权的网络空间不断壮大,而成为焦点。反过来,美国商务部在数据自由流动的进程中究竟代表何方利益也值得讨论。必须承认作为美国政府的官方机构,商务部在日常工作中的优先处理事项均与美国公司利益密切相关;在此基础上,我们必须再补充一点,提倡专属数据流的自由流动的政策适用并造福于美国内外的跨国资本。美国内外的跨国资本都依赖于跨境数据流与商业链。在这一过程中,美国商务部身体力行,试图为美国企业扫清各种发展障碍。它这样做,正代表了那些总部恰好设在美国的大型资本的利益诉求。在这一层面上,即便"无心插柳",可美国支持的是更为普遍的资产阶级利益。

我还需要更多的论据来阐述这一观点。多重市场因素削弱了相互竞争的跨国资本寻找并共享利益的能力(正如本书第二部分所言,各种美国资本的这一能力也遭到削弱②)。(削弱其能力的因素还包括)美国政府有时对美国公司的明显偏袒行为。一个值得关注的例子是,当美国贸易代表援引"政策原因"自 1987 年首次撤销了美国国际贸易委员会所做出的法律发现(legal finding)时,它明显表现出对于苹果(而非三星)的偏爱③。最后,如我们将在此处所见,充斥着现有战略与积累结构的各种假设并非一成不变;与此同时,我们也无需过于夸大美国政府的一致性。在美国发生的其他进程向我们揭示,制定互联网政策路线所引发的冲突,已导致美国权力结构出现内部分裂。

---

① Comments of eBay Inc., before the Department of Commerce Internet Policy Task Force, in the Matter of Global Free Flow of Information on the Internet, December 6, 2010, 无页码, available at http://www.ntia.doc.gov/files/ntia/comments/100921457-0457-01/attachments/eBay%20submission%20to%20DOC%20Free%20Flow%20NOI.pdf (accessed January 10, 2014).

② 另一例子请参见 Open Internet Advisory Committee, U.S. Federal Communications Commission, 2013 Annual Report, available at http://www.fcc.gov/encyclopedia/open-internet-advisory-committee (accessed January 10, 2014).

③ Brian Kahin, "Patently Geopolitical: The New Frontier of Government and Market Interaction," *Intellectual Property Watch*, August 26, 2013, available at http://www.ip-watch.org/2013/08/26/patently-geopolitical-the-new-frontier-of-government-and-market-interaction-2 (accessed January 10, 2014).

第 13 章
超越以美国为中心的互联网体系？

美国商务部围绕互联网通信的域名系统（Domain Name System, DNS）而展开的项目，形象地体现出当前互联网的地缘政治。这一由美国行政部门主导的项目折射出美国的境外政策方针，从而转变成其他国家一致向美国施加外交挑战的"主战场"。并且，由此导致的僵局随着美国在域名系统上所拥有的权力遭到意想不到的严重破坏，极有可能进一步恶化。

域名系统成型于1980年代（1994年得到进一步发展）。彼时，美国国防部同意将早期互联网拆分成一个封闭的军用系统与一个更为开放的民用系统。[1] 域名系统遂成为民用互联网的地址簿：它帮助人们方便友好地找寻某一特定计算机的地址。它保证每一用户只需输入日常语言所表述的域名便能轻松访问网站，而非通过数字网络服务器地址（即分配给每一台连接互联网的设备的网络协议地址）上网。（然而，随着"网络地址转换"[Network Address Translation]，以及动态网络协议地址分配技术不断发展，唯一分配制已不再盛行。）网络协议地址经过编码后存储在专门的路由器里，这些路由器之间的互操作性构成互联网服务。域名系统一方面具有等级结构，由中心统一协调与管理，与此同时，它却广泛分布于全球范围内。特定服务器保存的数据分为两种，一种是访问本地域名所需的数据，另一种则是用于处理储存在其他地方的信息的导航数据。美国商务部曾指出："域名系统所提供信息的精确性、完整性与可用性，对于绝大部分系统、服务或互联网应用程序而言，都是至关重要的"。[2]

甚至在这套标识系统现有的管理程序被正式确立之前，美国就已创建了一套多面

---

[1] A history of the DNS is provided in Milton L. Mueller, *Ruling the Root* (Cambridge, Mass.: MIT Press, 2002).
[2] U. S. Department of Commerce, "Request for Comments on the Internet Assigned Numbers Authority (IANA) Functions," Docket No. 110207099 – 1099 – 01, Federal Register 76, no. 38, February 25, 2011, 10569, available at http://www.ntia.doc.gov/files/ntia/publications/fr_ianafunctionsnoi_02252011.pdf (accessed January 10, 2014).

向、至今仍然尚未实现全面覆盖的互联网管控系统。互联网大为提倡的自愿主义保证了对核心技术标准发展进程的分享，而实际情况与理想原则背道而驰。（创建于1979年的）互联网工作任务组（Internet Engineering Task Force）负责协调志愿者的工作（部分资金来源于美国国防信息系统局［Defense Information Systems Agency］），而志愿者本身受到其雇主或赞助商的助助。直到2007年，16位管理互联网工作任务组事务的地区负责人中有14位来自美国，或者被美国企业雇佣，大部分"属于大企业的高管，或政府、学术机构的资深研究员"①。援引某则轻描淡写的评论，这"给美国互联网提供了某种保护"②。此外，美国非盈利企业的组建旨在安置域名服务器并管理相关网络性能，原本应当独立于政府机构而运作。然而，在这些企业工作的大部分员工却来自于美国国家标准与技术研究院（U.S. National Institute of Standards and Technology）、商务部、美国国家安全局以及国防部等政府机关③。2007年，互联网工作任务组里120位工作小组主席中有71%来自美国，而只有6%来自发展中国家；78%的核心技术专家受雇于思科这样的私人企业，4%的专家属于政府人员，6%来自于非政府组织④。

1997年，美国前总统克林顿向商务部下令，要求将域名服务器私有化，此举意味着美国互联网对域名服务器的控制机制正式确立下来。政府分别与威瑞信（VeriSign）等以盈利为目的的企业，以及互联网名称与数字地址分配机构这一创建于1998年的非盈利的私营机构签订合法合同。互联网名称与数字地址分配机构下设核心机构——互联网号码分配局（Internet Assigned Numbers Authority）。后者自互联网发展早期就已创建，以管理组成域名"根"的不可替代的标识符（irreplaceable identifiers）⑤。商务部同互联网名称与数字地址分配机构签订合同，让后者负责监管"互联网号码分配局的职能（行使情况）"，例如分配地址空间、处理顶级域名的授权请求（requests for delegation）。然而，商务部批准根区文件在完成之前可以对其进行有计划的修改。借此东风，威瑞信着手对主根区服务区进行改造，以保有权威性的根区文件，并能通过13台根域名服务器进行分配⑥。

---

① Harold Kwalwasser, "Internet Governance," in *Cyberpower and National Security*, ed. Franklin D. Kramer, Stuart H. Starr, and Larry K. Wentz (Washington, D. C. : National Defense University Press and Potomac Press, 2009), 506, 613n55, 508 (quote).

② Kwalwasser, "Internet Governance," 508.

③ Kwalwasser, "Internet Governance," 501.

④ J. Mathiason, *Internet Governance: The New Frontier of Global Institutions* (New York: Routledge, 2008), 36.

⑤ Kwalwasser, "Internet Governance," 493–509; the relations between these three organizations are briefly sketched in Department of Commerce, "IANA Functions," 10570; Milton L. Mueller, *Networks and States: The Global Politics of Internet Governance* (Cambridge, Mass. : MIT Press, 2010), 62–63; Laura DeNardis, *The Global War for Internet Governance* (New Haven, Conn. : Yale University Press, 2014), 47–55.

⑥ Kwalwasser, "Internet Governance," 497; DeNardis, *Global War*, 49–51.

签订这些合同后,保证境外互联网运行与发展的各项职能被正式确立下来。这些职能不仅包括全世界都在使用的互联网编号资源的分配,以及对访问顶级域名所需要的权威数据和相关的技术或政策事务进行调控和管理①。围绕这些程序以及为了支持它们而创建的各种机构,不少政治学者所提倡的"互联网全球治理"②体制正是源于美国,辐射全球。

作为这一治理机制的协调中心,互联网名称与数字地址分配机构——援引穆烈教授的观点——与现存的以国家为单位的国际传播协调机制之间形成"革命性的分离"③。互联网名称与数字地址分配机构面向全球,"集中化管理互联网"④,并透过私法契约将境外公司绑定在对域名系统的管理体制上⑤。地区性互联网注册机构被赋予管理地址的任务,这些地址分布在亚太、非洲、拉美与欧洲,归互联网名称与数字地址分配机构所有。一般的顶级域名由该机构的其他公司进行管理;而目前最为重要的、以".com"结尾的网址则归属美国公司威瑞信的管理范围。互联网名称与数字地址分配机构掌控互联网运营的政策制定,并推动(相关)技术发展;它与互联网工作任务组、互联网体系结构委员会(Internet Architecture Board,总部位于弗吉尼亚州雷斯顿的另一家非盈利组织互联网协会[the Internet Society]的附属机构)精诚合作⑥。万维网联盟(World Wide Web Consortium)虽不属于互联网名称与数字地址分配机构,却与之展开合作;万维网联盟主要关注万维网的国际标准的建立与发展。互联网名称与数字地址分配机构建立后数年(依然受到政府的合法监管),开始推广政策制定的多方利益模式(multi-stakeholder model),试图实现一种强势的民主程序。接下来我简单介绍一下这一模式。

自1998年起,互联网名称与数字地址分配机构的另一显著特征表现为"全球体制的单边建设",诚如穆烈所言,互联网名称与数字地址分配机构"仅受到唯一主权国家……即美国的监管,并对其负责"⑦。一些并不为公众所知的争论⑧强调了穆烈所说的"单边全球主义"⑨,而其他国家则认为流空间(space of flows)的运营、管理与进一步发展正在

---

① Department of Commerce, "IANA Functions," 10569.
② Hans Klein, "Private Governance for Global Communications: Technology, Contracts, and the Internet," in *The Emergent Global Information Policy Regime*, ed. Sandra Braman (New York: Palgrave Macmillan, 2004), 179-202.
③ Mueller, *Networks and States*, 60-61.
④ Mueller, *Networks and States*, 61.
⑤ Klein, "Private Governance for Global Communications."
⑥ R. Austein and B. Wijnen, "Structure of the IETF Administrative Support Activity," RFC 4071, Network Working Group, The Internet Society, April 2005, available at http://www.ietf.org/rfc/rfc4071.txt (accessed January 10, 2014).
⑦ Mueller, *Networks and States*, 10, 61.
⑧ Dan Schiller, *How to Think about Information* (Urbana: University of Illinois Press, 2007), 56, 137-39. 本书已有中文版,《信息拜物教:批判与解构》,北京:中国社会科学文献出版社2008年。
⑨ Mueller, *Networks and States*, 62.

走偏。网络的地缘政治①反复告诫人们历史上大国是如何试图掌控世界的信息流动以保障它们自身的经济与战略利益。尽管存在一些不透明的情况,境外互联网的发展正符合这一模式。

国家代码权威机构由美国学者乔恩·波斯特尔(Jon Postel)一手创办(或由他非正式全权代表)。波斯特尔一人承担了互联网号码分配局对数个国家多家机构所肩负的责任。国家代码权威机构吸引了许多政府的关注,这些政府都密切关注如何管理顶级域名(本书写作之时,大约有250个)这一发展迅速的领域。即便当"单边全球主义"模式确立下来,对美国掌控境外互联网的政治反对声一直没有停歇。2003至2005年,在信息社会世界峰会这一多边论坛上,巴西"扮演着反对领导者"的角色②。我在《信息拜物教》一书中已指出,数字化衰退出现之前,"互联网治理注定在未来的年月里,争议不断"③。如今,这番论断得以充分证实。

信息社会世界峰会最终促使美国作出一些让步,但结果与其说是与现有局面的彻底断裂,不如说是一切尚不明朗。美国不得不默许另一家新的组织机构的成立,即隶属于联合国的互联网治理论坛(Internet Governance Forum),后者正是在信息社会世界峰会上各方围绕全球互联网治理以及互联网名称与数字地址分配机构的运行环境等议题积极促成的结果。互联网名称与数字地址分配机构名义上提高了政府咨询委员会(成立于2002年)的地位,试图阻止更为激进的变革。随着互联网治理论坛与政府咨询委员会两家机构的成立,其他国家享有了一种对互联网治理机制的并非具有决定性的权威。这些国家如何以及是否借助互联网治理论坛与政府咨询委员会之力以诱发其他变革,尚不清楚。更加云山雾罩的,还有美国方面试图缓解其他国家的恐慌而做出的奇怪举动:2009年,互联网名称与数字地址分配机构同美国商务部的合同有所变化,以至于美国对互联网名称与数字地址分配机构的正式掌控权逐渐消退④。尽管上述(结构性)安排一定程度上遮蔽了深藏其中的权力关系,但美国行政机构始终没有失去对关键机构互联网号码分配局的管辖权。

---

① Dan Schiller, "Geopolitical – Economic Conflict and Network Infrastructures," *Chinese Journal of Communication* 4, no. 1 (2011):90 – 107.

② Mueller, *Networks and States*, 55 – 125, quote at 64; Abu Jafar Md. Shafiul Alam Bhuiyan, "Postcolonial States and Internet Governance:Possibilities of a Counter – Hegemonic Bloc?" PhD diss., Simon Fraser University,2010; Cees J. Hamelink, "Did WSIS Achieve Anything at All?" *Gazette: The International Journal for Communication Study* 66, no. 3 – 4 (2004): 281 – 90; Victor Pickard, "Neoliberal Visions and Revisions in Global Communications Policy from NWICO to WSIS," *Journal of Communication Inquiry* 31, no. 2 (2007), 118 – 39.

③ p. 56.

④ Bobbie Johnson, "US Relinquishes Control of the Internet," *The Guardian*, October 1, 2009 at guardian.co.uk. See the official document at http://www.icann.org/en/announcements/announcement – 30sep09 – en.htm#affirmation (accessed January 10, 2014).

美国商务部与互联网号码分配局签订合同,以行使域名服务器功能,并与威瑞信厘定合约,从而保障自己能够在主根区文件中进行写入或更改的操作。这两份合同都要求不定期更新。随着与互联网号码分配局的合同即将到期(2011年9月),一份替代性合同原本应当拟定出来。这向商务部提供了一个契机:它围绕是否以及如何修订现有法律文书等表面上似乎是技术与行政、而实际上是权力交织的问题,对外广泛征求公众意见。结果超乎寻常:美国的境外互联网政策遭遇各方言语克制却近乎狂暴的质疑。

要理解这一冲突,有必要简要讨论"多方利益"模式:该模式已经用于协调互联网治理,而且,它并非互联网名称与数字地址分配机构一家独有。例如,联合国下设的互联网治理论坛与欧盟的广播政策遵循的也正是类似的多方利益模式。然而,对这一创新的评价需谨慎。在麦金农看来,根据言论自由原则,多方利益模式提供了依靠政府之外的另一条友好路径。"倘若要保障公民自由,互联网治理不能仅仅仰仗政府来实现……民族国家体系并非合适的互联网治理模式"。[1] 互联网名称与数字地址分配机构虽然是非盈利性组织,却担负政治职能。在该机构内,国家连同私营企业、同业公会、非政府组织和个人,参与日常事务运作。但国家被赋予相对次要的角色:在互联网名称与数字地址分配机构理事会中,政府咨询委员会代表仅仅担任观察员,相较之下,其他成员则具有投票资格。互联网名称与数字地址分配机构的多方利益模式,因其同时降低国家与以条约为基础的国家间组织(例如国际电信联盟)的作用,而在全球化民主进程中被视为"公民社会"的推进者。

多方利益模式等同于民主责任?一言难尽。多方利益组织仿若一个场所,在其中,能听见各方的不同声音。由此,它保障每一个功能性的利益集团在政治体制中享有直接的代表权的权益。从这一层面出发,正如穆烈所言,这些多方利益组织构成了法团主义的一种变体。穆烈同意奥塔韦(Marina Ottaway)的观点,指出"法团主义正重新抬头,作为良方以解决互联网治理的种种新问题,它也是对当前跨国非政府组织数量激增及其粗暴状态加剧的一种回应"[2]。该提法极大地符合互联网名称与数字地址分配机构的情况,毕竟"机构内关系……远非平衡……并且使大企业聚集在一起反而让(内部)分裂更为明显"[3]。穆烈察觉到"多方利益集团的参与……往往在集团间的权力分配或它们在决策制定过程中所拥有的话事权等问题上难以达成一致"[4]。从代表与民主责任的角度考虑,多

---

[1] Rebecca MacKinnon, *Consent of the Networked: The Worldwide Struggle for Internet Freedom* (New York: Basic, 2012), 204, 210.

[2] Marina Ottaway, "Corporatism Goes Global: International Organizations, Nongovernmental Organization Networks, and Transnational Business," *Global Governance* 7, no. 3 (July – September 2001): 15 (强调部分为原文所加). 穆烈指出,互联网名称与数字地址分配机构的多方利益主义或许证明了一种松散形式的法团主义.

[3] Ottaway, "Corporatism Goes Global," 16.

[4] Mueller, *Networks and States*, 8.

方利益模式非但不是彻底的解决办法,更存在根本缺陷①。

显而易见,美国政府正是多方利益模式的首要支持者。美国行政部门在重重压力下坚称,应当保持互联网名称与数字地址分配机构的"多方利益模式",并且实际上,它应当推广至其他部门。举足轻重的人物——美国总统奥巴马曾对外宣称,"互联网治理不能仅限于政府,应当将各利益相关方囊括进来"。他指明,美国将"动员私营企业参与到互联网治理过程中来,这对多方利益模式而言至关重要"②。直至2014年,美国政府坚持不懈地构建一种"以私营企业为首的互联网治理多方利益模式"③。美国所奉行的多方利益主义的特质在于,以对民主权利的渴望为名,试图实现美国式的"多边全球主义"理念,并降低其他国家对境外互联网的影响力。可以肯定的是,多方利益模式给个人和非政府组织提供了表达观点的空间。然而,它本质职能旨在维系单一政府(即美国)在行使境外互联网治理上的首要地位,并能(有效地)隐藏这一现实情况。

除去美国行政部门,其他利益相关的权力部门也支持多方利益模式。在与贾里德·科恩(Jared Cohen,从国务院调至谷歌担任研究机构负责人)合写的一篇文章中,施密特(彼时仍是谷歌首席执行官④)相当正面地向互联网所构筑的"虚拟空间"表达出尊敬之情。随后,他们宣称,"政府、个体、非政府组织以及私营企业将彼此协调各方利益,直至形成平衡局面"⑤。在这一幅空洞的、被施密特与科恩赞许为"相互关联的产业"的多元主义图景里,"任何人无论你生活水平或国籍如何,都能访问互联网,都能发声或被赋权以推动变革"⑥。施密特与科恩将失地农民提升至与庞大的跨国公司同等高度的位置。然而,实际权力依然固若金汤:它仍牢牢掌握在美国资本与行政部门手上。

实际上,这一自诩民主却脆弱不堪的进程,掩盖并保护了旨在更新与延续以美国为首的数字资本主义体系的激进意图。2013年美国外交关系协会出台的一份报告更加显明地表达了上述意图:"美国做好充分准备,以享受其扩张并深入构建这一信息与数据共享的世界级平台所获得的各种好处,无论可知还是不可知的"⑦。因此,"多方利益治理"在修辞本质上具有某种欺骗性。它许诺向个体、非政府组织以及公民社会赋权,可实际上,它先发制人,阻止其他国家(无论是单一国家还是透过国家间条约组织[interstate

---

① I borrow from Mueller, *Networks and States*, 264.
② The White House, "International Strategy for Cyberspace: Prosperity, Security, and Openness in a Networked World," 10, 12.
③ U. S. Department of Commerce, National Telecommunications and Information Administration, "NTIA Announces Intent to Transition Key Internet Domain Name Functions," March 14, 2014, accessed at http://www.ntia.doc.gov/press-release/2014/ntia-announces-intent-to-transition-key-internet-domain-name-functions.
④ Scott Shane, "Groups to Help Online Activists in Authoritarian Countries," *New York Times*, June 12, 2012.
⑤ Eric Schmidt and Jared Cohen, "The Digital Disruption," *Foreign Affairs* 89, no. 6 (November-December 2010): 80.
⑥ Schmidt and Cohen, "Digital Disruption," 75.
⑦ John D. Negroponte, Samuel J. Palmisano, and Adam Segal, *Defending an Open, Global, Secure, and Resilient Internet* (New York: Council on Foreign Relations, June 2013), Independent Task Force Report no. 70, 66.

treaty organization]而组建的国家联盟)能与美国政府同等地参与到境外互联网管理过程中。与此同时,美国企业资本不断地将其需求与目标灌输到互联网治理过程中。①

如前所述,美国商务部就与互联网号码分配局签订新的合同而公开征集各方意见,企业、同业公会、非政府组织与个体,以及(反常的是)主权国家相继发表评论。一面是跨国企业对现状的维系,另一面则是部分国家以实际行动表明对现有的互联网权力结构的反对。以法团主义、美国主导的互联网治理机制为目标,重新实现多元主义政治理念的行动一定程度上已经并不具有说服力了。

美国国际商业委员会坚称,"互联网资源的技术协调,以及统一的域名系统的维系,对于我们每一个成员而言,都是至关重要的,因为它们大部分商务活动都是在互联网上展开"。美国国际商业委员会代表300家美国跨国企业与专业服务提供商,在它看来,执行互联网号码分配局职能的权力模式(互联网名称与数字地址分配机构、商务部与威瑞信)类似于现存的三权分立政治模式,同时它承认"部分利益相关方对现有模式忧虑重重"。与此相反,美国国际商业委员会表明,"我们支持现有模式,只要着重关注提高互联网号码分配局运作过程的透明度等特定问题,上述担忧(便可)迎刃而解。这些都应当在现有的模式与合同框架中加以解决"②。

"稳定性"与"安全"是当前秩序的利益相关企业最常使用的两个关键词。它们反复申明,这一境外互联网系统不能有任何改变。世界顶级互联网设备(路由器以及支持互联网性能与应用程序的一系列网络工具)提供商思科公司,便赫然在列。它确认了"五项核心基本原则":稳定性、信任、透明度、互操作性以及技术能力。互联网成功的建制化过程已经充分体现了上述五项原则。倘若重新规划互联网号码分配局的职能便削弱了五项原则,那么互联网运行有可能遭遇真正的破坏。当然这一情况不可能就这么发生:必须维持现状。与其他作为干预者的企业类似,思科承认应提高互联网运作机制的"透明度",从而增强现有体系的合法性③。

---

① 大公司同样在联合国教科文组织或国际电信联盟这样的多边机构中拥有正式地位,具体请参见 Viva Leye, "UNESCO, ICT Corporations and the Passion of ICT for Development: Modernization Resurrected," *Media, Culture and Society* 29, no. 6 (November 2007): 972–93; Dan Schiller, "The Legacy of Robert A. Brady: Antifascist Origins of the Political Economy of Communication," *Journal of Media Economics* 12, no. 2 (1999): 89–101.
② United States Council for International Business to Fiona Alexander, Associate Administrator, Office of International Affairs, National Telecommunications and Information Administration, Re: NTIA Notice of Inquiry, Request for Comments on the Internet Assigned Numbers Authority (IANA) Functions, March 31, 2011: 1, 2, available at http://www.ntia.doc.gov/files/ntia/comments/110207099-1099-01/attachments/FINAL%20USCIB%20comments%20on%20IANA%20NOI%20-%203-31-11.pdf (accessed January 10, 2014).
③ Cisco Systems, Inc., to Ms. Fiona Alexander, Associate Administrator, Office of International Affairs, National Telecommunications and Information Administration, Re: NTIA Notice of Inquiry, Request for Comments on the Internet Assigned Numbers Authority (IANA) Functions, March 28, 2011: 1–2, available at http://www.ntia.doc.gov/files/ntia/comments/110207099-1099-01/attachments/Cisco.pdf (accessed January 10, 2014).

不足为奇,谷歌也关注并确保域名系统管理的"稳定性与安全性"等问题。谷歌"坚信"互联网名称与数字地址分配机构应"继续成为互联网号码分配局职能的执行者"①。这一"由下至上的多方利益模式应当对所有利益相关者负责,并由互联网名称与数字地址分配机构具体实现,这样才能保证其有效性与重要性"。谷歌支持一项改革措施:透过把定义与发布权威地址数据等(原本属于威瑞信的)特定运行责任交付给互联网名称与数字地址分配机构这一方式,谷歌希望能增强它对互联网号码分配局职能的管理"随着这一改革措施逐渐付诸实施,互联网名称与数字地址分配机构所要求的变革,有可能只有在威瑞信承认后才会有所更改。倘若互联网名称与数字地址分配机构生成完整签署的根区,并将之安全地传输给威瑞信以作发布之用,那么整个过程的完整性将得到极大的提升"②。

这些晦涩难懂的技术议题背后,存在着政治权力不均衡的问题,后者已引发国际社会的高度关注:互联网名称与数字地址分配机构对外自卖自夸,坚持对透明度的追求,并尊重与之意见不合的"利益相关方",这与威瑞信同商务部直接签署合同以运作系统所需标识符的做法形成鲜明对比,甚至格格不入。谷歌暗示,既然全球互联网治理体制已经成功地实现建制化,那么商务部是时候让互联网名称与数字地址分配机构拥有独立权限——这可是商务部在互联网名称与数字地址分配机构成立伊始就曾许诺的。

谷歌强调,"对于美国国家电信和信息管理局而言,支持私营企业主导的互联网治理多方利益模式,具有重要的战略意义"③。除了表达对管理机制改革的支持外,谷歌还希望互联网名称与数字地址分配机构能拥有稳定持久的体制地位。就目前情况而言(从美国行政部门的角度来看,这一点正是建制化早期进程的敏感点),互联网名称与数字地址分配机构以服务商务部为宗旨,并与后者签订长达一年的基础合同,并附上四项为期一年的选择性条款以作更新之用。谷歌颇有先见之明地警告,这一安排"将导致毫无必要甚至具有潜在破坏性的不稳定局面",并容易引发"外界揣测,怀疑互联网号码分配局的权力将移交给另一家机构"。它对于互联网名称与数字地址分配局的内部组织进程非常不利,更显而易见地推动"其他利益相关方在国内与国际论坛上,踊跃地赞同互联网号码分配局的职能应当移交给当前治理结构之外的党派或组织时"。这意味着,当前管理结构的临时性,将激活异见国改变现有互联网治理模式的诉求。谷歌

---

① Vint Cerf, Chief Internet Evangelist, Google, Inc., to Fiona Alexander, Associate Administrator, Office of International Affairs, National Telecommunications and Information Administration, Re: NTIA Notice of Inquiry, Request for Comments on the Internet Assigned Numbers Authority (IANA) Functions, March 31, 2011: 1, available at http://www.ntia.doc.gov/files/ntia/comments/110207099-1099-01/attachments/ 20110331093955130.pdf (accessed January 10, 2014).

② Cerf, "NTIA Notice," 5.

③ Cerf, "NTIA Notice," 1.

谨慎地表示,"为期一年的选择性条款,将美国政府在互联网治理过程中的独特角色毫无必要地暴露在国际受众面前"。互联网名称与数字地址分配机构同美国电信和信息管理局所签订的"长期"协议,厘清了两大实体机构之间的"重要关系"(暗指"历久弥坚"),并强调"美国政府应当保障以私营企业为主导的治理模式的实现",从而有利于改善当前局势[1]。值得注意的是,谷歌丝毫没有提及剥夺商务部所拥有的大量职权等议题。商务部并未接受谷歌提议的事实,进一步确认了美国政府在互联网名称与数字地址分配机构中的影响力与实力。

其他评论者发出强大的异见声,直接挑战美国互联网的管理制度。当然,他们针对商务部发表评论这一行动本身,象征着局面正朝相反的方向发展。更非同寻常之处在于,多边条约组织国际电信联盟主动加入反对阵营中。国际电信联盟隶属于联合国,其成员包括192家政府机构(政府部门在该组织内的首要性遮蔽了企业深入渗透其中的事实)。过去数十年间,国际电信联盟一直是国际频谱与光缆电信政策的核心制定机构。实际上,它的管辖范围在20世纪中期不断扩大。相较之下,国际电信联盟从一开始就被排除在互联网治理之外,在部分成员的强烈要求下,它一直奋发蹈厉地在这一现代化的基础设施的政策制定过程中争取一席之地。它的努力持续受到打压。然而,在国际电信联盟内部及其背后,涌动着大量成员国对美国"单边全球主义"的不满情绪。如今,国际电信联盟将自己置放在一个极不相称的位置上,它向其中某个成员国的相关部门申请一项次要的管理职能(即域名.int的管理)[2]。或许我们无法更好地描述隐藏于这一过程中的权力动态关系。一个联合国授权的国际组织,代表全世界的国家,却落得被边缘化的乞求者的下场。商务部对国际电信联盟请求(实际上,这一请求已获得包括美国在内的所有成员国的一致通过)的直接忽视,更是雪上加霜[3]。在部分学者(包括像麦金农这样的有原则的民主党人)看来,这一局面无疑具有利好效应,"让联合国协调互联网的各项实际职能,是言论自由的退步"[4]。

或许是这样,但美国主导的局面从表面上就已损害了民主理念。对于世界上绝大部分地区而言,在美国放弃对互联网管理的单边控制前,它所宣扬的宪法保护及其对联合国机制的攻击,听起来极不诚恳、虚与委蛇。不少主权国家反对当前的互联网治

---

[1] Cerf, "NTIA Notice," 2.
[2] International Telecommunication Union, IANA NOI Response, Subject: Response to Request for Comments on the Internet Assigned Numbers Authority (IANA) Functions; National Telecommunications and Information Administration, docket no. 110207099 - 1099 - 01, RIN 0660 - XA23, March 30, 2011, 1 - 4, available at http://www.ntia.doc.gov/files/ntia/comments/110207099 - 1099 - 01/attachments/ITU_E910_IANA%20NOI%20response_30 - 03 - 2011_final.pdf (accessed January 10, 2014).
[3] 感谢理查德·希尔提供这一构想。
[4] MacKinnon, *Consent of the Networked*, 203.

理机制。肯尼亚政府主张,应当从美国商务部下属的美国国家电信和信息管理局对互联网号码分配局的掌控模式中"脱离"出来。肯尼亚政府宣称,一种真正意义上的"多方利益关系"要求能将真正代表全球和政府的各方组织联合起来。这些组织不仅包括根服务运营商、协议开发人员(包括互联网工作任务组)、五家区域互联网注册管理机构以及行使地址职能的互联网名称与数字地址分配机构,还包括国家代码顶级域名运营商以及政府咨询委员会。互联网号码分配局的管理机制必须应用全球代表与"国家政策(制定)进程"原则,以响应信息社会世界峰会通过的《突尼斯宣言》。实际上,"多方利益监督"模式应当建制化,并使用"联合国所有成员国的语言",覆盖更多范围,即"包括但不限于根区范围"[1]。肯尼亚扩大了其意欲改革的范围,例如将互联网工作任务组纳入其中以重组互联网治理机制。这是由于肯尼亚政府意识到在此之前,互联网工作任务组曾成功逃脱改革者的审查[2]。

印度的信息技术部(Department of Information Technology)所发表的评论,表明印度政府持类似立场。针对现有情况,印度指出:"互联网名称与数字地址分配机构所遵循的程序的确将包括政府、产业、公民社会以及其他利益相关方的实体机构都囊括进去"。互联网号码分配局的管理机制应当"体现更为广泛的代表性,从而保证整个生态与社区组织都能参与到(组织运作)透明度、责任的评估,以及提升工作效率的过程中"。这一扩大的群体更应包括区域互联网注册管理机构以及国家代码顶级域名。[3]

或许受其国内革命的影响,埃及竟然鼓起勇气,借其在互联网名称与数字地址分配机构下设的政府咨询委员会的代表之口,表达意见。埃及此举意在借力打力,以互联网名称与数字地址分配机构对"多方利益主义"的承诺之矛,攻当前互联网管理机制之盾。它宣称,"埃及支持互联网名称与数字地址分配机构继续行使互联网号码分配局的职能,并相信,互联网名称与数字地址分配机构因其由下至上的运行模式与所有利益相关方的加入,当之无愧地成为改进互联网号码分配局职能的部门,而非仅仅透过互联网名称与数字地址分配机构与单个政府之间签署协议改变现状"。埃及提交的意见书指出,"美国国家电信和信息管理局同商务部所掌握的最后审批权,将对整个过程的反馈、可预期性、

---

[1] Comments by Kenya on the Notice of Inquiry/Request for Comments on the Internet Assigned Numbers Authority (IANA) Functions by the National Telecommunications and Information Administration, U. S. Department of Commerce, 1,2,3, available at http://www. ntia. doc. gov/files/ntia/comments/110207099 – 1099 – 01/attachments/Kenya%20comments%20on%20Notice%20of%20Inquiry%20by%20NTIA%20on%20IANA%20Contract%20v4. pdf (accessed January 10,2014).

[2] Kwalwasser, "Internet Governance," 508.

[3] Government of India, Department of Information Technology, Sub: Request for Comments on the Internet Assigned Numbers Authority Functions—GoI Comments, available at http://www. ntia. doc. gov/federal – register – notices/2011/request – comments – internet – assigned – numbers – authority – iana – functions#comment – 28931 (accessed January 10,2014).

透明度与责任产生负面影响"。按照现有的组织架构,实际上,"互联网号码分配局更像是互联网名称与数字地址分配机构内部的一个黑匣子。政策如何影响以及如何体现互联网号码分配局的职能,政府咨询委员会原则如何反映在互联网号码分配局的授权与再授权过程中,一切尚未明朗"。然而,意见书认为,"只有取消单边合同监管(或缩小其范围),才有可能提高对整个社区的负责任程度;而只有增加透明度和责任程度,才能增强互联网号码分配局的职能"。互联网名称与数字地址分配机构所支持的各组织(例如国家代码域名支持组织[the Country Code Name Supporting Organization])及其咨询机构(例如政府咨询委员会)应当承担直接管理的责任①。只有美国被迫放弃其主导角色,更多的民主(或真正的民主)才能实现。

美国盟友墨西哥电信部部长的评论显得更加低眉顺目,意思却很明确:"我们相信,有必要强化互联网号码分配局职能的透明度与责任程度,以寻求新的机制,实现互联网号码分配局合同的演变"。这意味着,互联网名称与数字地址分配机构应当具有更加真实的代表性,互联网号码分配局的职能应当更加透明,"从而创造出更好的机制和程序以实现所有利益相关方的良性互动"②。

东亚国家的意见使整个异见图谱更为充实。其中,中国政府提交的建议或许最能体现互联网号码分配局所存在的权力分配不平衡问题。2010年一位高调的分析人士指出,"围绕赛博空间的信息流动而形成的冲突,将使危机不断的中美关系进一步复杂化"③。实际上,迄今为止,中美双方就全球互联网治理而相互抵牾数年④,这一冲突仍将持续。

总部设于北京的中国互联网络信息中心,负责全国的互联网运营情况。这次,它也利用"安全与稳定性""多方利益主义"之辞,反对美国各企业与商务部所声称的目标。中国互联网络信息中心清楚指出,互联网号码分配局应当独立于商务部与威瑞信,充分发挥作用。也就是说,互联网号码分配局应当转变成一家真正独立的组织,或由独立组

---

① Manal Ismail Egypt GAC Representative Director, International Technical Co-ordination National Telecom Regulatory Authority, to Fiona M. Alexander, Associate Administrator, Office of International Affairs National Telecommunications and Information Administration, U. S. Department of Commerce, March 31, 2011, 1-4, available at https://web.archive.org/web/20120925231524/http://www.ntia.doc.gov/files/ntia/comments/110207099-1099-01/attachments/Egypt%20Response%20to%20NTIA%20NoI%20on%20IANA%20Functions.pdf (accessed January 10, 2014).

② Omar Charfen Tommasi, El Director General Ajunto, Secretaria de Comunicaciones y Transportes, Estados Unidos Mexicanos, to Sra. Fiona Alexander, Associate Administrator, Office of International Affairs, National Telecommunications and Infor-mation Administration, Annex 2-1, available at http://www.ntia.doc.gov/federal-register-notices/2011/request-comments-internet-assigned-numbers-authority-iana-functions#comment-28931 (accessed January 10, 2014).

③ Ian Bremmer, "Democracy in Cyberspace," *Foreign Affairs* 89 no. 6 (November-December 2010):90.

④ Hong Shen, "Road to Cyber-Sovereigntism? China's Policy toward Global Internet Governance: From WSIS to WCIT-12," 未出版论文, University of Illinois at Urbana-Champaign, August 2013.

织所运作,然后交由全球互联网社区自身进行监管。同时,互联网号码分配局应当强化其多方利益主义模式,从而保证所有根服务器运营商遵守互联网社区所制定的各项政策与指导意见①。中国互联网络信息中心主任李晓东在附加的一封邮件中再次申明,最佳的多方利益模式以改变商务部单独监管模式为己任,以推动互联网号码分配局转变成一家真正独立或由独立组织所运营、并受全球互联网社区所监管的组织为目标②。这份报告并未具体阐明如何实现上述目标。然而,随着情势的发展,有必要强调,中国同印度、墨西哥、肯尼亚与埃及所提交的意见书,在这一点上将达成共识。

前国家互联网信息办公室主任王晨,在 2011 年 8 月北京所举办的一次会议上宣布,"各国互联网彼此相连,又分属不同主权范围"。西方批评家大多关注国家如何滥用其"主权管辖"(sovereign jurisdiction)以实施镇压。这的确令人担忧。然而,主权同样保证国家有充分的理由主张互联网管理机制应当从国际层面上进行重组。王晨认为,"各国"就互联网议题,"迫切需要加强国际合作"。王晨无懈可击地反驳了美方论调,犀利地指出,"互联网领域的国际交流与合作,应体现完全平等、相互尊重、互助互利的原则,反对以'网络自由'为名,行'互联网强权'之实"。在他看来,"公开和普遍参与的方式"和"共同制定国际规则"是互联网政策制定的首要原则。最后,他指出,中国"愿意积极参与这一过程"③。

另一家中国互联网组织提交了类似的意见书,展示中国在全球互联网治理上的坚定决心④。创建于 2008 年的非盈利性机构政务和公益机构域名注册管理中心(China Organizational Name Administration Center)得到政府授权,管理以".cn"结尾的政务与公益机构的域名注册事务。政务和公益机构域名注册管理中心向外界承认,机构"积极地参与到全球互联网社区事务中"。该中心以一种融合了政治与市场的修辞阐明,"互联网号码分配局必须整合多方利益模式,并建立起正式机制,以方便搜集互联网号码分配局功能

---

① Xiaodong Lee, Deputy Director General and Chief Technology Officer, CNNIC, March 31, 2011, Request for Comments on the Internet Assigned Numbers Authority (IANA) Functions, docket no. 110207099 – 1099 – 01, p. 2 – 3, available at http://www.ntia.doc.gov/files/ntia/comments/110207099 – 1099 – 01/attachments/CNNIC% 20comments% 20on% 20IANA% 20Funcionts.pdf (accessed January 10,2014).

② Xiaodong Lee,"Request for Comments."

③ Wang Chen, Minister of the State Internet Information Office, China,"Promote Internet Development and Safeguard Internet Security,"Keynote Speech at the 4th UK – China Internet Roundtable, September 29, 2011, Beijing, ChinaDaily.com.cn, available at http://www.chinadaily.com.cn/china/2011 – 09/29/content_13818671.htm (accessed January 10, 2104). 中文版请参见 http://news.xinhuanet.com/world/2011 – 09/29/c_122106372.htm:译者注。

④ Internet Society of China Comments on the IANA Functions, available at http://www.ntia.doc.gov/files/ntia/internet_society_of_china_comments_on_the_sow_draft_en.pdf (accessed January 10,2014); and China Organizational Name Administration Center, to Fiona M. Alexander, Associate Administrator, Office of International Affairs, National Telecommunications and Information Administration, U.S. Department of Commerce, March 31, 2011, available at http://www.ntia.doc.gov/files/ntia/comments/110207099 – 1099 – 01/attachments/CONAC% 27s% 20response% 20to% 20NOI.pdf.

用户的输入与反馈情况,从而从整体上提升用户体验。同时,应当发布更多有关互联网号码分配局性能与管理的信息,以提升其透明度,有助于各利益相关方能监管分配局的职能运作情况"。然而,政务和公益机构域名注册管理中心认为,互联网名称与数字地址分配机构现有的官员,应当启动组织的结构性变革,从而创造出一种"互联网号码分配局的职能合同的新模式"①。互联网名称与数字地址分配机构的领导者只有获得授权,才能开启一系列意义重大的变革。

尽管穆烈教授反对国家中心模式,但他体认到,"世界范围内大多数政府所期望的"路径,"正是签订合同过程多边化。美国原本应与其他政府共享对互联网号码分配局职能的行使权,无论基于一国一票的原则,还是透过某些特权政府所组成的小团体或俱乐部的形式"②。值得注意的是,上述国家达成多大程度上的共识尚不清楚,这一主张背后,往往受到外在政治与经济的压力。然而,各方向美国商务提交的各种建议书表明,其他国家的忧虑并没有消退,而且这些建议书无法弃如敝屣。它们是否再次证实在反对美国的单边全球主义之外,统一的政治目标正在形成?

实际上,这些美国式项目囊括了整个贫穷世界(非洲、中东、南亚、东亚与拉美)。难道这只是一种巧合?尽管它将反帝国主义这一仍被广泛接受的遗产带入互联网政策制定过程中,可无论如何,它绝不代表第三世界政治蓝图的重生(1980年代已然过去)。当然,它也不会是反资本主义的"联合阵线"。这些国家都被整合进跨国资本主义体系之中,并且大部分领导人致力于融入跨国资本主义体系里。在普拉沙德看来,随着跨国资本主义体系在1980至1990年代的不断演进,第三世界政治蓝图已经转变成某种"具有南方特色的新自由主义"③。南方委员会(the South Commission)、印度巴西南非对话论坛(IBSA)以及中国与俄罗斯相继加入的金砖五国等的倡议,无非是处于萌芽状态或潜在的政治运动。它们将实际存在的跨国资本主义视为理所当然,却主张在这一体系中获取更多的权力。要实现政治统一已属不易,要维系政治统一更是难上加难。上述国家中出现的社会政治抗争(它们不断与国际趋势[international direction]相互影响)进一步强化了这一混沌的局面。所有这一切都表明,无论"具有南方特色的新自由主义"如何发展,它的领导人都共享同一理念,即削弱美国对境外互联网的单边统治权力。

---

① China Organizational Name Administration Center, to U. S. Department of Commerce:1,3,4.
② Comments of the Internet Governance Project on the NTIA's "Request for Comments on the Internet Assigned Numbers Authority (IANA) Functions," March 31,2011, available at http://www.ntia.doc.gov/federal-register-notices/2011/request-comments-internet-assigned-numbers-authority-iana-functions#comment-28973 (accessed January 10,2014).
③ Vijay Prashad, *The Poorer Nations: A Possible History of the Global South* (London:Verso,2012).

在公开征集意见的阶段结束后，美国领导人表现出对这一倡议的重视。2011年5月，主管通信及信息事务的商务部部长助理劳伦斯·斯特里克林承认，"在接下来的五年内，互联网所面临的最大挑战正是其政治可持续性，它迫使我们直面如下问题，民族国家在多方利益模式中究竟扮演什么样的集体性角色"。斯特里克林坚决地重申，"美国坚定不移地反对建立一个由多民族国家管理并掌控的互联网治理结构"①。

2011年5月至6月初在巴黎举行的八国集团峰会上，美国极为强硬地表示出对多方利益治理模式的偏好，而反对国家间管辖权。巴黎这一地点更能说明问题：八国集团的谱系可以追溯至1975年美国、法国以及主要贸易伙伴对全球石油危机所采取的联合回应。它并非二十国集团，后者成员国包括了互联网号码分配局的异见国，例如中国、印度与巴西。并且，在八国集团正式发表宣言之前，法国公共关系与广告公司阳狮集团组织了一场名为"电子八国"（eG8）的非比寻常的预备会议②。此次会议上，包括互联网与媒体领导者易趣、脸书、新闻集团、微软、谷歌与亚马逊的行业代表等在内的千余名与会者，与国际领导人进行紧密接触。施密特在会上试图向萨科齐（以及默多克）上一堂生动的实例课，阐述政府规制在多大程度上能够应用于互联网领域这一议题③。尽管出现不少争吵，但八国集团在多维尔召开的会议所出台的官方宣言，证实了美国的偏好："在互联网经济的部分领军人物在场的情况下，我们领导人第一次在某些核心原则上达成一致，这些原则包括自由、对隐私权与知识产权的尊重、多方利益治理模式、网络安全以及防止网络犯罪等，共建一个强大而繁荣的互联网世界"④。接下来发生的事件表明，宣言承诺要实现的"对隐私权的尊重"原则，显得格外矫饰虚情。

阅读八国集团宣言，仿若阅读美国商务部下设的互联网政策任务组一年前就已使用的剧本：

> 全球数字经济已成为强有力的经济驱动，以及增长与创新的引擎。宽带互联网是当前经济活动的核心基础设施。我们国家要从数字经济中获益，需要抓住这千载难逢的契机，例如云计算、社交媒体以及公民出版，它们能推进创新、保证增长。随着我们采取更多富有创新力的互联网服务，我们在推进交互性和

---

① Lawrence E. Strickling, Keynote Remarks before the Global Internet Governance Academic Network, Washington, D. C., May 5, 2011, 3（quote）, 4（quote）, available at http://www.ntia.doc.gov/speechtestimony/2011/remarks - assistant - secretary - strickling - american - universitys - giganet - conference（accessed January 10, 2014）.
② MacKinnon, *Consent of the Networked*, 197.
③ "'e - G - 8' Summit Split on Policing Internet," *China Post*, May 26, 2011, available at http://www.chinapost.com.tw/international/2011/05/26/303835/e - G - 8 - summit.htm（accessed January 10, 2014）.
④ G8 Declaration, "Renewed Commitment for Freedom and Democracy," G8 Summit of Deauville, May 26 - 27, 2011, available at http://www.nato.int/nato_static/assets/pdf/ pdf_2011_05/20110926_110526 - G8 - Summit - Deauville.pdf（accessed January 10, 2014）.

融合的层面,在涉及保护私人数据、网络中立、跨境数据流、信息与通信技术安全以及知识产权等议题的公共政策层面,将遭遇更多挑战①。

宣言发表不到一个月,经合组织出台《互联网政策制定原则公报》(Communiqué on Principles for Internet Policy Making)。这份公报在三年前《首尔宣言》的基础上发展而来,强调"信息自由流动"的必要性,推进"跨境服务"与"多方利益合作的政策制定模式"②。

美国商务部丝毫没有松懈。就互联网号码分配局的职能,它马不停蹄地公布了一份《关于调查的进一步通知》(Further Notice of Inquiry),似乎有意炫耀美国在"关键性的互联网资源"上所拥有的广泛权力③。然而,国际社会的反对声持续不断。中国提交给商务部的意见书更加单刀直入,纳米比亚也加入到异见国行列。④

中国互联网协会直接指责"美国单边控制的现状",并毫不讳言地指出,"遗憾的是",美国商务部所提交的修改草案并未"就各互联网社群最关心的问题予以实质性的改进"。这份意见书同时用英文与中文写就,耐人寻味⑤。中国工信部郑重声明,必须寻找新的路径,"从而保证所有国家都能平等地参与到互联网关键资源的管理中";它向信息社会世界峰会公开请求,提倡互联网治理的多边原则⑥。

中国互联网协会的这份意见书,正是为回应美国商务部的号召而提交的;2011年6月中旬,在审阅了各方响应"调查通知"所提交的80余份意见书后,美国商务部发布《关于调查的进一步通知》,向全球公开征集对"工作说明书草案"的意见。美国国家电信和信息管理局针对这些意见书,展开商议;它有意对外承认,"当务之急在于,必须着手处理所有的利益相关方(包括各国政府)在一个多方利益的范式下如何行事,并使得各方都对

---

① G8 Declaration, "Renewed Commitment."
② "Communiqué on Principles for Internet Policy – Making," OECD High – Level Meeting on "The Internet Economy: Generating Innovation and Growth," June 28 – 29, 2011, Paris, France, available at http://www.oecd.org/internet/innovation/48289796.pdf.
③ The Internet Governance Project commented that the IANA contract "must not become ... a mechanism by which the U. S. government attempts to influence or second – guess the policies developed by ICANN." "Comments of the Internet Governance Project (IGP) on the Further Notice of Inquiry on the Internet Assigned Numbers Authority Functions," July 28, 2011, available at http://www.internetgovernance.org/wordpress/wp – content/uploads/iana – contract – fnoi – igpcomments.pdf (accessed January 10, 2014).
④ China Internet Network Information Center (CNNIC), Re: Further Notice Inquiry on the IANA Functions, July 28, 2011, available at http://www.ntia.doc.gov/files/ntia/cnnic_comments_on_fnoi.pdf (accessed January 10, 2014).
⑤ Internet Society of China Comments on the SOW Draft, Eng., July 28, 2011; "Internet Society of China Comments on the SOW Draft," available at http://www.ntia.doc.gov/files/ntia/internet_society_of_china_comments_on_the_sow_draft_en.pdf (accessed January 10, 2014). 可参见引用协会提交的意见中文稿 https://www.ntia.doc.gov/files/ntia/internet_society_of_china_comments_on_the_sow_draft_cn.pdf;译者注。
⑥ "MIIT of China Response to the Further Notice of Inquiry on the IANA Functions," July 28, 2011, available at http://www.ntia.doc.gov/files/ntia/miitcomments_on_iana_functions.pdf (accessed January 10, 2014).

自身利益得到充分满足而感到满意这一问题。解决该问题,对建构一个强有力的多方利益模式,对保障互联网的政治可持续性,实现信息、商品与服务的自由流动而言,至关重要。美国国家电信和信息管理局致力于互联网的开放、透明度与多方利益模式,这一点在它处理采购问题上体现得十分明显"①。然而,美国国家电信和信息管理局也相当独断地声称,它将无法忍受美国对互联网号码分配局的控制政策有任何改变或松动,"美国依然坚守(美国国家电信和信息管理局)2005 年所发布的《美国关于互联网域名和地址系统的原则声明》(U. S. Principles on the Internet's Domain Name and Addressing System),依然致力于维护这份声明的历史地位,并不会采取任何对高效的域名服务系统产生负面影响的行动……在《关于调查的进一步通知》发布后,美国国家电信和信息管理局重申,并未与互联网名称与数字地址分配机构协商讨论改革互联网号码分配局职能的问题,甚至讨论或协商的意图都没有"②。美国国家电信和信息管理局在声明草案中做出部分让步:例如,承认国家代码运营商希望成为政策制定者的诉求的合理性;并且,它希望号召外界对其所提交的变革计划发表意见。因此,围绕数字资本主义的运行权力结构而形成的矛盾冲突,毫无消退的迹象。

实际上,这些矛盾冲突愈演愈烈。2011 年 6 月,美国国家电信和信息管理局局长兼主管通信及信息事务的商务部部长助理劳伦斯·斯特里克林发表评论,回顾过去发生的一系列事件。他重申,"我们应当'同舟共济'。过去一年发生的事件仅仅确认了行动的必要性。我们已目睹在线信息的自由流动所受到的越来越多的限制、不同标准组织之间的争论以及国际组织与某些政府要求更直接管制互联网的声明"。这些情况的出现,无非让斯特里克林更坚定地认为,必须坚持现有的多方利益治理模式,并预料到这一立场将持续遭遇挑战。斯特里克林强调:

> 我们要想办法让各国政府自愿地加入到多方利益模式的阵营中来,哪怕它们不热情也没关系。一面是部分国家坚持要求采取相关措施,使国际电信联盟拥有否决互联网名称与数字地址分配机构委员会决策的权力;另一面是,美国更笃定地反对推翻现有的治理模式,即构建并推广一个强调开放、速度与创新的互联网。使互联网名称与数字地址分配机构等主导性的互联网组织与互联网工作任务组服膺于以条约为基础的传统规制模式,例如国际电信联盟,必将导致不利于经济发展的铁腕政策的出台与强制实施,以及当前互联网体制所容

---

① Department of Commerce, National Telecommunications and Information Administration (IANA), docket no. 11207099 – 1319 – 02, RIN 0660 – XA23, "The Internet Assigned Numbers Authority (IANA) Functions," *Federal Register* 76, no. 114 (June 14, 2011), 34660.

② Department of Commerce, "IANA Functions", 34660.

许的弹性的消失:所有这一切将威胁到过去数十年间我们所享受到的增长与创新。美国政府将与其他国家携手并进,更有效地确定政府所扮演的利益相关者的角色,从而保护现有的全球互联网机构。我们不希望联合国或条约组织取代互联网机构。①

认为上述话语支持人权并反对国家的那些观点,都有些想入非非。人权固然重要,但核心问题不在于此。问题在于,国际体系里各国拥有管控关键性互联网资源的权力的不平衡:这正是美国所推行的"单边全球主义"。接下来数月,围绕全球互联网治理的矛盾不断升级。

美国跨国企业大力支持美国政府的强硬立场。2011年年末,软件与信息产业协会(the Software and Information Industry Association)与全国对外贸易理事会(the National Foreign Trade Council)联手"推进数据的跨国与全球性流动",并援引经合组织2011年发布的公报(如今已成为一份里程碑式的文件),暗指美国政策与跨国资本之间的表面合流②。实际上,的确有一项当务之急,"围绕数字商品、服务或信息的跨境流动,全球贸易尚未形成透明且一致的框架,这使得企业或个体不得不着手处理一堆国家内部、双边或全球的贸易纷争问题"。需要采取干预行为,既能协调现有的体制,又能为"保障更大程度的互联网跨境协作的网络新技术"的出现铺平道路③。

2012年3月,美国国家电信和信息管理局对外宣布,取消此前与互联网号码分配局签署合同而公开征集建议书的行动,因为"我们没有收到符合全球社区要求的建议书。商务部原本打算再次发起征求建议书活动(具体哪一天尚未确定),以满足全球互联网社区的需求"④——此举似乎将管理局所拥有的掌控权丢还给它的批评者。一方面,管理局的这一举动激发外界对其动机的各种揣测,甚至有可能破坏大资本与美国商务部的表面

---

① Lawrence E. Strickling, "What Kind of Internet Do You Want?" Keynote Remarks before Internet Society's INET Series, New York, June 14, 2011, available at http://www.ntia.doc.gov/speechtestimony/2011/keynote-remarks-assistant-secretary-strickling-internet-societys-inet-conference (accessed February 18, 2014).
② Mark MacCarthy, "SIAA Joins Call for U.S. Action to Promote Cross-Border Data Flows," November 3, 2011, available at http://www.siia.net/blog/index.php/2011/11/siia-joins-call-for-u-s-action-to-promote-cross-border-data-flows (accessed January 10, 2014).
③ SIAA, "Promoting Cross-Border Data Flows: Priorities for the Business Community," 1, available at http://www.nftc.org/default/Innovation/PromotingCrossBorder DataFlowsNFTC.pdf (accessed January 10, 2014).
④ NTIA, "Notice-Cancelled IANA Functions-Request for Proposal SA1301-12-RP-IANA," March 10, 2012, available at http://www.ntia.doc.gov/other-publication/2012/notice-internet-assigned-numbers-authority-iana-functions-request-proposal-rf (accessed January 10, 2014).

"合流"所形成的利益共同体①;另一方面,美国国家电信和信息管理局次月就互联网号码分配局职能签署合同,再次发起征集建议书行动,2012年7月,与互联网名称与数字地址分配机构签署一份新合同②。

与此同时,2012年6月,中国移动与中国电信的三位工程师向互联网工作任务组提交了一份关于建设"自治互联网"的建议书③。按照穆烈的看法,此举旨在"改变互联网标准,并利用域名系统,将互联网划分成几个进行自治管理的国家网络"④。工程师专门指出现有域名系统的"垄断控制权",指控其"不适于自治";同时,在现有的域名系统里,不可能建立起"拥有独立的根域名服务器"的"国家互联网网络"。这份建议书的技术假设以及给出的解决途径很有可能是错的,它的意义与其说是技术性的,毋宁认为是政治性的。它表明,尽管名义上,中国仍然强调现有的全球互联网治理机制,但它一直没有放弃重新调整以美国为主导的互联网的诉求⑤。

与此同时,美国正跃跃欲试,先发制人。政策制定者采取攻势,宣称互联网多边管控模式的提倡者在整个2012年都在谋划政策改变,并有可能在即将举办的国际电信联盟会议上进行这些争辩⑥。斯特里克林与联邦通讯委员会委员罗伯特·麦克道尔(Robert

---

① 商务部是否可能正在疏导此前颇有政治影响力的商业集团所表达的不满情绪? 全国广告商协会的四百多家会员单位代表全球数万品牌,每年的营销、传播与广告成本近2 500亿美元;该协会写信给商务部,表达协会及其会员单位对互联网名称与数字地址分配机构履行职责的方式的"深切担忧",尤其对互联网名称与数字地址分配机构2011年6月20日启动的"通用顶级域名计划"的担忧。互联网名称与数字地址分配机构核准可能无穷多数量的新的顶级域名,从而成功实现了新域名(名义上)的积累,并反对专属于跨国企业商标所有者的网络财产。对此,全国广告协会激烈地回应,"尽管互联网名称与数字地址分配机构尚未确定通用顶级域名计划的利益超出其成本支出,又或者通用顶级域名计划有可能造成消费者的困惑、主权削弱、域名抢注现象、对网络安全与隐私问题的践踏以及其他恶意行为,但互联网名称与地址分配机构武断地执行该计划,将引发一系列问题,促使我们质疑该机构是否具备资格制定核心政策,或执行互联网号码分配局的职能,至少我们缺乏一套相互制衡的机制,以约束互联网名称与地址分配机构日益膨胀的权力",具体请参见 Robert Liodice, President and CEO, Association of National Advertisers, to Fiona M. Alexander, Associate Administrator, Office of International Affairs, NTIA, "Re: Further Notice of Inquiry on the Internet Assigned Numbers Authority Functions Docket No. 110207099 – 1319 – 02 RIN 0660 – XA23," July 29, 2011. Letter marked "Privileged and Confidential: Subject to Attorney – Client and Work Product Privileges." Available at http://www.ntia.doc.gov/files/ntia/ana_sub_correction.pdf (accessed January 10, 2014).

② NTIA, "Commerce Department Awards Contract for Management of Key Internet Functions to ICANN," July 2, 2012, available at http://www.ntia.doc.gov/press – release/ 2012/commerce – department – awards – contract – management – key – internet – functions – icann (accessed January 10, 2014).

③ DNS Extension for Autonomous Internet (AIP) draft – diao – aip – dns – 00. txt IETF proposal, June 13, 2012 at https://tools.ietf.org/html/draft – diao – aip – dns – 00 (accessed January 10, 2014). The proposal was submitted again in June 2013. 可参见三位工程师的建议书: https://tools.ietf.org/html/draft – diao – aip – dns – 00;译者注 http://202.119.108.161:93/modules/showContent.aspx? title = &Word = &DocGUID = dc1e533d812248ca90a4091b780e6c79.

④ Milton Mueller, "Proposed New IETF Standard Would Create a Nationally Partitioned 'Internet,'" Internet Governance Project, June 18, 2012, available at http://www.internetgovernance.org/2012/06/18/proposed – new – ietf – standard – would – create – a – nationally – partitioned – internet (accessed January 10, 2014). See also Andrew Sullivan, "ICANN 44: Examining the AIP Draft Proposal," available at http://dyn.com/blog/icann – 44 – preview – examining – the – aip – internet – draft – proposal (accessed January 10, 2014).

⑤ Thanks to Shen Hong for this formulation.

⑥ I follow Anders, "Who Controls the Internet?", *TechnoLlama*, June 1, 2012, at www.technollama.co.uk.

M. McDowell)打响"开头炮":2011年9月至2012年1月间斯特里克林做了一系列公开演讲①,麦克道尔为《华尔街日报》撰写了备受赞誉的专栏文章《论联合国对互联网自由的威胁》②。随后,关于美国必须抵制政府管控而继续坚持现有的互联网治理模式的提案,也在国会中提出。一份两党国会宣言声称,美国行政部门"应当继续致力于巩固美国在互联网治理中的角色,它清楚地体现在美国一致且明确的互联网政策中,即推广不受政府管控的全球互联网理念,保存并发扬成功的多方利益主义的全球互联网治理模式"③。美国国务院与联邦通讯委员会的高级政策制定者,以及互联网协会与谷歌公司代表出席众议院举行的听证会,并表达了基本相同的观点④。2012年6月20日美国众议院能源和商务委员会(the House Energy and Commerce Committee)出台一份美国国会决议案(H. Con. Res. 127),"表达国会的看法,即互联网应当不受国际规制的束缚,并且美国应当继续致力于当前'多方利益'治理模式"。这份议案得到民主、共和两党的一致赞同,专门"否决了原本计划12月在迪拜举办的国际电信世界大会(World Conference on International Telecommunications)上进行讨论的国际建议书,这些建议书将互联网视为一种老式的电话服务"。在国际电信世界大会举行的数月前,已有人指出,此次大会将是开放互联网理念的提倡者同俄罗斯、伊朗、中国等国家之间的一场划时代交锋。这些术语如此僵化,以至于欧洲电信公司的一位高管称此次大会为"宣传之战"⑤。

请允许我再次强调,言论自由,绝无小事。无论我们身居何处,我们都有理由担心,

---

① "Opening Session Remarks by Lawrence E. Strickling," Internet Governance Forum, Nairobi, Kenya, September 27,2011, available at http://www.ntia.doc.gov/headlines/2011/opening-session-remarks-assistant-secretary-strickling-internet-governance-forum (accessed February 22,2014); "Remarks by Lawrence E. Strickling," PLI/FCBA Telecommunications Policy and Regulation Institute, Washington, D. C., December 8,2011, available at http://www.ntia.doc.gov/speechtestimony/2011/remarks-assistant-secretary-strickling-practising-law-institutes-29th-annual-te (accessed February 22,2014); "Remarks by Lawrence E. Strickling," Brookings Institution Center for Technology Innovation Meeting on "Principles of Internet Governance: An Agenda for Economic Growth and Innovation," Washington, D. C., January 11,2012, available at http://www.ntia.doc.gov/speechtestimony/2012/remarks-assistant-secretary-strickling-brookings-institutions-center-technology (accessed February 22,2014).
② Robert M. McDowell, "The U. N. Threat to Internet Freedom," *Wall Street Journal*, February 2,2012, available at http://online.wsj.com/news/articles/SB10001424052970204792404577229074023195322 (accessed January 10,2014).
③ U. S. Congress, House of Representatives,112th Cong.,2d Sess. H. Con. Res, May 30,2012, House Energy and Commerce Committee, "Bipartisan Leaders of the Committee Introduce Resolution to Preserve and Protect a Global Internet Free from Government Control," press release, May 30,2012 at www.energycommerce.house.gov/press-release/bipartisan-leaders-committee-introduce-resolution-preserve-and-protect-global-internet (accessed January 10,2014).
④ See Testimony of Ambassador Philip Verveer, Deputy Assistant Secretary of State and United States Coordinator for International Communications and Information Policy; and Statement of Commissioner Robert M. McDowell, Federal Communications Commission, before the U. S. House of Representatives, Committee on Energy and Commerce, Subcommittee on Communications and Technology, Hearing on International Proposals to Regulate the Internet, May 31,2012.
⑤ Rachel Sanderson and Daniel Thomas, "US Accused of Telecoms Pact Propaganda," *FT.com*, December 16,2013, available at http://www.ft.com/cms/s/0/86d4baf4-4774-11e2-8c34-00144feab49a.html#axzz2r3C4tlb1; for details, including discussion of how the ITU's constitution prioritizes freedom of speech, see Richard Hill, *The New International Telecommunication Regulations and the Internet: A Commentary and Legislative History* (Zurich: Schulthess,2013).

互联网的相对开放有可能遭遇破坏、腐蚀、限制与蚕食。正如上述一连串的事情所显示那般，这并不必然地表明，国家审查者或"防火墙"正是那些破坏者。然而，"互联网自由"再次转移问题焦点。"互联网自由"理念颇具操控性与算计色彩，它号召我们将基本的人权托付给一群深具影响力、自私自利的社会行动者。

12月上旬在迪拜召开的国际电信世界大会充分体现了波谲云诡的互联网地缘政治①。在面对国际电信联盟成员是否应当授权该组织负责监管互联网（类似过去数十年间监管其他形式的国际传播的责任）这个问题时，美国回答"不应当"。然而，这只是某种修辞层面的问题，因为迪拜会议没有收到一份与此相关的正式提议；美国最终占尽上风，也不足为奇。修订后的国际电信联盟文件，并未在全球互联网治理中授予该组织以正式职位。但是，大部分国家投票表决，并附上一份决议，"邀请成员国在不同的国际电信联盟论坛上，各自阐述它们对国际互联网的技术、发展与公共政策议题的看法与立场"。这份决议得以"一致"通过，这里的"一致"是指没有国家正式提出反对意见②。位《纽约时报》记者撰文指出，美国"甚至反对形式上的互联网监管"③，因此它拒绝在条约上签字。欧盟所有国家、英国、澳大利亚、日本、印度、肯尼亚、哥伦比亚、加拿大等55个国家跟随美国，拒不签字。不过，倘若美国占据上风，那么这场事关全球互联网治理的战争局面就变得扑朔迷离：超过三分之二的与会国（共89个国家）已经签署文件。许多非签字国声称，它们将展开进一步磋商，再决定是否签署条约。这无疑表明，转折点即将出现④。

12月的国际电信世界大会商议的内容涉及面广，并包括不少相互重叠的议题⑤。其中之一是，互联网服务公司（例如谷歌）与传输海量数据流的网络运营商和网络服务提供商（例如威瑞森、德国电信）之间的贸易条件。这场商业争斗包含更加广泛、更为重要的政策议题，我在本书第二部分已经讨论过它们：例如谁应当支付网络基础设施的不断现代化——它才能保证网络服务的扩大与扩张——所需的成本。一项支持内容提供商向网络

---

① 关于稍后发生的事情，请参见 Dan Schiller, "Masters of the Internet," *Le Monde diplomatique*, February 2013, 6, 也请参见 http://www.counterpunch.org/2013/02/07/masters-of-the-internet (accessed January 10, 2014). 要如实了解这些商议所导致的结果，请参见 Richard Hill, "WCIT: Failure or Success, Impasse or Way Forward?", *International Journal of Law and Information Technology* 21, no. 3 (Autumn 2013): 313–28.

② International Telecommunication Union, "Final Acts World Conference on International Telecommunications (Dubai, 2012)," resolution 3, "To foster an enabling environment for the greater growth of the Internet," 20, available at http://www.itu.int/pub/S-CONF-WCIT-2012/en (accessed January 10, 2014); see Hill, "WCIT: failure or success, impasse or way forward," 313. 可参见 https://www.itu.int/en/wcit-12/Documents/final-acts-wcit-12-zh.pdf, 第 PLEN/3 号决议（2012年，迪拜）：译者注。

③ Eric Pfanner, "Message, If Murky, from U.S. to World," *New York Times*, December 15, 2012.

④ Hill, "New International."

⑤ Dwayne Winseck, "Big New Global Threat to the Internet or Paper Tiger? The ITU and Global Internet Regulation," parts 1–4, June 10–19, 2012, available at https://dwmw.wordpress.com/2012/06/10/big-new-global-threat-to-the-internet-or-paper-tiger-the-itu-and-global-internet-regulation-part-i (accessed January 10, 2014).

运营商付费的法令,原本将严重影响网络中立政策,可此次大会避免此项法令的出台——尽管它是一众电信公司追求的目标,甚至在某些国家或地区已悄然出现。

国际电信世界大会讨论的另一重大议题则是,谁有权将互联网整合进当前跨国资本主义政治经济体系中。我们有可能相信,美国官员将强化他们的双边游说活动,从而向异见者敞开怀抱。印度①与肯尼亚加入美国阵营,反对国际电信世界大会条约;然而,韩国与墨西哥,以及美国在阿拉伯地区的盟国没有持反对意见,这一点同样说明问题——对美国"全球单边主义"的政治挑战已全面展开。《华尔街日报》评论员称迪拜大会是"美国所遭遇的第一次数字化惨败"②。

尽管此次大会一定程度上淡出公众视野,但会后不同国家之间的矛盾依然存在。一方面,俄罗斯在2013年5月主办了一场高级别国际会议,国际电信联盟秘书长哈玛德·图埃(Hamadoun Toure)博士与其他与会者共同探讨迪拜的国际电信世界大会是否应当"被视为……转折点这一问题,毕竟,会后各国围绕互联网管控,直接展开政治对抗"③。会上,与会者提出"达成共识的代价是什么?"④,这是与美国典型论调截然相反的问题。在这一点上,俄罗斯的".ru"国家代码负责人安德烈·科列斯尼科夫(Andrey Kolesnikov)点名表扬中国,认为中国"从未高调宣扬并争取自己的国际地位(哪怕在国际电信世界大会上也是如此)或四处联盟,而是大力推进国内信息技术产业的迅猛发展"⑤。

世界信息技术与服务联盟(The World Information Technology and Services Alliance)是一家贸易组织,其成员由各类公司组成,涉及面广泛。它曾担心,"全球企业将有可能身处一个不确定的规制环境中,其根源始于2012年国际电信世界大会上各国之间的纷争与矛盾",同时它坚定不移地表达了对"多方利益对话"(而非政府管控)模式的支持⑥。美国官员也进行重新部署。当某位学者在哥伦比亚大学举办的会议上指出,"互联网治

---

① "印度外交部在大多数互联网治理议题上,采取最传统的主权独立原则,但来自印度市民社会组织以及私营部门的压力,迫使印度政府投票反对国际电信世界大会条约。"请参见 Milton Mueller and Ben Wagner,"Finding a Formula for Brazil: Representation and Legitimacy in Internet Governance"(Philadelphia: Annenberg School for Communication Center for Global Communication Studies Internet Policy Observatory, 2014), 4.
② L. Gordon Crovitz, "America's First Big Digital Defeat," *Wall Street Journal*, December 17, 2012.
③ PIR Center (Russian Center for Policy Studies), "Global Internet Governance after Dubai," June 10, 2013. available at http://www.pircenter.org/en/news/6466 – global – internet – governance – after – dubai – summit (accessed January 10, 2014).
④ PIR Center, Program for "Internet Governance after WCIT – 2012: Mapping Key Global Trends and Assessing Russia's National Interests," available at http://www.pircenter.org/en/events/1809 – pir – centers – international – seminar – internet – governance – after – wcit2012 – mapping – key – global – trends – and – assessing – russia – s – national – interests (accessed January 10, 2014).
⑤ PIR Center, "Global Internet Governance after Dubai."
⑥ World Information Technology and Services Alliance (WITSA), "Special Report on ITU WCIT – 2012," January 2013, available at http://www.witsa.org/v2/media_center/pdf/ITU_Dubai_WCIT12_outcome_report_Final.pdf (accessed January 10, 2014).

理的联邦模式"如今有可能超越美国主导的境外互联网治理模式[1]时,斯特里克林毫不犹豫地提出异议。"联邦模式"的具体内容与程序尚不确定,而且我们也会揣测美国官员私下如何看待这一建议。无论如何,2013 年 6 月向美国外交关系委员会(U. S. Council on Foreign Relations)所提交的一份高级别任务组报告中,真真切切地表达了对全球互联网治理现状的担忧之情[2]。这份报告出台后不久,斯诺登向外界曝光了美国国家安全局对全球互联网流量的无孔不入的监控。斯诺登事件对全球政治版图造成极大震动,并终结了美国试图先发制人的美梦。

斯诺登事件影响深远,已超过监控问题本身,进而"动摇国际互联网治理的基础"[3]。这并非因为斯诺登向外界曝光了新的秘密,而是事件本身暴露了长期被忽视的议题。美国对国际通信体系的监控(美国国安局从 1952 年就批准的项目)可追溯至 20 世纪早期[4]。1945 年,美国军方二十四小时监控系统截获参与联合国成立大会的代表之间的外交电报[5]。1970 年代中期,滥用职权的情况美国情报部门(包括国安局代号"三叶草"[Shamrock]的计划)遭到美国参议员弗兰克·丘奇(Frank Church)的调查。1990 年代,有报道指出,美国国安局与英国、加拿大、澳大利亚、新西兰结成"五眼"(Five Eyes)合作关系,共同启动一项信号情报计划以监控和截获国际卫星通信。这一监控计划所波及的范围,以及它是用于外交与军事目的还是向美国企业提供具有商业价值的情报等细节,统统在欧洲对"梯队"计划(Echelon)展开调查时,浮出水面[6]。斯诺登事件爆发之前,许多报告已经揭露,美国国安局通过其分布广泛的"情报收集中心"以及设在美国犹他州布拉夫戴尔市的超大数据中心,全方位监控卫星与有线系统的电子传输内容[7]。最后,有一点毋庸置疑,美国政府迫不及待地攻击那些支持言论自由的人——告密者和泄密者[8]。

---

[1] Negroponte, Palmisano, and Segal, "Defending," 13, 67.

[2] Lawrence E. Strickling, Keynote Address, Conference on the Future of Internet Governance after Dubai, Columbia University Institute of Tele‑Information, New York, June 20, 2013. The program is publicized at http://www8. gsb. columbia. edu/citi/thefuture oftheinternet.

[3] Mueller and Wagner, "Finding a Formula," 1.

[4] James Bamford, "They Know Much More Than You Think," *New York Review of Books* 60, no. 13 (August 15, 2013), 4; Alfred M. McCoy, "Imperial Illusions: Information Infrastructure and the Future of U. S. Global Power," in *Endless Empire: Spain's Retreat, Europe's Eclipse, America's Decline*, ed. Alfred W. McCoy, Josep M. Fradera, and Stephen Jacobson (Madison: University of Wisconsin Press, 2012), 360–86.

[5] Perry Anderson, "American Foreign Policy and Its Thinkers," *New Left Review* 83 (September/October 2013): 23.

[6] This is recounted in the relevant Wikipedia entry "ECHELON," http://en. wikipedia. org/wiki/ECHELON. 有关于此的精彩分析,请参见 James Bamford, Body of Secrets (New York: Anchor, 2002).

[7] James Bamford, "The NSA Is Building the Country's Biggest Spy Center (Watch What You Say)," *Wired*, March 15, 2012, available at http://www. wired. com/threatlevel/ 2012/03/ff_nsadatacenter/all/1 (accessed January 10, 2014).

[8] Leonard Downie Jr., "The Obama Administration and the Press," *Committee to Protect Journalists*, October 10, 2013, available at http://cpj. org/reports/2013/10/obama–and–the–press–us–leaks–surveillance–post–911. php (accessed January 10, 2014).

斯诺登的爆料产生深远影响，主要体现在三个相互关联的方面：首先，斯诺登披露的资料让全世界了解到美国正系统性地利用其在境外互联网治理上的独特地位，为所欲为。2013年前，大家公认互联网由美国主导，与此同时，美国政府早已掩盖其所具有的互联网实力，人们只能断续有限地了解美国的互联网实力。美国国安局是全美雇佣最多数学家的机构，大约3.5万名数学家供职于国安局，年度预算高达108亿美元，由此成为全美情报复合体中最大的组成部分。现如今，有证据显示，国安局的"战略任务"不仅包括外交、军事与反恐，它也致力于"确保美国的经济优势与政策战略"。这或许才是国安局2010年不仅监控委内瑞拉政府以及负责经济的十位高管的私人信件，并同时寻求相对于日本和巴西的"经济优势"的原因①。针对英美两国情报机构的指控逐渐浮出水面，这些指控认为，英美情报部门监控负责反托拉斯调查的欧盟委员会委员，其中一项调查牵涉谷歌②。

少数勇敢的记者将斯诺登的文件发送给世界各大媒体，试图向世界传递如下信息：美国政府与顶尖互联网企业联手（尽管有时看起来很隐秘），以构建美国政府内部人士所说的"通信情报的黄金时代"③。美国国安局借助被外界大肆报道的"棱镜"计划，得以访问通信与互联网公司的各项数据，其他"更为隐蔽和更具侵犯性的"计划使得国安局能够直接进入所有电子通信都必须使用的光缆与相关基础设施④。在此之前，国内外民众的通信活动都不曾像今天这般遭遇大规模的入侵：据报道，国安局能够监控流经美国的互联网流量的75%⑤。国安局大规模监控项目所辐射的领域包括电子邮件讯息、社交网站、网站流量、信用卡交易以及电话通讯；国安局正从谷歌、微软电子邮件、雅虎和脸书等网站上搜集全部电子邮件地址⑥。魔兽世界（World of Warcraft）和第二人生（Second Life）以

---

① Scott Shane, "No Morsel Too Miniscule for All–Consuming N. S. A. ," *New York Times*, November 3, 2013.
② George Parker and Richard McGregor, "Brussels Furious at Ally Spying Claim," *Financial Times*, December 21/22, 2013.
③ James Risen and Laura Poitras, "N. S. A. Report Outlined Goals for More Power," *New York Times*, November 23, 2013; Jason Healey, ed. , *A Fierce Domain: Conflict in Cyberspace, 1986 to 2012* (Vienna, Va. : Cyber Conflict Studies Association and Atlantic Council, 2013), 87.
④ Bamford, "They Know Much More Than You Think," 6; Craig Timberg and Barton Gellman, "NSA Paying U. S. Companies for Access to Communications Networks," *Washington Post*, August 29, 2013, available at http://www.washingtonpost.com/world/national–security/nsa–paying–us–companies–for–access–to–communications–networks/2013/08/29/5641a4b6–10c2–11e3–bdf6–e4fc677d94a1_story.html (accessed January 10, 2014); Ed Pilkington, "Phone Companies Remain Silent over Legality of NSA Data Collection," The Guardian, September 18, 2013, available at http://www.theguardian.com/world/2013/sep/18/phone–companies–silent–nsa–data–collection (accessed January 10, 2014).
⑤ CBS/AP, "German Magazine: NSA Spied on United Nations," August 26, 2013, available at http://www.cbsnews.com/news/german–magazine–nsa–spied–on–united–nations (accessed January 10, 2014).
⑥ Barton Gellman and Ashkan Soltani, "NSA Collects Millions of E–mail Address Books Globally," *Washington Post*, October 14, 2013, available at http://www.washingtonpost.com/world/national–security/nsa–collects–millions–of–e–mail–address–books–globally/2013/10/14/8e58b5be–34f9–11e3–80c6–7e6dd8d22d8f_story.html (accessed January 10, 2014).

及其他在线游戏已经遭到过滤,大概原因是,每一游戏似乎都有可能成为潜在的被恐怖分子加以利用的"目标密集的通信网络"。所以,国安局也监控了那些容易泄露信息的智能手机应用程序的数据流,首当其冲的便是手游"愤怒的小鸟"①。国安局早已具备访问那些位于德国、南非、俄罗斯、中国和新加坡等国家或地区原本应当受到保护的数据中心的能力②。据说,国安局利用位于波哥大、加斯拉斯、墨西哥城、巴拿马城以及巴西利亚等地的美国大使馆内的情报站,以监控当地人民和政府③。除此之外,国安局还监控某些国家的领导人,在欧盟驻华盛顿市区办事处安装窃听器,侵入欧盟内部计算机网络,并黑进联合国通信系统④。如此看来,数月前,朱利安·阿桑奇(Julian Assange)对外宣称,政府与互联网中介商之间明显或不明显的合作行为早已将万维网转变成一架"监控引擎",这一说法无疑是正确的⑤。

其次,公众对美国政府监控互联网行为的反对,如今已成为一种政治不稳定的因素,因为点滴式(drip-feed)的深层曝光所引发的公众愤怒的"反制"已经汇聚成一场国内与国际大讨论⑥。玻利维亚总统埃沃·莫拉莱斯(Evo Morales)专机在从莫斯科向拉巴斯(La Paz)返航途中,因为美国干预(看起来,美国政府相信莫拉莱斯政府有可能向斯诺登提供政治庇护)而迫降于澳大利亚⑦。欧洲不少国家的民选领导人面对这一政治倒退,认为在政治上有必要(同时也是机遇)针对美国国安局大规模的监控计划做出战略性回应⑧。法国利用斯诺登事件,在欧盟与美国关于跨大西洋贸易协定的谈判中深入推进其"文化例外"政策,并积极扩展其自身的数字监控计划。一方面,不少欧洲立法者主张必须实行更为严格的数据保护标准,并且,这些标准应成为即将出台的贸易协定的内容;另一方面,其他立法者建议暂时搁置包含从欧盟向美国安全机构进行银行数据转移条款的

---

① Mark Mazzetti and Justin Elliott,"Spies Infiltrate a Fantasy Realm of Online Games,"*New York Times*,December 10,2013;James Glanz,Jeff Larson,and Andrew W. Lehren,"Spy Agencies Tap Data Streaming from Phone Apps,"*New York Times*,January 28,2014.
② Risen and Poitras,"N. S. A. Report."
③ 据报道,整体上,美国国安局在全球 80 家大使馆及领事馆里设有"监听处",具体请参见 CBS/AP,"NSA Spied."
④ CBS/AP,"NSA Spied."
⑤ Julian Assange,Cypherpunks:Freedom and the Future of the Internet. (New York:O/R,2012).
⑥ Alfred McCoy,"Surveillance Blowback:The Making of the U. S. Surveillance State,1898-2020,"*Popular Resistance*,July 15,2013,available at http://www. popularresistance. org/ surveillance-blowback-the-making-of-the-us-surveillance-state-1898-2020 (accessed January 10,2014).
⑦ Benjamin Dangl,"U. S. Spying and Resistance in Latin America,"*CounterPunch*,July 19-21,2013,available at http://www. counterpunch. org/2013/07/19/us-spying-and-resistance-in-latin-america (accessed January 10,2014).
⑧ Quentin Peel,"Europe Calls for Strict Europe-Wide Law on Protecting Personal Data,"*Financial Times*,July 15,2013.

"环球同业银行金融电讯协会"(SWIFT)协定①。墨西哥、德国、法国与西班牙领导人受到监控的消息相继被曝光,这些国家各自照会其美国外交大使②。德国的隐私事务专员要求审查欧洲互联网是否受到欧盟保护;欧盟委员会发布一份报告后,德国宣称互联网治理模式过于以美国为中心,欧盟应当采取措施深化其在互联网治理中的作用③。巴西与德国共同起草了一份有关互联网隐私权的联合国决议。④ 印度建议政府工作人员不使用谷歌邮件服务,并警告其驻伦敦的外交人员在准备敏感性文件时,应使用打字机而不是计算机⑤。同样,印度官员指责多方利益模式就是一场骗局,并且他们再次发起互联网号码分配局管理模式多边化行动,试图"将互联网从美国控制中解放出来"⑥。包括阿根廷总统克里斯蒂娜·费尔南德斯·德基什内尔(Christina Fernandez Kirchner)与巴西总统迪尔玛·罗塞夫在内的南美国家领导人抗议南方共同市场(Mercosur),认为国家主权受到

---

① James Fontanella – Khan and James Politi, "Data Scandal Clouds Trade Talks," *Financial Times*, June 10, 2013; Hugh Carney, "France Expands Digital Spying," Financial Times, December 12, 2013; Gregor Peter Schmitz, "SWIFT Suspension? EU Parliament Furious about NSA Bank Spying," *Spiegel Online*, September 18, 2013, available at http://www.spiegel.de/international/europe/nsa – spying – european – parliamentarians – call – for – swift – suspension – a – 922920.html (accessed January 10, 2014).
② BBC News Europe, "Snowden Leaks: France Summons U. S. Envoy over Spying Claims," BBC, October 21, 2013, available at http://www.bbc.co.uk/news/world – europe – 24607880 (accessed January 10, 2014); Paul Lewis and Angelique Chrisafis, "Barack Obama Calls Francois Hollande Following NSA Revelations in France," *The Guardian*, October 21, 2013, available at http://www.theguardian.com/world/2013/oct/21/us – french – surveillance – legitimate – questions (accessed January 10, 2014); Jens Glüsing, Laura Poitras, Marcel Rosenbach and Holger Stark, "Fresh Leak on US Spying: NSA Accessed Mexican President's Email," *Spiegel Online*, October 20, 2013, available at www.spiegel.de/international/world/nsa – hacked – email – account – of – mexican – president – a – 928817.html (accessed January 10, 2014).
③ Matthew Taylor, Nick Hopkins, and Jemima Kiss, "NSA Surveillance May Cause Break – Up of the Internet, Experts Warn," *The Guardian*, November 1, 2013, available at http://www.theguardian.com/world/2013/nov/01/nsa – surveillance – cause – internet – breakup – edward – snowden (accessed January 10, 2014); Ian Traynor, "Internet Governance Too US – centric, Says European Commission," *The Guardian*, February 12, 2014, available at http://www.theguardian.com/technology/2014/feb/12/internet – governance – us – european – commission (accessed February 18, 2014); European Commission, "Communication from the Commission to the European Parliament, the Council, the European Economic and Social Committee and the Committee of the Regions, Internet Policy and Governance Europe's Role in Shaping the Future of Internet Governance" (Brussels, COM (2014) 72/4), available at http://ec.europa.eu/information_society/newsroom/cf/dae/document.cfm?doc_id=4453 (accessed February 18, 2014).
④ Taylor, Hopkins, and Kiss, "NSA Surveillance."
⑤ "Germany, Brazil Work on Draft UN Resolution to End Excessive Spying," *Global Post*, October 26, 2013, available at www.globalpost.com/dispatch/news/regions/europe/ 131026/germany – brazil – US – draft – un – resolution – spying (accessed January 10, 2014); Nick Hopkins and Matthew Taylor, "Edward Snowden Revelations Prompt UN Investigation into Surveillance," *The Guardian*, December 2, 2013, available at http://www.theguardian.com/world/2013/dec/02/edward – snowden – un – investigation – surveillance (accessed February 18, 2014).
⑥ Sandeep Joshi, "India to Push for Freeing Internet from U. S. Control," *The Hindu*, December 7, 2013, available at http://www.thehindu.com/sci – tech/technology/internet/india – to – push – for – freeing – internet – from – us – control/article5434095.ece (accessed February 24, 2014).

侵犯，并向联合国大会提出类似指控①。

面对此情此景，美国政府处于相对被动的局面。荣·怀登(Ron Wyden)以及其他少数坚持原则的立法者以践踏人权为由，反对国安局自行扩大权限。与此同时，深受挫败的国会领导人沆瀣一气，密谋寻找政治掩护，企图继续支持国安局②。作为2016年美国总统候选人，希拉里·克林顿"挺身而出"，抛出一套说辞(她可能希望公众认为这套说辞是经过深思熟虑的)：是时候就监控问题展开一场"理性的、成人般的对话"——可这并非真正的纠偏行动③。美国联邦调查局以防止针对美国的网络攻击为名，试图扭转议题方向④。甚至在美国政府决定起诉斯诺登违反间谍法案后，最初的民调显示，美国人更倾向于将斯诺登视为一位"英雄"而非"叛徒"⑤。这种情绪不断发酵⑥。《纽约时报》发表社论，认为斯诺登应被视为"告密者"，以获得宽大处理，或者接受辩诉交易⑦。欧洲议会在调查美国政府监控行为时，甚至邀请斯诺登透过视频作证⑧。

一方面，美国领导人仓促应对各种危机；另一方面，2013年秋再次爆出巴西、墨西哥、

---

① Joe Leahy, "Rousseff Attacks Foreign Spying and Calls for Code to Protect Internet Privacy," *Financial Times*, September 25, 2013; "Latin America Demands Answers from U. S. on Spying," *Agence France-Press*, July 11, 2013, available at http://www.rawstory.com/rs/2013/07/11/latin-america-demands-answers-from-u-s-on-spying; Julian Borger, "Brazilian President: US Surveillance a 'Breach of International Law,'" *The Guardian*, September 24, 2013, available at http://www.theguardian.com/world/2013/sep/24/brazil-president-un-speech-nsa-surveillance (accessed January 10, 2014); "UN vs. NSA: 21 Nations Discuss Resolutions Restraining US Spying," *Voice of Russia*, October 26, 2013, available at http://voiceofrussia.com/news/2013_10_26/UN-against-NSA-21-nations-discuss-resolution-restraining-US-spying-6298 (accessed January 10, 2014).

② Geoff Dyer, "Feinstein Urges 'Total Review' of Intelligence," *Financial Times*, October 29, 2013; Spencer Ackerman, "Feinstein Promotes Bill to Strengthen NSA's Hand on War-rantless Searches," *The Guardian*, November 15, 2013, available at http://www.theguardian.com/world/2013/nov/15/feinstein-bill-nsa-warrantless-searches-surveillance (accessed January 10, 2014).

③ Saeed Kamali Dehghan, Nicholas Watt, Alan Travis, and Nick Hopkins, "Hillary Clinton: We Need to Talk Sensibly about Spying," *The Guardian*, October 11, 2013, available at http://www.theguardian.com/world/2013/oct/11/hillary-clinton-spying (accessed January 10, 2014).

④ Spencer Ackerman, "Cyber-Attacks Eclipsing Terrorism as Gravest Domestic Threat—FBI," *The Guardian*, November 14, 2013, available at http://www.theguardian.com/world/2013/nov/14/cyber-attacks-terrorism-domestic-threat-fbi (accessed January 10, 2014).

⑤ Reuters/Ipsos poll, reported in Alessandra Prentice and Steve Gutterman, "Snowden Still at Airport, Ecuador Asylum Decision Could Take Months," *Reuters*, June 26, 2013, available at http://uk.reuters.com/article/2013/06/26/uk-usa-security-snowden-idUKBRE95P0H820130626 (accessed January 10, 2014).

⑥ Ezra Klein, "Edward Snowden, Patriot," *Washington Post*, August 9, 2013, available at http://www.washingtonpost.com/blogs/wonkblog/wp/2013/08/09/edward-snowden-patriot (accessed January 10, 2014); Bruce Joffe, "Letter: Let's Honor Snowden as a Hero," *Salt Lake Tribune*, November 16, 2013, available at http://www.sltrib.com/sltrib/opinion/57119133-82/hero-snowden-nsa-accusations.html.csp (accessed January 10, 2014).

⑦ "Edward Snowden, Whistle-Blower," *New York Times*, January 2, 2014.

⑧ Associated Press, "European Parliament Invites Edward Snowden to Testify via Video," *The Guardian*, January 9, 2014, available at http://www.theguardian.com/world/2014/jan/09/edward-snowden-invited-testify-video-european-parliament-nsa-surveillance (accessed February 18, 2014).

德国与法国(可能还有其他国家)的总统与首相的通信受到监控的消息①。巴西总统罗塞夫在联合国大会上坚称,全球互联网治理模式应当进行全面改革②。在美国和澳大利亚大使馆秘密收集北京、雅加达和吉隆坡等地通信情报,以及美国国安局搜集数十亿份印度互联网与电话通信信息(这使得印度在金砖五国中成为国安局的头号监控目标)的行为相继被曝光后,亚洲多个国家政府要求美国对此做出解释③。

有关消息的曝光所引发的讨论已超越权利议题,而直接延伸至对权力结构的反思。巴西的互联网容量占整个拉丁美洲的四分之三,因此它提交一系列提议以降低对美国主导的互联网的依赖,并试图促进本国互联网产业的发展④。这些提议包括:增加国内互联网带宽,建立国际互联网连接并使之多元化,支持国内内容生产的同时发展本国的电子邮件服务,鼓励使用国产网络设备等⑤。本地数据存储条款写进《互联网宪法》(Marco Civil de Internet),并将其递交给巴西众议院⑥,不料此举即刻引发美国互联网中

---

① BBC News Europe, "Snowden Leaks"; Glusing, Poitras, Rosenbach, and Stark, "Fresh Leak."
② Borger, "Brazilian President"; "UN vs. NSA."
③ Associated Press, "Asian Countries Demand Answers over Reports of Spying from Embassies," *The Globe and Mail*, October 31, 2013, available at http://www.ottawastar.com/asian-countries-demand-answers-over-reports-of-spying-from-embassies (accessed January 10, 2014); Glenn Greenwald and Shobhan Saxena, "India among Top Targets of Spying by NSA," *The Hindu*, September 23, 2013, available at http://www.thehindu.com/news/national/india-among-top-targets-of-spying-by-nsa/article5157526.ece (accessed January 10, 2014). Thanks to Manjunath Pendakur for this reference.
④ Tamara Pearson, "Venezuela and Mercosur Discuss Mechanisms to Prevent US Government Spying," Venezuelanalysis.com, September 18, 2013, available at http://ven-ezuelanalysis.com/news/10030 (accessed January 10, 2014); Amar Toor, "Cutting the Cord: Brazil's Bold Plan to Combat the NSA," *The Verge*, September 25, 2013, available at http://www.theverge.com/2013/9/25/4769534/brazil-to-build-internet-cable-to-avoid-us-nsa-spying (accessed January 10, 2014); "Brazil Plans to Go Offline from US-centric Internet," *The Hindu*, September 17, 2013, available at www.thehindu.com/news/international/world/brazil-plans-to-go-offline-from-US-centric-Internet/article5137689.ece (accessed January 10, 2014); Sreeram Chaulia, "Snowden Fallout: India's Meow, Brazil's Roar," *RT*, September 29, 2013, available at http://rt.com/op-edge/india-brazil-china-nsa-fallout-448 (accessed January 10, 2014); Robert Muggah, "After NSA Scandal, Will Brazil Try to Unravel the Internet?" *The Globe and Mail*, September 19, 2013, available at http://www.theglobeandmail.com/globe-debate/after-nsa-scandal-will-brazil-try-to-unravel-the-internet/article14407678 (accessed January 10, 2014); Walker Simon, "South America Studies How to Curb U.S. 'Spying': Ecuador," *Reuters*, September 25, 2013, http://www.reuters.com/article/2013/09/26/us-ecuador-spying-id USBRE98P01P20130926 (accessed January 10, 2014).
⑤ Bill Woodcock, "On Internet, Brazil Is Beating US at Its Own Game," *Al Jazeera America*, September 20, 2013, available at http://america.aljazeera.com/articles/2013/9/20/brazil-internet-dilmarousseffnsa.html (accessed January 10, 2014); "SACS Angola-Brazil Cable Ready Mid-2015; Telebras Onboard, Shelves US Link," *TeleGeography*, Comms Update, November 15, 2013.
⑥ Karis Hustad, "In Light of NSA Spying, Brazil May Take a Step Back from World Wide Web," CSMonitor.com, November 12, 2013, available at http://www.csmonitor.com/Innovation/2013/1112/In-light-of-NSA-spying-Brazil-may-take-a-step-back-from-World-Wide-Web (accessed January 10, 2014).

介商的大举抗议①。德国各大电话与互联网公司所组成的联盟提议,应当在全国层面重组德国电子邮件服务与网站访问系统,由此保证这一特定的网络流量只停留在德国境内,而不会流经美国的互联网交换中心②。出于对美国工业间谍活动的担忧,德国迫不及待地(至少作为暂时性的策略)将数据保护限制条款加入欧盟与美国彼时正在协商起草的《跨大西洋贸易与投资伙伴协定》(Transatlantic Trade and Investment Partnership)中③。德国总理安格拉·默克尔同意建立欧洲数据网络的提议,后者将保护网络通信不受美国间谍机构的监控④。欧盟委员会主张应采取"具体可行的措施,从而解决互联网名称与数字地址分配机构以及互联网号码分配局职能的全球化问题"⑤。

最后,长期反对美国在境外互联网治理上所奉行的"单边全球主义"模式的力量,最终集腋成裘,再次掀起有关互联网号码分配局职能的争斗。一直以来处于分化状态的各方政经势力,在这场针对美国间谍活动的国际怒火中,再次赢得新的"弹药",以至于——诚如穆烈所言——"美国作为中立的互联网管理员的信誉严重受损"⑥。联合国下属机构互联网治理论坛(被整合进美国主导的互联网名称与数字地址分配机构体系)正是在美国监控事件被曝光的阴影下,于十月在巴厘岛举行年会。这场年会共包括135场研讨会与分会场,有来自111个国家或地区的1 500名与会者⑦。美国所秉持的互联网自由的论调早已支离破碎,其道德权威遭遇严重危机。而与会者正思索建立"后斯诺登时代的互联网"的可能性⑧。更有深意的是,专门负责协调互联网技术基础设施的组织聚集在乌拉圭首都蒙得维的亚,共同"提倡应加快互联网名称与数字地址分配机构以及互联网号码分配局职能的全球化进程,进而创造出一个包括政府在内的所有利益相关方都能平等参

---

① Amanda Holpuch,"Brazil's Controversial Plan to Extricate the Internet from US Control,"*The Guardian*,September 20,2013,available at http://www.theguardian.com/world/2013/sep/20/brazil-dilma-rousseff-internet-us-control(accessed January 10,2014). 也请参见 "Canadian Spies Targeted Brazil's Mines and Energy Ministry:Report,"*The Globe and Mail*,October 6, 2013, available at http://www.brazilsun.com/index.php/sid/217563656/scat/24437442923341fl(accessed January 10,2014).

② Michael Birnbaum,"Germany Looks at Keeping its Internet,E-mail Traffic Inside Its Borders,"*Washington Post*,November 1,2013,available at http://www.washingtonpost.com/world/europe/germany-looks-at-keeping-its-internet-e-mail-traffic-inside-its-borders/2013/10/31/981104fe-424f-11e3-a751-f032898f2dbc_story.html?wpisrc=emailtoafriend(accessed January 10,2014).

③ Stefan Wagstyl,Jeevan Vasagar,and James Fontanella-Khan,"German Spy Backlash Threatens EU-US Pact,"*Financial Times*,November 4,2013;Sam Schechner,"Oceans Apart over Privacy,"*Wall Street Journal*,January 9,2014.

④ Alison Smale,"Merkel Backs Plan to Keep European Data in Europe",*New York Times*,February 16,2014.

⑤ European Commission,"Internet Policy and Governance,"5.

⑥ In Geoff Dyer and Richard Waters,"Spying Threatens Internet,Say Experts,"*Financial Times*,November 1,2013.

⑦ Rita A. Widiadana,"Surveillance Takes Center Stage as IGF Ends,"*Jakarta Post*,October 26,2013,available at http://www.thejakartapost.com/news/2013/10/26/surveillance-takes-center-stage-igf-ends.html(accessed January 10,2014).

⑧ Ayee Macaraig,"Distrust and the Post-Snowden Internet,"*Rappler*,October 27,2013,available at http://www.rappler.com/world/regions/asia-pacific/42326-internet-governance-forum-wrap(accessed January 10,2014).

与的环境"①。除了互联网号码分配局,其他所有的专业团体(包括地区性网址分配组织、互联网架构委员会、互联网工作任务组、互联网协会、万维网联盟,尤其是互联网名称与数字地址分配机构)都参与到互联网协作与发展的进程中,并对这一历史性突破表示支持。

同一时间,随着有关美国国安局与英国政府通信总部(Government Communication Headquarters)联合侵入雅虎与谷歌在世界各地的数据中心以窃取和复制海量数据流的新闻见诸报端,互联网中介商开始与美国政府分道扬镳:《纽约时报》登文表示,监听丑闻已然"威胁到(互联网中介商的)商业活动,后者完全仰仗于消费者与公司将数字生活全盘交托给它们的那份信任感"②。诚如某篇新闻头条所发出的疑问:"脸书止步于哪,而国安局起步于哪?"③美国互联网中介商试图重新成为政府侵入行为的强烈反对者。埃里克·施密特借助香港平台表示抗议,而谷歌则向国安局、白宫与国会代表正式发起投诉④。然而,这一公关闪电战是否有效,尚未得知。美国互联网公司代表的跨国资本利益所持续遭受的损害,已威胁到它们的云服务及加诸云服务上的商业应用程序。

这是一个极为不稳定的时刻,变革的方向十分紧要,却仍不明朗,或许我们即将迎来历史转折点。多管齐下并倾向于建立跨国数字资本主义体系的美国互联网政策不仅在国内,更在国外遭遇重重危机:美国被迫重新调整其政策⑤。然而,除了美国,很难说还有谁将或能够扛起主导或改革现有政策的重担。有趣的是,巴西自告奋勇地站出来,对外宣称它将在2014年4月举办一场"互联网治理的未来:全球各利益相关方会议"⑥。这一举动究竟是摆脱美国主导的互联网体系的尝试,还是虚晃一枪?是否有可能出现国家与企业之间的联合,它们的联合又是否能够出台一份完全不同的全球互联网治理政策?这又将美国置于何处?官员、战略家以及独立学者都在思考一个问题:巴西的倡议是否有

---

① ICANN,"Montevideo Statement on the Future of Internet Cooperation," October 7, 2013, available at http://www.icann.org/en/news/announcements/announcement – 07oct13 – en. htm (accessed January 10, 2014). 可参见 https://www.icann.org/news/announcement – 2013 – 10 – 07 – en, https://www.icann.org/news/announcement – 2013 – 10 – 07 – zh
② Claire Cain Miller,"Angry over U. S. Surveillance, Tech Giants Bolster Defenses," *New York Times*, November 1, 2013. 也可参见 http://cn.nytstyle.com/technology/20131104/t04pushback/dual/:译者注。
③ Monika Bauerlein and Clara Jeffery,"Where Does Facebook Stop and the NSA Begin?" *Mother Jones*, October 31, 2013, available at http://www.motherjones.com/media/2013/10/facebook – personal – data – online – privacy – social – norm (accessed January 10, 2014).
④ Rory Carroll,"Google Chairman: NSA Spying on Our Data Centres 'Outrageous'," *The Guardian*, November 4, 2013, available at http://www.theguardian.com/technology/2013/nov/04/eric – schmidt – nsa – spying – data – centres – outrageous (accessed January 10, 2014).
⑤ Ambassador Daniel A. Sepulveda, Deputy Assistant Secretary of State and U. S. Coordinator for International Communications and Information Policy,"Internet Governance 2020: Geopolitics and the Future of the Internet," Center for Strategic and International Studies, Washington, D. C., January 23, 2014, available at http://translations.state.gov/st/english/texttrans/2014/01/20140125291640.html#axzz2tyInxSuz (accessed February 21, 2014).
⑥ http://netmundial.br/zh/about/:译者注。

可能化解矛盾,并帮助重建现状的合法性,或者超越现状①?

在主导性的美国话语体系里,有一个问题依然具有试金石的意义:随着不同国家对互联网施加更多的司法管辖控制,它们是否有可能分化或撕裂彼此协作的互联网;可在当下,其他问题显得更加意义深远、令人讶异。美国公司与国家在境外互联网治理上所拥有的权力最终会被削弱吗?倘若如此,这将导致一场重大变革,其引发的重要后果将直接导向其他问题:美国的单边全球主义的替代物是什么?互联网名称与数字地址分配机构的法团主义"多方利益模式"演变成或转变成一种波及全球的体制,还是建立起互联网治理的多边模式?抑或,随着美国主导的互联网治理及其此前的盟友继续与中国和俄罗斯等心怀不满的利益相关方展开竞争,之前并不稳定的僵局是否将产生新的转机?美国领导层如何回应上述各不相同的改革提议?欧盟、南方共同市场、金砖五国、上海合作组织等其他权力组织将在接下来的倡议行动中扮演什么样的角色?只有当该书付梓出版后,我们才能知晓美国主导的互联网治理模式是否有可能进行变革,以及如何进行变革。结果肯定存在惊喜。然而,核心问题并非埃里克·施密特所说的"分化的互联网的幽灵"②,即互联网的"巴尔干化",而是在重构过程中,谁的政治经济利益占据主导位置,(最主要的是)我们如何以及在多大程度上想象和建立代表与问责等民主原则。

以上具有深远意义的问题仍忽略了某一面向,它使我们再次关注一个并非单打独斗、铁板一块的美国政府。美国国安局的监听丑闻向我们揭示,美国行政部门同美国网络与互联网公司之间的利益远非和谐一致那么简单。美国互联网企业所遭受的威胁,不仅促使它们寻找各种途径,试图与美国政府保持一定的政治距离,而且,它们宣誓"加强"各自系统,公开呼吁更为严格的法律以钳制美国政府间谍计划与后台监控项目③——实

---

① Mueller and Wagner, "Finding a Formula for Brazil"; Ryan Cox, "We Have 18 Months to Find New Governance for a Single Internet, Says ICANN," *Silicon Angle*, January 10, 2014, available at http://siliconangle.com/blog/2014/01/10/icanns-fadi-chehade-says-we-have-18-months-to-find-new-governance-for-a-single-internet-or-else/ (accessed February 21, 2014); Internet Governance Project, "US Cautiously Encourages IANA Reform, Brazil Meeting," January 26, 2014, available at http://www.internetgovernance.org/2014/01/26/us-cautiously-encourages-iana-reform-brazil-meeting/ (accessed February 21, 2014); Richard Hill, "The Future of Internet Governance: Dystopia, Utopia, or Realpolitik?" in *Global Internet Governance in Transition*, ed. Lorenzo Pupillo (Berlin: Springer, forthcoming).

② Amanda Holpuch, "Google's Eric Schmidt Says Government Spying Is 'The Nature of Our Society'," *The Guardian*, September 13, 2013, available at http://www.theguardian.com/world/2013/sep/13/eric-schmidt-google-nsa-surveillance.

③ Matthew J. Schwartz, "NSA Surveillance Fallout Costs IT Industry Billions," *Information Week*, November 27, 2013, available at http://www.informationweek.com/security/security-monitoring/nsa-surveillance-fallout-costs-it-industry-billions/d/d-id/1112838 (accessed February 18, 2014); Jim Sensenbrenner, "The NSA Overreach Poses a Serious Threat to Our Economy," *The Guardian*, November 20, 2013, available at http://www.theguardian.com/commentisfree/2013/nov/20/jim-sensenbrenner-nsa-overreach-hurts-business (accessed February 18, 2014); Richard McGregor and Richard Waters, "Tech Groups Demand Limits on Spy Sweeps," *Financial Times*, December 9, 2013; Claire Cain Miller, "Angry Over U.S. Surveillance, Tech Giants Bolster Defenses," *New York Times*, November 1, 2013.

际上,微软甚至夸下海口,宣称它将允许其系统的海外用户在美国领土外的服务器上存储个人数据[1]。奥巴马总统不顾美国国内舆论对国安局数据搜集政策的反对声,执意支持国安局的监控项目,并宣称"我们的隐私所遭遇的挑战并非仅仅来自政府"[2],意欲转移焦点,推诿责任。在美国互联网资本与美国政府之间的裂缝中,其他拥有权势的国家政要也表示,应当警惕他们长期视为互联网战略脆弱性的那些因素。同样,美国长期奉行的全球互联网治理模式所遭遇的挑战,不仅来自国际,更来自国内。

---

[1] James Fontanella-Khan and Richard Waters, "Microsoft to Shield Foreign Users' Data," *Financial Times*, January 23, 2014.

[2] Spencer Ackerman, "NSA: Six Out of 10 Americans Want Reform of Data Collection, Says Poll," *The Guardian*, January 16, 2014, available at http://www.theguardian.com/world/2014/jan/16/nsa-americans-reform-data-collection (accessed February 18, 2014); Richard Waters, "Obama Drags Tech Companies Deeper into Mire of Surveillance," *Financial Times*, January 21, 2014.

第 14 章
积累与遏制

美国行政部门隐秘且持续的动员,对现有互联网造成鲜为人知的挑战。这些挑战议题与军方和安全部门所遭遇的网络冲突有关。正如数十年前的空军力量,当前我们需要重新评估网络冲突中网络武器的战略必要性。

1990年代以及接下来的十年,网络攻击四处上演,有时产生相当严重的后果[1]。2007年5月,爱沙尼亚银行业与政府网站因遭受可能来自俄罗斯的攻击而被迫关闭。据说,2007年,以色列使用网络武器(或许是一种硬件特洛伊木马)摧毁叙利亚防空体系,进而投掷炸弹破坏其核设施[2]。美国分析家指责中国黑客数次侵入美国军方、企业承包商以及数字服务系统[3],并声称中国黑客早已将"逻辑炸弹"秘密植入美国网络中,以供后续使用[4]。其中一位分析者认为,"来自中国的网络攻击,已导致海量的私营部门专属数据丢失,更不用说敏感的军事信息,例如F-35新式战斗机的工程数据"[5]。美国海、空以及海

---

[1] 迄今为止,最佳评论当属 Jason Healey, ed., A Fierce Domain: Conflict in Cyberspace, 1986 to 2012 (Vienna, Va.: Cyber Conflict Studies Association and Atlantic Council, 2013)。

[2] Julian E. Barnes, "Pentagon Digs In on Cyberwar Front," *Wall Street Journal*, July 6, 2012.

[3] Geoff Dyer and Joseph Menn, "Chinese and Russian Cyberspies Threaten US, Say Intelligence Chiefs", *Financial Times*, November 4, 2011; Joseph Menn and Geoff Dyer, "US Goes Public with Spying Frustrations," *Financial Times*, November 4, 2011.

[4] Siobhan Gorman, "Electricity Grid in U.S. Penetrated by Spies," *Wall Street Journal*, April 8, 2009, available at http://online.wsj.com/news/articles/SB123914805204099085 (accessed January 10, 2014).

[5] Kenneth Lieberthal, "Understanding Strategic Distrust: The U.S. Side," in *Address-ing U.S.-China Strategic Distrust*, by Kenneth Lieberthal and Wang Jisi, 27 (Washington, D.C.: John L. Thornton China Center at Brookings), monograph series 4 (March 2012), 27; for a more extensive tally, see Bryan Krekel, Patton Adams, and George Bakos, "Occupying the Information High Ground: Chinese Capabilities for Computer Network Operations and Cyber-Espionage," prepared for the U.S.-China Economic and Security Review Commission by Northrop Grumman, March 7, 2012; and James Andrew Lewis, Center for Strategic and International Studies, "Significant Cyber Events Since 2006," available at http://csis.org/publication/cyber-events-2006 (accessed January 10, 2014). 也可参见 http://www.brookings.edu/~/media/research/files/papers/2012/3/30-us-china-lieberthal/0330_china_lieberthal_chinese.pdf;译者注。

军陆战队已经订购共计 2 500 架 F-35 战斗机,总额超过 3 000 亿美元①。这笔巨大的开支,以及它所允诺的主导性优势,是否大打折扣?并且,在这一新的战场上,间谍与战争的分界线在哪里?

社会与技术因素使得人们很难核实实际情况。很少有公司或行政部门愿意公开承认它们的网络遭到黑客入侵;同样,军事官员与承包商公司以国家利益为名,很少曝光网络武器,却往往落得本位主义之嫌。并且,高级网络黑客有可能成功抹去其痕迹,所以公司与国家机构或许并未意识到自身的网络早已被入侵,或压根不知道侵入者身份,甚至连国籍也无从得知。无论被侵入的程度如何,这些网络平台成为制造夸张与散布恐慌的近乎完美的场所,尤其在"9·11"事件以后,它们在美国民众心中播下焦虑与困惑的种子。

美国网络冲突政策的发展史上,有不少相对为人所熟知的里程碑式的事件。1991 年海湾战争被某位内部人士包装成信息战的分水岭,尽管这一评论是否为真还有待商榷②。不论实际情况如何,1990 年代正是大规模秘密准备武器,也是武器攻防能力不断提升的年代。美国军方积极研发网络武器技术,为即将到来的信息或网络战训练专有人才。美国网络冲突规划中,"起飞时期"的"标志性事件"(某位权威作者将时间追溯至 1998 年)是当年出台的第 63 号总统决议令。随后在这位作者称之为"军事化"③的时期内,一系列组织变革相继发生:"军事化"时期起始于 2003 年,"标志性事件"则是尚未公开的文件《建设安全网络空间的国家战略》(National Strategy for a Secure Cyber-space)。2002 年 7 月,《第 16 号国家安全总统令》要求政府制定标准,以决定何时以及如何展开针对敌方网络的网络攻击。2003 年《国防部信息作战路线图》(DOD Information Operations Roadmap)建议,美国应当签署一份关于展开进攻的政策声明。2006 年《网络空间行动的国家军事战略》则公开宣称"网络空间作为网络战争的领域……必须采取攻势"④。国家不断扩展,重组进攻任务并对此加以改善,可重要的是,国安局在"互联网武器化"的进程中扮演导航者的角色⑤。同样,随着新的想法出现,技术不断变革,"某一政府对另一国家的电脑

---

① Richard A. Clarke and Robert K. Knake, *Cyber War: The Next Threat to National Security and What to Do About It* (New York: HarperCollins, 2010), 233.
② Clarke and Knake, *Cyber War*.
③ Healey, *Fierce Domain*, 41, 77.
④ National Security Presidential Directives, Department of Defense Roadmap and quote in William A. Owens, Kenneth W. Dam, and Herbert S. Lin, eds., Committee on Offensive Information Warfare, National Research Council, *Technologies, Policy, Law, and Ethics Regarding U.S. Acquisition and Use of Cyberattack Capabilities* (Washington, D.C.: National Academies Press, 2009), 10, 216.
⑤ Healey, *Fierce Domain*, 45, 65, 113; Nicholas Weaver, "Our Government Has Weaponized the Internet: Here's How They Did It," Wired.com, November 13, 2013, available at http://www.wired.com/opinion/2013/11/this-is-how-the-internet-backbone-has-been-turned-into-a-weapon (accessed February 4, 2014).

或网络的未经批准的入侵,或其他任何影响电脑系统的非法行动,其目的在于增加、改变或伪造数据,或引发电脑崩溃或破坏电脑系统、网络设备以及电脑系统控制的对象",在此情形下,重塑网络威慑,旨在为网络冲突的各种工具提供发展空间①。

2008年1月,布什总统发布一份尚未完全解密的《第54号国家安全总统令》/《第23号国土安全总统令》,该文件还有另一个名称《国家网际安全综合倡议》(Comprehensive National Cybersecurity Initiative)。为此,国会拨款170亿美元,用于资助这份倡议的5年预算②。2009年,奥巴马政府公布一份《网络安全评估报告》(Cyberspace Policy Review):这份报告发出警告,"国家正处于十字路口",并号召"全国就网络安全展开对话"③。国家研究委员会(The National Research Council)已在2006年召集成立进攻信息战专家委员会,并于2009年发布报告。该委员会认为,"在网络空间中,持续的单边主导地位不现实,美国也很难完全实现"④。只是这份报告不仅遭遇雪藏,并很快被其他事件所湮没。

一项颇有助益的发现指出,"保密状态严重阻碍了人们对美国网络进攻的实质与内涵的广泛理解和争论";专家委员会的建议与《网络安全评估报告》不谋而合,依然可圈可点,即美国政府应当"就网络进攻政策展开一场广泛的、无需遮遮掩掩的全国性争论或讨论"⑤。然而,尽管出现一系列军事与情报分析、报纸报道、智库研究甚至开展国会听证会,可美国仍未就某些根本性问题(它们正是民主问责的绝对性前提)发起讨论——政府除了决定着手处理那些有可能构成或导向战争的冲突外,基本上对其他重要议题不闻不问。

一方面,美国军方对网络的依赖与日俱增;另一方面,一个急速增长、以盈利为目的的机构复合体正开发、管理并协调网络连接激活的武器装备。

正如网络已侵入金融、生产与通信领域一般,网络也很早成为现代化战争机器的内在组成部分。这已非向艾布兰坦克(Abrams tanks)或布莱德雷战车(Bradley fighting vehicles)配备数字瞄准器或通信功能这么简单⑥。网络早已全面扩散至发动战争的各项功能中。2010年,美国国防部副部长威廉·林恩将军(William Lynn)如是总结军方采用网络连接性的程度:"信息技术能够让美国军方无所不能——物流支撑、对军队的全球指挥与

---

① Clarke and Knake, *Cyber War*, 228.
② Owens, Dam, and Lin, *Technologies, Policy, Law, and Ethics Regarding U. S. Acquisition and Use of Cyberattack Capabilities*, viii, 25; David E. Sanger, John Markoff, and Thom Shanker, "U. S. Steps Up Effort on Digital Defenses," New York Times, April 28, 2009, available at http://www.nytimes.com/2009/04/28/us/28cyber.html?pagewanted=all&_r=0 (accessed January 10, 2014).
③ The White House, "Cyberspace Policy Review: Assuring a Trusted and Resilient Information and Communications Infrastructure," iii, i, available at http://www.whitehouse.gov/assets/documents/Cyberspace_Policy_Review_final.pdf (accessed January 10, 2014).
④ Owens, Dam, and Lin, *Technologies*, 5.
⑤ Owens, Dam, and Lin, *Technologies*, 28, 58-59.
⑥ Christopher Drew, "Military Is Said to Make Progress in Modernizing," *New York Times*, October 28, 2011.

掌控、情报的实时提供以及远程操作。每一项功能都高度依赖于军方的全球主干通信网络，该网络涵盖了横跨数十个国家、上百个安置中心的，15 000张网络、700万台电脑设备。共有9万名全职工作人员维护该主干通信的正常运行"①。截至2013年，国防部从多家供应商所购得并运行的移动设备共计60万余台②。国防部的信息技术预算（2011年高达360亿美元）占联邦政府在信息技术上的总开销（800亿美元）的将近一半——这还没有计算情报部门所产生的花销③。新资金的"注入"用于满足国家的紧要需求，旨在"保护"国家当前不可或缺的网络基础设施：例如此前所提及的盐湖城附近的数据中心——该中心由国安局的陆军工程兵团（Army Corps of Engineers）花费12亿美元建造，以平衡国安局在马里兰州米德堡市设立的基地所展开的全球间谍行动所产生的数据负载④。

为了供应所需武器装备，军备竞赛又开辟新的战线。诺斯洛普·格鲁门（Northrop Grumman）、通用动力（General Dynamics）、洛克希德·马丁（Lockheed Martin）、波音（Boeing）和雷神（Raytheon）等美国最大的军事承包商，相继与美国军方或情报部门签订重要的"网络合同"。2011年，诺斯洛普·格鲁门将"网络"视为其四大增长型市场之一，它预估联邦政府在网络攻防上所花费的总金额高达将100亿美元，而且该数字将有增无减⑤。相关法律出台明显倾向于公司供应商，在2011年的一项法案中称后者为"网络安全供应商"⑥。网络安全联盟（the Internet Security Alliance）以贸易协会的身份，与军事承包商建立机构联系⑦——后者反过来"斥巨资"建立《金融时报》所说的"网络——工业复合体"。该领域开始出现大规模并购行为，大华盛顿地区所有受雇的信息技术员工共计28万——远超硅谷或纽约⑧。奥巴马总统深入贯彻前任总统所草拟的规划，创建网络司令部（Cyber Command），总部设在米德堡国安局大楼附近。在司令部周围，数百家公司如雨后春笋纷纷涌现。包括英法两国在内的其他数十个国家，继美国脚步，相继建造自己的

---

① William J. Lynn III, "Defending a New Domain," *Foreign Affairs* 89, no. 5 (September – October 2010), 98.
② John Ribeiro, "US Defense Department Approves Apple's iOS Devices for Its Networks," *IDG News Service*, April 19, 2013, available at http://www.pcworld.idg.com.au/article/462295/us_defense_department_approves_apple_ios_devices_its_networks (accessed January 10, 2014).
③ Booz Allen Hamilton, "RightIT: A Proven Approach to Achieve Cost – Effective IT Capabilities", available at http://www.boozallen.com/media/file/RightIT_Factsheet.pdf (accessed January 10, 2014).
④ Pam Benson, "Utah Will Be Site of Huge Cyber Protection Facility," *CNN*, January 12, 2011, available at http://www.cnn.com/2011/POLITICS/01/12/cyber.defense.center (accessed January 10, 2014); James Bamford, "The Black Box," *Wired*, April 2012, 78 – 85 + .
⑤ Christopher Drew and John Markoff, "Contractors Vie for Plum Work, Hacking for U.S"., *New York Times*, May 31, 2009, available at http://www.nytimes.com/2009/05/31/us/31cyber.html?pagewanted = all (accessed January 10, 2014); Joseph Menn, "Defence Trains Sights on Threat to Internet," *Financial Times*, October 11, 2011.
⑥ U.S. House of Representatives, 112th Cong., 1st Sess., "Cyber Intelligence Sharing and Protection Act of 2011," H. R. 3523, November 30, 2011.
⑦ Dan Schiller, *How To Think about Information* (Urbana: University of Illinois Press, 2007), 53 – 54.
⑧ Menn, "Defence."

网络司令部①。

　　网络攻势被整合进美国军事战略这一情况并非即刻成为公共事件:网络空间的军事化议题早已逃脱日渐式微的公共讨论的审查。《纽约时报》使用一则颇有艺术气息的标题《叫停的 2003 伊拉克战争计划表明美国对网络战争风险的恐惧》。该标题暗示,出于对人类福祉的牵挂,美国最终决定在进攻伊拉克之前暂时不发动针对伊拉克金融体系的网络进攻。实际上,《纽约时报》在报道中揭露,美国做此决定,主要出于"附带伤害"的考量,即(如果发动网络进攻)有可能引发"世界范围内的金融浩劫,从中东蔓延至欧洲甚至美国"②。当然,我们现在清楚了,美国无需网络战争来摧毁自己的金融体系。然而,2011 年 10 月,《纽约时报》撰文透露,奥巴马政府曾"数次讨论"是否应当在 3 月启动针对利比亚的军事进攻,例如"发动网络攻击破坏卡扎菲政府的防空系统甚至使之瘫痪"。这项计划再次被搁浅,不过被搁浅的理由不再是为了人类福祉,而是对行动的不确定性的担忧:根据《纽约时报》的披露,部分军方人员极力反对这次进攻行动,他们"质疑在如此仓促的情况下能否发动进攻"③。然而,《华盛顿邮报》根据斯诺登所提供的一份被封存的情报预算表,认为 2011 年美国虽然放弃网络进攻利比亚的计划,可同年,间谍机构早已发动不少于 231 次的网络进攻④。

　　美国马丁·登普西将军(Martin Dempsey)在其专著中表明,"摧毁敌人需要将空间与网络空间作战完全纳入传统的海陆空战场里……它们对军事力量的规划具有关键性意义"⑤。一位北约高级官员指出,"很明显,未来所有的冲突或战争都将与摧毁信息技术系统有关,因为通信系统,以及高精尖武器系统的操作都有赖于信息技术"⑥。在提出"广泛

---

① Menn", Defence."同样,军方的网络战争训练计划迅速扩张;单就海军部队的信息主导中心一家机构,每年就训练 2.5 万名学员。Julian E. Barnes, "Pentagon Digs In on Cyberwar Front," *Wall Street Journal*, July 6, 2012.

② John Markoff and Thom Shanker, "Halted '03 Iraq Plan Illustrates U. S. Fear of Cyberwar Risk," *New York Times*, August 1, 2009, available at http://www.nytimes.com/2009/08/02/us/politics/02cyber.html?_r=0 (accessed January 10, 2014). 早先发生的事例也已曝光。1990 年代末,相关新闻报道披露,美国对塞尔维亚通信网络的攻击,无意间中断了国际通信卫星组织的通信活动。

③ Eric Schmitt and Thom Shanker, "U. S. Weighed Use of Cyberattacks to Weaken Libya," *New York Times*, October 18, 2012.

④ Barton Gellman and Ellen Nakashima, "The Black Budget: U. S. Spy Agencies Mounted 231 Offensive Cyber – Operations in 2011, Documents Show," *Washington Post*, August 30, 2013, available at http://www.washingtonpost.com/world/national – security/ us – spy – agencies – mounted – 231 – offensive – cyber – operations – in – 2011 – documents – show/2013/08/30/d090a6ae – 119e – 11e3 – b4cb – fd7ce041d814_story.html (accessed January 10, 2014).

⑤ In Nick Hopkins, "Militarisation of Cyberspace: How the Global Power Struggle Moved Online," *The Guardian*, April 16, 2012, available at http://www.theguardian.com/technology/2012/apr/16/militarisation – of – cyberspace – power – struggle (accessed January 10, 2014); also, Nicholas Weaver, "Our Government Has Weaponized the Internet. Here's How They Did It," *Wired*, November 13, 2013, available at http://www.wired.com/opinion/2013/11/this – is – how – the – internet – backbone – has – been – turned – into – a – weapon (accessed January 10, 2014).

⑥ Jamie Shea, in Carola Hoyos, "Fresh Enemy Emerges in the Battle against Cyberattacks," *Financial Times*, March 12, 2012.

的全国性讨论"建议的三年后,《金融时报》一篇社论仅仅号召英美两国政府"应当在各自所具有的网络实力问题上,更加开诚布公"①。

(美国)虽然做了某些关键性决策,却缺少任何实际的问责。最突出的一点在于,坊间数月间都在猜测究竟是谁开发出代号为"震网"(Stuxnet)的军用级别的计算机病毒,以及2010年它是如何出现在开放互联网平台上的。随后,美国与以色列被坐实为该病毒的开发者。从小布什时代一直到奥巴马政府,两国的军事情报服务部门并肩携手,在成功破坏伊朗设在纳坦兹的核设施的过程中,开发出原始代号为"奥运会"的病毒。大卫·桑格(David E. Sanger)在《纽约时报》的头版撰文指出,"奥巴马从其上任的首月起,就已经秘密下令,针对运行伊朗主要核浓缩设备的计算机系统,实施精准攻击"②。"奥运会"病毒的使用,已成为"美国史上最令人震撼的新武器现场试验"③,它标志着美国这个世界上最依赖网络的国家已下定决心主导网络新式战场——正如二战时它在广岛和长崎投下原子弹那般。奥巴马政府并未终止对网络武器的使用,因为网络武器还需要被用于对付伊朗以及其他国家④。有报道声称,代号为"火焰"(Flame)的另一病毒已经研制出来,旨在破坏伊朗高级官员所使用的电脑⑤。如此前所提,美国也针对中国、俄罗斯以及朝鲜发起了一系列网络攻击⑥。

由于我们所得到的资料较少,时间相对滞后,且经过大幅度修改,因此很难完全掌握总统做出"秘密带领美国进入网络战争新时代"⑦决策的整个过程。大卫·桑格暗示,以色列的施压,是使用"奥运会"病毒精准打击伊朗的因素之一⑧。无论实际情况如何,其他潜在的因素使网络攻击成为一项更加普遍的选择。第一个因素是,网络武器的魅力部分源自于如下事实,即它们似乎能降低战争的成本。针对纳坦兹所展开的网络攻击虽然比向大众所说的要更为昂贵、复杂以及耗时,可它无需派驻"地面部队"就能发动"有力"进攻,更避免因派驻"地面部队"而不得不动用昂贵的后勤与再补给力量(在美对阿富汗战

---

① "Telling the Truth about Cyberwarfare," editorial, *Financial Times*, June 27, 2012.
② David E. Sanger, "Obama Order Set Off Wave of Cyberattacks against Iran," *New York Times*, June 1, 2012; David E. Sanger, *Confront and Conceal: Obama's Secret Wars and Surprising Use of American Power* (New York: Crown, 2012), 203-5.
③ Sanger, *Confront and Conceal*, 190.
④ Sanger stated in his news story that "parts" of this effort "continue to this day," adding in his book that "there is no reason to believe that America's cyber wars have ceased." Sanger, "Obama Order"; and Sanger, *Confront and Conceal*, 207, 188-225.
⑤ "Telling the Truth."
⑥ Barton Gellman and Ellen Nakashima, "U. S. Spy Agencies Mounted 231 Offensive Cyber-Operations in 2011, Documents Show," *Washington Post*, August 30, 2013, available at http://www.washingtonpost.com/world/national-security/us-spy-agencies-mounted-231-offensive-cyber-operations-in-2011-documents-show/2013/08/30/d090a6ae-119e-11e3-b4cb-fd7ce041d814_story.html (accessed January 10, 2014); Healey, *Fierce Domain*, 64-87.
⑦ Sanger, *Confront and Conceal*, xvi.
⑧ Sanger, *Confront and Conceal*.

争中,每周大约花费20亿美元)这一情形的发生。因此,在当前数字化衰退所导向的"紧缩时代"下(甚至连美军的开支都遭到缩减①),网络战争是最适合的作战方式。

第二个因素是,网络武器与无人机使公民甚至他们的立法代表介入战争的程度降至最低。大卫·桑格指出,这些新式武器"极大地扩展了"总统发动"秘密战争的能力",并使"每天实施不间断、低烈度战争(甚至算不上战争)"成为可能②。美国的网络战士或许希望,有朝一日在不造成本国伤亡(而丝毫不顾对其他国家所造成的"附带伤害")的前提下,能够使用这些新型武器。毕竟,这样才可能不会引发国内的强烈抗议——这才是永久战争年代下的永久考量。

第三个因素具有决定性,因为它是前两个因素的基础:美国所拥有的全球军事主导权依然是高于一切(实际上也是无可动摇)的官方承诺。二战结束以来,美国的战略使命在于,代表跨国资本长远(以及经常是即时的)利益而在全球积极排兵布阵。如今,这一使命里已包括网络进攻这项内容。对于美国领导者而言,任何敌手要主导该战场都是不可容忍的:这并非源于美国的夜郎自大,而是与美国在充当世界警察的过程中,长期致力于利用"攻击性防守的特权"③密不可分的。

然而,让我们回到攻击性网络武器委员会(the Committee on Offensive Cyber Weapons)的调查,一切"易说难做"。在《奇爱博士》所描绘的世界里,美国军事决策往往倾向于将一次主动有效的进攻(尽管造成棘手的问题)视为高级目标。网络进攻有可能战略性地利用位于第三世界国家(或地区)的计算机资源,借助网络的互操作性形成境外互联网络。这一事实不仅可能使非交战国卷入战争中,还在应对任何一个国家(或地区)可能发起的网络进攻过程中,向一触即发的局势增加关键的不确定性因素。根据理查德·克拉克(Richard A. Clarke)的观察,针对美国的网络进攻,"极有可能发端于美国本土,所以我们很难预测,并加以阻止":来自美国和其他国家(或地区)的网络战争,渗透于民用网络,将"逻辑炸弹"植入电力系统,"向基础设施种下破坏性的种子"④。

因此,美国防御网络进攻的需求引发了一系列深远的衍生效应。分析家认为,只有解决了防御性安全这一根本问题,才能确保使用进攻型网络武器的战略意义⑤:尽管如此——诚如我们所见——哪怕没有解决防御性安全的问题,也丝毫不能阻止美国使用进

---

① Sanger, *Confront and Conceal*, 420, 243, 355. Largely implicit, this theme imparts a somewhat melancholy tone to portions of Henry Kissinger, *On China* (New York: Penguin, 2011).
② Sanger, *Confront and Conceal*, 244 – 45.
③ A. T. Mahan, *The Influence of Sea Power Upon History*, 1660 – 1783 (London, 1890), 87, 转引自 Perry Anderson, "American Foreign Policy and its Thinkers", *New Left Review*, 84 (September/October, 2013): 9.
④ Clarke and Knake, *Cyber War*, 260, 259; 也请参见 Weaver, "Our Government."
⑤ White House, "Cyberspace Policy Review"; Clarke and Knake, *Cyber War*; Joseph Menn, "Power Grid Looks Exposed to Assault," *Financial Times*, October 12, 2011.

攻型网络武器。一定程度上,这是因为美国的网络进攻促使其他国家加紧开发自身的网络武器①。更紧要的是,网络武器领域存在根本性的信息不对称:作为数字资本主义的始作俑者,美国在传统军事与核武器上所拥有的绝对优势,反而使它疲于应付各种网络进攻。

即便美国因其对网络的高度依赖而从网络空间去军事化的协定中获益匪浅,美国也绝不会选择网络空间的去军事化这一方案。美国向来回避从政治层面解决问题,而倾向于进行技术和组织层面的小修小补。克林顿政府一方面不断加强网络连接性的应用程序的开发,另一方面,它启动反军事化项目,用以取代此前长期存在的联邦政府"保卫核心基础设施"升级计划——该计划主要涵盖深植于通信、能源、交通与金融商品链中的网络。克林顿之后的几届政府将这一升级计划持续到底。大卫·桑格指出,"每当提及网络,奥巴马及其智囊团总是将话题引到网络防御上:譬如,如何强化并保护美国的电力系统、银行系统以及其他关键性的基础设施"②。因此,美国政府深化并拓展数字资本主义的各种举动,本身已表明其所奉行的长期战略的"不安全"状态。

因为美国长期致力于拓展资本的自由度,进而开发并应用了网络连接性程序;因为大部分互联网系统与服务用于支持每一种商品链,并深植于当前的政治经济结构(包括军事核心机构)之中;因为各种网络组建而成的一整套网络系统,延伸至境外;因为——诚如奥巴马政府出台的《网络安全评估报告》所强调——"数字基础设施建设考虑更多的不是安全性,而是互操作性与效率问题"③;还有,因为上述所有因素都发生在一个被霸权关系与根深蒂固的不平等所彻底分裂的世界里,所以,美国政府要保卫社会不受网络行动的破坏,无异于天方夜谭。《网络安全评估报告》表明,"越来越多的国家或地区……危害、窃取、篡改或毁坏信息,并逐渐摧毁美国互联网体系"④。一系列政府报告与新闻报道提供了应对方案,可核心(也是紧要)问题在于,随着美国使用网络武器,联邦政府反而需要投入更多,才能保卫本国的网络体系⑤。

---

① Misha Glenny,"We Will Rue the Cavalier Deployment of Stuxnet,"*Financial Times*,June 7,2012.
② Sanger,*Confront and Conceal*,247.
③ White House,"Cyberspace Policy Review",iii. 也可参见 http://www.cetin.net.cn/cetin2/servlet/cetin/action/HtmlDocumentAction? baseid = 1&docno = 392024:译者注。
④ White House,"Cyberspace Policy Review,"iii.
⑤ U. S. Government Accountability Office (GAO),"Internet Infrastructure:Challenges in Developing a Public/Private Recovery Plan,"September 13,2006,available at www. gao. gov/cgi – bin/getrpt? GAO – 06 – 1100T (accessed January 10,2014);U. S. GAO,"Coordination of Federal Cyber Security Research and Development,"September 2006,GAO – 06 – 811;U. S. GAO,"DHS Leadership Needed to Enhance Cybersecurity,"September 13,2006,GAO 06 – 1087T;U. S. GAO,"CyberSecurity:Continued Attention Needed to Protect Our Nation's Critical Infrastructure."GAO 11 – 865T,July 26,2011;Menn,"Power Grid";Executive Order 13636,"Improving Critical Infrastructure Cyber – Security,"*Federal Register*,February 19,2013,available at https://www. federalregister. gov/ articles/2013/02/19/2013 – 03915/improving – critical – infrastructure – cybersecurity (accessed January 10,2014).

美国政府依然围绕"关键性的基础设施"①大做文章。与此同时,随着美国政治经济结构越来越依赖于网络,以及人们清楚地意识到互联网的薄弱性折射的正是它的内部设计(这并未包括其他公共网络所使用的安全措施),美国政府也积极寻求建立一个覆盖面更广的保护罩②。出于扩大防御范围的需要,互联网政策任务组在2010至2012年对已经被确定为关键性的基础设施的相关领域,即所谓的"互联网与信息创新部门",进行安全审查③。防御范围的扩大工程,并非局限于此。国防部开始同国土安全部协调网络防御事宜④。同样,美国的网络安全战略框架开始向国外延伸。美国与加拿大、澳大利亚以及英国等相关部门紧密合作,并向北约组织提交一份网络防御议程⑤。2012年年初,北约28个成员国签署一份网络防御协议,旨在"保护其分布于50个地点的网络"⑥。2012年,所有北约的网络,无论民用还是军事,统一被整合进北约的网络事件回应中心(Cyber Incident Response Center)。当然,美国新成立的网络司令部也开始关注日本、韩国以及新西兰⑦——这是北约之外的另一个世界。2014年,斯诺登事件对上述组织和协议将产生何种影响,一切尚不可知。

一场围绕网络是如何被整合进(当前的)政治经济结构而展开的"广泛的全国性讨论"依然存在,尚未停歇。然而,在2012年总统大选期间,我们看不到关于这场讨论的任何痕迹。相反,经过刻意修饰的宣传以及无处不在的媒体,营造了一种替代性的氛围,即仅仅围绕"如何"而非"为何"大做文章。在许多有意义的细节上,民主党不同意共和党:例如,是否应当赋予互联网服务供应商第一梯队而不是政府机构以执行深度审查的权力,军事部门与企业之间的信息共享是否享受到充分的保护措施。尽管分歧不断,但宣传话语基本表达了两党试图保护基于网络连接的跨国资本主义(利益)的愿望。在此情境下,关于美国互联网的脆弱性的宣称,反而成为互联网将进行彻底变革(wrenching changes)的托辞。长期担任白宫国家安全助手的理查德·克拉克正是从这些角度理解该

---

① "Senators Spar with Power Industry:Is It Safe from Cyber – Attack?"CSMonitor. com,July 17,2012,available at http://www. csmonitor. com/USA/2012/0717/Senators – spar – with – power – industry – Is – it – safe – from – cyberattack (accessed January 10,2014).
② David Talbot,"The Internet Is Broken," *MIT Technology Review*,February 15,2006,available at http://www. technology-review. com/news/405318/the – internet – is – broken (accessed January 10,2014).
③ U. S. Department of Commerce,docket no. 110527305 – 1303 – 02,"Cybersecurity,Innovation,and the Internet Economy," *Federal Register* 76,no. 115(Wednesday,June 15,2011):34965 – 67,available at http://www. ntia. doc. gov/federal – register – notice/2011/cybersecurity – innovation – and – internet – economy (accessed January 10,2014).
④ Cheryl Pellerin,"DOD,Partners Better Prepared for Cyber Attacks," *American Forces Press Service*,October 18,2011,available at http://www. defense. gov/News/NewsArticle. aspx? ID = 65709 (accessed January 10,2014).
⑤ Cheryl Pellerin,"White House Launches U. S. International Cyber Strategy," *American Forces Press Service*,May 17,2011,available at http://www. defense. gov/news/newsarticle . aspx? id = 63966 (accessed January 10,2014).
⑥ Carola Hoyos,"Fresh Enemy Emerges in the Battle against Cyberattacks," *Financial Times*,March 12,2012.
⑦ Cheryl Pellerin,"DOD Expands International Cyber Cooperation,Official Says," *American Forces Press Service*,April 10,2012,available at http://www. defense. gov/News/NewsArticle. aspx? ID = 67889 (accessed January 10,2014).

议题的：例如他对国内网络基础设施的建设是否能够保障美国"借助我们新型的网络战士发起进攻、赢得网络空间的主导优势"，存在疑虑①。克拉克主张应采取国际军备控制措施，以限制网络战争对平民的（不利）影响。但是，他坚决认为，任何协定应当"允许美国继续在其擅长的领域内发挥作用，例如第一时间对军事目标发动网络战争"②。毫无疑问，美国依然在利用其所拥有的"攻击性防守的特权"③。

美国遭受网络攻击的可能性极大。并且，从目标方来看，网络冲突的未来十分可怕。随着网络基础设施渗透进政治与社会生活中，整个社会变得更加脆弱。银行、学校、红绿灯、超市、医院甚至家庭：每一个依赖网络的组织的运作及其性能，都相继受到影响，甚至有可能遭遇灭顶之灾。诚如奥汀格（Oettinger）④早在1980年代就已构想的那般，要对战争保持心明眼亮的分析态度，就必须将"平民与军方之间的界限逐渐淡化"这一命题视为公理。然而，他却不会承认，网络武器意味着平民和日常生活的毁灭⑤。某位权威人士指出，尽管"没有人会在"网络冲突中"丧生"，"可网络战争依然有可能残民害物"，因为国家"将更多实体性的基础设施网络化，例如智能电网"⑥。

要确保更高级别的网络安全，可以遵循两种途径。一种方案是，通过技术、法律与组织的途径，重新调整对网络的依赖程度——当然，这必须以数字资本主义已经发展到无法叫停的程度为前提条件。克拉克钟情于这一方案，他直言不讳地表示，"目前，要降低我们对网络系统的依赖，近乎蹇人升天"⑦。另一种方案则是，发起一项全球性运动，从而达成一项禁止使用网络武器的综合性协议。不得不承认，该方案要取得成功，必须彻底扭转影响深远的美国政策，从而调整有可能招致他国进攻的主导性关系。对美国而言，第一步措施应当是，从全球数百家国外军事基地中撤军，并废除"军事结构"协定。然而，在大多数美国政策制定者看来，这种方案无异于缘木求鱼。

建立在信息全面共享基础上的多边对话，是着手处理网络空间境外管辖权的安全性问题的先决条件⑧。数字化衰退所导致的不断恶化的政治经济关系，反而有可能浇灭（多边对话的）微弱希望。美国国内，不断恶化的政经关系，加上庞大的军事工业以及无处不在的政治献金腐败现象，同样不利于官方所提倡的"广泛的全国性讨论"。那么，是什么

---

① Clarke and Knake, *Cyber War*, 178.
② Clarke and Knake, *Cyber War*, 243.
③ Mahan, "American Foreign Policy", 9.
④ Anthony G. Oettinger, "Information Resources: Knowledge and Power in the 21st Century," *Science*, July 4, 1980: 197.
⑤ Clarke and Knake, Cyber War, xi, xiii.
⑥ Healey, *Fierce Domain*, 85, 21.
⑦ Clarke and Knake, *Cyber War*, 149.
⑧ Richard Hill, *The New International Telecommunication Regulations and the Internet: A Commentary and Legislative History* (Zurich: Schulthess, 2013).

取代了民主问责与决策过程?

奥巴马政府上下齐心,试图在体制和技术的层面重新调整互联网职能。这些举措往往在秘密且技术不透明的情况下得以实施,并与惯常做法保持一致,十分符合马特拉对当前发展轨迹的总结:"世界体系网络的领导者,对不平等现象采取一种暴力性的管理办法,而非对当前存在再生产不平等现象的世界体系公开宣战,抑或重建早已千疮百孔的团结机制"[1]。美国联邦政府"保卫"国家网络的倡议,充斥着令人生畏的内容。

我们很容易提出问题,却难以把握其产生的复杂的衍生效应:实际上很难保护军事网络与企业商品链不受到任何攻击,毕竟,这些系统与现有的互联网相互连接、相互运作。这一威胁看起来将产生十分深远的影响,以至于前白宫安全顾问克拉克于2010年对外宣称,"考虑到我们防御网络战争的漏洞的不对等,倘若不存在网络战争,美国可以发展得更好"[2]。然而,那些弥补网络漏洞的举措,需要付出不菲代价。对此,实际上,民主党无法接受。强化"网络安全"的政策,必将孕育出镇压式的威权。

早在"9·11"事件之前,政府采取先发制人的举措,所依据的理由往往是黑客与国家资助的网络进攻的存在。此前,我已经提及保卫网络基础设施的各种项目。大概从1998年3月开始,似乎由俄罗斯发起了针对五角大楼、美国国家航空航天局,以及私立大学和研究实验室的数百台电脑的持续攻击。这促使美国国防部下令,即便是无需保密的通信,也应当"通过八台大型电子网关,以方便监控"。十年后,美国政府出台《可信网络通信指令》(Trusted Internet Communication Directive),该指令要求整个联邦政府的通信都应当经由特定通道[3]。"9·11"事件发生后,类似规定层出不穷。《爱国者法案》以及一系列附加措施所营造的,似乎是一种永久性的"例外状态"。借此,政府僭称拥有一切采取行动对抗任何威胁(无论是真实的还是想象的)的权利。聊举发生在斯诺登事件前一年的案例:2011年,手机运营商向外透露,美国执法机关曾向他们提出130万次要求(大多数都是要求获取多位用户信息),申请获取用户信息。《纽约时报》称该数字"令人震惊"[4],以此证明这是一次"手机监控大爆炸"事件:手机运营商每天向执法机关提供数千次的用户信息或记录。斯诺登事件的爆发使我们了解到,这些行为仅仅是冰山一角:攻

---

[1] Herbert I. Schiller, *Information and the Crisis Economy* (Norwood, N. J.: Ablex, 1984), 15 – 26; Armand Mattelart, *The Globalization of Surveillance* (Cambridge: Polity, 2010), 3.
[2] Clarke and Knake, *Cyber War*, 226.
[3] Healey, *Fierce Domain*, 49 – 50.
[4] Eric Lichtblau, "Cell Carriers Called On More in Surveillance," *New York Times*, July 9, 2012.

防兼备的国安局侵入数亿户①电子邮件、电话、短信、聊天讯息、博客以及其他的电子通信平台。其侵入的通信平台不仅涵盖国内,更涉及国外②。

当维系美国军方采购的商品链实现跨国化以后,建立全面覆盖的监控机制具有了合理性(实际上,刻不容缓)。2008 年,小布什总统签署《第 54 号总统决议令》:这是一份保卫美国不受网络战争侵扰的秘密纲领,其中一项与"供应链安全"有关③。五角大楼的"委托铸造"(Trusted Foundry)项目里,美国公司制造的电脑芯片,仅仅占军方年度采购集成电路总开销 35 亿美元的 2%。由于全球外包生产的电脑硬件相比美国本土制造的电脑硬件更容易遭到篡改,前者很有可能成为特洛伊木马④。奥巴马将这份纲领继续发扬光大,但意识到,它已经引发更为普遍的问题:"商业信息与通信技术市场的全球化,反而向那些试图通过渗透供应链而非法访问、篡改数据或终止通信等方式有意伤害美国的人,大开方便之门。必须针对产品、系统与服务的整个生命周期,以战略性与综合性的眼光,管理国内外供应链可能引发的各种风险"⑤。当然,美国公司面对此类风险,可以假借爱国之名,排挤外国竞争者,以换取美国政府订单。然而,威胁管理也包含其他维度。

2010 年 3 月,白宫签署了一份有关网络安全的决议,该决议大部分内容源于小布什政府所启动的秘密项目⑥。"防火墙"以及能检测到任何试图进入数据包的行为的"入侵

---

① "NSA Inspector General Report on Email and Internet Data Collection under Stellar Wind—Full Document," *The Guardian*, June 27, 2013, available at http://www.guardian.co.uk/world/interactive/2013/jun/27/nsa-inspector-general-report-document-data-collection (accessed January 10, 2014); Glenn Greenwald and Spencer Ackerman, "NSA Collected Americans' Email Records in Bulk for Two Years under Obama," *The Guardian*, June 27, 2013, available at http://www.guardian.co.uk/world/2013/jun/27/nsa-data-mining-authorised-obama (accessed January 10, 2014); "The NSA Files," *The Guardian*, available at http://www.guardian.co.uk/world/the-nsa-files (accessed January 10, 2014); Ian Traynor and Dan Roberts, "Barack Obama Seeks to Limit EU Fallout over US Spying Claims," *The Guardian*, July 1, 2013, available at http://www.theguardian.com/world/2013/jul/01/barack-obama-eu-fallout-us-spying-claims (accessed January 10, 2014).
② Craig Timberg and Ellen Nakashima, "Agreements with Private Companies Protect U.S. Access to Cables' Data for Surveillance," *Washington Post*, July 7, 2013, http://www.washingtonpost.com/business/technology/agreements-with-private-companies-protect-us-access-to-cables-data-for-surveillance/2013/07/06/aa5d017a-df77-11e2-b2d4-ea6d8f477a01_story.html (accessed January 10, 2014); Tom Engelhardt, "How to Be a Rogue Super-Power," TomDispatch.com, July 16, 2013, available at http://www.tomdispatch.com/blog/175725/tomgram%3A_engelhardt%2C_can_edward_snowden_be_deterred (accessed January 10, 2014).
③ Clarke and Knake, 95; see also U.S. GAO, "DOD Supply Chain: Preliminary Observations Indicate That Counterfeit Electronic Parts Can Be Found on Internet Purchasing Platforms." GAO 12-213T, November 8, 2011, available at http://www.gao.gov/products/GAO-12-213T (accessed January 10, 2014).
④ John Markoff, "Old Trick Threatens the Newest Weapons," *New York Times*, October 27, 2009, available at http://www.nytimes.com/2009/10/27/science/27trojan.html?pagewanted=all (accessed January 10, 2014).
⑤ Executive Office of the President, "The Comprehensive National Cybersecurity Initiative," September 1, 2010, Objective 11, 5, available at http://www.whitehouse.gov/sites/default/files/cybersecurity.pdf (accessed January 10, 2014).
⑥ Executive Office of the President, "Comprehensive." John Markoff, "U.S. to Reveal Rules on Internet Security," *New York Times*, March 2, 2010, available at http://www.nytimes.com/2010/03/02/science/02cyber.html (accessed January 10, 2014).

防护系统"被安装到政府网络里。美国出台相关法律,以期在主要的互联网服务供应商那里,尽快应用数据包深度检测技术。诸如"安全域名"(Secure DNS)或"域名系统安全扩展"(DNSSEC)等技术,被拿来应急,用以保障每位网络用户能够"确信与之交流的个体或组织的身份,既非作假,又非伪造"①。政府采取类似的措施,内容涉及互联网协议的架构、用于发送数据包的边界网关协议,以及万维网的技术标准、硬件漏洞等②。这些深奥难懂的技术措施,是否足以排除安全漏洞③?该问题的某一维度向我们揭示出,那些试图推广强加密方案的举措,不断受到主导性资本的拒斥。

商务部下属的互联网政策任务组负责网络安全事宜,试图就当前形势出台相关报告,并提出系统性的官方解决方案。分属通信商品链上不同环节的公司纷纷参与其中。美国电话电报公司、思科、谷歌、美国国际商用机器公司、贝宝以及威瑞信相继提交意见。主要的贸易协会也发表看法,它们的成员代表各方资本:例如商业软件联盟(Business Software Alliance)、蜂窝电信工业协会(Cellular Telecommunications Industry Association)、美国信息技术产业理事会(Information Technology Industry Council)、互联网安全联盟(Internet Security Alliance)、反信息滥用工作组(Messaging Anti–Abuse Working Group)、在线信任联盟(Online Trust Alliance)以及技术美国等④。2011年5月奥巴马总统发布《网络空间国际战略》(International Strategy for Cyberspace)。一个月后,商务部出台一份名为《绿皮书》的现状报告⑤。该绿皮书有三大特点值得关注。

《绿皮书》的第一大特点是设立了一种三方管理"网络安全"的方法。军事网络归国防部、国安局及其公司承包商管理。其他的政府网络以及所谓的"关键性的基础设施"(例如能源、交通、银行业与通信)则交由国土安全部联合首席信息官委员会(CIO Council)共同管辖;首席信息官委员会成员是28个联邦政府机构或部门的高层信息主管。商务部(尤其是美国国家标准技术研究所)则负责协调"互联网与信息创新部门"的网络安

---

① John Markoff, "A Stronger Net Security System Is Deployed," *New York Times*, June 25, 2011.
② S. Kent and K. Seo, BBN Technologies, "Security Architecture for the Internet Protocol," Network Working Group RFC 4301, IETF, December 2005. "因为互联网技术不断发展,随着旧系统被淘汰或被新系统所取代,路由表必须持续更新。边界网关协议(BGP)是指服务于全球互联网这一目的的协议。如果该协议失效,部分互联网有可能在一段时间内(几分钟或几小时)无法使用。"请参见 Rick Kuhn, Kotikalapudi Sriram, and Doug Montgomery, "Border Gateway Protocol Security: Recommendations of the National Institute of Standards and Technology," NIST Special Publication 800–54, July 2007, I–1. 也请参见 U. S. Department of Commerce, Internet Policy Task Force, "Cyber Security, Innovation and the Internet Economy," June 2011, "Appendix B: Widely Recognized Security Standards and Practices," 54–64 (hereinafter DoC, "CyberSecurity"), available at http://www.nist.gov/itl/upload/Cybersecurity_Green–Paper_FinalVersion.pdf (accessed January 10, 2014); and Clarke and Knake, *Cyber War*, 74–101.
③ Clarke and Knake, *Cyber War*, 83.
④ Department of Commerce", CyberSecurity, "Appendix C: "Notice of Inquiry Respondents."
⑤ The White House, "International Strategy for Cyberspace: Prosperity, Security, and Openness in a Networked World," May 2011, available at http://www.whitehouse.gov/sites/default/files/rss_viewer/international_strategy_for_cyberspace.pdf (accessed January 10, 2014); Department of Commerce, "CyberSecurity."

全事宜;"互联网与信息创新部门"涵盖商业信息服务与内容提供商、交易服务、存储与主机服务,以及诸如应用程序、浏览器、社交媒体以及搜索服务等"用户支持"服务供应商①。这三大行政部门与网络司令部、国安局展开通力合作②,建立起"横跨多个政府部门、30余家安全工具供应商以及大量终端用户组织的私人/公共协作机制"③。由于互联网是由各个隶属于公司和政府机构的网络所组成的一整套具有互操作性的网络体系,因此,只有国家与资本之间的全面协作(又被称为"公私合作",产生"信任"),才能"最有效地"主导"网络安全事宜"④。在与互联网所形成的特定关系上,这种"公私合作"关系早在克林顿政府时期就已出现,以该政府推出的《全球电子商务纲要》为标志⑤。那么,奥巴马政府所采用的"公私合作"关系是否有助于形成此前所说"组织化的、统一的(危机)回应模式"⑥,即各方利益的结构性融合? 或者这只是一种简单的混杂,从而受制于冲突与不稳定状态?

商务部出台的《绿皮书》的第二大特点,可以暂时回答上述问题。与其说企业评论者根据原则抵制政府批准的网络安全防护措施,毋宁认为,他们倾向于认同这种安排,只要后者被视为一种外部效应,一项由纳税人所承担的成本。这并非唯一可能的解决途径:安全性问题的成本也可以转嫁到公司身上。实际上,企业往往划拨大量资金,用于维护内部网络安全。然而,在它们的内部网之外,这些企业为何要肩负重任,负责各不连属、耗资巨大的网络安全事宜? (这反而与金融行业的某些引发数字化衰退的做法有几分类似:信用违约掉期以及其他金融衍生产品,可能降低了个别企业的风险,却极大地增加了金融体系的风险)。政府应当介入。政府应当启动相关项目,用于诊断内在于边界网关协议中的安全风险,这有助于实现网络的互操作性。互联网工作任务组(这是一个由志愿者所组成的组织,原本中立地代表全球社群)与国土安全部以及商务部下属的国家标准技术研究所展开合作,(对网络风险)进行一系列密集的分析⑦。

然而,由于企业评论者一致认定,政府不应当插手额外的规制事宜,因此无法保证这一回应措施的范围与一致性。政府只能提出"安全性"措施的有关建议,而不能执行这些

---

① DoC,"CyberSecurity,"14.
② David E. Sanger and Eric Schmitt,"Rise Is Seen in Cyberattacks Targeting U. S. Infrastructure,"*New York Times*,July 27,2012.
③ DoC,"CyberSecurity,"18.
④ DoC,"CyberSecurity,"iv – v,30.
⑤ Matthew Crain,"The Revolution Will Be Commercialized:Finance,Public Policy,and the Construction of Internet Advertising,"PhD diss.,University of Illinois Urbana – Champaign,2013;DoC,"CyberSecurity,"39,40.
⑥ U. S. Executive Office of the President,"Cybersecurity Initiative,"1.
⑦ DoC,"CyberSecurity,61 – 62;NIST's statutory responsibilities in this area were codified by the Federal Information Security Management Act (FISMA) of 2002,Public Law 107 – 347.

措施。拥有全美85%的关键性基础设施的资本①，极力反对联邦政府催促它们"加强"网络系统与服务建设的行为。企业如此反对，不是因为它们吝惜此类规制所需的大笔资金，更与保卫公民自由这一相较于其他国家的吹毛求疵而显得愈发重要的议题毫无关系。实际上，它们的反对源自于1980年代与1990年代互联网启动商业化进程以来逐渐形成的一种假设性共识：在互联网以及其他领域内，资本应当享受绝对自由，它凌驾于公共需求之上；而任何必要的措施，完全应当由政府买单②。将规制强加于互联网(互联网已被视为当代复兴资本主义的最重要的平台)，正是对上述信条的极度蔑视。

企业的反对导致政府与企业间形成长时间的、相互对立的僵局，而非前后一致的政策的出台。从2009年开始，奥巴马政府批准国土安全部具备对国内关键性基础设施执行最低网络安全标准的权力。按照《纽约时报》的解释，这些关键性基础设施"一旦遭损，将导致重大伤亡或经济损失"③。强制性规定的长期缺位，曾引发军方与公民的激烈批评。在他们看来，激励机制与自愿原则不足以保卫美国人民的安全④。然而，政府在2011年曾两次开展网络安全立法工作，不料成为大众抗议的牺牲品⑤。2012年间⑥，就是否应当实施强制性规定一事，中央政府内部纷争不断。奥巴马总统发表社论，公开支持"全面的网络安全立法工作"以解决"燃眉之急，即国家安全问题"⑦；与此同时，大量自由派与共和党人(以及美国商会和其他商业说客)竭力反对作为执法者的国土安全部的权限进一步扩大⑧。2013年，复苏的严格立法工作只开展了一次就再度遭到扼杀⑨。商务部的

---

① This widely used figure is cited, for example, in Menn, "Defence."
② Clarke and Knake, *Cyber War*, 146.
③ Michael S. Schmidt, "New Revisions Weaken Senate Cybersecurity Bill," *New York Times*, July 28, 2012.
④ Schmidt, "New Revisions Weaken Senate Cybersecurity Bill"; 112th Congress, 2d Session, U. S. Senate, Committee on Homeland Security and Governmental Affairs, Testimony of James A. Lewis, Center for Strategic and International Studies, on "Securing America's Future: The Cybersecurity Act of 2012," February 16, 2012, available at http://www.hsgac.senate.gov/hearings/securing-americas-future-the-cybersecurity-act-of-2012 (accessed January 10, 2014).
⑤ David Moon, Patrick Ruffini, and David Segal, *Hacking Politics: How Geeks, Progressives, the Tea Party, Gamers, Anarchists and Suits Teamed Up to Defeat SOPA and Save the Internet* (New York: O/R, 2013).
⑥ 112th Congress, 2d Session, U. S. Senate Committee on Homeland Security and Governmental Affairs, "Press Conference: Co-sponsors Discuss Revised Cyber-Security Act S. 3414," July 24, 2012, available at http://www.hsgac.senate.gov/issues/cybersecurity (accessed January 10, 2014).
⑦ Barack Obama, "Taking the Cyberattack Threat Seriously," *Wall Street Journal*, July 19, 2012, available at http://online.wsj.com/news/articles/SB10000872396390444330904577535492693044650 (accessed January 10, 2014).
⑧ Siobhan Gorman, "Cyber Bill Relies on Voluntary Security," *Wall Street Journal*, July 25, 2012.
⑨ Gerry Smith, "Senate Won't Vote On CISPA, Deals Blow to Controversial Cyber Bill," *Huffington Post*, April 25, 2013, available at http://www.huffingtonpost.com/2013/04/25/cispa-cyber-bill_n_3158221.html (accessed January 10, 2014).

立身之本在于,它代表美国商界利益;它依然继续支持"多方利益路径"与"自愿行为准则"①。

这一问题在境外所引发的衍生效应,便是《绿皮书》所具有的第三大核心特征——也是纷争的来源。《绿皮书》宣称,"网络安全不是由国家边界所定义的,以及美国无法不从全球范围进行战略考量等事实,是一个能引发各方讨论的宏大话题……并直接影响商务部如何看待自己在网络安全中的角色"。有一项提案建议,美国应当在国务院内部设立网络安全大使一职。果不其然,国务院很快设立了网络事务协调员的职位②。此举与奥巴马总统所强调的"必须关注国际网络空间政策的外交层面"这一观点,可谓不谋而合③。信息反滥用工作组(Messaging Anti-Abuse Working Group)要求,商务部应当"在海外组建自己的专业技术'地面部队',它由具备网络知识和专业技能的雇员所组成"④。他们为那些"遭遇严重威胁的国家"提供教育、技术、国际标准推广以及其他形式的支持⑤。总统本人也以"发展"为名,数次发起倡议⑥。对帝国主义发展史稍微有所了解的人可能会察觉出,上述一系列举措与传教士所进行的教育改革,又或者与二战后所兴起的最初的"发展"项目(用历史学家布莱德利·辛普森[Bradley Simpson]的话说,这些项目就是"枪炮经济学家"[economists with guns]⑦)之间,存在些许关联。

在奥巴马总统的振臂一呼(即2011年5月发布的《网络空间国际战略》[International Strategy for Cyberspace])中,被夹在"外交"与"发展"话语之间的,还有第三个关键词——"防御"。奥巴马宣称,"一张遍布全球的网络必须具备遍布全球的预警机制",以及"不断增加的电脑网络防御机制"⑧。借助"持续的运作与政策关系",与"技术和军事防御领域里的协作",美国完全可以利用其当全球军事实力,提升其境外网络安全性。美国政府

---

① DoC, "CyberSecurity," v, vi; and Testimony of Fiona M. Alexander, Associate Administrator, Office of International Affairs, National Telecommunications and Information Administration, U. S. Department of Commerce, before the Committee on Energy and Commerce, Subcommittee on Communications and Technology, United States House of Representatives, Hearing on "Cybersecurity: Threats to Communications Networks and Public - Sector Responses," March 28, 2012, 1, available at http://www.ntia.doc.gov/speechtestimony/2012/testimony - associate - administrator - alexander - cybersecurity - threats - communication (accessed January 10, 2014); White House, "International Strategy for Cyberspace."
② DoC, "CyberSecurity," 44 and n154.
③ White House, "International Strategy for Cyberspace," 11.
④ Messaging Anti - Abuse Working Group, "Comment," 7, in DoC, "CyberSecurity," 45, available at http://www.nist.gov/itl/upload/MAAWG_DoC_Internet_Task_Force - 2011 - 08.pdf (accessed January 10, 2014).
⑤ DoC, "CyberSecurity," 45.
⑥ White House, "International Strategy for Cyberspace," 14.
⑦ Bradley R. Simpson, *Economists with Guns: Authoritarian Development and U. S. - Indonesian Relations*, 1960 - 1968 (Stanford, Calif.: Stanford University Press, 2008); for the overall U. S. - guided discourse of "development," see Michael E. Latham, Modernization as Ideology: American Social Science and "Nation Building" in the Kennedy Era (Durham: University of North Carolina Press, 2000).
⑧ White House, *International Strategy for Cyberspace*, 13.

提出的一整套方案将是多边合作性质的；国际组织与机构积极参与和介入，并由美国主导。这些国际组织包括：美洲国家组织（Organization of American States）、东南亚国家联盟（Association of Southeast Asian Nations）、欧洲安全与合作组织（Organization for Cooperation and Security in Europe）、非洲联盟（African Union）、经济合作与发展组织、八国集团（Group of Eight）、北大西洋公约组织、欧盟以及亚太经济合作组织（Asia - Pacific Economic Cooperation Organization）①。"子午线进程"（Meridian Process）也开展相关工作，该项目围绕"关键信息基础设施保护计划"（Critical Infrastructure Information Protection）而推进更为紧密的国际合作，并以信息共享为己任。2011年子午线大会（Meridian Conference）在卡塔尔举办（前三届的举办地分别为中国台湾、美国与新加坡），主题是"关键信息基础设施保护与国际依附关系"。大会筹备委员会由来自卡塔尔、德国、匈牙利、日本、荷兰、新加坡、中国台湾、英国、阿根廷以及美国的代表所组成②。《网络空间国际战略》中还有不少双边协定，估计与"军事结构"协定有关——后者厘定条款，以保障美国在数十个国家设立数百家军事基地③。在这个范围内，政府"与行业展开磋商"的工作将"增强全球化的供应链的安全性，后者正是自由开放的贸易所依赖的条件"④。同样，这也是美国国家安全局监控项目契入的框架。只有完整的、全球的、全方位的电子情报网才有可能发出威胁警告，这些警告有可能起源于或出现在遍布全球的、互操作性的网络中的任何地方。

这些雄心勃勃的举措就足够了吗？一种排外的思潮开始崛起，它强调应当重建互联网，从而吸纳各种技术变革。这些技术变革旨在修复围绕协议而形成的"错误初始设计"，原本的协议强调网络的互操作性以信任与匿名性为基础。一项名为"凤凰计划"（Project Phoenix）的方案，包含生物识别系统与键盘加密机制，赢得了贝宝公司安全主管的赞许。谷歌副总裁温顿·瑟夫（Vinton Cerf）曾参与设计原始互联网协议，对"彻底清除理念"也产生兴趣⑤。

这样一种激进的重构方案是否能付出实施（先不论其能否成功），一切还是未知数。然而，从2010至2014年，一个在机构上紧密结合的网络——工业复合体一直试图往这个方向推进改革。正如美国公民自由协会所言，侵入性的、全面覆盖的在线监控项目"实际上"被赋予了"一种毫无限制的权力，它可以布下天罗地网，搜集美国人的国际邮件与电

---

① White House, "International Strategy for Cyberspace," 18, 21.
② "Meridian 2011 Summary," *Meridian Newsletter* 6, no. 1 (January 31, 2012), 2, available at http://www.meridian.org.
③ White House, "International Strategy for Cyberspace," 18.
④ White House, "International Strategy for Cyberspace," 19.
⑤ Joseph Menn, "Founding Father Wants Secure 'Internet 2'," FT.com, October 11, 2011, available at http://www.ft.com/intl/cms/s/2/9b28f1ec - eaa9 - 11e0 - aeca - 00144feab49a.html#axzz2kpB5vznV (accessed January 10, 2014).

话记录,而无需搜查令或接受任何质疑"①。理查德·克拉克曾对如下事实耿耿于怀,即与美国不同,"中国政府有权也有能力把中国的网络与世界其他地方断开;如果与美国交恶,中国政府有可能这么做"②。据《金融时报》报道,波音子公司的某主管曾问过同样的问题,"倘若中国能够阻止任何数据包进入该国,我们无法进入,我们怎么赢?"③不是中国也不是伊朗,而是来自美国海军战争学院(Naval War College)的一位教授于是简单地断定,由情报机构所监控的互联网"将按照各国边界进行重建"④。克拉克提出若干建议:除了政府应当集中行使网络安全职能外,美国应当开发出更安全的网络设计。尤其是,美国应当开发出他所说的、以监控为主的"军事互联网协议"(Military Internet Protocol);美国应当建造专有网络,后者同互联网和使用协议、应用程序以及与之不相容的操作系统等之间要实现"非实时连接"。克拉克坚称,"那些致力于构建一张大型的任何人去任何地方的、相互连接的网络的人们,肯定不喜欢我的建议,但变革即将来临"⑤。伊恩·布雷默(Ian Bremmer)预测,跨国公司有可能在"各国政府所密切监控的、相互连接的内部网"⑥中学会如何协调它们的运作。我们切莫低估它们的能力。

当其他国家提出上述建议时,美国政府曾表示强烈反对,即便如此,按照国界、连接限制等标准重建互联网的想法,在美国本土却有不少信徒。然而,如果境外互联网被分成各个部分,或碎片化,那么跨境数据流(跨国商品链建诸其上)以及向云计算(通过中心化的数据中心传输服务)的快速迁移,以及甚至"信息的自由流动"意识形态,都将有可能引发网络冲突。

美国官员中,对上述两种方案各有拥护者:碎片化互联网从而"加强"美国网络建设的提议者,与旨在保护全球网络的互操作性的提倡者,大有人在。奥巴马总统公开反对"碎片化的互联网",但他试图掩饰"自由流动"政策同国际军事、外交与发展网络安全倡议之间存在的紧张关系⑦。2013 年,一份向外交关系委员会提交的高级别的任务组报告言之凿凿地声称,"全球互联网正不断经历碎片化过程,它逐渐分裂成国家互联网(na-

---

① American Civil Liberties Union, "Administration Seeks Easy Access to Americans' Private Online Communications," September 27,2010, available at https://www.aclu.org/technology – and – liberty/administration – seeks – easy – access – americans – private – online – communications (accessed January 10,2014). 也请参见 Electronic Privacy Information Center, at www.epig.org; Thom Shanker and David E. Sanger, "Privacy May Be a Victim in Cyberdefense Plan," *New York Times*, June 13,2009, available at http://www.nytimes.com/2009/06/13/us/politics/13cyber.html? pagewanted = all (accessed January 10,2014).
② Clarke and Knake, *Cyber War*,146.
③ Greg Oslan at Boeing's Narus unit, in Joseph Menn, "Online Privacy Risks Becoming an Early Casualty," *Financial Times*, October 11,2011.
④ Menn, "Online Privacy."
⑤ Clarke and Knake, *Cyber War*,276.
⑥ Ian Bremmer, "Democracy in Cyberspace," *Foreign Affairs* 89, no. 6 (November – December 2010),92.
⑦ White House, "International Strategy," 3,8 (fragmented) and generally.

tional Internets),这并不利于美国"。该报告的结论显示,"通过组建网络联盟、将信息的自由流动写入未来所有的贸易协定里,以及强调一种包容笃定的互联网治理模式等方式,华盛顿方面能够有效地限制互联网碎片化所带来的不利影响"。然而,该报告还指出,"未来的趋势不容乐观"[1]。

斯诺登事件戏剧性地增加了更多的不确定性。一家设立于华盛顿的研究机构召集商界代表,与美国国务院国际通信和信息政策(International Communications and Information Policy)前协调员共同商讨"棱镜计划对数字贸易政策的影响",并警告美国政府"对数字通信无处不在的隐秘监控……有可能影响美国政府和技术部门对抗反竞争政策的能力;像服务器本地化等反竞争政策将严重阻碍信息的自由流动,并有可能使那些希望实施反竞争政策的国家(或地区)合法化"[2]。随即,这一机构暗示,斯诺登对监控计划的曝光所产生的影响在于,云服务供应商或许会损失数百亿美元的收入[3]。2013年第三季度显示:实际上,美国公司思科在巴西和俄罗斯所获新订单的数量分别下降了25%和30%;并且,这些网络设备的跨国供应商不得不面对"'国安局利用美国科技公司的强势地位拓展其监控范围'这一爆料",以及美国在网络空间中所具备的进攻实力"而引发的怒火"[4]。

2013年6月在美国召开的一次学术会议上出现的论争,也应当放在这一情境下加以考量;该学术会议的主题为:"联邦互联网"有可能成为美国领导人相对可以接受的方案,以取代现有的美国主导的境外互联网体系[5]。"联邦互联网"提议的具体内容并没有详细展开,其实施的可能性也不得而知。然而(即便以后换成其他名字),它依然显示出一种主动性,以产生一种完全不同的、有利的美国政策协同效应。美国军事规划者继续坚持要求对互联网进行彻底改造,以适应"攻击性防守"模式;与此同时,美国的经济外交政策仍然强调,互操作性的网络应当成为不受限的外商投资、处于变动中的跨境商品链,以及跨国企业信息流的核心枢纽。是否有可能设计出一种手段,用以调和国家遏制与资本积累这两种不同的政策需求之间的矛盾?

---

[1] John D. Negroponte, Samuel J. Palmisano, and Adam Segal, "Defending an Open, Global, Secure, and Resilient Internet," May 2011, 13, 67, available at http://www.whitehouse.gov/sites/default/files/rss_viewer/international_strategy_for_cyberspace.pdf (accessed January 10, 2014). Emphasis in original.

[2] Information Technology and Innovation Foundation, "The Impact of PRISM on Digital Trade Policy," July 24, 2013, Washington, D.C., announcement available at http://www.itif.org/events/impact-prism-digital-trade-policy (accessed January 10, 2014).

[3] Information Technology and Innovation Foundation, "How Much Will PRISM Cost U.S. Cloud Computing Providers?" August 5, 2013, available at http://mpictcenter.blogspot.com/2013/08/itif-how-much-will-prism-cost-us-cloud.html (accessed January 10, 2014).

[4] Richard Waters, "Cisco Cites EM Backlash over NSA Leaks as It Warns on Sales," *Financial Times*, November 14, 2013.

[5] "The Future of Internet Governance after Dubai: Are We Heading to a Federated Internet?" Columbia University Institute for Tele-Information, June 20, 2013.

这是众多深奥且无解的问题中的一个。当然，相互冲突的美国政策目标，也同其他社会和政策行动者所设定的目标和规划相互影响。这种影响不仅仅局限于美国国内，还拓展至国际。同样，围绕控制与引导境外互联网而展开的争斗，将有可能产生许多意想不到的偶然性后果。本书的最后一章将讨论各种重要力量，在它们的推动下，数字资本主义的未来令人忧心。

第15章
从地缘政治到社会政治冲突

政治经济的历史发展受到由上至下、国家主导的地缘政治的型塑,同时并非完全受到这一型塑力量的掌控。其中,起决定性作用并充满活力的因素是,某个特定社会内部以及全球范围内社会力量之间的政治制衡关系。

大卫·哈维问道,"资产阶级在面对一系列经济、社会、政治、地缘以及环境危机时,能否实现权力的再生产?"他认为,资产阶级或许能够扭转乾坤,但(倘若果真如此)只能是社会与政治冲突所导致的结果。对此,哈维有自己的解释:为了保障资产阶级的(重建)计划取得成功,"资产阶级权力的地缘格局与部门构架必须进行彻底且痛苦的改革。倘若历史能提供某种指南的话,那么资产阶级只要没有改变其自身的特性,并将积累转向另一条轨迹或转移到新的空间(例如东亚地区),便难以维系既有的权力"[1]。这一重组的过程,不仅因其展开规模的庞大,更因其参与主体间的矛盾,而充满各种偶然与意外。

我们已经看到,凸显积累的数字化场所已经导致信息的地缘政治的日渐碎片化。诸多国家试图形成对以美国为中心的境外互联网的多边控制局势,此番尝试既是对(现有的)国际体系的结构性改变,也是重建政治经济、解决彼此冲突的诉求——重建工作有可能为某些特定的资本或资产阶级获取超大份额的利润。

数字化衰退的出现,引发国际体系的变革,这正是政治经济关系发生变革的表现。华盛顿共识赋予美国为全球政治经济设置规则的权力,这一共识最终被抛弃。当恐慌来临,似乎20国集团(其中包括日本等五个亚洲国家)作为新兴的经济政策制定实体,大有取代小型的大西洋七国集团之势[2]。即便在这一趋势有所消退的情况下,升任国际货币

---

[1] David Harvey, *The Enigma of Capital* (New York: Oxford University Press, 2010), 215–16.
[2] Martin Wolf, "The West No Longer Holds All the Cards," *Financial Times*. Special Report "G20 in Pittsburgh," September 24, 2009; Edward Luce, "Tensions over IMF Threaten to Mar G20," *Financial Times*, September 25, 2009; Krishna Guha, Edward Luce, Chris Giles, and Gideon Rachman, "Scepticism over G20 Pledge of New Era," *Financial Times*, September 26–27, 2009: 1.

基金组织主席的克里斯蒂娜·拉加德(Christine Lagarde)认为有必要向巴西、印度和中国主动示好以争取它们的支持。很快,中国成为经过重组的国际货币基金组织里配额排名第三的成员国,巴西、印度和俄罗斯的配额也有所提升①。同样,其他多边组织和政策制定机构也(有选择地,更多是相冲突地)向现在被称为"大的新兴市场"(以中国为首)开放。另一方面,美国和欧盟主导的世界贸易组织的多哈回合谈判在南方国家的齐声反对下,最终破产②。经济政策上的反对意见不断发酵。"讽刺的是,需要对自经济大萧条以来的深重危机负全责、至今尚未完全解决自身问题的某些国家,竟然如此迫不及待地妄图制定世界其他地方的行动法则"③,这是巴西财政部长吉多·曼特加(Guido Mantega)2012 年所做出的尖刻评论。美国国家情报委员会(National Intelligence Council)已经预计,"美国的相对实力……将有所下降,因此美国所掌握的筹码将进一步缩减"④。美国权力不断遭遇挑战,然而关键之处在于,它依旧固若金汤。诚如一位记者 2012 年所言,"权力结构仍然最大限度地折射出这个世界的原有状态"⑤。倘若美国正处于不断衰落的阶段,那么至今也没有其他权力作为全球霸权(即资本的规则制定者与推动者)能够完全替代它。在世界贸易组织的支持下,美国尝试修订 1996 年的《信息技术协议》(Information Technology Agreement)⑥。它也试图就跨大西洋和跨太平洋贸易协议展开谈判,借此巧妙地避开世界贸易组织以及其他多边机构所形成的全球制度。然而,上述三类措施在本书写作期间遭受各方压力⑦。

众多评论者认为,中国迫切希望成为下一个全球霸权。可(事实是)美国经济总体上依然是中国的三倍,与此同时,中国资本必定在充斥着生产能力过剩(现象)并受跨国企业全权掌控的全球经济体中,强势地实现其跨国化发展诉求⑧。即便中国无意追逐全球

---

① International Monetary Fund,"Factsheet: IMF Quotas," March 31, 2013, available at http://www.imf.org/external/np/exr/facts/quotas.htm (accessed January 10, 2014).
② Vijay Prashad, *The Poorer Nations: A Possible History of the Global South* (London: Verso, 2012), 189–91.
③ Claire Jones,"Power Structures: Emerging Nations Seek Better Balance," *Financial Times*, June 18, 2012.
④ Scott Shane,"Global Forecast by American Intelligence Expects Al Qaeda's Appeal to Falter," *New York Times*, November 21, 2008; National Intelligence Council,"Global Trends 2025: A Transformed World," available at http://www.aicpa.org/research/cpahorizons2025/globalforces/downloadabledocuments/globaltrends.pdf (accessed January 10, 2014).
⑤ Claire Jones,"Power Structures: Emerging Nations Seek Better Balance," *Financial Times*, June 18, 2012.
⑥ Doug Palmer,"U.S. Seeks Expanded Information-Technology Pact," *Politico*, November 11, 2013, available at http://www.politico.com/story/2013/11/us-pact-trade-info-technology-99631.html (accessed January 10, 2014).
⑦ Alex Hern and Dominic Rushe,"WikiLeaks Publishes Secret Draft Chapter of Trans-Pacific Partnership," *The Guardian*, November 13, 2013, available at http://www.theguardian.com/media/2013/nov/13/wikileaks-trans-pacific-partnership-chapter-secret (accessed January 10, 2014).
⑧ Peter Nolan and Jin Zhang,"Global Competition after the Financial Crisis," *New Left Review* 64 (July–August 2010): 97–108. 2013 年,钢铁、炼油以及(第一章所分析的)汽车等全球三大行业均面临大规模生产过剩的问题. 请参见 "An Inferno of Unprofitability," *The Economist*, July 6, 2013; Guy Chazan and Ed Crooks,"Refining Overcapacity Hits Shell, Total and ExxonMobil," *Financial Times*, November 1, 2013.

霸主地位（就其自身而言也非小事①），中国的军事或金融机构也难以承担主导全球的重任。并且，中国的贸易顺差早已用于供养美国以及欧盟等两大出口市场，而非重建其发展严重不平衡、高度依赖投资与出口（等三驾马车）的政治经济结构。（考虑事项）优先级别的转变并不那么容易实现，尽管有迹象显示，习近平政府有意启动相关的改革措施②。中国在一个存在各种抵抗的国际环境下提出并实现其所追求与坚持的外交、政治以及意识形态立场。

不可否认，中国已然成为全球经济版图中两大增长极之一。另一增长极不是地域性而是部门性的：信息与通信产业③。这两大增长极如何互动、如何联合？尤其是，中国自身的信息产业在国内拥有什么样的地位？我将集中阐述这一问题，从而厘清数字资本主义某些紧急的压力点。

中国的工业化尽管与20世纪晚期商品链的跨国重组有关，但诚如洪宇所分析那般，它本质上还是信息化的④。虽然中国的政治体制容许国内各个行业向大量的外商直接投资开放，可它在设定准入国内具有战略意义的通信与信息产业的门槛上所取得的成功，同样令人瞩目⑤。

2010年的4月至6月间，作为顶级制造商，联想荣登台式电脑出货量最高宝座：其一半销量以及全部利润均来自国内市场。《金融时报》如此评价，"从西方（市场）撤退，看起来很明智"⑥；接下来几年里，联想强势的销售记录一直有赖于其国内市场⑦。相较之下，谷歌与新闻集团不得不克服各自因为从中国市场中撤出而引发的不利局面⑧。脸书

---

① Lin Chun, *China and Global Capitalism：Reflections on Marxism，History，and Contemporary Politics*（New York：Palgrave，2013）.
② Michael Pettis, *The Great Rebalancing：Trade，Conflict，and the Perilous Road Ahead for the World Economy*（Princeton，N. J.：Princeton University Press，2013）；Peter Nolan, *Is China Buying the World?*（London：Polity，2012）.
③ 关于较早的分析，请参见 Dan Schiller, *How To Think about Information*（Urbana：University of Illinois Press，2007），177-97.
④ Yu Hong, "Information Society with Chinese Characteristics – Discursive Construction of the Neo – industrialization Strategy in the People's Daily," *Javnost – The Public* 15, no. 3（2008）：3，23-38，available at http://www.javnost-thepublic.org/article/2008/3/2/（accessed February 21，2014）；Yu Hong, *Labor, Class Formation, and China's Informationized Policy of Economic Development*（Lanham, Md.：Rowman and Littlefield, 2011）.
⑤ Yuezhi Zhao, "China's Pursuits of Indigenous Innovations in Information Technology Developments：Hopes, Follies, and Uncertainties," *Chinese Journal of Communication* 3, no. 3（September 2010）：266-89.
⑥ "Lenovo," The Lex Column, *Financial Times*, August 20, 2010.
⑦ Chris Nuttall and Maija Palmer, "Ailing HP Takes ＄8bn Writedown," *Financial Times*, August 9, 2012.
⑧ Dan Schiller and Christian Sandvig, "Google v. China：Principled, Brave, or Business as Usual?" *Huffington Post*, April 5, 2010, available at http://www.huffingtonpost.com/dan-schiller/google-v-china-principled_b_524727.html（accessed January 10, 2014）；Kathrin Hille and Tom Mitchell, "News Corp Admits Defeat in China with Sale of TV Channels," *Financial Times*, August 10, 2010；Kathrin Hille, "Functionality Remains Top Priority for Chinese Group," *Financial Times*, September 2, 2010；David Barboza, "New China Search Engine Will Be State – Controlled," *New York Times*, August 14, 2010.

依旧保持旁观态度,却一直企图进入中国①。中国电商的主导者不是亚马逊,而是阿里巴巴。包括彭博、路透社、纽约时报以及华尔街日报等在内的占主导地位的西方金融新闻网站,在中国都处于进退维谷的状态②。随着美国互联网中介商继续保持观望态度,其他种类的资本跃跃欲试,不但成为各类网络设备与服务的提供商,更成功占领国内各大市场,这些资本包括:中央电视台与上海文广集团、阿里巴巴、腾讯、百度、中国移动与中国电信、华为、中兴与小米(主打低价红米智能手机,向外界宣称,制作的第一批共计十万台红米手机曾在 90 秒内售罄③)、新华网、搜狐、优酷以及人人网。

  无论如何这并不意味着经济上的闭关锁国。中国互联网与通信公司的名字经常出现在美国纳斯达克股票市场上,有的公司甚至找到途径进入开曼群岛或维尔京群岛。正如杨信庄所言,大部分公司的所有权结构并不透明,包括大部分美国私募股权与对冲基金以及各类主权财富基金在内的位置显要的机构投资者④。电商巨头阿里巴巴的未来估值足以与脸书相抗衡,而日本软银(SoftBank)掌握其 35% 的股权⑤;同样,日本软银也拥有人人网总公司美国千橡集团(Oak Pacific Interactive.)相当一部分股权,而百度与搜狐身后,也涌现出英国投资基金普信资产(T. Rowe Price)与奥本海默(Oppenheimer)等投资商的身影。腾讯运营四家外商独资企业。由上可见,中国的互联网公司相当自由地利用境外投资资本;反过来,这些资本急不可耐地试图从不断膨胀的中国市场上分得一杯羹。

  然而,这并非国外资本介入中国互联网并从中赢利的唯一方式。中国批准跨国互联网中介商能够直接进入国内某些特定的行业分支(industry segments):例如,微软进入操作系统软件市场,苹果准入移动设备市场⑥。美国国际商用机器公司生产的大型计算机完全占领中国"第一梯队"国有银行市场,由此,甲骨文与德国软件公司(SAP)成为它们最主要的商业软件提供商⑦。2011 年,中国中央人民政府提供的电子政务服务所使用的

---

① Facebook,Inc.,Form 10 – Q,U. S. Securities and Exchange Commission,June 30,2013,48.
② Kathy Chu and William Launder,"U. S. Media Firms Stymied in China," *Wall Street Journal*,December 7 – 8,2013.
③ Sarah Mishkin,"＄10bn Xiaomi Beats Apple in China," *Financial Times*,August 24,2013.
④ ShinJoung Yeo,"Behind the Search Box:The Political Economy of the Global Search Engine Industry," draft PhD diss.,University of Illinois,Urbana – Champaign,2013.
⑤ Brian Deagon,"Alibaba IPO Looms:Inside China's eBay – Amazon – Google," Investors. com,January 31,2014,available at http://news. investors. com/technology/013114 – 688253 – alibaba – group – humongous – ipo – looms – amid – rapid – growth. htm? ref = mp (accessed February 22,2014);Paul J. Davies,"Alibaba Board Wrestles over Listed Future," *Financial Times*,September 9,2013.
⑥ Tom Mitchell,Song Jung – a,and James Crabtree,"Apple Seeks Leap Forward in Biggest Market," *Financial Times*,September 12,2013;Gregg Keizer,"China Mobile – Apple iPhone Pact 'Very Big Deal'," *Computer world*,December 5,2013,available at http://www. computerworld. com/s/article/9244557/China_Mobile_Apple_iPhone_pact_very _big_ deal (accessed February 22,2014).
⑦ Nolan,*Is China Buying the World?*,118.

软件与硬件产品有近一半来自国外①。随着中国逐步取代美国拥有全球最大的国内电影市场,中国逐渐成为好莱坞的全球枢纽②。好莱坞担心中国观众的(文化)倾向有可能偏离它自身"对立体以及巨幕立体电影的高预算幻想(high-budget fantasies)",而偏向国内放映(模式)③。

正因为这种渗透性,信息、通信与文化领域也被中国政府视为"支柱型产业",这意味着它们在中国经济政策的整体框架中被赋予战略优先地位④。这一关键的经济增长极已初见规模,并牵引国家实施旨在实现额外增长的全方位发展规划。2010年中央经济工作会议指出,内容数字化以及与民营资本加强合作,将成为接下来的发展重点⑤。据媒体报道,2013年,中国的工信部计划投资3 250亿美元,将在2020年前用于扩建并升级全国有线和无线宽带基础设施⑥。中国的云计算平台、应用程序以及主机与存储,在得到超过200家中国公司的技术支持,并成为国务院"十二五"规划中的战略型产业的利好条件下,获得快速增长⑦。洪宇等学者强调,中国政府意识到"整体上,数字媒体(尤其是互联网)对国民经济发展至关重要"⑧,因此对它进行一系列发展战略部署。

如同美国政府,中国政府在互联网行业培育大型资本。胡锦涛(2010年)与习近平(2012年)先后公开访问腾讯(总部位于深圳,其聊天平台[QQ]用户数高达七亿,首席执

---

① Leigh Ann Ragland et al., Center for Intelligence Research and Analysis, "Red Cloud Rising: Cloud Computing in China," Research Report Prepared on Behalf of the U. S. – China Economic and Security Review Commission, September 5, 2013:47.
② Toby Miller et al., *Global Hollywood II* (London: BFI, 2005).
③ Michael Cieply, "U. S. Box Office Heroes Proving Mortal in China," *New York Times*, April 22, 2013; Matthew Garrahan, "China Reels in Hollywood as Multiplex Screens Thrive," *Financial Times*, April 25, 2013.
④ Yu Hong, "Reading the Twelfth Five – Year Plan: China's Communication – Driven Mode of Economic Restructuring," *International Journal of Communication* 5 (2011): 1045 – 57; Yu Hong, "Between Corporate Development and Public Service: The Cultural System Reform in the Chinese Media Sector," *Media, Culture and Society*, 2014 (forthcoming); Yu Hong, Francois Bar, and Zheng An, "Chinese Telecommunications on the Threshold of Convergence: Contexts, Possibilities and Limitations of Forging a Nation – Centric Growth Model," *Telecommunications Policy* 36, no. 10 – 11 (November – December 2012): 914 – 28; Yuezhi Zhao, Communication in China (Lanham, Md.: Rowman and Littlefield, 2008).
⑤ 官方所提供的可能不足以采信的数据指出,2009年中国"文化产业"市值1 200亿美元. 具体请参见"The 10 Most Important Business Policies of the Year," *China Daily*, December 23, 2010, available at http://www.chinadaily.com.cn/bizchina/2010 – 12/23/content_11746341.htm (accessed January 10, 2014); Chen Limin, "Cultural Industry Likely to Flourish under State Plans," *China Daily*, December 16, 2010; Yu Hong, "Corporate Development."
⑥ "China to Shell Out USD325bn on Broadband Development," *TeleGeography*, CommsUpdate, September 19, 2013; "China Sets New Targets for Broadband," *TeleGeography*, CommsUpdate, August 19, 2013; "Fiber in New Homes to be Compulsory," *TeleGeography*, CommsUpdate, January 16, 2013; "China Telecom's LTE Spending to Pass USD7bn in 2014," *TeleGeography*, CommsUpdate, November 26, 2013; "China Hands over TD – LTE Concessions Paving the Way for China Mobile Launch," *TeleGeography*, CommsUpdate, December 4, 2013.
⑦ Ragland et al., "Red Cloud Rising," 13, 49.
⑧ Hu Yong et al., "Mapping Digital Media: China," *Open Society Foundations*, October 2012, available at http://www.opensocietyfoundations.org/reports/mapping – digital – media – china (accessed February 22, 2014).

行官马化腾个人资产据估计约为64亿美元①),此举堪比奥巴马与埃里克·施密特的亲切交谈。同样与美国类似,中国政府经常介入到国内市场的准入条件的制定过程中②。例如,微软与苹果均(被要求)在产品的设计上进行战略性妥协,以换取在国内销售产品的资格③。无线通信巨头中国移动(2013年客户数已达7.4亿)在第四代移动网络设备上的资本投资规模已远超威瑞森、美国电话电报公司以及沃达丰。它开始转向支持设立国有技术标准,以保障中国企业拥有专利权。在《华尔街日报》看来,这一举动"很快产生了关于(技术)标准的临界值(standard critical mass)",并极有可能使"中国在全球无线通信产业的运营问题上,拥有更大的话事权"④。中国最重要的经济规划与规制部门——国家发改委,针对全球最大手机芯片制造商美国高通公司(Qualcomm)所开展的反垄断调查⑤,与此关联甚密。

使中国企业的专业化管理与外商投资组合、直接投资者以及中国政府相互联系的各种(社会)关系和所有制结构,都是不透明的。尽管这些利益的重要性无法明说且不稳定,以至于中国的信息产业所引发的权力制衡问题难以一语定之,但中国政府支持国内资本占领国内市场已是不争之事实。中国在引导国内信息与通信市场上所取得的成功,必须被视为一项例外的历史成就。

过去数十年间,虽然法国正式出台"文化例外"政策以保护本国音乐与电影产业发展,并且,最近一段时间坚称,倘若数字媒体服务获得同样保护,那么文化例外的"第二条款"(Act Two)才有可能奏效,然而,法国从未将上述理念完全付诸实施。英国超前发展的计算机产业最终落得缓慢衰亡的结局,此后,英国基本上放弃这些理念。2013年年末,德国软件企业(SAP)董事长对外宣称:"(早知欧洲信息技术产业处于萎靡不振的局面),当初欧洲人怎么会在20年前任其衰亡?"⑥(有必要指出德国软件企业[SAP]董事长孟鼎铭[Bill McDermott]正是美国人⑦)战后西欧资本主义的重建所导致的结果是,在不断演

---

① Simon Montlake,"Chinese Leaders Knock On Internet Giants' Doors As Transition Unfolds," *Forbes*, December 13, 2013, available at http://www.forbes.com/sites/simonmontlake/2012/12/13/chinese-leaders-knock-on-internet-giants-doors-as-transition-unfolds/ (accessed February 22, 2014).
② 要了解与美国企业相匹敌的公开亮相的对手的情况,请参见 "Huawei Sees Resolution of U. S. Security Concern Taking a Decade", Bloomberg.com, October 17, 2013, available at http://www.bloomberg.com/news/2013-10-18/huawei-sees-resolution-of-u-s-security-concern-taking-a-decade.html (accessed February 22, 2014).
③ 关于微软情况,请参见 Clarke and Knake, Cyber-War; for Apple, Ronald J. Deibert, *Black Code: Inside the Battle for Cyberspace* (Toronto: Signal [McLelland and Stewart], 2013), 79.
④ Paul Mozur, "China Mobile Calls on Its Clout for 4G Standards," *Wall Street Journal*, August 16, 2013.
⑤ Supantha Mukherjee and Neha Alawadhi, "China Probe May Be Aimed at Qualcomm's 4G Royalties," *Reuters*, November 26, 2013, available at http://www.reuters.com/article/2013/11/26/us-qualcomm-china-idUS-BRE9A0OE820131126 (accessed February 22, 2014).
⑥ Hasso Plattner, quoted in Chris Bryant, "NSA Claims Put German Business on Guard," *Financial Times*, November 1, 2013.
⑦ Shira Ovide, "SAP to Have One CEO, an American," *Wall Street Journal*, July 22, 2013.

变的通信与信息领域里开发小众市场(mere niches)。这些小众市场要么衰败(例如法国布尔[Bull]有限公司),要么遭遇抛弃(如诺基亚将手机制造部门卖给微软),要么只是失去发展活力(例如阿尔卡特)①。德国软件企业(SAP)与爱立信则是例外。日本近年来的发展情况可与欧洲相提并论:尽管日本此前制定一项产业计划以推动国内计算机产业的发展壮大②,并数十年如一日地致力于电子硬件的发展;然而,截至2010年,索尼、松下以及其他曾经雄霸一方的电子企业不得不在与苹果、三星以及华为、中兴的激烈竞争中败下阵来。

中国的情况也非全然具有特殊性。"信息的去殖民化"曾激励第三世界的政治抗争与发展蓝图一直到1980年代才逐渐走向没落;没落的原因来自于美国所施加的强大压力,以及许多贫困国家社会阶级关系的固化等事实③。然而,部分第三世界国家所提出的进口替代政策,却成功地培育了国内信息产业(creating elements of national information industries),这些要素为接下来的政治宏图奠定了新的基础。巴西在整个1970年代所奉行的"市场储备"政策为其锻造了(坚实的)情报学实力,却在1990年后改弦易辙,实行提供补贴、减免赋税以及降低关税等措施,旨在重构其市场以吸收外商(主要是美国)科技公司的投资资本。在与戴尔、索尼、惠普与联想一起组建世界第三大计算机市场后,鸿海科技集团如今在巴西开厂装配苹果手机④。然而,即便巴西贯彻经济政策以适应国内市场,那些已然崛起的本土信息技术企业仍然通过特许与经销协议,与跨国信息技术提供商联手。与此同时,国家管理部门依然关注互联网发展问题。截至2013年,巴西已经成功实现对互联网基础设施的本地主导权,并且巴西企业在国内外所发挥的作用越来越大⑤。从这一角度看,罗塞夫总统主动抵制美国监控的行为,一定程度上更像代表巴西本土的高科技企业的利益所作出的一种经济外交姿态。

1970至1980年代,印度的卫星项目与计算机产业同样表达了该国追求国民经济独立发展的诉求。此后,随着印度领导人激进地向全球市场投怀送抱,以印孚瑟斯(Infosys)、塔塔咨询服务公司(TCS)以及威普罗(Wipro)为代表的印度本土信息技术软件与企

---

① Richard Milne, "Nokia Faces Fresh Test of Endurance," *Financial Times*, September 4, 2013; Adam Thomson, "Combes Seizes Alcatel's Last Chance," *Financial Times*, October 9, 2013.
② Marie Anchordoguy, *Computers, Inc.: Japan's Challenge To IBM*, Harvard East Asian Monograph 144 (Cambridge: Council on East Asian Studies of Harvard University, and Harvard University Press, 1989).
③ Vijay Prashad, The Darker Nations (New York: New Press, 2007); Dan Schiller, *How To Think about Information*, 36–57.
④ Bill Vlasic, Hiroko Tabuchi, and Charles Duhigg, "An American Model for Tech Jobs?" *New York Times*, August 5, 2012. 与其说巴西屈服于跨国资本,毋宁认为,它以比较小经济体所能享受到的更优惠的条件,整合进跨国资本体系里.
⑤ Sara Schoonmaker, *High-Tech Trade Wars: U. S. - Brazilian Conflicts in the Global Economy* (Pittsburgh: University of Pittsburgh Press, 2002); Bill Woodcock, "On Internet, Brazil Is Beating US at Its Own Game," *Al Jazeera America*, September 20, 2013, available at http://america.aljazeera.com/articles/2013/9/20/brazil-internet-dilmaroussefnsa.html (accessed January 10, 2014).

业流程外包公司(business process outsourcing company)在全球市场强势崛起,并成为货真价实的跨国供应商——尽管有人指出,最近他们向国外资本出让优先权①。韩国开发了令人艳羡的数字游戏利基市场,并孕育出在全球消费性电子产品市场拥有一席之地的本土冠军企业——三星:它联手谷歌共同向苹果自留地即高端手机市场发起挑战②。台湾的信息技术产业发端于1973年工业技术研究院(the Industrial Technology Research Institute)的创建。如今,它以拥有微电子芯片制造商集成电路制造公司(TSMC)、两家个人电脑制造商宏碁(Acer)与华硕(ASUSTEK),以及低利润制造商广达(Quanta)、纬创(Wistron)、仁宝(Compal)与鸿海③而自豪。台湾的芯片制造至2012年已是拥有630亿美元市值的产业,占全球半导体总销量的五分之一。即便芯片制造商的大型客户(例如苹果和三星)利用其所提供的技术以产生令人讶异的利润,这些制造商也处于相互竞争的局面④。我们的确需要对上述或其他国家的互联网产业进行对比分析,包括受俄罗斯—前苏联影响深远的国家计划经济与科技教育被国家现代化项目所取代,例如"电子俄罗斯"(Electronic Russia,2002-2012)与"前往俄罗斯"(Go Russia,2009)。而国内资本在互联网服务的本土市场中仍发挥超大作用⑤。

然而,中国提供了一个由国家主导的信息通信技术产业的发展版本:它影响深远、具有多面性并取得成功⑥。改革开放时期,中国政府监管信息与通信产业的国内资本的发展权力没有被削减。截至2010年,除美国之外,只有中国培育出多面的、拥有尖端技术的信息与通信产业,它由大型且依然不断增长的国内市场所统摄,并受到强势政府的管

---

① Vivek Chibber, *Locked In Place: State-Building and Late Industrialization in India* (Princeton, N. J.: Princeton University Press, 2003); Jyoti Saraswati, *Dot. Compradors: Power and Policy in the Development of the Indian Software Industry* (London: Pluto, 2012); and Pradip Ninan Thomas, *Digital India: Understanding Information, Communication and Social Change* (New Delhi: Sage, 2012). 印度一直有选择地推进信息通信技术的本地化发展. 请参见"India to Pay Out INR100bn to Local Vendors," *TeleGeography*, CommsUpdate, October 28, 2013.
② Dal Yong Jin, *Korea's Online Gaming Empire* (Cambridge, Mass.: MIT Press, 2010); Dal Yong Jin, *Hands On/Hands Off: The Korean State and the Market Liberalization of the Communication Industry* (Cresskill, N. J.: Hampton, 2010); Kwang-Suk Lee, "A Final Flowering of the Developmental State: The IT Policy Experiment of the Korean Information Infrastructure, 1995-2005," University of Wollongong Research Online, 2009, available at http://ro.uow.edu.au/cgi/viewcontent.cgi? article=1247&context=artspapers (accessed February 22, 2014); Kwang-Suk Lee, *IT Development in Korea: A Broadband Nirvana?* (London: Routledge, 2012); Cheol Gi Bae, "The Transformation of the Korean Wireless Telecommunications Policy: Interplays Between the State, Transnational Forces, Business, and Networked Users," PhD diss., University of Illinois at Urbana-Champaign, 2013.
③ "After the Personal Computer," *The Economist*, July 6, 2013; "Chips," The Lex Column, *Financial Times*, July 19, 2013.
④ Eric Pfanner, "Taiwan Chip Industry Powers the Tech World, but Struggles for Status", *New York Times*, September 16, 2013.
⑤ Valentin Makarov, Stefan Schandera, and Jean-Paul Simon, "The ICT Landscape in BRICS Countries: 5. Russian Federation," *Digiworld Economic Journal* 87 (2012), 163, available at http://is.jrc.ec.europa.eu/pages/documents/CS87_Feat_SIMON_et_al.pdf (accessed January 10, 2014).
⑥ Jack Linchuan Qiu, "China's Network Society: A Three-Phase Trajectory—As-teroids, Bees, Coliseums," Presentation to Centre for the Study of Global Media and Democracy, Goldsmiths, University of London, May 29, 2013.

控。出于上述原因,中国商业机构与政府部门同时作为日渐重要的行动者,出现在全球数字资本主义版图中(2013年年底,中国对外宣称,它将重组国家安全结构,使后者进一步与美国模式保持一致,从而更有效地应对国内与国际挑战①)。

中国制定疏导国内市场从而造福于国内企业的相关政策,并非只是信息与通信产业独有的现象。油及化工产品、航空航天、汽车装备、能源生产与分配、军工设备、银行业以及基因组学等毫不相干的其他产业的发展同样取得成功,尽管如彼得·诺兰所言,显得不可思议②。这意味着,中国政策在高速增长的信息与通信产业里的有效性,对外国资本(尤其是美国)而言,构成了间歇性的沉重负担。

中国国内市场的各种准入限制,让跨国资本循着快速增长的轨迹进行扩张的举动处处受到掣肘,这反过来使得这些限制成为美国国内政治势力(攻击中国)的常用借口。美国的政策制定者要求中国必须将自己定位于这一交易关系的接收端。2011年希拉里曾敦促美国各大企业"应主张,在向中国市场出口产品时必须机会均等……同时应确保投资于中国、高达500亿美元的美国资本必须为新的市场与投资机遇奠定坚实的基础"。这位国务卿进一步阐述了该议程,"中国仍然需要进一步深化改革……从而终结针对美国以及其他外国企业或创新技术的各种歧视行为,并对国外企业一视同仁,废除一系列不利于或盗用外国知识产权的措施"③。然而,美国试图占有中国高速增长的信息与通信市场份额的目标,却始终未能实现。

一种互惠互利的趋势十分明显。中国成功保护国内市场或为其划定边界的行为,给中国资本提供了一部分活动空间。然而,一旦资本在国内市场获得成功(这并非提前下结论,例如2014年国家资助的操作系统提供商红旗软件倒闭④),那么中国各大通信企业更需要走出国门,进入全球市场。它们希望"走出去"(即打入世界市场)的抱负,与它们的业绩表现并不相符,尽管2007年后中国对外直接投资呈现疯狂增长趋势,以至于2012年中国企业花费570亿美元用于境外收购⑤。因此,通信与信息领域的中国资本,同美

---

① Jeremy Page,"China Deepens Xi's Powers with New Security Plan,"*Wall Street Journal*,November 12,2013,available at http://online.wsj.com/news/articles/SB20001424052702304644104579193921242308990(accessed January 10,2014);Sui-Lee Wee and Ben Blanchard,"China to Revamp Security in Face of Threats at Home,Abroad,"*Reuters*,November 12,2013,available at http://uk.reuters.com/article/2013/11/12/uk-china-reform-politics-idUKBRE9AB0Q420131112(accessed January 10,2014).
② Nolan,Is China Buying The World?,59-60;Michael Specter,"The Gene Factory,"*New Yorker*,January 6,2014,34-43.
③ Hillary Clinton,"America's Pacific Century,"*Foreign Policy*(November 2011);60,available at http://www.foreignpolicy.com/articles/2011/10/11/americas_pacific_century(accessed January 10,2014).
④ Adrian Wan,"Chinese Software Pioneer Red Flag Bites the Dust,"*South China Morning Post*,February 14,2014,available at http://www.scmp.com/business/china-business/article/1427823/chinese-software-pioneer-red-flag-bites-dust(accessed February 22,2014).感谢唐旻提供这一链接。
⑤ Simon Rabinovitch and Leslie Hook,"Chinese Groups Step Up Push for Global Deals",*Financial Times*,December 11,2012.

国、欧洲以及日本跨国企业并不处于同一量级上。在某些例外情形下,中国的通信企业才敢以全球企业自居。2009年,网络设备供应商华为从新接的订单中获益300亿美元,这些订单不仅来自中国,还有欧洲与非洲,从这一层面上讲,华为已成为世界最大的移动基础设施供应商。中国第二大网络设备制造商中兴同样跻身于世界级企业行列①。此前我提到的联想集团,作为全球企业,它一直处于不断增长的态势中,例如2014年年初,它以23亿美元收购美国国际商用机器公司的服务器业务,以29亿美元收购谷歌的摩托罗拉移动业务②。

然而,大部分国外通信与信息合资企业并非扮演那么关键的角色。中国电信在巴西设立分部,主要向两国的跨国企业提供互联网与外包服务③。同样,中国电信与美国电话电报公司达成网络的相互连通的协议,也是以向企业用户提供跨境服务为目的④。腾讯微信与谷歌达成一项协议,以扩大其在亚洲、南非、西班牙与美国的用户规模⑤。矢志不渝地致力于电影业的大连万达集团,2012年收购美国的电影院线(AMC娱乐)⑥。总之,中国的通信与信息企业在国际上依然受到来自以美国为中心的数字资本主义所施加的强大压力与限制⑦。

这些压力与限制包括政府强加的政治限制,以及横跨各个盈利行业的跨国企业所设立的准入门槛。针对(国外)政府(主导)的信息通信技术的收购行为,美国政府启动了一项"网络间谍"审核程序,主要针对华为与中兴两家中国供应商。美国立法者敦促国内企业开展收购行为,甚至明目张胆地联合其他国家寻求帮助⑧。据维基网站揭露,2009年3月希拉里曾询问澳大利亚总理陆克文(Kevin Rudd):"你如何强硬地与你的银行家

---

① Kathrin Hille,"China's ZTE Seals E200m Mobile Deal with Telenor," *Financial Times*,August 23,2010.
② Charles Clover,"Lenovo to Buy IBM's x86," *Financial Times*,January 24,2014;Richard Waters and Charles Clover,"Lenovo Dials into US Market," *Financial Times*,January 31,2014.
③ Joe Leahy,"China Telecom Moves to Secure Foothold in Brazil," *Financial Times*,June 14,2012.
④ Kathrin Hille,"China Telecom Gains Access to AT&T's Networks," *Financial Times*,November 30,2011,available at http://www.ft.com/intl/cms/s/0/b5f1e728-1b6d-11e1-85f8-00144feabdc0.html#axzz1ffP3fhLZ (accessed January 14,2014).
⑤ Juro Osawa,"China's WeChat App Targets U.S. Users," WSJ.com,January 27,2014,available at http://blogs.wsj.com/digits/2014/01/27/chinas-wechat-app-targets-u-s-users/ (accessed February 22,2014).
⑥ Keith Bradsher,"Chinese Titan Takes Aim At Hollywood," *New York Times*,September 23,2013.
⑦ Broadly, I follow Nolan, *Is China Buying The World?*
⑧ "US Introduces Cyber-Espionage Clause to Funding Law to Lock Out Chinese Vendors," *TeleGeography*,CommsUpdate,March 28,2013;Richard McGregor,"Huawei Deal With S. Korea Is Threat to US-Seoul Defence Ties,Warn Senators," *Financial Times*,December 4,2013.

相处?"①这是一个试探性的问题(尽管通过这次大型收购,中国仍然拥有一部分美国国债)②。尽管中美双方开展多次贸易会谈以降低投资门槛,并已经存在中国对美国的直接投资(如2013年中),但中国资本的增长依然要面对来自美国的各种令人窒息的限制。美国当局已经否决中国对美国石油、猪肉与网络路由器等本土产业的直接投资;并且,美国政府一直坚守互联网产业这块"战略"阵地,不容中国资本有任何染指的机会,毕竟这是数字资本主义的主要增长极。华为在2013年被迫撤离政治敏感的美国市场前,曾数次探底③。

政治经济结构构成了中国资本在扩张过程中所遭遇的全球(而非仅仅是国家)阻力。只有那么一小撮诺兰所形容的"系统整合者"即跨国企业,主导了从航空航天、半导体到软饮料等各个行业的全球市场④。这些跨国企业中有3/4的总部设在富裕国家。过去数十年间,它们通过兼并与收购、研发以及品牌营销等方式,独掌商业大权。我在第一部分已指出,如今它们拥有强大的跨境生产体系,尤其是延伸至中国的生产线⑤。这里所说的跨国企业,最近也是最贴切的例子,就是美国大型互联网企业。

然而,它们的出现所导致的情况,并非简单的停滞,而是形成一种反复无常的场域。美国企业为了应对数字化衰退的第一轮打击,囤积大量流动资本,以防止遭遇更深层次、不可预计的风险。因此,2011年美国企业拥有1.9万亿资产(这可是半个世纪以来美国企业总资产的最高值),"对资产负债情况完全坐视不管"⑥。尽管经济增长放缓,可美国与欧洲企业⑦在2012年年初拥有现金储备共计2万亿欧元,2013年这一数字还在增长⑧。其中,获得超高利润的高科技公司拥有最大份额。仅仅苹果、微软与谷歌等三家公

---

① State Department cable, February 28, 2009, classified "Confidential," in David E. Sanger, *Confront and Conceal* (New York: Crown, 2012), 369.
② 另一位作者指明,"美国欠中国数万亿美元债务,使美国尴尬地被视为其主要竞争对手的金融哀求者(financial supplicant)"。具体请参见 Alan Dupont, "An Asian Security Standoff," *The National Interest*, May/June 2012, 56. This said, however, as Peter Nolan emphasizes, at $1.2 trillion in June 2011, China's share of U.S. government debt—the largest share by any foreign holder—amounted to about 12 percent of the total. Nolan, *Is China Buying the World?*, 4, and n4.
③ Andrew Parker, "Huawei Eyes Deals Worth $30 Billion," *Financial Times*, March 9, 2009; Amol Sharma and Sara Silver, "Huawei Tries to Crack U.S. Market," *Wall Street Journal*, March 26, 2009; Kevin J. O'Brien, "Upstart Chinese Telecom Company Rattles Industry as It Rises to No. 2," *New York Times*, November 30, 2009; David Barboza, "Scrutiny for Chinese Telecom Bid," *New York Times*, August 23, 2010; Stephanie Kirchgaessner, "Challenge to Huawei's US ambitions," *Financial Times*, August 22, 2010: 9; "Huawei Sees Resolution of U.S. Security Concern Taking a Decade." *Bloomberg News*, October 17, 2013. 也可参见 Peter Nolan, Is China Buying the World?.
④ 也可参见 John Bellamy Foster and Robert W. McChesney, *The Endless Crisis: How Monopoly - Finance Capital Produces Stagnation and Upheaval from the USA to China* (New York: Monthly Review Press, 2012), 155 – 83.
⑤ Nolan and Zhang, "Global Competition"; Nolan, *Is China Buying The World?*.
⑥ Richard Milne and Anousha Sakoui, "Rivers of Riches," *Financial Times*, May 23, 2011.
⑦ John Authers, "Corporate America Cannot Cut Its Way to Prosperity," *Financial Times*, July 23, 2012.
⑧ Tony Jackson "Cash - Hoarding Companies Seem Unable to Splash Out," *Financial Times*, March 12, 2012: 14; Anousha Sakoui, "Concentrated Cash Pile Puts Recovery in Hands of the Few," *Financial Times*, January 22, 2014; Ed Crooks, "'Animal Spirits' of Spending Jostle for Release," *Financial Times*, January 24, 2014.

司在2010年12月所拥有的现金流就高达900亿美元①。这些巨额的流动资产仍将持续增长,置各种风险于不顾。截至2012年6月,单苹果一家企业就掌握了1 117亿美元现金流,2013年第三季度这一数字飙升至1 470亿美元②。美国的科技公司总共坐拥7 750亿美元资产③。这到底是发展强劲还是日渐式微的迹象呢?

尽管高科技企业的兼并与收购行为此起彼伏④,尽管奥巴马总统在2011年年初敦促美国各大企业应"参与到游戏中"⑤,尽管投资者对亚马逊极尽容忍(亚马逊以牺牲利润为代价来吸引投资)⑥,高级管理人员仍阻止大部分货币资本回流到非金融投资领域中。2013年年底一位记者指出,"虽然存在资本的低成本运营,可丝毫没有任何迹象表明资本开支开始复苏"⑦。随着美国资本开支的萎靡态势一直持续到2014年,《金融时报》对这一场被坊间称为"延长的企业投资罢工"⑧(该术语与罗斯福主政时期的经济大萧条有关)甚为恼火。根本问题在于(这也是在经济大萧条中屡见不鲜的问题),企业难以辨识出足够多的盈利机遇。相反,它们宁愿关注能够囤积多少(资金),以及在股东红利与股票回购上花费多少。2002至2012年,思科在股票回购上共花费720亿美元,"与它在收购上所花费的资金相比,可谓小巫见大巫"⑨。由于受到巧取豪夺的投资商的重重压力,苹果采取了类似的行动⑩。假使互联网资本获准能更加自由地流入中国的信息与通信产业,那么它们也就不愁没有资金可利用了。

当然,大体上,打破现有僵局不是没有可能的。中美当局可以精诚合作,以释放这些庞大的资金储备,并帮助它们流入国内以及国外市场。实际上,暗度陈仓的情况时有发生:美国的对冲基金一直向中国互联网公司进行投资,例如,微软与华为联手向非洲推销各种使用视窗系统的低端智能手机⑪。然而,上述这些行为,实在微不足道。中美两国政

---

① Jenna Wortham and Evelyn M. Rusli, "Silicon Valley Showing Signs of New Bubble," *New York Times*, December 4, 2010.
② Jessica E. Vascellaro and Ian Sherr, "Rare Miss for Apple as iPhone Sales Cool," *Wall Street Journal*, July 25, 2012; Anousha Sakoui, "Pressure Builds for Groups to Put Their Cash Hoards to Work," *Financial Times*, January 22, 2014. 2013年中,仅仅六家企业(苹果、微软、谷歌、思科、甲骨文与高通)就坐拥全美非金融机构1.5万亿资产的1/4。请参见 Richard Waters, "Tech Sector Still Sitting on a Mountain of Wealth," *Financial Times*, January 22, 2014.
③ Sakoui, "Pressure Builds."
④ Hannah Kuchler and Tim Bradshaw, "WhatsApp Pushes Tech Deal Total to ＄50bn," Financial Times, February 21, 2014.
⑤ Reported in Milne and Sakoui, "Rivers of Riches."
⑥ Nick Wingfield, "Amazon's Profit Falls as It Spends Heavily on Projects," *New York Times*, April 26, 2013.
⑦ Henny Sender, "Pessimism over US and the Dollar Will be Shortlived," *Financial Times*, November 2–3, 2013.
⑧ Ed Crooks, "US Capital Spending Set to Slow to Four-Year Low in Sign of Caution," *Financial Times*, January 24, 2014; "America's Corporate Investment Drought" (editorial), *Financial Times*, January 24, 2014.
⑨ "Cisco," The Lex Column, *Financial Times*, March 16, 2012.
⑩ "Apple/Icahn," The Lex Column, *Financial Times*, December 6, 2013.
⑪ Kevin J. O'Brien, "Microsoft and Huawei of China to Unite to Sell Low-Cost Windows Smartphones in Africa," *New York Times*, February 5, 2013.

府从中牵线,外商直接投资、兼并其他的合资企业以及中美资本间的合并难道不可能推进信息产业的增长吗?

跨国资本所形成的场域并非一个中立的政治经济空间。是美国还是中国资本主导之前所提及的合并呢?谁收购谁?中美双方能准入对方市场的程度分别是多少?在这一新兴的赢利产业(无论是"大数据"分析学、云计算还是基因组学)中,哪家公司能赢得最后的胜利,获得有利的市场地位?如何制定税收、利润汇回以及投资的基本规则?"重大再平衡"(great rebalancing)[1]所耗费的成本以及收益如何平摊?解决上述问题的尝试如何与更宏观、正在发生变革的跨国政治经济结构(当然,它包括 scores of additional states,其中每个国家都面临来自国内的重重压力)相互交织?

带着这些问题,我们从基本事实出发。推动数字资本主义重组进程的地缘政治,它的形成不仅源于国家与大公司的各种战略措施,本质上,它更依随国家或国际随时变动的力量对比关系(balance of social forces)而发生相应的变化。普遍性的危机与数字资本主义的增长模式预示着,互联网的地缘政治令人担忧,并仍将问题重重。

国际上,美国资本与政府同它们那些贪得无厌的贸易伙伴一道,寻求既得优势的扩大化。它们主张,包括美国与欧洲在内的低增长地区的人们应当在生活标准、环境质量、社会供给以及民主自由等问题上做出妥协。一面是美国与欧洲资本主义转移金融崩溃风险的行为招致口诛笔伐,一面则是政治与企业领导者利用危机大做文章,不惜动用国家权力以实施"紧缩"政策。(福山奉劝茶党不要继续行妖魔化联邦政府之事,在他看来,当前我们需要一个"强大国家"的权力,以实现"民族复兴"[2])针对工薪阶层与"非正式"行业工人的一系列举措,透露出一种威权主义的色彩。随着苛捐杂税进入人们的日常生活,人们对资本的阶级政策的抗议行为也将逐渐升级。

部分系统经理(system managers)已较早地认识到这一点。多米尼克·斯特劳斯-卡恩(Dominique Strauss-Kahn)在由世界货币基金组织与国际劳工组织(International Labour Organization)所召开的一场特别会议上指出,"他们说,世界范围内大概有2.1亿人口处于失业状态,这是有史以来官方记载的最高失业人口记录"。截至2010年,世界货币基金组织发出警告,因为这一失业危机,美国与欧洲正遭受"爆发大规模社会动荡"的风险[3]。随着希腊、法国、英国、西班牙、葡萄牙与意大利相继发生社会抗议行动,反对代表资本利益的国家政策,这一预言开始得到验证。在美国,占领行动所引发的一系列示威游行极大地改变了政治话语的版图:原本混杂着阶级教义与华尔街政党权益的话语在

---

[1] Pettis, *Great Rebalancing*.
[2] Francis Fukuyama, "Conservatives Must Fall Back in Love with the State," *Financial Times*, July 21–22, 2012.
[3] Dominique Strauss-Kahn, "Saving the Lost Generation," *IMF Direct*, September 14, 2010, available at http://blog-imf-direct.imf.org/2010/09/14/saving-the-lost-generation (accessed January 10, 2014).

短短数周内,逐渐转向由企业尤其是银行等利润掠夺者所引发的经济不平等与不公正现象①。当经济不景气依然持续,对现状的抵制也相应地存在。世界货币基金组织货币和资本市场部门主管何塞·比尼亚尔斯(José Viñals)指出,自 2011 年年中开始,欧洲"正进入危机的新阶段,我称之为危机的政治阶段"②。从雅典到奥克兰,从约翰内斯堡到首尔,从里斯本、马德里到圣保罗,各地民众反对现有政策的抗议行动此起彼伏,这表明,"危机的政治阶段"尚未结束。代表资本利益的紧缩政策激活了人民的反抗能量,因为他们(尤其是年轻人)在当下的生活中看不到未来。2013 年 11 月,希腊工人发动了一场反对紧缩政策的 24 小时大罢工③。一直持续到 2014 年的各种社会抗议并未引发跨国资本主义制度的政治变革,但这并不表明它不会发生任何变化。

然而,这一局面需要进一步详述。社会政治抗争并非仅仅作为经济衰退以及由此产生的紧缩政策的附属物而出现,或甚至仅仅源自于不平等与统治这一长久的社会形式(forms of inequality and domination),它还是更为显明的(发展)趋势必然导致的结果,即数字化衰退。一方面,美国当前的经济政策依然凸显以网络为基础的利润项目(profit projects)的优先性,这类似于 1930 年出台的应对模式,甚至如某位主流评论员所言,"这是一个失落的十年"④。时任美国国家经济委员会(National Economic Council)主任的劳伦斯·萨默斯(Lawrence Summers)指出,"数字化基础设施,将成为知识经济中竞争优势的核心要素"⑤。另一方面,围绕数字网络拓展利润机制空间的行为,也不可避免地引发社会抗议。

商品化进程(即培育生产利润的产业)并非建立在各派既得利益的共识基础上。以网络为基础的系统与服务的典型特征是破坏性,因为它们以掠夺公共产品(例如文化、教育、政府与生命的共享资源)为前提⑥。迈克尔·佩罗曼(Michael Perelman)与大卫·哈维称这一种与资本主义历史一样悠久的巧取豪夺行为为"剥夺式积累"⑦。数字资本主义的几乎每一部门不仅延续了资本对共享资源的(通常是不公正的)占有功能,更同时引发

---

① David Harvey, *Rebel Cities: From the Right to the City to the Urban Revolution* (London: Verso, 2012), 159.
② 转引自 Joe Leahy and Chris Giles, "IMF Warns on Growing Global Risks," FT.com, June 17, 2011, available at http://www.ft.com/intl/cms/s/0/a2a1834a-98cd-11e0-bd66-00144feab49a.html#axzz1PYLWMMOs (accessed January 10, 2014).
③ "General Strike against Cuts Brings Greece to a Halt," *BBC News Europe*, November 6, 2013, available at http://www.bbc.co.uk/news/world-europe-24832847 (accessed January 10, 2014).
④ James Mackintosh, "The World Is Halfway through a Lost Decade," *Financial Times*, August 12, 2012.
⑤ Lawrence H. Summers, "Technological Opportunities, Job Creation, and Economic Growth," Remarks at the New America Foundation on the President's Spectrum Initiative, June 28, 2010, 3.
⑥ Ursula Huws, "Crisis as Capitalist Opportunity: New Accumulation through Public Service Commodification," in Leo Panitch, Greg Albo, and Vivek Chibber, eds., *The Crisis and the Left*, Socialist Register 2012 (Pontypool, Wales: Merlin, 2011), 64-84.
⑦ Michael Perelman, *The Invention of Capitalism: Classical Political Economy and the Secret History of Primitive Accumulation* (Durham, N.C.: Duke University Press, 2000); Harvey, *Enigma of Capital*.

反向的社会运动与抗议行为。这一反向运动正作为另一参与者,加入当前的历史进程中。

以教育为例。在美国,计算机辅助教育可以追溯到 1959 年,彼时伊利诺伊大学启动一项维持数年的计划(军方、企业以及恪守原则的教育家深度介入这项计划[事实不总是单向度的])①。这项以网络为技术基础的教育计划,吸引了不少国际追随者。1968 年墨西哥引领的"电视学校运动"(tele – school movement)作为新学校建成之前的过渡方案,(其影响)却一直波及 2012 年:当时墨西哥五个儿童中至少有一个正在上电视学校②。截至 1980 年代中期,要发现初生的在线教育产业并非难事,我在《数字资本主义》一书中已经就此展开过讨论③。这一产业自诞生之日起便不断发展壮大,一直持续到数字化衰退阶段。无论是中国还是智利,韩国还是南非,美国、印度、墨西哥还是巴西,教育产品与服务的私营承办商都宣称他们希望打造一个市值数万亿美元的跨国教育市场。

互联网的连接性是公共产品商品化过程的核心。在贫穷国家,教育资源通常供不应求,私营(教育)机构将自身置于完全开放的领域。《华尔街日报》登载的一篇文章指出,"公共教育的缺口反而为非公共机构创造了机遇"④。尽管不少学生抗议,试图能享受非营利性教育服务⑤,可扩大入学率的任务被移交到企业手上⑥。在发达国家市场经济环境下,公共产品商品化的进程却面临着完全不同的历史条件。政府对公共教育的资助构成了一种近乎普世性的体系(可以肯定,它完全受制于阶层不平等),而公立大学招收了一大批大专学生。在这一情境下,商品化进程往往与诋毁、改革公共教育系统甚至取消对其资助等行为齐头并进⑦。

随着数字化衰退成为某种托辞,以方便私营企业"准入"教育行业,各种责难声蔓延于教育系统的各个层面。在学龄前教育领域,不少市政当局将纳税人的钱从公共部门转

---

① D. Alpert and D. Bitzer, "Advances in Computer – Based Education: A Progress Report on the PLATO Program," University of Illinois, Computer – based Education Research Laboratory CERL Report X – 10, Urbana, July 1969.
② Anna Vigna, "Mexico's Teleschools," *Le Monde diplomatique*, March 2012, 12.
③ Dan Schiller, *Digital Capitalism: Networking the Global Market System* (Cambridge, Mass.: MIT Press, 1999), 143 – 202.
④ Paulo Trevisani, "Brazil Welcomes For – Profit Schools as Aspiring Professionals Seek Skills," *Wall Street Journal*, June 27, 2011. 从美墨关系角度进行的学术讨论,请参见 Lora E. Taub and Dan Schiller, "Networking the North American Higher Education Industry," in Continental Order? Integrating North America for Cyber – Capitalism, ed. Vincent Mosco and Dan Schiller (Lanham, Md.: Rowman and Littlefield, 2001), 163 – 88.
⑤ "Protests for Expansion of Public Higher Education in Sri Lanka," *Inside Higher Ed*, March 13, 2013, available at http://www.insidehighered.com/quicktakes/2013/03/13/protests – expansion – public – higher – ed – sri – lanka (accessed January 10, 2014).
⑥ Andrew England, "Parents Race to Enroll Children as Low Cost Private Schools Boom in S. Africa," *Financial Times*, February 15, 2012; Joe Leahy, "Private Education Offers Lucrative Pickings in Brazil," *Financial Times*, September 29, 2011.
⑦ Aisha Labi, "Europe's Austerity Measures Take Their Toll on Academe," *Chronicle of Higher Education*, April 29, 2012, available at http://chronicle.com/article/Europes – Austerity – Measures/131739 (accessed January 10, 2014).

移至私营教育机构,这势必影响现有的阶级规模与属性①。在小学教育领域,某些城市(作为美国第三大学区,芝加哥是最典型的城市)草率地关闭数十所公立小学,完全置数万社区居民与加入工会的教师的抗议行为于不顾②。与此同时,由于三分之一的美国家庭年收入不超过三万美元,子女与父母生活在一起,家庭没有安装网络宽带,结果麦当劳因其拥有 1.2 万家安装无线网络的连锁快餐店,竟然成为这些家庭子女热衷于选择的学习场所③。社区大学招收全美近 44% 的大学生,其中包括大量贫困与少数族裔学生。如今国家对它的财政补贴(即联邦基金)逐渐下降④。同样,公立大学所获得的公共资源也慢慢减少。作为拥有全美最先进的公立大学体系的地区,加州在 1960 年总体规划中就已着手实施"无学费"政策⑤。50 年后,免费享受大学教育的理念正遭受严重破坏。2013 年,作为全美最后一批实行免学杂费政策的大学之一,库珀联盟学院(Cooper Union)对外宣布,它将向本科生收取入学费用⑥。这些新情况都是对美国工人阶级的打击,他们享受不同阶段的精英教育的可能性,更是微乎其微⑦。

美国的筹资模式揭示出政府与资本再次结盟:随着公共教育丧失其原有的基本资源,并成为更大范围的倒行逆施政策(批评者恰如其分地称之为"有意失败"⑧的一部分),联邦政府提供给就读于私立大学的大学生的贷款,全部流入企业的腰包⑨。这一(盈利)动机对凤凰城大学、教育管理集团(高盛控制该集团 41% 股份,招收 15 万名学生)等私营机构而言,充满诱惑。因此,私立大学的大部分收入并非由它们在市场上取得的成功所致,而是来自于政府。事实证明,相当一部分私立大学向学生许以虚假的承诺,从而扩大其入学率,而其学生贷款违约率高出公立大学足足一倍⑩。当这些情况被曝光后⑪,

---

① Motoko Rich, "Private Preschools See More Public Funds as Classes Grow," *New York Times*, June 24, 2013.
② Steven Yaccino and Motoko Rich, "Chicago Makes It Official, with 54 Schools to Be Closed," *New York Times*, March 22, 2013; Steven Yaccino, "Protests Fail to Deter Chicago from Shutting 49 Schools," *New York Times*, May 23, 2013.
③ Anton Troianovski, "The Web-Deprived Study at McDonald's," *Wall Street Journal*, January 29, 2013.
④ David Leonhardt, "Through Enrolling More Poor Students, 2-Year Colleges Get Less of Federal Pie," *New York Times*, May 23, 2013.
⑤ Robert Lindsey, "California Weighs End of Free College Education," *New York Times*, December 28, 1982.
⑥ Ariel Kaminer, "College Ends Free Tuition, and an Era," *New York Times*, April 24, 2013.
⑦ 2006 年,据统计,200 家 4 年制精英教育学校里,大约 5% 的学生来自底层社会. 请参见 Leonhardt, "Poor Students."
⑧ Noam Chomsky, "The Assault on Public Education," *Truthout*, April 4, 2012, available at http://truth-out.org/opinion/item/8305-the-assault-on-public-education (accessed January 10, 2014). Chomsky cites Josh Bivens, *Failure by Design* (Washington, D. C., Economic Policy Institute, 2011), available at http://www.epi.org/publication/failure-by-design (accessed January 10, 2014).
⑨ Floyd Norris, "Colleges for Profit Are Growing, with U.S. Aid," *New York Times*, May 25, 2012.
⑩ Tamar Lewin, "For-Profit College Group Sued As U.S. Portrays Wide Fraud," *New York Times*, August 9, 2011.
⑪ U.S. Senate, 112th Cong., 2d Sess., Committee on Health, Education, Labor and Pensions, *For-Profit Higher Education: The Failure to Safeguard the Federal Investment and Ensure Student Success*, Committee Print S 112-37, 4 vols. (Washington, D. C.: GPO, July 2012).

以盈利为目的的(私立)大学入学率开始下跌①。

然而,仅仅通过增加大规模财政补贴的方式,从而增加公共教育机构应对当前危机的可能性,依然渺乎微哉。相反,公共教育机构的董事会成员大多具有商业头脑,在他们的驱使下,机构管理者急不可耐地与商业性的网络课程供应商展开合作。三大网络课程供应商(Coursera、edX、Udacity)作为新兴企业,依托于大学,共同将一种新型商品(大学课程)转化成超额利润增长点②。它们所提供的密集型网路课程(或称之为慕课)吸引了大量公众的关注③,随后,它们推出能够帮助学生获取大学学分的课程教育服务④。诸如黑板(Blackboard)或明灯(Moodle)等"学习管理系统"承办商也积极开发周边的教育产品。

无论是国际教学、培训和评估学习标准(ITT)的教育服务产品、凤凰城大学,还是德锐理工学院(DeVry Institute of Technology)、克瑞林学院公司(Corinthian Colleges)、楷博高等教育(Kaplan Higher Education)、培生教育集团(Pearson Education),这些私营教育企业纷纷强势地进军海外市场。德锐与培生进军巴西,培生向中国市场投资⑤。调研显示,在中国,四分之三的小学生接受处于灰色地带(通常以利润为导向)的海外机构所提供的课堂外教育⑥。同样,日本与韩国也以开办众多远程教育机构而自豪。美国承办商对这些已然成熟的市场颇为眼红。美国在线教育供应商优德米(Udemy),其百万学生用户有一半来自国外。它的网站使用九种语言(包括中文),主要以那些希望通过假期课程培训(例如它所推出的最受欢迎的课程是如何使用微软办公软件 Excel)后时薪能达到十美元的(普通人)为目标用户⑦。苹果等互联网公司⑧以及新闻集团等大型媒体巨头也开始涉足该领域。新闻集团曾对外宣称,旗下的教育分支机构将与美国电话电报公司合作,"以准入这一价值数十亿美元的公共教育市场":例如,它向从幼儿园到高中的学生推销"各类数字化学习工具"。推动新闻集团进军教育行业的头号人物当属乔尔·I. 克莱恩(Joel I. Klein),在入职新闻集团之前,他曾担任纽约市学校校长(New York City's schools),随后

---

① Melissa Korn,"For – Profit Schools Increasingly Find the Party Is Over,"*Wall Street Journal*,August 23,2011.
② John Markoff,"Online Education Venture Lures Cash Infusion and Deals with 5 Top Universities,"*New York Times*,April 18,2012.
③ 例外情况,请参见 Edward Luce,"Moocs Are No Magic Bullet for Educating Americans,"*Financial Times*,November 25,2013.
④ Tamar Lewin,"Universities Team with Online Course Provider,"*New York Times*,May 30,2013.
⑤ Trevisani,"Brazil,"B6.
⑥ Richard Garner,"Chalk Talk:Impressive Results in the Far East – A 'Shadow' over Plans to Improve Our Schools?"*The Independent*,February 5,2014,available at http://www.independent.co.uk/news/education/schools/chalk – talk – impressive – results – in – the – far – east – a – shadow – over – plans – to – improve – our – schools – 9110187.html (accessed February 23,2014).
⑦ April Dembosky,"US Online Learning Groups Seek to Push Borders,"*Financial Times*,August 5,2013.
⑧ Andrew Edgcliffe – Johnson,"Apple Opens New Era in Digital Learning,"*Financial Times*,January 20,2012.

加入新闻集团成为默多克的重要幕僚(并帮助他在英国消除因手机窃听丑闻而招致的威胁)①。放眼整个世界,这些网络教育承办商以救助者形象出现,不仅拓宽(人们)受教育的途径,并有意使之与作为正规教育象征的精英教育与阶级特权相脱离。从这个意义上说,它们取得了成功。讽刺的是,它们也降低了技术工人的价值,这反而为资本主义社会关系的再生产奠定了更庞大的基础。

并非所有的教育机构在这一变革过程中都保持默许态度。《纽约时报》的一位记者强调,"对教育者而言,数字化学习工具是一个充满争议的话题。许多教师要么视之为扩大学生规模的一种方式,要么认为它给工作带来额外负担,甚至有可能导致教师职位缩减"②。大学教授也表示了某种担忧,无论是圣何塞州立大学还是哈佛大学,大部分教师对目前以挣学分为目的、以利润为导向的大学课程抱有难过、焦虑甚至愤怒之态度③。公共教育财政补贴的削减,引发了各地学生的齐声抗议,无论是在英国、智利,还是魁北克或中国台湾。过去一年里,智利学生举行示威游行,要求降低学费,曾鼓舞数千名学生参与行动④;智利总统米歇尔·巴奇莱(Michelle Bachelet)"出面回应学生游行,并承诺,政府将提高企业税收,部分用以投入教育改革"⑤。在魁北克,政府批准大学学费上涨75%,学生组织激进的社会运动,并于2012年使魁北克省政府倒台⑥。

正如商品化对其他公共产品的破坏一样,公共教育资源私有化的整体进程,引发了多方面的反对行动。我没有记录下这些运动所涉及的范围与种类。在强调紧缩政策、类似于1980年代的私有化模式的加持下,在2010至2011年间世界范围内总值数亿美元的国家资产被变卖的情况下⑦,文化遗产、政府服务、制药、医疗以及农业生物技术相继遭遇商品化的洗礼。印度将政府福利补贴(连同银行账户与手机服务)与身份程序(an ID

---

① Amy Chozick, "News Corp. Has a Tablet for Schools," *New York Times*, March 6, 2013, available at http://www.nytimes.com/2013/03/06/business/media/news-corp-has-a-tablet-for-schools.html?pagewanted=all&_r=0 (accessed January 10, 2014).
② Amy Chozick, "News Corp. Brands Unit for Education as Amplify," *New York Times*, July 24, 2012.
③ Steve Kolowich, "Harvard Professors Call for Greater Oversight of MOOCs," *Chronicle of Higher Education*, May 24, 2013, available at http://chronicle.com/blogs/wiredcampus/harvard-professors-call-for-greater-oversight-of-moocs/43953 (accessed January 10, 2014).
④ For a progress report see Alexei Barrionuevo, "With Kiss-Ins and Dances, Young Chileans Push for Reform," *New York Times*, August 5, 2011; for Quebec, Matthew Brett, "The Student Movement: Radical Priorities," *The Bullet*, Socialist Project E-Bulletin No. 619, April 19, 2012.
⑤ Associated Press, "Policy Proposals of Top Two Candidates in Chile's Presidential Vote", December 16, 2013, available at http://article.wn.com/view/2013/11/17/Policy_proposals_of_top_2_candidates_in_Chile_s_presidential/#/video (accessed January 10, 2014).
⑥ Richard Seymour, "Quebec's Students Provide a Lesson in Protest Politics," *The Guardian*, September 7, 2012, available at http://www.guardian.co.uk/commentisfree/2012/sep/07/quebec-students-lesson-protest-politics (accessed January 10, 2014); Xavier Lafrance and Alan Sears, "Campus Fightbacks in the Age of Austerity: Learning from Quebec Students," *The Bullet*, Socialist Project E-Bulletin No. 771, February 9, 2013.
⑦ Gill Plimmer, "It's Back to the 1980s as Privatization Fever Takes a Grip," *Financial Times*, June 27, 2011.

program)相互绑定,此举有可能打造出一个世界最大型的、以视网膜扫描与指纹为主要内容的生物识别数据库①。名为"医疗的信息技术未来"的项目,旨在依托商业性基因序列测定成本的迅速降低,并使用西班牙 Integromics 以及瑞典 Qlucore 等生物信息公司所提供的软件,将脱氧核糖核酸(DNA)分析整合进疾病管理系统中②。相关的丑闻事件层出不穷:政府采购信息技术系统竟然将英国人的医疗记录上传至网上③;数字化存档并非如其当初承诺的那般有效地降低成本④;制药企业并未向外界公布其研究的商业赞助方,这一违背医疗伦理的行为在制药行业早已屡见不鲜⑤;将病人病例上传网上从而侵犯个人隐私权⑥。全球范围内向转基因食品发起的战争,偶尔见诸报端⑦。谷歌图书在将学术图书馆近 2 000 万册藏书扫描入(数据)库后,也不得不暂时放慢脚步,着手处理由此带来的法律纠纷⑧。然而,这丝毫没有阻挡以利润为导向的大规模数字化图书资源的步伐⑨。艺术与文化生产也与时俱进地被整合进总体性的经济话语体系中:据官方统计,2011 年,"艺术与文化部门"向美国国民生产总值贡献了 5 040 亿美元⑩,令人惊愕。在这一情境下,美国政府所出台的各项政策,以及美国法院所做出的各项裁决,通常具有全球意义。

  商品化进程的各个层面,都遭遇到各种形式的抵抗。21 世纪初,许多国家出现"知情权"运动(最典型的例子当属印度),这些运动孕育了覆盖面更广的"近用权"倡议,后者

---

① Lydia Polgreen,"Scanning 2. 4 Billion Eyes,India Tries to Connect Poor to Growth,"*New York Times*,September 2,2011. 要了解印度电子政务的发展,请参见 Thomas,Digital India.
② Clive Cookson,"Industry Braced for Information Deluge,"*Financial Times*,Health Life Sciences Special Report,June 27,2011.
③ Nicholas Timmins,"Only the Bare Bones,"*Financial Times*,May 17,2011.
④ Steve Lohr,"Digital Records May Not Cut Health Costs,Study Cautions,"*New York Times*,March 6,2012.
⑤ Duff Wilson,"Medical Industry Ties Often Undisclosed in Journals,"*New York Times*,September 14,2010;Abigail Zuger,"A Drumbeat on Profit Takers,"*New York Times*,March 20,2012. 2012 年,12 家医药公司向医生支付的薪金高达十亿美元,以此影响他们开特定的处方药. 具体请参见 Andrew Jack,"US Doctors Paid ﹩1bn Last Year by Drugs Groups,"*Financial Times*,May 23,2013.
⑥ Kevin Sack,"Medical Data of Thousands Posted Online,"*New York Times*,September 9,2011.
⑦ Amy Harmon and Andrew Pollack,"Battle Brewing over Labeling of Genetically Modified Food,"*New York Times*,May 25,2012.
⑧ Jennifer Howard,"Google Begins to Scale Back Its Scanning of Books from University Libraries,"*Chronicle of Higher Education*,March 9,2012,available at http://chronicle.com/ article/Google – Begins – to – Scale – Back/131109 (accessed January 10,2014).
⑨ Katrina Fenlon,"Corporate Mass Digitization and Cultural Heritage:From Public Relations to Content Accumulation,"未出版论文,Graduate School of Library and Information Science,University of Illinois at Urbana – Champaign,October 2013.
⑩ U. S. Department of Commerce,Bureau of Economic Analysis and National Endowment for the Arts,"U. S. Bureau of Economic Analysis and National Endowment for the Arts Release Preliminary Report on Impact of Arts and Culture on U. S. Economy,"BEA – 13 – 58,December 5,2013,available at http://arts. gov/news/2013/us – bureau – economic – analysis – and – national – endowment – arts – release – preliminary – report – impact (accessed February 23,2014).

涵盖从自由软件到生物科技的各个领域①。

正如哈维所强调的,公共产品的商品化进程来势汹汹,必须将之与建成环境的变化相联系。社会生活得以展开的物质空间,其构建与偶尔的重建工作,一直需要大量的资金投入。从历史上看,物质空间主要是指公路、高速公路、街道、桥梁与房屋,以及港口设备、机场、水坝、生活用水、医院、污水与垃圾处理系统,还有电网与通信网络等。当前,经过改造的信息基础设施成为重塑建成环境的核心基础,以承受现有商品与新兴商品的分配。我在第一和第二部分中已经指出,投资现如今都已转向这些体量巨大的网络基础设施。但这绝非仅仅只是一次物理过程,或"投资的"止痛药。社会关系在世界范围内不平衡的发展,不仅嵌入到既有环境中,更经常遭遇暴力性的重构,以服膺于不断扩张的商品化进程。

全球范围内,商品化转型的进程往往以征收农地为前提②:无论是南苏丹、刚果民主共和国,还是印尼、阿根廷或是中国。中国的个案尤其重要。随着中国大量农民向东南沿海迁移,它们已经转变成工薪阶层。2011 年,中国公民大多居住在城市而非农村地区;仅仅 30 年前,不到 20% 的中国人居住在城市。从全球层面上看,2008 年世界的城市人口已经超过农村人口③;并且,在拉美、非洲与南亚地区,四处扩张、粗制滥建的超大型城市成为各种社会冲突的场所,这些冲突往往因为权利和社会公正等问题而爆发。与之相较,中国的城镇化进程却是从头开始。

2010 年,中国取代美国成为世界头号建筑大国。当年,中国政府花费逾万亿美元,试图开放金融闸口转移经济危机④。随着水泥与建材机械设备销量的上升,房地产价格开始飙升。经济学家开始讨论中国的建筑热是否显示了传统的投机性泡沫的动力学特

---

① Alasdair Roberts, *Blacked Out: Government Secrecy in the Information Age* (New York: Cambridge University Press, 2006); Pradip Ninan Thomas, *Political Economy of Communications in India: The Good, the Bad and the Ugly* (New Delhi: Sage, 2010); Pradip Ninan Thomas and Jan Servaes, eds., *Intellectual Property Rights and Communications in Asia: Conflicting Traditions* (New Delhi: Sage, 2006); Gaelle Krikorian and Amy Kapczynski, eds., *Access to Knowledge in the Age of Intellectual Property* (Cambridge, Mass.: MIT Press, 2010).
② Fred Magdoff, "21st Century Land Grabs: Accumulation by Agricultural Dispossession," *Monthly Review* 65, no. 6 (November 2013): 1–18.
③ Jamil Anderlini, "Milestone Passed as More Chinese Live in Cities than in Countryside," *Financial Times*, January 18, 2012; Zhou Xin and Koh Gui Qing, "China City Dwellers Exceed Villagers for First Time," *Reuters*, January 17, 2012, available at http://www.reuters.com/article/2012/01/17/us-china-population-idUSTRE80G0DB20120117 (accessed January 10, 2014); Chandran Nair, "Reverse the Urbanization Policies That Empty Asia's Countryside," *Financial Times*, March 22, 2013.
④ Ed Hammond and Jamil Anderlini, "China Builds Way to Top of Construction League," FT.com, March 2, 2011, available at http://www.ft.com/intl/cms/s/0/f9c3e0ca-44ed-11e0-80e7-00144feab49a.html#axzz2kvAKpOQQ (accessed January 10, 2014).

征①。有人预测这是一场"硬着陆"②。经济政策成为优先事务,正如它所引发的政治衍生效应也成为当务之急。

中国的城镇化进程推动了一大批针对中型新兴城市的融合发展方案的出台:"不仅像北京、上海和香港这样的大城市,二线城市也开始启动大规模、不可思议的基础设施建设工程。"③长沙这个拥有人口700万、位于华中地区的城市,2012年对外公布城市建设方案,宣称将花费1 300亿美元用于机场与道路建设、废物处理以及其他项目④。2011年,重庆推出"智慧互联社区"(2015年推出"互联网+智慧社区"口号:译者注)理念,不仅引进智能能源技术,更制定电子政务计划,并推进教育与医疗服务供给模式的改革创新⑤。在接下来的10年里,世界范围内(基础设施)的建设预计耗资百万亿美元⑥。这些建设项目有可能引发疯狂的通货膨胀现象,并表明(哈维很早就已指出),"城镇化已成为吸收资本与剩余劳动力的重要方式",特别是"中国的城镇化热,在刺激各种消费产品的增长与全球经济复苏上,发挥着核心作用"⑦。

数字化衰退只会按照有利于资本的方式加以克服,例如废除现有的(产品)供给结构(尽管公共产品的供给严重不足且不公平),以支持高科技、利润导向的替代产品。这不是民主自觉(遑论政治和谐)的处方。社会不能只充斥着一种理念,即公共产品必须受资本支配。剥夺性积累方式剥削了那些已然遭受剥削的人群,以造福于那些已然剥削他人的人群。诚如格雷戈·肖特韦尔所言,倘若"自由主义者为事业而战,激进分子为生活而战",那么随着剥夺性积累渗透至社会的方方面面,它极有可能导致激进分子数量的增加⑧。他们所采取的激进形式,以及有可能对更为宏观的政治经济结构所产生的影响,则是更有意义的开放式问题,留待我们继续考察。

通信与信息有可能再次推动经济增长,这一点远远不够。我们必须追问:这是谁的增长?哪一种增长?以及,随着环境议题愈发紧要,增长多少?对这些问题的最普遍的回答,却难以得到世界绝大多数人的认同。并且对全体人类而言,这些都是不可持续的。只有意识到,数字资本主义无论哪一种形式,都不会造福于人类;也只有数字资本主义所引发的具体行动,才能帮助我们找到希望之源。

---

① Merryn Somerset Webb, "The Caustic Soda Connection", House and Home, *Financial Times*, July 29, 2012.
② Martin Wolf, "Risks of a Hard Landing for China," *Financial Times*, July 3, 2013.
③ Edwin Heathcote, "Visions Differ as World Cities Build for the Future," *Financial Times*, September 14, 2011.
④ Simon Rabinovitch, "Chinese City Starts Projects to Fuel Growth," *Financial Times*, August 7, 2012.
⑤ Rebecca MacKinnon, *Consent of the Networked: The Worldwide Struggle for Internet Freedom* (New York: Basic, 2012), 170;也请参见 Yuezhi Zhao, "The Struggle for Socialism in China: The Bo Xilai Saga and Beyond," *Monthly Review*, 64, no. 5 (2012), available at http://monthlyreview.org/author/yuezhizhao (accessed January 10, 2014).
⑥ Ed Hammond and Jamil Anderlini, "China Builds Way to Top of Construction League," *Financial Times*, March 2, 2011.
⑦ David Harvey, *Rebel Cities: From the Right to the City to the Urban Revolution* (London: Verso, 2012), 42, 60.
⑧ Gregg Shotwell, *Autoworkers under the Gun* (Chicago: Haymarket, 2011), 101.

"数字化衰退:信息技术与经济危机"
ⓒ2014 by Dan Schiller
Reprinted by arrangement with the University of Illinois Press
中文简体版权由中国传媒大学出版社有限责任公司持有

图书在版编目(CIP)数据

数字化衰退:信息技术与经济危机/(美)丹·席勒著;吴畅畅译.—北京:中国传媒大学出版社,2017.8
(传播·地缘·政治/赵月枝,张志华主编)
书名原文:Digital Depression:Information Technology and Economic Crisis
ISBN 978-7-5657-1853-3

Ⅰ.①数… Ⅱ.①丹… ②吴… Ⅲ.①信息技术－关系－经济危机－研究
Ⅳ.①F014.82

中国版本图书馆 CIP 数据核字(2016)第 260401 号

数字化衰退:信息技术与经济危机
SHUZIHUA SHUAITUI:XINXI JISHU YU JINGJI WEIJI

著　　者	〔美〕丹·席勒(Dan Schiller)
译　　者	吴畅畅
责任编辑	赵丽华　唐　颖
特约编辑	刘广东　王梦露　张湘悦
封面设计	风得信·阿东
责任印制	曹　辉
出版发行	中国传媒大学出版社
社　　址	北京市朝阳区定福庄东街1号　邮编:100024
电　　话	86-10-65450528　65450532　传真:65779405
网　　址	http://www.cucp.com.cn
经　　销	全国新华书店
印　　刷	北京中科印刷有限公司
开　　本	787mm×1092mm　1/16
印　　张	17.25
字　　数	327千字
版　　次	2017年8月第1版　2017年8月第1次印刷
书　　号	ISBN 978-7-5657-1853-3/F·1853　定价　69.00元

版权所有　　翻印必究　　印装错误　　负责调换